East Asia
History, Politics, Sociology, Culture

Edited by
Edward Beauchamp
University of Hawaii

A Routledge Series

East Asia: History, Politics, Sociology, Culture

Edward Beauchamp, *General Editor*

The Bible and the Gun
Christianity in South China, 1860-1900
Joseph Tse-Hei Lee

An American Editor in Early Revolutionary China
John William Powell and the China Weekly/Monthly Review
Neil L. O'Brien

Between Sacrifice and Desire
National Identity and the Governing of Femininity in Vietnam
Ashley Pettus

New Culture in a New World
The May Fourth Movement and the Chinese Diaspora in Singapore, 1919–1932
David L. Kenley

Alliance in Anxiety
Détente and the Sino-American-Japanese Triangle
Go Ito

State and Society in China's Democratic Transition
Confucianism, Leninism, and Economic Development
Xiaoqin Guo

In Search of an Identity
The Politics of History as a School Subject in Hong Kong, 1960s–2002
Edward Vickers

Pitfall or Panacea
The Irony of US Power in Occupied Japan, 1945–1952
Yoneyuki Sugita

The Renaissance of Takefu
How People and the Local Past Changed the Civic Life of a Regional Japanese Town
Guven Peter Witteveen

Managing Transitions
The Chinese Communist Party, United Front Work, Corporatism, and Hegemony
Gerry Groot

The Prospects for a Regional Human Rights Mechanism in East Asia
Hidetoshi Hashimoto

American Women Missionaries at Kobe College, 1873–1909
Noriko Ishii

A Path toward Gender Equality
State Feminism in Japan
Yoshie Kobayashi

Postsocialist Cinema in Post-Mao China
The Cultural Revolution after the Cultural Revolution
Chris Berry

Building Cultural Nationalism In Malaysia
Identity, Representation, and Citizenship
Timothy P. Daniels

Liberal Rights and Political Culture
Envisioning Democracy in China
Zhenghuan Zhou

The Origins of Left-wing Cinema in China, 1932–37
Vivien Shen

Making a Market Economy
The Institutional Transformation of a Freshwater Fishery in a Chinese Community
Ning Wang

Global Media
The Televison Revolution in Asia
James D. White

Global Media
The Television Revolution in Asia

James D. White

First published 2005 by Routledge
605 Third Avenue, New York, NY 10017
2 Park Square, Milton Park, Abingdon, Oxon OX14 4RN

Routledge is an imprint of the Taylor & Francis Group, an informa business

Library of Congress Cataloging-In-Publication Data

White, James D. (James Daniel)
Global media : the television revolution in Asia / by James D. White.--1st ed.
p. cm. -- (East asia)
Includes bibliographical references and index.
ISBN 0-415-97306-6
1. Television broadcasting--China. 2. Television broadcasting--Japan. 3. Television broadcasting policy--China. 4. Television broadcasting policy--Japan. 5. Nihon Håosåo Kyåokai. 6. Zhong yang dian shi tai (Beijing, China) I. Title. II. Series: East Asia (New York, N.Y.)

PN1992.3.C6W48 2005
384.55'095'090511--dc22 2004025355

ISBN 13: 978-0-415-88404-4 (pbk)
ISBN 13: 978-0-415-97306-9 (hbk)

Publisher's Note
The publisher has gone to great lengths to ensure the quality of this reprint but points out that some imperfections in the original may be apparent.

For Jianglan, Jonathan and Jerome, who make it all worthwhile

Contents

List of Tables and Figures

TABLES

FIGURES

Acknowledgments

This book is based on my dissertation entitled "Balancing the Flow in a World of Information: Three Case Studies of Information Flows in Japan, China and Hong Kong." Accordingly I want to thank my dissertation committee for their guidance and patience, including Joan Johnson-Freese, Meheroo Jussawalla, Peter Manicas and Deane Neubauer. A special note of appreciation goes to the chairperson, Jim Dator, who was always available for advice and encouragement, and to Pat Steinhoff—not only did she give detailed and very helpful comments, but also she was instrumental in helping preserve the integrity of the manuscript. I would like to thank the 60 plus people, from all walks of life, who agreed to be interviewed for this research and who in a real sense made it possible.

I have received advice, support and encouragement from many friends and colleagues, and it is a great pleasure to have the opportunity to acknowledge them. In particular I must thank Karen and Pat Laidler in Hong Kong, who were ever generous in offering a base for my trips to Asia and also gave useful perspective on the changes happening in Hong Kong and China; and Mary and Donald Wood in London, who also gave me both encouragement and a place of refuge on trips to Europe. Over the years Mary ran a virtual clipping service for my research, which helped greatly in building the international perspective essential for a work looking at globalization. My good friends in Tokyo, John Provo and Russ McCulloch, gave me useful perspective and practical support, invaluable when trying to stay abreast of the complexities of Japan.

I must also express my gratitude to Joseph Man Chan (Hong Kong), Brien Hallett (Honolulu), Sohail Inayatullah (Queensland), Ellis Krauss (San Diego) and Manfred Steger (Illinois). All of them were generous with their time and their feedback on the many different aspects of this work, from globalization to futures to the media in China and Japan. Finally I would like to acknowledge my former coworkers in the Globalization Research

Center at the University of Hawai'i, who did much to stimulate my thinking about globalization, in particular the members of the Globalization Atlas and Portal Project team and the production crew of the television series "Living in a Global World."

Practical support for some of the field research was received from the following institutions: the Pacific Telecommunications Council, Honolulu, for travel support to Tokyo, Hong Kong and Bangkok in 1994; the Center for Chinese Studies, University of Hawaii, as part of its Peking University Exchange Program, which supported research in Hong Kong, Yunnan, and Beijing in 1997; and the Eu Tong Sen Memorial Exchange Program, University of Hawaii, which supported research in Hong Kong and Tokyo in 1998.

The biggest burden of over-ambitious research falls on those who have to deal with the consequences of absences, physical and mental. My wife Jianglan and my children Jonathan and Jerome handled this unfair load for too long. Their love and affection is what made this work possible.

Introduction

The genesis of this book was my interest in an immodest proposal. In the 1980s I was working in Japan, heavily involved with the media, both Japanese and international. Journalists love to gossip, so through conversations at the Foreign Correspondent's Club in central Tokyo I was early aware that the Japanese national public broadcaster, NHK, was developing plans to launch a 24-hour news service. I was very interested in this idea, as a step towards rectifying what seemed to me a heavy imbalance. While there was a demonstrably limited amount of accurate information about Asia circulating through the mass media in the West, I could compare that with the Asian media's extensive coverage of political, economic and social issues in the West. Information was flowing, from West to East and from East to West, but the flows were clearly unbalanced.

The NHK plans appeared to develop rapidly. They had the support of the President of NHK, Keiji Shima, who was rumored to be negotiating with ABC of the United States and with the BBC, in an attempt to get them to join as production and distribution partners. The service even had a putative name, GNN (Global News Network), which made it plain that one major purpose was to set up a rival to the rapidly expanding CNN.

As quickly as they had begun, the rumors died down. Shima lost his position, and the GNN proposal was shelved. This only heightened my curiosity, however. Why had NHK, one of the richest and most powerful broadcasting organizations in the world, been unable to push the idea of an international news channel even to the starting line, especially at a time when media curiosity about the various Asian economic "miracles" was at a height? Was there no way that an Asian point of view could be presented and heard in the West? Who "owned" the news? At a time when globalization as a theme for discussion was becoming popular in the media, were the terms of the debate to be effectively dictated by the West?

In the course of attempting to find answers to these questions, my focus widened, as I saw that the GNN case history did not stand alone, but was linked to other events both in Japan and elsewhere in Asia, especially China and Hong Kong. The real threat to the television status quo was not in fact CNN's Ted Turner, but rather an archrival, Rupert Murdoch. In 1994, having had a major impact on the media situation in the U.K. and in the U.S., Murdoch made his entry onto the stage of Asian television when he bought a controlling share in STAR TV, the first pan-Asian television service. STAR TV[1] had been made possible by Asiasat, the first satellite to cover the region, itself a strange hybrid of Hong Kong entrepreneurialism supported by a mix of wealthy Hong Kong Chinese, the Hong Kong British colonial establishment and mainland Chinese finance. Suddenly it was owned by an Australian with announced ambitions to set up a global television network. Questions about who owns and operates the media, and in whose interest, were given fresh currency. At the same time the Internet was growing exponentially, offering a completely new way to deliver and receive news, including television.

I also became convinced that the events I was looking at reflected in part attempts to deal with macro processes of change which can be labeled 'globalization.' From that perspective, the condition of the television industry, of the production of news, and in particular of the public service broadcaster appear in a symbolic role, metaphors for the reconfiguration of relationships between the global and the local.

However, the initial spark of intellectual curiosity remained: can a perceived imbalance in understanding between cultures be redressed? Is there any possibility of international (between nations) communications becoming a two-way street? At the same time as I was researching this book I was acting as producer and writer of a television series, entitled "Living in a Global World," which looked at many different aspects of globalization, based on interviews with a wide range of thinkers in the field, academic and non-academic. If I try to choose one key word which emerged from all those interviews it was "balance"—the need for it, or the lack of it, in the processes of globalization as we know it now.

Recent events have only reinforced the ambivalence surrounding the situation of information flows between cultures. If the 1991 Gulf war pushed CNN into the center of the international stage, the 2003 Iraq war found another and unexpected broadcast star, the Arabic satellite news channel Al-Jazeera. While CNN competed with Fox News and CNBC for the jingoism awards in their coverage of the "war for Iraqi freedom," Al-Jazeera showed the bloody side of the conflict, attracting the vehement criticism of the British and American governments. Jehane Noujaim, an Egyptian-American film-maker made a documentary, "Control Room," about the TV station as it covered the war. In an interview he explained why he wanted to make the film:

> I have traveled back and forth between the U.S. and the Middle East my whole life, and I've always been interested in the fact that there are completely different stories (in the two regions concerning) the same world events. How is it possible to have a peaceful world, people talking to each other and understanding each other, when there are completely different views being told to the people? (Schecter, 2004)

Ultimately balance or fairness was at the center of Shima's rationale for setting up GNN, just as it is the primary rationale for Al-Jazeera, which claims "to cover all viewpoints with objectivity, integrity and balance."

THREE CASE HISTORIES

This book has an empirical/historical core. Empirically, my goal is to describe the actual situation concerning information flows as revealed through a comparative study of three television case histories in Asia. The primary case histories focus on the roles of the national public service broadcasters of Japan and China, NHK and CCTV, and their reactions to globalization. A supplementary story looks at the checkered history of STAR TV and more generally of the activities of Rupert Murdoch's News Corporation in Asia, both seen as exemplars of a specific aspect of globalization, the emergence of the global corporation.

These case histories are based on an extensive review of the literature, and on interview-based field research in Tokyo, Beijing, Kunming, Hong Kong, Honolulu and London, mostly carried out in 1997 and 1998, and updated by visits to Japan, China and Hong Kong in 2002.

It is my suggestion that the ongoing discussion on globalization has tended to be more descriptive and speculative than analytical or empirical.[2] I have attempted to give my contribution to this discussion a factual anchor, by linking my conclusions on the nature of globalization directly to the findings of my research. All three case histories are based on interviews with leading participants in exemplar events:

- the attempts to set up GNN, and to 'internationalize' news at NHK;
- CCTV's defense of its 'turf,' under pressure from bureaucratic upheavals such as the creation of the Ministry of Information Industries in 1998 and the emergence of major commercial rivals like Beijing TV,

at the same time as it has itself become a major revenue earner and its role has changed following China's entry into the WTO; and
- the establishment, sale and erratic progress of STAR TV.

This is contextualized through a broader discussion about the role of public service broadcasters, and of information and communication generally. Finally, my approach has a futures orientation from the outset, and concludes with a causal layered analysis of the case histories, which is used to revisit the initial theoretical mapping, in an imaginative attempt to gauge some of the impact of these complex, fast-moving changes.

By looking at the case histories in some detail, my intent is to depict some of the workings of political power and the media. By delineating the pattern, or structure, of specific examples of the processes of globalization, and to attempt to describe their impact, I hope to suggest ways in which such patterns might change in the future.

Pattern delineation is based on asking, first, which sets of actors are helping to demarcate time-space boundaries through policy, regulation, ownership and personal practices, in a context where "satellite, digital and fibre optic communications are supplying new definitions of, and imperatives for, time and space" (Ferguson, 1990: 170). The description of pattern and the identification of which actors are involved, and the process of their involvement, I take to be basic first steps in trying to see how the complex system of globalization works, in practice. Careful observation is designed to describe histories, recognize patterns, and identify themes: in turn, these are the early building blocks for the development of the metaphors we need to help navigate our way forward, which I see as the essential mission of futures studies.

In Japan, the actors include state organs like the former Ministry of Posts and Telecommunications; quasi-governmental organizations like the national public broadcaster, NHK; and a cast of numerous others, including the commercial TV stations, the manufacturers of electronic equipment, the national space industry, cable and satellite operators, and program suppliers, both domestic and foreign. Finally, there is the audience for national and international television.

In China and Hong Kong, this study looks at the constant adjustments in the positions of the former Ministry of Radio, Film and Television, of the national broadcaster CCTV, and of local TV stations, as they dealt with general changes in Chinese society and the specific impact of the first commercial TV satellite station in Asia, STAR TV from Hong Kong. The nature of the players is generally similar to those in Japan, with both public and the private sector actors, and with the manufacturers of 'hard' equipment like satellite dishes and the operators of communications networks like cable TV, as well as the suppliers of the 'soft': information, news and entertainment (my focus is primarily on the 'soft').

Because I am looking at flows, which by their nature have at least the potential to flow out as well as in, I also examine how both NHK and CCTV are attempting to remake themselves as international broadcasters. Again, it is important not to lose sight of the audience, at home or abroad.

Both case histories involve a highly varied cast of international actors, many of them not Asian. They include multinational corporations like CNN and the Hughes Corporation, transnationals like News Corporation and Asiasat, and national public corporations like the BBC, which are re-inventing themselves as hybrid public commercial organizations.

For all these diverse organizations there is one key variable: they all have to operate in a context which is no longer bounded by the nation-state. For the young industry of television, this is a new situation. For ancient countries like China, it is also a situation seemingly fraught with challenges to an always complex society.

WHAT IS AT STAKE?

After pattern delineation, my second line of inquiry is based on asking what is at stake for the state, for the commercial interests, for the producers and for the 'consumers' of 'information flows.' This question is fundamental, in order to tackle larger contextual issues about the nature of globalization or the impact of information in modern society.

At the level of the nation-state, the debate on information flows has long been framed in terms as abstract as its own phraseology. Reference is made to national security or to cultural imperialism, in its turn an abstraction based on a simplistic equating of the state with a heavily constructed concept or co-option of culture. But as revealed through the case studies, the real priorities for the government bureaucrats charged with policy development and implementation are often at once more pragmatic and more mundane. The nation-state (or the elements that constitute it) can no longer be equated with a larger cultural order, or a one-size-fits-all economic paradigm.

In both China and Japan, government officials were plainly as much interested in bureaucratic turf battles and fights over who was to gain advantage from administering the new technologies like the Internet and overseeing the expanding role of television as they were with larger questions of national interest. In China a layer of complexity was added by the overwhelming question of how, in reality, a totalitarian state bureaucracy handles "one country, two systems," in the sense that official China still lays dubious claim to be both socialist and capitalist.

One reality that both situations seemed to share was fragmentation of what had appeared as stable situations. Both NHK and CCTV had long enjoyed a position of security, whether measured in economic terms (an assured income from license fees for NHK, government subsidy for CCTV); social terms (a position as the stable reference point for information on how the world of the nation was running); cultural terms (key participant in the "imagined community" of the people); or technological terms (NHK was the defender of the nation's technological honor in developing high-definition TV, while both CCTV and NHK played important roles as the representative of the nation in the development of a 'necessary' (for the nation) technology like satellites.

Globalization threatened those positions. Commercial rivals seemed to undermine the rationale for a public broadcaster, as did technological developments like the Internet. Multiple sources of news and data rendered a monopoly position on information untenable, and the very notion of globalization fundamentally upset the whole idea of community, which suddenly could be as big as the audience for world cup soccer or Princess Diana's funeral, or as specific as viewers of a channel devoted to golf or subscribers to an online discussion group, situated everywhere and nowhere.

In both countries there was a sense of having to deal with a force beyond anybody's control, a tiger leaping towards the latest level of modernization, ridden by organizations wielding technological developments which were a reality well before the bureaucracy or the legislature in either country was able to comprehend the consequences of their deployment. Attempting to call the shots on which direction the tiger might jump was a complex, risky business. Japanese officials interviewed for this research sometimes seemed daunted by the task, while those involved in establishing STAR TV described themselves as making something up—pan-Asian television—as they were going along.

Internationally, what was at stake had since the sixties been expressed in terms of one freedom or another, most commonly of choice or of access to information. In the 1980s this rubric had largely been swept aside by a new ideology, of "open" markets, which usually meant the right to enter another nation's markets.

Television had moved or been pushed into the arms of the global marketplace, creating a new international broadcast industry, which sometimes seemed beyond the reach of national governments to control. The situation raised fundamental questions of political and cultural sovereignty, as, for example, the concept of "language-area" superseded the territorial state as the target audience for broadcasting, already a well-established reality with Cantonese-speaking China. Again, the technology—in this case, that of cable and satellites—had developed at such a pace that "rogue" commercial broadcasters (and even rogue commercial satellites) were in operation before international law was able to catch up.

While the new rhetoric implied a stepping away from traditional kinds of regulation, the nation-state continued its battle to hold the center. In Japan, the actual result of de facto international television arriving in the home was effective re-regulation, while in China the intention was plainly to continue the center's attempts to exert control. It remains open to question how successful such regulation or attempts to control will be in the long term, because the object of the regulation or control—in this case, television—is caught up in changes well beyond the capability of the nation-state to command, to the degree that the structure of the industry itself may be transformed. As Tracey puts it, "Broadcasting in general, and NHK in particular, is no more than a bit player in a game of global proportions and yet it finds itself faced with theoretical decommissioning precisely because of these wider events" (Tracey, 1998: 224).

At the same time, globalization must be seen as a process, and one which is embedded in inherited social structures and relationships. The process of change is itself in no way orderly or linear, and there is no guarantee that it will produce anything necessarily "new": but equally, the notion that future directions are inevitably or inexorably connected with the "old" is in no way self-evident.

As a result, when that process is tracked through the case study approach used here, the findings can be surprising. It is notable, for example, that the position of STAR TV today—after many years and huge expenditures and considerable shifts in policy—is not dissimilar to the parameters for the Asian operation of GNN sketched out in 1990. In 2004 the president of NHK announced plans for a 24-hour news service, specifically citing the examples of CNN and BBC. Maybe GNN was simply an idea ahead of its time.

In summary, this volume examines the distribution of information around the globe through a study of the history and contemporary situation of two Asian national television broadcasters and one international media conglomerate with pretensions to be 'global.' My specific focus is on the creation of international news. Major findings include:

- The changes that have engulfed television can be seen as emblematic of globalization at work. Institutions like NHK and CCTV are in the front line of dealing with globalization, and the debates about the role of public service broadcasters reflect both the threat and the potential of globalization.

- Globalization pressures—be they commercial, technological or symbolic—lead to the fragmentation of heretofore apparently stable situations, but the resultant changes are not predictable, and should not be regarded as resulting in an inevitable homogeneity.
- The context for these changes is one no longer bounded by the nation-state.
- Non-state actors are often the drivers of change, in large part because of their adaptability in the face of rapid technological developments and of a global situation of great complexity—but they are not necessarily the beneficiaries of change. At the same time the more nimble state organs may well flourish under the new regime suggested by globalization, or lead resistance to it.
- A constant preoccupation of the nation-state is how to handle information, control of which is a means of wielding power. Globally, flows of information are plainly controlled by a few institutions and dominated by a handful of nations, but the potential for this control to be subverted is growing.

Chapter One

The Globalization Context

APPROACHING GLOBALIZATION: SIX CHARACTERISTICS

This section describes six characteristics of globalization I believe to be germane to this study, supported by and giving context to the case studies. It is followed by a description of some of the processes of globalization, also referenced to the case histories.

I take an explicitly non-reductionist approach to research, what Mosca describes as "multiply determined." I opt not to attribute historical or social change to an essential economic or cultural cause, as it seems to me that globalization by definition cannot be examined through isolated practices. This is also the first of the six characteristics of globalization.

Complexity cannot be reduced to a core essentiality

There is a well-entrenched tendency—by critics as well as by endorsers of the phenomenon—to see globalization in economic terms. As applied to the media, the term 'globalization' is apt to be embedded in the language of political economy, and to focus on the financial power of the media conglomerates. The impression given is that of unstoppable juggernauts beaming their consumerist messages around the world (see Negrine and Papathanassopoulos, 1990; Mosco, 1996; Martin and Schumann, 1997; Greider, 1997). The examples—and the general conclusions drawn from them—tend to be taken from the Western media context. However, when applied to specific case histories of how the process of globalization actually impacts the local, these paradigmatic views may not always square with the reality revealed by closer examination of events and consequences.

The fate of public service broadcasters in a globalized world is an interesting example. In fact the most popular operational model for television was (and mostly still is) to function as some kind of public agency, until quite recently operating largely outside market economics (with the U.S. situation as an exception). Despite being forced to face a highly competitive environment in recent years, few if any public broadcasters have disappeared.[1]

Certainly, they have been forced to adapt. The swing factor was the expansion of information carrying capacity, whether by cable or satellite or, following digitalization, by conventional broadcast channels.

Nevertheless, the public service broadcasters have been remarkable robust in the face of great pressure to change. They are also institutions of weight: according to IDATE (2000, 2001, 2003), three public broadcasters (ARD, NHK and BBC) regularly appear in the top 13 media groups in the world. CCTV and the Indian *Prasar Bharati* might also be included, if there were a meaningful way of comparing the value of their networks and resources with those outside China and India.

Success is relative

As revealed through the case study approach, a note of caution needs to be introduced into consideration of the role of giant media corporations. A simple listing of investments and shareholding and gross revenues should not be equated with invulnerability or inevitability.

In fact, the Western media and communications conglomerates have often been remarkably unsuccessful, at least in Asia. As examples, leading American media operations have failed outright (DirecTV in Japan), have been forced to radically change their corporate strategy in order to survive (MTV in Asia), or had meager success at best (News Corporation in Japan, Time Warner in China and Japan). The conglomerate featured in the STAR TV case study, Rupert Murdoch's News Corporation, is the media company that has tried hardest to ride the global wave into Asia, with limited success, and at the expense of a huge investment and at the cost of sacrificing any idea of editorial independence.

The remarkable flip-flops in policy that characterize Rupert Murdoch's corporate history in China or Japan—contrasted with the relatively consistent policy development of NHK and CCTV—demonstrate that the story of global mass media systems is still being written.

Globalization is about relationships

In one sense globalization is about communications, which in turn is about relationships (what Castells calls networks). These are characterized by their self-referential, interdependent, dynamic and ever-changing nature.

On the micro scale, Burawoy et al (2000) have attempted to map out a "global ethnography." The intention is to show how "concrete, lived experience can sharpen the abstraction of globalization theories into more precise and meaningful conceptual tools" (xiv). In describing the processes of global television, it is easy to lose sight of the person in the sitting room looking at the television. Cultural, economic, social and political influences arrive in the home unannounced and sometimes uninvited—but not unchanged in the process of transmission, nor in the manner of reception.

The complexity of the phenomenon of globalization is also revealed on the macro scale, where the resistances to it may be as meaningful as its superficially apparent success. As revealed by taking a detailed look at cases studies, globalization is a complex interplay between economic, cultural and political factors. The political stage on which this takes place is still primarily that of the nation-state. Referencing the CCTV case history, the politics and economics may be an interacting mix of the national (the MRFT being engulfed by the MII) and the local (the rise to prominence of regional TV stations like Shanghai TV).

And while national governments as a whole often may be slow to react to rapidly changing situations—which is a characteristic of globalization—specific institutions of government (like the Japanese Ministry of Posts and Telecommunications) or institutions associated with the government (like the BBC, NHK or CCTV) may be much more successful not only in reacting but in fact in turning the environment of change to their advantage. Public broadcasters start from a position of considerable strength in the societies in which they are embedded, and often have a symbiotic affinity with one another. NHK and CCTV, for example, have long had a close working relationship, and employees of both often use strikingly similar language to describe the sensitive place their organizations occupy in their respective societies.

Political power has been reconfigured

In the political domain, the role of the state is in the process of changing in fundamental ways, and in many cases is being fragmented due to the state's inability to react with suppleness to ongoing processes of change which are distinguished by speed, by interconnectedness and by the compression of space. This is a situation of constant, necessary flux (Sassen, 1996).

Traditional political and economic barometers are inadequate to measure the scope of what is going on, in particular when sovereignty-free actors, like multinationals and certain NGOs, effectively operate their own micro economic systems.[2] If television broadcasting is seen as a process, then what is happening with global television is a development of that process to the point where judicial or territorial barriers are "accommodated" or sidelined or radically reconfigured.

A contradictory process

Television is a technology, and technological developments matter. At the moment where technologies reach a take-off point, they make possible the tremendous accelerations in speed, extensions in reach and lowerings in cost of all forms of communications (including transportation) which in turn produce global linkages, the strands out of which the web of globalization is spun.

However technology is ultimately a means to an end, which can shape it in numerous different ways, most often in terms of culture. Ultimately globalization has a major impact on culture, which is also the source of the most important resistances to it. Television is emblematic of this ambivalence.

On the one hand, television could serve as the glue for a new universal culture—or as the vehicle for global advertising, an acolyte to the global market. On the other hand, the evidence to date is that global television only succeeds in proportion to the extent it caters to the local. National public television broadcasters, as an example, have not only survived but often flourished in the face of globalization. One of the many conundrums of globalization is that it seems to encourage regionalization and localization, an intrinsic tension. In that sense globalization is about the reworking of the relationship between the local and the global. Globalization is a contradictory process.

The global and the local

Globalization is most often equated with growing global economic integration, which at its most rudimentary is characterized by the Financial Times of London as "falling trade barriers, co-ordinated economic policies and single currencies" (Patel, 2001). It is also commonly identified with Americanization, or more precisely the alignment of other economies, currencies and stock markets with that of the U.S. By spring 2001, for example, correlation between U.S. and foreign stocks had reached 0.75 (where 1 represents synchronized movement and 0 indicates relative independence) (ibid.: 5).

This sense of things coming together is also probably the commonest perception underlying globalization in its conceptualization as something larger than a purely economic phenomenon. In an interview David Harvey[3] speculated on how the term globalization achieved its sudden popularity, and identified the publication of the famous NASA "Earthrise" photo in 1968 as a moment of transformation, the presentation of an iconic image which told the inhabitants of the earth how small and vulnerable was the space we share. Indeed, the language used to describe globalization is all about integration and time and space compression, about economic, social and technological forces weaving a real world wide web, so that "what happens here" can be directly and instantaneously impacted by a distant event.

Giddens (1994, 1999, 2000) in particular has focused on how the local interacts with the global when "things come together."[4] He sees the emergence of globalization influenced above all by developments in systems of communication and transportation. These in many cases had their roots in the 19th century, as witness the development of international time standards, driven by the needs of the railway and the telegraph (Palmer, 2002). The globalization difference was created in large measure by the birth of instantaneous electronic communication on a global scale, signaled by the rapid development of communication satellite technology from the 1960s on.

Giddens also points out that globalization is not only about large-scale systems, but also about the impact on the local, and conversely how "local lifestyle habits have become globally consequential" (1994: 5). He goes on to argue that globalization is a complex mixture of processes, which often act in contradictory ways. A focus on one part of the operation of the media in one particular region as presented in this book allows us to see how the constitutive elements of globalization interact with each other, be they cultural, or economic, or political, or social. It also paints a picture of a process that is not unidirectional. For globalization develops regional centers of power, and institutional alternatives to the status quo, which may or may not form the context for the future, but which certainly impact the way the processes develop.

Another lens to look through is provided by Michael Shapiro, with his concept of the "sovereignty-exchange nexus" (1991, 1992). Globalization is about the reconfiguration of historically fixed relationships between localizing and globalizing forces, the "most pervasive modern tension . . . between the various impulses behind sovereignty norms and those behind relations of exchange" (1992: 5). Different social entities engage in identity securing projects, in attempts to adjust to the new configurations and the fragmentation of existing values in the to and fro of sovereignty (local) and exchange (global). This provides a useful theoretical reference point for the case studies outlined in this research, and also serves as a succinct description of the bind in which the public service broadcasters find themselves in a globalized world.

In her discussion of the "spatialities and temporalities of the global," Sakia Sassen (2000) underlines the significance of the ways in which the global and the local overlap and interact.

> Much of social science has operated with the assumption of the nation-state as a container, representing a unified spatiotemporality. Much of history, however, has failed to confirm this assumption . . . and the global restructurings of today threaten to erode the usefulness of this proposition for what is an expanding arena of sociological reality (215).

Her point is to use an examination of the workings of globalization as a critique of an idea commonly embedded in the social sciences, that the national and the non-national are somehow mutually exclusive. Sassen proposes a different perspective, one well supported by the case histories of global television that follow:

> Thinking about the global in terms of distinct spatialities embedded in the territory of the national yet retaining their own specificity helps us analytically to apprehend that a global dynamic or process may partly operate through a national institution (228).

National institutions, such as public service broadcasters, can internalize the global and become part of a global space.

Actually making the connection between local sites and global dynamics is a daunting task, one for which ethnographers are well suited, as their task is to study others in their own space and time. This starting point fits in neatly with Sassen's (1991) linking of the global city of high-flying executives and bankers with the armies of immigrants that make their lives possible. Burawoy (2000: 29) describes three strategies adopted by his team of 'global ethnographers' to counter the tendency to see globalization as something huge, powerful and inevitable. I have attempted to apply all three strategies to my examination of national public service broadcasters pushed onto a global stage. One is to see global forces as constituted at a distance, and therefore to focus on the ways in which they are resisted or negotiated. The second is to see those forces themselves as the product of flows of people, things and ideas, the actual global connections between sites. The third, which I shall address in my final chapter on futures, is to see those forces and connections as imaginative constructs, a realization that leads to the possibility of countervailing movements exposing the hollowness of the wizard of globalization, and taking control of a no longer distant world.

THE PROCESSES OF GLOBALIZATION

In the section that follows I shall attempt to outline some of the processes of globalization that emerge from a review of the literature on globalization, and which serve as reference points for the narratives of globalization in action which constitute the case histories.

WAVES OF TRANSFORMATION

The three characteristics Giddens has identified as typifying modernity are the pace of change, the scope of change and the new nature of institutions, with modern cities cited as an example. They lead to his vision of a world of change. "As different areas of the globe are drawn into interconnection with one another, waves of social transformation crash across virtually the whole of the earth's surface" (1990: 6).

The waves of economic and social transformation are not necessarily all generated in the West, although the western social sciences tend to wear cultural blinkers in this regard. The West continues to see itself as the center of the world: the east is still 'far' and the 'Orient' is still an object of knowledge and of power, as Said described it (1978). This is a schema which has long rankled with other regions of the world, especially those with strong cultural traditions of their own. In the 1990s Asian readers turned books like "The Japan That Can Say No" (Ishihara and Morita, 1991 and 1989), "The China That Can Say No" (Song, Zhang, and Qiao, 1996), and even "The Asia That Can Say No" (Mahathir and Ishihara, 1994)[5] into best sellers. More recently the sudden emergence of highly popular Arab satellite TV stations like al-Jazeera and al-Arabiya, broadcasting on satellites with names like Arabsat and Nilesat can be seen as part of the same reaction. As long as the West holds the institutional power that permits it to construct Asian or Arab Other(s)—in other words as long as the dice are loaded and the relationship is unequal—the blinkers will stay on.

But one consequence of globalization is that the resistances to that power take on a new strength and vitality. In describing how the subset of Japanese intellectual discourse known as "discussion about the Japanese" (*nihonjinron*) have developed, Morely and Robins show how it has moved from a definition of Japan's identity in terms of deviations from Western norms to a point where "the Japanese would occupy the position of the centre and of the subject which determines other particularities in its own universal term" (1995: 164). This is precisely what Shima's Global News Network was all about: diagrammatic maps showing how the satellite news network would have worked reveal Tokyo positioned on top of that globe (see figure 1, p. 133).

Such resistances are not met with good grace. At a time when Japan was seen as a potent rival to the United States, Fallows could write about "Containing Japan" (1989). Huntington's famous 1993 Foreign Affairs article ruminating on "The Clash of Civilizations" especially focused on the rise of China posing a fundamental challenge to the American-dominated status quo. The second Bush administration went out of its way to denigrate and even silence al-Jazeera and al-Arabiya during the 2003 war in Iraq.

Maybe the biggest lesson that can be learnt from the checkered history of STAR TV, which is at the center of this book, is that this resistance is real enough to alter the nature of the flow in dramatic and fundamental ways. Despite an investment measured in billions of dollars, STAR TV's pretensions to be a regional broadcaster covering one third of the world's population were reduced to becoming "a conglomeration of half a dozen local broadcasters slugging it out market by market" (Granitsas, 2000). STAR TV's original business model, in so far as there was one, was founded on the notion of Hong Kong as a communications hub, with a primary but ill-defined audience of middle-class Asians, who were imagined by STAR TV's Chinese owners to be primarily Chinese. In the event, STAR TV's biggest success was in India, a fact that its owners, Chinese and Australian/American, had difficulty adjusting to. At least in its potential, globalization can be about de-centering. The waves of transformation can break in unexpected ways.

WHERE IS THE NATION, THE STATE, THE NATION-STATE?

One of the intellectual traditions of the social sciences is a tendency to focus on one dominant rationale to explain the global rush of events. For Wallerstein and many others, it is primarily economic, or more narrowly, capitalist, or some subset of this thinking, such as the tension between security requirements and economic interests, or the demands of an apparently omnipotent market place. The inclination is to start with the nation-state as the unit of analysis and ignore larger cultural communities, such as the great world religions; or scorn the smaller units, such as ethnic minorities; or belittle the increasing number of organizations which can choose not to "see" the nation-state or to step around it, such as is sometimes the case with the international communications organizations that are the subject of this study; or underestimate institutions that reject the authority of a particular nation-state, such as the Falun Gong.

I am not here supporting the notion of Smith (1990), Appadurai (1996) and others, that the nation-state has effectively lost much of its significance or is on the way to becoming obsolete. As is clear from the example of the manner in which the former Ministry of Posts and Telecommunications (MPT) in Japan has effectively remade itself in order to deal with the new realities of international communications, there is every reason to believe the sovereign state—or some elements of it—is quite capable of living with a globally connected world, and indeed of thriving on the connections. For the time being, this seems to be the case with the national public service broadcasters that appear in this study.

But as Hobsbawm (1983: 13) has argued, we are dealing with an *invented* tradition, an exercise in social engineering. The nation-state still has an important role, and the connections between states still matter, but in order to survive in a world of exponential change, they and their constituent components, such as political parties, have to recreate themselves, constantly.

Already there exist virtual parallel worlds (or as Appadurai terms them, "imagined worlds"), where developments are fast and social connections are made with no reference to flags or borders or national self-interest, as well as the "cultural communes" identified by Castells (1997) as providing viable alternatives for the construction of meaning in a global society. As Castells describes it, control of the nation-state becomes just one way among many to assert power. The nation-state as an institution has no privileged right to continue as it was while the world of which it is a constituent part changes. In Raymond Williams' words, "the nation-state in its classical European forms is at once too large and too small for the range of real social purposes" (1983: 197).

Sassen (2000) sees the global as a partial condition, a project in the making, but warns against any conclusion that the global and the national are discrete conditions, excluding each other. On the contrary, it is the fact that they constantly overlap and interact that distinguishes the world we live in. At the same time, in their close analysis of how the quantitive indicators of globalization have often been misinterpreted or their extent and novelty exaggerated Sutcliffe and Glyn (1999) conclude that, while it is reasonable to assume that changing global structures will tend to alter the political areas in which local or national autonomy exists, this can not be equated with the idea of globalization simply rendering the politics of smaller units, such as the national state, redundant.

In one sense, the fact that television signals transmitted by satellite ignore national boundaries is only one reminder among many that the post-Westphalian world of nation-states has never been quite what it appears. A fairly neutral definition of nation-state might run along the lines of "a political entity consisting of a people with some common cultural experience (nation) who also share a common political authority (state) recognized by other sovereignties (nation-states)." The key concepts here revolve around ideas of cultural homogeneity and political unity but as Dittmer and Kim (1993) point out these have no universal validity, either in terms of ethnic group membership (a majority of contemporary nation-states have very large "minority" populations), or with regard to physical boundary and linguistic community (in half the countries of the world less than 70 percent of the population speak the same language). In order to reach a claimed 98% of the population, India's national radio network AIR broadcasts in 21 regional languages (Gill, 2001).

Historically, however, television has been national, an identification central to the whole notion of the public service broadcaster and traditionally a measure of the success of the reach of commercial broadcasters. The national broadcaster is also part of an ongoing process, and has come to play an important role in the construction of the relationship between nation and state. But the environment in which that process develops has changed.

The new context in which international television is being developed is a "global system marked by a variety of borders, frontiers, and bridges among states and other entities such as corporations, organizations, and diasporic communities" (Nagel, 2000: 160). Nagel goes on to list and supply examples of political, economic, cultural, social and legal boundaries and to identify at least one substructure that underlies the global system that rarely draws attention, the "global economy of desire" (to which I would add the global infrastructure of crime).

Reflecting on some of the consequences of changes (or the perception of changes) in the status of the nation-state as they impact the world of broadcasting, Dyson, Humphreys et al (1988) point to a paradigm change in regulatory policies, from a conception of regulation as "trusteeship" for the national cultural heritage to regulation as an exercise in 'international gamesmanship" (308).

> West European governments seemed to be involved in a difficult but common learning process: learning about the implications for national power and prosperity of international interdependency, learning from domestic problems of policy design and implementation, and being 'taught' by new media conglomerates which displayed great knowledge and political sophistication and were often emerging as well-coordinated 'global' actors (328).

While I believe it to be true that the pathfinders in the 'learning process' are indeed often the commercial media concerns, I question the notion that they are any more sophisticated or well-coordinated, or indeed truly global, than their national public service rivals. Globalization does not necessarily handicap the institutions of the state: on the contrary, it may ultimately make them stronger, albeit transformed.

YEARNING TO BE SOVEREIGNTY FREE

Overall the state is more and more hampered by its mandate. Rosenau (1990) makes a cogent case that:

> states are limited by the very considerations that are usually regarded as the source of their strengths. To regard a state as bound by its sovereign

> responsibilities—the need to monitor the vast array of issues that compromise the global agenda and then to allocate resources among them in order to preserve and enhance its integrity and welfare—is to underscore its vulnerabilities and its inability to concentrate prerogatives and energies upon a few selective goals (36).

The corollary is that *sovereignty-free* actors, including multinational corporations, international organizations and certain ethnic and religious groups, can concentrate their resources on the pursuit of limited objectives. CNN is an excellent example of such an actor, able to invent and reinvent itself as an international news organization, to the point where for a decade after Tiananmen Square it was widely acknowledged as often helping to shape the international events it reported on: a remarkable metamorphosis for a local television station from Georgia.

Other examples might include the world's first global policeman, the Drug Enforcement Agency, which has turned its *raison d'être,* America's "War on Drugs," into a worldwide jihad; or an international emergency relief agency like Médecins Sans Frontières, which, with its promise to deliver "borderless" medical care, very consciously tries to avoid playing the national political games of its famous progenitor, the Red Cross.

The less an actor is able to concentrate and be "sovereignty-free," the greater its loss of effectiveness, and the higher its inability to deal with parallel imagined worlds. The oldest UN body, and arguably one of its most successful, is the International Telecommunication Union (ITU), which long flourished precisely because of its narrow focus on what used to be a clearly defined field, with the definitions written by the monopoly telecoms carriers of the rich nation-states. Today the ITU has to deal with a fast-moving world, where international telecommunications are open to a wide variety of opportunistic commercial concerns,[6] and used for applications like the World Wide Web which were not even conceived of until 1989.

As a result, when the Secretary-General of the ITU gives a speech on globalization he has to give equal weight to the notion that the ITU is founded on the principle of national sovereignty and to an insistence that a key function of the ITU is "to minimize the obstacles that prevent the development of a global market for telecommunications services," obstacles which include "national boundaries, restrictive practices, risk avoidance and plain ignorance of what opportunities are available" (Tarjanne, 1994: 7). In other words, he has to uphold the legitimacy of the nation-state system, at the same time as boosting a major cause for the loss of that legitimacy.

One consequence of having to serve two masters may be an extremely laborious decision making process, which is incapable of keeping abreast of technological development. Thus the development of global standards for high-definition television was effectively driven by regional standards organizations (European, Japanese and American), which have the heavy involvement of interested multinationals (Dupagne and Seel, 1998).

Another result is that organizations with a wider remit, like the supranational World Trade Organization, end up taking over issues directly relevant to global communications, such as the Trade-Related Aspects of Intellectual Property Rights (TRIPS—effective from January, 1995) and the 1997 WTO telecommunications agreement (requiring the 68 signatory countries to open their markets to foreign telecoms companies). They also have a heavy influence on the development of an organization like the World Intellectual Property Organization (WIPO), which since 1996 has become the global watchdog defining and enforcing protections for intellectual property rights on the Internet.

This concept, that the disembedding of social institutions which Giddens (1991) comments on has become a boon to those actors in a position to take advantage of it, is an important key to some of the apparent anomalies of globalization. It helps explain, for example, why Taiwan, virtually alone among the nations of East Asia, was able not only to avoid the acute recession which affected all its neighbors in 1998, but instead register an economic growth rate that ranked fifth in the world. Thanks to the efforts of the People's Republic of China, Taiwan is effectively locked out of most of the major international bodies, and it is this status as the outsider which does not belong that enabled it to flourish while all its neighbors were suffering (Economist, 1998).[7]

It also provides a context to the strange history of STAR TV, a gadfly company originally owned by a Hong Kong Chinese entrepreneur, which launched a pan-Asian television service on a reconditioned satellite owned in equal part by the entrepreneur's father, by an investment arm of the Chinese government, and by a colonial era British Hong Kong telecoms company. STAR TV was able to find and develop audiences in Asia at a speed which was literally beyond the capability of local governments to regulate. This nimbleness was a matter of corporate policy, driven by necessity: however, the company was totally unprepared for and even unaware of its own initial success.[8] In the process of this chaotic development, STAR TV demonstrated clearly how inadequate were old notions of broadcasting sovereignty. Together cable and satellite broadcasting have in many cases rendered obsolete the idea that the state, small or large, can strictly regulate the broadcasting industry.

Where does this leave the national public service broadcaster? Would the BBC be what it is without the first "B"? Although BBC World lays claim to being independent and international, in reality its only raison d'etre is its association with the BBC. On the other hand, did Shima's idea of a *Global* News Network ever stand a chance of success, with its presumed lack of a national base—or was that indeed a misnomer, as Japanese finance would presumably have insisted on Japanese control?

The history of a company like News Corporation in Asia seems to provide the answer about whether broadcast companies, no matter how buccaneering they appear, really function independent of the nation. As Wark (1994) points out, the opposite appears to be the case:

> the more global capitalism becomes, and the more it desires the global market, the more it also requires the state to administer the referents the market connects and coordinates, and to police the veracity of information companies issue about themselves. Free-market utopians thought they could escape from the state along the vectors of the globalized market, and indeed they have escaped antiquated state regulation. Marxist pessimists correctly saw the dangers in all this for democratic governments and national social forces like trade unions, but missed one paradoxical aspect of this movement. As capital moves in an ever more global space, trying to free itself from the regulatory net of individual states, it flies by one set of nets into a space where it needs another beneath it. It needs a new administration of the referents without which globalization is always incomplete. (210)

ACKNOWLEDGING COMPLEXITY

In the globalization literature, references to complexity are ubiquitous. For Appadurai (1996), it is a complex interactive system; for Smith (1990: 177) today's emerging global culture is "context-less, a true melange of disparate components drawn from everywhere and nowhere"; for Giddens (1990: 64) globalization is the "intensification of worldwide social relations," with the distant impinging on and shaping the local, and vice versa.

It is argued here that the complexity has "thickened" radically in the last 20 to 30 years, so that, for example, an industry and a popular cultural institution like television has gone from a traditional, national, relatively straightforward base to become part of "very complex politico-economic systems comprised of hundred or even thousands of individual participants and the organizations they represent" (Dupagne and Seel, 1998: 294).

The challenge is to construct a narrative or a framework open enough in conceptualization that it is able to deal with the global condition, in all its complexity. Giddens (1990) has called for a move away from the reliance on the idea of a defined, bounded system, a "society," to an analysis of how social life is ordered, and social relations are "stretched," across time and space, in a process which fragments as it coordinates. The examples looked at in this volume show such stretching in progress, as television broadcasting moved from being a stable communication order, bounded by the nation-state which created it, to become part of a situation in which economic connections do not necessarily parallel political power structures, and both are built on underlying cultural tectonic plates. Those plates can be successfully ignored, up to the point where they move and rub against each other, when suddenly they become the most important element of all, strong enough to topple any edifice of power.

I believe an acknowledgement of that complexity is important, in particular as much of the communications literature has a political economy base, which seems to distort the drawing of a clear picture of global media. As Nicholas Garnham (1986) points out, the problem with cultural and information goods is that, because their use value is limitless, i.e. cannot be destroyed or consumed by use, it is extremely difficult to attach an exchange value to them. Marx clearly foresaw difficulties in subsuming non-material production under capitalism, and Marxism, neo or classical, also has problems in grappling with the notion of an information economy

> Historical materialist theories are inadequate to deal with the real practical challenges they face largely because they offer reductionist explanations which favour either a simple economic determinism or an ideological autonomy, thus failing to analyse and explain precisely that which makes the object of analysis centrally significant, namely the relationship between the economic and the ideological (Garnham: 16)

There are numerous consequences of an unproblematic acceptance of the base/superstructure model. One simply states that the mass-media are ideological tools of ruling class domination either through direct ownership or, as in the case of broadcasting, via ruling class control of the State. Another privileges determinacy, seeing TV news as economically determined and performing an ideological function within a political framework. Yet another concludes that the audience is indeed a commodity, essentially passive receptors (see Schiller, Smythe, Pilger, Greider and others).

Little of this is supported by the case histories. There are numerous conflicts between the local and the global on the political front, typified by the Shima story; on the economic, exemplified by Murdoch and his News Corporation; and on the cultural, as represented by the widely different ways societies like Japan or India reacted to the arrival unannounced of satellite signals emanating from Hong Kong.

The point here is to recognize a self-evident reality. In talking about globalization we are dealing with a very large system, which can not be simply explained by a reference to a part of the system, or even by the sum of the parts of the system, as far as we can know them.

SELF-REFERENTIAL AND INTERDEPENDENT

In addition to complexity, another striking feature of the new global picture is its self-referential quality. The current apotheosis of this tendency is the World Wide Web, where the hypertext markup language (HTML) makes it theoretically possible for everything to connect with everything else. At the level of national policy making, there is also evidence that globalization has produced a competitive dynamic between national regulators, which helps explain the extraordinary speed with which the Thatcherite credo of "privatisation" swept the world. The effect may be to generate a negative reaction—Vogel (1996) argues convincingly that this was as likely to result in "the reorganization of government control" as in any true deregulation—but the point is the efficacy with which the idea became part of the political discourse. In Japan, for example, it eventually resulted in the dismantling of traditional structures such as the Japanese National Railway system and in much talk of privatizing NHK, which serves as a constant subtext to the NHK case history.

In the world of finance modern communications technology makes more information about prices in markets more widely available at ever greater speed, which has had the anomalous effect of making the system more volatile, as shocks are amplified when banking and finance firms automatically and instantaneously react to the information on how much the value of their positions has been impacted, in an endless knock-on effect (Economist, 1999 (3): 66).

Movements of people, goods and ideas around the world are certainly not new, and have often produced remarkable results, whether it be the transformation of the United States by nineteenth century immigration, or the inspiration modern painters in the West drew from newly-discovered African sculptures or from Japanese woodblock prints used as wrapping paper. What is new here, as Lubbers (1998) and others have argued, is the degree of dependency and interaction between different spheres.

The self-referential quality of globalization generates its own tensions. In his essay describing his experience of being in Beijing at the time of Tiananmen, and becoming part of the news making process, Calhoun notes how the international media came to constitute a public sphere , a 'placeless space' of international information flows. In this space, there was a "remarkable sense of the press building on itself," with falsehoods circulating as truth, and history being recast as it was recorded (1989: 61).

On the macro level, globalization can directly affect national policy making. In tracking the 14-year-long history of attempts to reform NTT (Nippon Telegraph and Telephone Corporation), the world's largest telephone company, Yoshimatsu (1998) traces the roots of the compromise eventually reached at the end of 1996 to the fears of the corporation's leaders that it was missing the chance to participate in the sea changes taking place in the world telecommunications market that year. Following the US Congress's passage of amendments to the telecommunication laws in February 1996, which effectively deregulated American domestic communication, all the major Western telecommunications carriers had rushed into global alliances. NTT was excluded, because of Article 1 in the NTT Law that expressly forbad involvement in international telecommunications services, at the same time as AT&T and others suddenly appeared in the Japanese market.[9]

These interconnections are not equal. Attempting to describe the "global, networked economy," Castells (2000) points out that the new levels of connectivity which underlie globalization are at once highly inclusive of the information that is needed and equally ruthless in ignoring the peripheral.

The 'inclusive/exclusive' effect is plainly apparent in the production of international news. Christiane Amanpour, one of CNN's most famous international correspondents, acknowledges that there are "some countries to which we never go. African countries are examples." (Flournoy and Stewart, 1997: 67). Suddenly, there is nothing to refer to.

A NON-LINEAR, MULTI-CENTRIC WORLD

This "endless variable geometry" is a cat's cradle of cross-referencing nodes, the antithesis of linearity. This aspect is another distinguishing feature of globalization, what Rosenau (1990) calls a "multi-centric world."

One of the problems faced in attempting to write about transnational television signals, and more generally, information flows is, well, that they flow. At the same time they do not move in a way that can be depicted by connecting straight lines on a graph. A common, and misleading, depiction of the way satellites work is to show a satellite dish "pointing" at a satellite, with the uplink signal represented by a dotted line, which is shown to bounce off the satellite (always depicted in a fixed position), there to proceed in another straight line down to a receiving dish. There are many technical inaccuracies in this picture: satellites have to be constantly monitored and closely controlled to keep them in roughly the same position, and, in the case of television, the downlink signal "lands" inside a giant, irregularly shaped footprint which ignores boundaries and borders and can span continents. The strength of the signal and the clarity of its reception can vary enormously inside that footprint. A communication satellite is itself basically a radio relay station, but one which operates in a highly hostile environment, subject to temperature extremes and varying solar conditions, and without the possibility of repair or servicing.

Also ignored is the reality of what happens to the signal when it lands: how is it used, who uses it, and how the information carried by the signal is received. This is a very inexact process: the group of entrepreneurs who launched STAR TV were apparently unaware of the impact their television programming was having in China until a junior engineer visited a trade show in Sichuan, and found the open space in front of the exhibition hall full of satellite dishes all relaying the STAR TV signal. In a sense, the STAR TV business had created itself, as informal networks of reception equipment manufacturers and suppliers linked up with cable head operators to offer this novel programming from Hong Kong, arriving from the same satellite that carried the national broadcaster CCTV, and therefore only one click of a dial away from it.

From this and other examples in this volume, we can see that the relationships described are not balanced, or in proportion. They are richly dynamic and subject to change, change which is a function of the process. The act of playing the game changes the rules. And they are recursive or self-referential, with the behavior of one pattern guided by the behavior of another which is a part of it or intricately connected to it.

This description in itself represents a challenge to what has long been theoretical orthodoxy in international communication research, a depiction of the sender, the information sent, and the recipient as connected units, like beads on a string. This was early challenged by Kenneth Arrow and his followers (see Heller et al 1986), who later developed a view of the economy as an evolving complex system (Anderson et al, 1988).

Current research into mapping or modeling the Internet may indicate another path for describing information flows: treat them as if they are natural phenomena (Barabasi, 2002). One conclusion of the Internet research is that it is scale-free, a fractal design that has emerged without any central planning or organization. Another is that links in the Internet are "preferentially attached." A router that has many links to it is likely to attract more links: one that does not, will not. Such nodes with many connections are known as hubs. Because of hubs, new nodes can be added at incredible speed, the every-day story of the Internet, without impacting the number of connections needed to get from one node to another. These observations may give clues on novel approaches to globalization research in general, and information flows in particular. Could a well-linked router or hub be compared to a public service television system like CCTV's?

CONSTANT, NECESSARY FLUX

McLuhan's (1967) "inventory of effects" of our "electrically-configured world" included the shift from "the habit of data classification to the mode of pattern recognition." This is a shift which has happened in the physical sciences in a far more meaningful way than in the social sciences[10], in particular through applications of chaos and complexity theory, which represent a major move away from linear, reductionist thinking (see Gleick, 1987, and Waldrop, 1992). The work of Barabasi—a physicist—demonstrates that social networks, species, corporations, cells and home pages on the Internet have many intriguing similarities. As Mosco points out: "It is not just ironic that social scientists continue to call for building theory around causal, determinist models long after much of the scientific establishment has questioned this goal" (1996: 8).

Waldrop's description (1992: 145) shows how one of the social sciences, economics, has slowly opened up to the concept of "evolutionary economics," adopting ideas from physics, such as complex adaptive systems. Such systems feature "agents" (for example, families, or companies, or nations) acting in environments produced by interactions with other agents in the systems (such as ant colonies, trading groups, or political parties). There is no master control for these systems, just as there is no master neuron for the brain.

A complex adaptive system is marked by its intricate organization, and the fact that it is constantly reorganizing itself. In one such system, the human brain, connections between neurons are strengthened or weakened as the individual grows and learns. In another, a government bureaucracy, a department like the Japanese Ministry of Posts and Telecommunications will prosper or falter as individuals are promoted, the organizational chart is changed, or links with other entities are built or broken. In a third, a consultancy to entertainment companies uses complexity theory research as the basis for "artificial-life systems" to predict how movies and CDs will perform in the market place (Colton, 1999: 67).

In Giddens' formulation, structure is depicted as both enabling and constraining: complexity theory adds the notion that there is no way of predicting how a particular action will pan out. While enormously wealthy individuals or institutions may try to structure the globe in ways they see as fitting to their ends, they are as likely to be themselves restructured: indeed, failure to adapt may well result in the loss of power or wealth.

It is also relevant to refer to Gould's reshaping of evolutionary theory to allow for change and selection to occur at multiple levels, impacting genes, cell lineages, organisms, demes, species and clades, and to encompass a very broad scope and to acknowledge the role of unique and arbitrary historical events (Gould, 2002).

The argument here is about recognizing the contingent nature of life, and allowing for the entry of dream and myth. Freeman Dyson (1997) illustrates this beautifully with his stories about the interaction of technology and human affairs, including computers, digital astronomy and the genome project, but nowhere more succinctly than in the history of flying in the 1920s, when two radically different technologies were competing for survival—in the beginning they were called heavier-than-air and lighter-than-air. The airplane and the airship were not only physically different in shape and size but also sociologically different. The airplane grew out of dreams of personal adventure. The airship grew out of dreams of empire. The image in the minds of airplane-builders was a bird. The image in the minds of airship-builders was an oceanliner (Dyson: 18). In the event, of course, the airplane 'won, ' but the point is the result of the race was not pre-determined.

This kind of thinking is a challenge to a "conservative" neoclassical framework in economics, with its insistence on perfectly rational players functioning in a marketplace which is characterized by equilibrium, where ultimately everything should be reducible to a mathematical formula. It forces a focus on problems of process, of evolution, and of pattern formation—processes and formations which will never stop, because if they do it will mean the system is dead.

At the same time it is an approach which offers a way to come to terms with what is variously referred to as "a process of uneven development that fragments as it coordinates" (Giddens, 1990: 175); "a world defined by lack of clarity" (Emmott, 1997: 1); "global networks of wealth, power, information, and images, which circulate and transmute in a system of variable geometry and dematerialized geography" (Castells, 1997: 359); or "the anarchic disorder of today's turbo-capitalism—a world of dynamic creativity, rapid innovation, increasing inequality, and colossal capital markets that nobody controls" (Luttwak, 1998).

TECHNOLOGICAL TAKE-OFF POINTS

I have already referred to how the convergence of new and old technologies underpins the ever-shifting, self-referential, complex cat's cradle that is globalization. In the case histories I will be looking at, the impact of new technology on existing institutions, on policy development and implementation, and on the ways people in society both construct and perceive their worlds is evident.

I do not wish to substitute one kind of determinism (economic) for another (technological), but rather to reinforce the point made by Freeman Dyson, that we should allow a space for human creativity, and not simply equate scientific or technological innovation with the demands of the market place. As Giddens explains it:

> The internet, digital technology and developments in the life sciences all have a strong input from scientific innovation, which is a creative process rather than a destructive one. I would tend to see the equilibrium tendencies in capitalism as in tension with scientific innovation and technological change. Both are essentially unpredictable and therefore have no particular connection to market-clearing qualities . . . Technological change sometimes has the effect of producing a sort of quantum leap, forcing a sort of restructuring of the whole of the capitalist economy. A quantum leap of this kind is happening through the impact of the information revolution at the moment (2000: 20).

It has always been so. Anderson (1991) has described how "print-capitalism," the creation of mass reading publics by the printing and publishing industries, effectively reduced the number of "print languages" in which information could be economically distributed across regions, so that the different French or Chinese or Spanish peoples, different because of the huge variations in local vernaculars and cultural traditions, could communicate among themselves via print in languages of state. Technology was developed to the point where a breakthrough occurred: a giant leap in the amount of information available, and in the numbers of people with access to that information.

What McCluhan was trying to emphasize, with his famous metaphor of a global village, was that television also created one of those takeoff points. Like mass printing, television was another leap in information access, and it also marked a major transition in the manner of information delivery. It took satellites to make McCluhan's global village a real-time reality, and seen from a distance the consequences are likely to be as dramatic as the invention of the printing press.[11] At the very least, they include a sea change in the nature of the nation-state, as one of its foundation stones, print language, has been superseded by a new language of electronic images.[12] To the degree that the concept of a 'national language' has been used to bolster the legitimacy of the state in a country like China, where ethnic and linguistic division always lurks just below the surface, such changes have the potential to weaken the power of the state, at the very least.

When developments in technology are coupled with socio-economic developments such as the collapse of the communist ideal or the triumphant ride of neo-liberalism, the force of change is remarkable both in its speed and its power to challenge the status quo.

On the one hand, public broadcasters like the BBC and NHK have had to react to assaults on the very principles of public service and autonomy upon which they were built, as the ideas of privatization and deregulation have quickly won political acceptance in the name of making government more cost-effective and more responsive to the citizen/consumer.

On the other hand, they have had to deal with the reality of satellites, which have punched holes in the very notion of a national television service, and with the development of new technologies such as optic fiber, which have made irrelevant some of the foundations upon which they were built, for example the notions that they are state-appointed guardians of a scarce resource, or that different communications media such as telephony and television must by their very nature be separate.

For those charged with policy making, such technological developments can be confusing. Thus the Chinese government banned the sale of satellite dishes after millions were installed. When Japanese Ministry of Post and Telecommunications officials were interviewed for this book in 1998 they denied the possibility of using DBS satellites for Internet communications, simply because satellites were not supposed to do that, although they were already being used for the purpose in the United States.

Not only the ability but also the need to control may be impacted in direct proportion to the increased capacity to communicate provided by new technology. The government of China has to constantly struggle with an ingrained tendency to control, when to do so may be to deny the possibility of making full use of the technology. The result is a dizzying stream of often contradictory regulations on use of the Internet, of dubious effectiveness.

In this context technology has another level of meaning and another role, as a contributor to a sense of identity. "What would the West be without its vaunted technological supremacy?" ask Morely and Robins (1995: 167). Technological potency has become a benchmark of modernity, and much of the fear and resentment that surrounded the rise to economic prominence of Asia in the decade up to the mid-1990s (and the quiet satisfaction subsequent to the bursting of the economic bubble in the late 1990s) was due to concern that Asia was challenging that supremacy, and if successful would put itself in a position to set the agenda for the future, the dream of a Pacific century.

CULTURE COUNTS

Writing about the impact of the internationalization of television on notions of national sovereignty, Negrine and Papathanassopoulos (1990) observe that from "the lack of fit between cultural and political sovereignty, and the difficulty of defining 'national identity' in a divided world—one is left with a very complex picture of political systems and cultural systems co-existing within an international order" (56).

In this view, satellite TV signals may be available across frontiers, without fundamentally upsetting a political status quo, as more elemental economic and cultural forces have already destroyed the separateness of the nation. When the Chinese government issues a ban on the installation of satellite TV dishes (after millions have been installed), and the ban is completely ignored, it is relevant to query whether issues of political or cultural sovereignty were ever at stake. In fact, trade in cultural commodities is hardly new: the difference is that the trade is now on an unprecedented scale, and modern technology offers the kind of distribution systems which effectively translate into unlimited access.

In looking at the ways technologies like television or satellites are used, it is essential to locate them not only in political or economic organization but also in culture. Just as the reluctance or inability of successive Japanese government to tackle its economic problems directly can be traced to a combination of political paralysis, cultural desire for a consensus compromise to minimize the damage done, and lobbying from powerful economic pressure groups, so do organizational and cultural factors directly influence the manner in which information flows from outside Japan are handled by the authorities, used by commercial concerns and received by the Japanese public.

This mix of factors, in constantly shifting interplay, is an essential, distinguishing characteristic of globalization. Thus, the question of the status of NHK or CCTV is, on one level, a matter of politics, as both organizations are in different ways an integral part of a political system. Because organizing and maintaining a national broadcast system with international ambitions is hugely expensive, financial considerations are also vitally important, especially as both television services have to deal with costly technological developments as well as operate in an environment of competition with aggressive commercial concerns. But their *key* defining characteristic is the fact that they are both public service broadcasters, and as Tracey insists (1998: 16): "A key assumption behind public service broadcasting, only rarely made explicit, is that broadcasting entails important moral and intellectual questions and ambitions which are separate from any technological or financial considerations." Since the heyday of Thatcher and Reagan the very idea of public culture has been challenged on ideological grounds, and public television has born the brunt of those gale-force winds of cultural change.

There is a rich ambivalence built into any contemplation of globalization at work. Looking at the example of the globalization of media, Herman and McChesney (1997: 8) suggest three positive effects—the energizing effect global media has had on the often stodgy national media monopolies, the development of something like a universal popular culture, and the relaying of certain Western values, such as questioning of authority, which may have a major beneficial influence. Against this, they warn of the commercial model of the media supplanting the notion of broadcasting in the public good, and the inevitable way in which such commercial media serve the god of the global market place. These are a mix of political, economic and cultural considerations, but I would argue that underpinning them all, whether positive or negative, is Williams' "pattern of meanings and values through which people conduct their whole lives." In the end, most people would probably welcome the notion of a global market place, if it translates into a better life for them and their families. Their discomfort starts with the ideology which accompanies it, one which is very clear and usually very Western, and which often seems to ignore their sense of self and identity.

If the case histories examined in this work can be extrapolated onto a wider stage, we might also see culture as being the dam that breaks the flow of the globalization river. Parker (1995:83) describes how the "relativity of language and culture is acting as a powerful gate-keeper, impeding the penetration of English-language enterprises such as CNN International and BBC (World)." In Parker's account, an ironic consequence of the globalization of television has been a strengthening of local television, in particular the national public broadcasters, which have relegated foreign programming to small audiences in the off-hours by focusing on their strengths in producing programs, including news, with local appeal.

The experience of Rupert Murdoch's News Corporation is illustrative. In his attempts to overhaul STAR TV and achieve the kind of success he has enjoyed with BSkyB in Britain, he concentrated his efforts on China and India. In both cases little progress was achieved until he developed local programming, worked with local producers and, most importantly, switched to use of Mandarin Chinese and Hindi. The logic seems to be to continue and deepen that trend, as the next move should be to develop broadcasts in regional languages or dialects, in particular Cantonese and Tamil. It seems that the more Murdoch acknowledges the culture on the ground—not the potential market of millions as seen from outer space or from twirling a globe on a fingertip—the better his chances of success.

Chapter Two
Information, Television and News

CONNECT OR DISCONNECT

Since Daniel Bell told us in 1973 that post-industrial society was coming and that we were entering a world where knowledge is the basis of social organization, the concept of the information society has become common currency, swept along by the exponential growth in accessible computing power and the rapid expansion of telecommunications capacity.

But information is itself a controversial term. Although it tends to be used by Nicholas Negroponte and others as if it has some objective authenticity, it is in fact not neutral, a reality immediately apparent when it is communicated. Williams reminds us that the perennial controversy at the core of communication studies—about the role of the sender and the impact on the recipient[1]—is embedded in the word 'communication' itself, which can range from meaning 'transmit,' a one-way process, to 'share,' (as in communicant) a mutual process of the exchange of information (Williams, 1983: 72).

Pilger, for example, positions himself at the extreme end of the one-way process spectrum, when he questions whether the western media are nothing more than propagandists, "whose narcissism, dissembling language and omissions often prevent us from understanding the meaning of contemporary events" (Pilger, 1998: 4). For less polemical reasons, this view is shared by Negroponte, who describes broadcast television as "an example of a medium in which all the intelligence is at the point of origin. The transmitter determines everything and the receiver just takes what it gets" (1996: 19). Part of what Shima claimed to be doing when he made the GNN proposal was precisely to allow for an element of sharing at the point of transmission, so that an Asian (= Japanese) view could be given proportionate weight in the representations of the information age.

Suggesting the process of communication may be subtler than the above views imply, Farmer questions how dumb the receiver is, pointing out that differences in culture result in information being processed in radically distinct ways in different societies, and, using examples drawn from American coverage of the Tiananmen Square protests, indicates how difficult it is to "see" an accurate picture of events (Farmer, 1990). In his musings on "How Culture Conditions the Colours We See," Umberto Eco takes the analysis further, arguing that the culture which provides the context for our lives also prioritizes the information we are able to digest.[2]

> a signification system allows its possible users to isolate and name what is relevant to them from a given point of view . . . a given culture organizes the world according to given practices, or practical purposes, and consequently considers as pertinent different aspects of the world. Pertinence is a function of our practices . . . To say that a signification system makes communication processes possible means that one can usually communicate only about those cultural units that a given signification system has made pertinent (Eco, 1991: 163).

Friedman describes the practical consequences of this as he traces some of the modern roots of Arab hatred of Israel, and in particular the story that 4,000 Jews were warned not to go into the World Trade Center on September 11, 2001, a fable widely believed in the Muslim world, and one created and spread entirely over the Internet.

> thanks to the Internet and satellite TV, the world is being wired together technologically, but not socially, politically or culturally. We are now seeing and hearing one another faster and better, but with no corresponding improvement in our ability to learn from, or understand one another. So integration, at this stage is producing more anger than anything else (Friedman, 2002: 2).

Looking at the 2003 Iraq war, Gladney questions the famous McLuhan metaphor to ask whether the global village has in fact become disconnected, as coverage of the war pointed to the existence of "dual media spheres that gave people the world over their choice of which reality to have confirmed as they searched for news of the Iraq war" (Gladney, 2004: 23).

In short, while a term like 'information age' has become a truism, the basis for meaning embedded in the term demands questioning, especially at the point where it is transmitted. Shima saw the way the international information society was being constructed and developed as representing another specific example of Western hegemony[3]—and when we talk about one facet of that society, news production and distribution, largely an Anglo-American construct (for the media represent a major part of the information society). He was asking for a seat in the transmission control room—a position that the Al-Jazeera station now seems to have taken.

HOW DEEP A CHANGE?

One characteristic of the construction of the information society (and indeed of globalization) is to equate it with an unstoppable juggernaut or what Castells describes as "The Automaton," in his analysis of information technology and financial globalization (2000). Especially in the "West" the voices of opposition to this powerful force are few and lonely.[4] There is a feeling of inevitability about what is happening, epitomized by the exponential growth in the number of Internet hosts increasing by a factor of 1100 in the ten years between 1988 and 1998, from 213 in 1981, to 109.5 million in 2000 (see Table 1).

The commonest reaction to such remarkable figures is one of triumphalism:

> Information technology has created an entirely new economy, an information economy, as different from the industrial economy as the industrial was from the agricultural. And when the sources of the wealth of nations change, the politics of nations change as well . . . Information has forever changed the way the world works (Wriston, 1992: 186)

Table 1: Growth in Number of Internet Host Computers

Year	Host computers (number)
1981	213
1982	235
1983	562
1984	1,024
1985	2,308
1986	5,089
1987	28,174
1988	80,000
1989	159,000
1990	376,000
1991	727,000
1992	1,313,000
1993	2,217,000
1994	5,846,000
1995	14,352,000
1996	21,819,000
1997	29,670,000
1998	43,230,000
1999	72,398,092
2000	109,574,429

Sources: a) Vital Signs 1998; b) http://www.isc.org/ds/host-count-history.html

The notion that we have put the industrial age behind us and are part of a major change in "civilization" was first popularized by Alvin Toffler in 1980 with "The Third Wave," a book of remarkable influence.[5] In an interview Toffler specified the advent of satellites and universal television as some of the key exemplars of the change (Zwingle, 1999).

However, there is reason to query how deep the transformation has been, whether "not just the forms of economic activity have changed, but the axial principles that define the society have also changed" (Tracey, 1998: 194). The question whether we are witness to (or part of) a change which is by nature evolutionary or in some sense revolutionary is tied to an ongoing debate about technology and its effect on society, relevant to the discussion here about the impact of news delivered by technologies such as satellites and the Internet.

Technological determinism, described as social thinking that privileges the technological component of a social system over all others (Parsons and Frieden, 1998) is prevalent in much of communications studies, notably in the work of Innis and McLuhan. The view that technological innovations are steering us down specific social or economic paths has been popularized by writers like Negroponte (1995) and Gates (1995), who are in a sense disciples of Toffler. Communications are usually included in these route maps for the future, with predictions that the days of mass media are numbered, new communications systems are being born, and the social consequences are boundless—and benign.

The opposition to this view questions whether there has been any real disjuncture with the past at all. Schiller, for example, insists on a traditional Marxist analysis which sees the technological improvements that have produced the information society as an inevitable concomitant to capitalism's endless drive to increase efficiency and profitability. Robins and Webster (1999) question whether the expansion of work based on information, as identified by Reich, Castells and others, can be equated with any fundamental change in the nature of capitalism, other than the birth of a sub-variety they term 'informational capitalism.' Pilger derides the very concept of the information age as a myth, claiming that in fact "we live in a media age, in which the available information is repetitive, 'safe' and limited by invisible boundaries" (1998: 4).

The debate has been given renewed currency by the ubiquity of the phenomena of globalization, and the fact that speedy communications are regularly spotlighted as one of its key distinguishing features. In particular, the effects of the global spread of information technology are still unclear, as it has mutated in so many ways, in particular with computer-based communication technology. Chapman has speculated that the communications explosion we are a part of is tantamount to "a massive parallel computing system of pandemonic architecture, multi-purpose components, and evolutionary cacophonic competing ideas" (1993: 31), on a scale which allows it to have the emergent property of consciousness.

Such a suggestion may appear extreme, but the very idea—let alone the reality—of a world girdled by satellites, where a telephone is something that slips into as pocket, was only a dream until quite recently. In global communications it does seem we may be approaching one of the 'transformation points,' the routinized intersections of practices in the structural relations of social systems that Giddens has written about (1984), or even more controversially one of the punctuation points postulated by Gould and Eldredge (Gould, 2002).

But a radical innovation or transformation point does not necessarily result in the kind of utopian change predicted by Toffler and Negroponte. The ambivalence that lies at the heart of globalization and the complexity that characterizes it can also be applied to any so-called information society.

On the one hand, we may want to speculate on a developing global village and on "what kinds of patterns of communication and belief emerge . . . in a very large—perhaps worldwide—population, so that it can function, in some sense as a community" (Bateson, 1990: 150). Raymond Williams reflected on this issue early, pointing out in *Towards 2000* (1983) that it would require new forms of society allowing for multiple identities. And while the notion of enhanced community may be attractive, it is also problematic, in that one man's community may be another's alien force.

The idea of an all-conquering new global paradigm can be located as part of a well established Panglossian tradition in Western social science, which tends to see "the modern" as part of an unbroken process of social transformation stretching from seventeenth-century Europe to the modern-day globalized world, as defined by the "West." This is the Europeanization of culture and knowledge that Edward Said has delineated, or as Sardar describes it, "colonizing the future." Amartya Sen argues trenchantly that we must resist the diagnosis of globalization as a phenomenon of quintessentially Western origin: "the confounding of globalization with Westernization is not only ahistorical, it also distracts attention from the many potential benefits of global integration" (Sen, 2002: A6).

In this context, it is instructive to pay attention again to the father of the phrase 'global village.' Marshal McLuhan was not quite as starry-eyed about the technology of communications as he is sometimes depicted, but had a clear view of the agency involved. In *Understanding Media: The*

Extensions of Man (1965) the key words are speed, power and control. The same notion was summarized by Tehranian in the phrase "technologies of power" (1990).

There is a disconcerting lesson to be learnt from the history of Murdoch's adventures in China (see Chapter 5), which traces a perfect trajectory from high hopes and avowed intentions of fundamental social change to blatant submission to the status quo.

Shima's complaint and Sardar's fears about CNN as the symbolic colonizer of international time and global space remain valid. Murdoch's News Corporation spreads around the globe and CNN and the BBC World Service Television[6] are widely available. They have been joined, however, by other voices—from Germany, from Japan, from China and, most dramatically, from Dubai. The history of information and communications is still being written.

INFORMATION + COMMUNICATION = POWER

An analysis of what the notion that information "flows" actually means did not emerge until the theory of communication and control in organizations of all kind was popularized by Norbert Wiener with the term "cybernetics" (Wiener, 1961). Wiener and others argued that "all organizations are alike in certain fundamental characteristics and that every organization is held together by communication" (Deutsch, 1963: 77).[7] Deutsch elaborated on this to describe communications as the "nerves of government" and propose "that governments and parties—that is, political systems or networks of decision and control—are dependent on processes of communication" (Deutsch: 145). In effect, communication—the transmission of information—makes the institution, and thereby the society.

There is little argument about the prime role communication technology now plays in policy development in all industrial societies, no matter their ranking. Whether in China or Cambodia, information and communication industries have become central.[8] Although by the 1970s a member of the United States Mission to the OECD was already quoted as saying, "Trade doesn't follow the flag anymore, it follows the communication system"(O'Brien and Helleiner, 1980: 457), Jussawalla points out that information was not recognized as a core element in economic development until the early 1980s. By then almost all the service industries identified as important exporters by the U.S. Department of Commerce were characterized by their intensive use of information as a factor of production (1993: 105). According to an OTA report from 1982 almost half of all United States economic activity at that time resulted from the collection, organization, analysis, and dissemination of information and information-related services (Martinez, 1985:23). Preston lists a number of major studies appearing throughout the 1980s and 1990s, all pointing to the ever growing importance of the information economy (Preston, 2001: 53–6).[9]

By 1998 the main conclusions of a United Nations study assessing the implications of emerging global and national information societies were blunt about the consequences for the developing world.

> Information and communication technologies (ICTs) will become crucially important for sustainable development in developing countries. Although the costs of using ICTs to build national information infrastructures to contribute to innovative knowledge societies are high, the costs of not doing so are likely to be higher (Credé and Mansell, 1998: ix).

The major reason why information and communication stand center stage in a globalized world is the access they offer to power (Deutsch, 1963; Martinez, 1985 ; Giddens, 1985; Arquilla and Ronfeldt, 1997).

As Giddens sees it the size and complexity of the nation state is on such a scale that it is engaged in a constant fight to maintain control, and one way to achieve this is through control of communication and information resources. Mowlana describes the consequences in apocalyptic terms, as he sees a global society, where those who "hold mastery of information and ready capital, rather than military might, dictate the course of the world" (Mowlana, 1997:19).

> In the arena of economic and political power . . . information has assumed its place besides petroleum, strategic metals , and uranium as an international resource to be bartered, boycotted, and blackmailed . . . Information means power and its manipulation can have far-reaching effects on economic, social, and political developments. (Ibid:7)

The state strategic argument is an interesting one, in particular as American strategic theorists can be blunt in their description of what is at stake.

> Knowledge more than ever before, is power. The one country that can best lead the information revolution will be more powerful than any other. For the foreseeable future that country is the United States . . . (with) its ability to collect, process, act upon, and disseminate information, an edge that will almost certainly grow over the next decade. (Nye and Owens, 1996: 20)

This is an edge that many in Asia and the Arab world are acutely aware of, that not only is accurate, timely information itself become a valuable commodity, but that "control over information flow and over the vehicles for propagation of popular taste and culture have likewise become vital weapons in competitive struggle" (Harvey, 1990: 160). It is a conundrum that governments have to face: on the one hand, an up-to-date communications system is essential in order to be an effective player in a globalized world, but on the other these systems constantly threaten to undermine political control, traditional values and moral systems.

Harold Innis early noted in *The Bias of Communication* (1951), that whoever controls time, space and the information that moves through it, or who can appear to control it, has immense power. Schiller (1969) and Mowlana (1993) continue to see global information and communication order as the ideological and cultural battlefield of contemporary international politics. Both views are reinforced by contemporary events, where the emergence of Arab satellite television stations prepared to take an independent stance has introduced a new dimension to the global media situation. The Al-Jazeera television network has succeeded in upsetting Arab governments just as much as the Bush administration, simply by its commitment to air every point of view.

MASS MEDIA

The notions outlined above, that controlling access to information is power, and that communications represent relationships, inform the role of the mass media. The mass media have become omnipresent channels for the circulation of information and communications of various kinds. It is easy to forget how ubiquitous they are. As De Certeau (1991) reminds us, from the time of waking to the moments before sleep, chances are the media are with us: radio, television, newspaper, Internet, magazine, book.

The Frankfurt School of critical social theory focused early on the importance of mass communications, shaped as the members all were by the historical events of the first half of the 20th century, in particular the role media and propaganda played in the emergence of Stalinism in the Soviet Union and the rapid ascendancy of fascism in Germany. Horkheimer and Adorno (1972), in particular, described the commodification of cultural forms, resulting in the production of cultural goods like movies tailored for mass consumption, in turn leading to the "dumbing down" of the individual, and the loss of the power of critical thinking. These ideas of mass communications as just another extension of the all-engulfing cloak of capitalist development, and of the recipients of the communication as passive consumers, essentially manipulated and controlled at will, underpin a lot of the discussions of the "power of the media," despite trenchant criticism by

Thompson and others. It feeds one of the commonest characterizations of globalization, the idea of a web of domination that the individual is totally ensnared by.

Thompson(1990) points out the fundamental flaws here are an overly consensual image of modern societies, and an overly integrated conception of the modern individual. The processes both of production and distribution of, say, television news, and its appropriation and integration into the social contexts and interpretative frameworks of the recipients are varied and complex. Simply put, there is no guarantee of successful delivery of the media message. Ikeda recounts the famous story of how the Japanese Prime Minster Sato ordered the press out of his final news conference in 1972, insisting that he wanted "to talk to the people" through television, which he proceeded to do, uninterrupted by questions from reporters. However NHK broadcast the entire event, including his dismissal of the press, and his reputation with the Japanese public was seriously damaged (Ikeda, 2001: 264). As the media have become increasingly global in nature, the complexity of the delivery systems and the uncertainly of how the message will be received have increased exponentially.

Arguably a more sophisticated approach to the development of media institutions and their role in the development of modern societies lies in the work of Jürgen Habermas, in particular his concept of "the public sphere." The basic notion refers to an earlier time when the media (i.e. the press) were part of a process of criticism, discussion and debate about the governance and direction of society. This critical potential has effectively been muted or sidelined by the emergence of powerful state and commercial organizations.

Habermas takes his argument further, to describe how the media are party to the "manufacturing of consent" that Chomsky warns us of, and that the media industries encourage a 'false consciousness' and a 'false consensus':

> Intelligent criticism of publicly discussed affairs gives way before a mood of conformity with publicly presented persons or personifications; consent coincides with good will evoked by publicity (Habermas, 1989 : 195).

Again a criticism of this view must be based on a denial of the passivity of the consumers of media messages, and an affirmation of the complexity of the media situation. I follow Thompson in seeing the general notion of the public sphere as still useful in describing an arena of communication that is neither state controlled nor commerce dominated. However it is necessary to acknowledge the extent to which technology has totally changed the communication landscape: even if the idea of an Internet discussion group may in some ways reflect the ideal of a salon or a coffee house from a bygone age that Habermas seems to postulate, the reality is different in so many obvious ways, starting with the absence of face-to-face communication. In particular, Habermas' focus is almost exclusively on an idealized depiction of the print media, which themselves are in the process of being transformed by digital technology.

TELEVISION

Ted Turner launched the now famous station by saying to his employees, "See, we're gonna take the news and put it on the satellite, and then we're gonna beam it down into Russia, and we're gonna bring world peace, and we're gonna get rich in the process! Thank you very much! Good luck!" (Whittemore, 1990: 124).

The immediate reaction to Turner's reported comments may be amusement at his hubris, but on reflection it reveals a pointed truth: the media play an important role in the operation of globalization, involving us as both observers and participants in a complex, interactive process.

As described in Chapter 1 globalization is defined by its ever-growing complexity. This complexity is reflected in the recent history of the media, illustrated by both the ownership and the birthing grounds of new media organizations. In their analysis of the ownership of the American media, Compaine and Gomery point out that between 1980 and 1998 as many media conglomerates shrunk or disappeared as merged or grew, newer players entered the stage, and a number of major international firms joined the list, where in 1980 there had been none (2000: 488). In short, the media have become part of "very complex politico-economic systems comprised of hundreds or even thousands of individual participants and the organizations they represent" (Dupagne and Seel, 1998: 294).

In the case of national television organizations, complexity does not apply to their ownership, where there is a well-developed and well-documented tendency to oligopoly, in the United States (Bagdikian, 1992; Compaine and Gomery, 2000), in Britain (Franklin, 1997), in Italy (Robertson, 2001) and elsewhere. However, as with media conglomerates in general, it is a mistake to see this picture as static—on the contrary ownership is volatile and subject to abrupt change. One of the biggest changes mapped out by Compaigne and Gomery is the arrival on the American media scene of foreign-owned conglomerates, such as Bertelsmann, News Corporation, Sony and Vivendi.

The media themselves are impacted by globalization in a variety of ways. The commonest archetype for television broadcasting has been the public service model, which puts television on a bigger stage than it would occupy simply as a process to deliver entertainment or news. CCTV, NHK and the BBC and their like came to act as conscious embodiments of the national psyche, as interpreted by a social elite, in a relatively unproblematic fashion. Globalization and globalism[10] have opened that comfortable arrangement to question, while vastly extending television's international reach.

The nature of established television organizations has changed dramatically, as they have spread their reach around the globe. For example, in 2003 CNN International could be seen in "more than"200 countries and territories worldwide, claiming 165 million television households; BBC World was viewable in 200 countries, reaching 254 million homes; MTV claimed to be the world's most widely distributed network, with 384 million households in about 140 countries; Deutsche Welle TV was broadcast in 124 countries; and NHK could be seen in 175 countries and territories.[11]

TELEVISION WAS NATIONAL

The idea of international television is a comparatively recent development. The commonest identified turning point was the international coverage of the Kennedy assassination in 1963, when twenty-three countries in all received the news by satellite from America. Takashima (1995) has recorded the feeling that this was the day Japanese international television journalism took its first step. For the first time, television was global.

It took a long time for policy to catch up with technology, however. For the 20 years following the Kennedy assassination, discussions about television continued to be limited to a traditional, national, relatively straightforward forum, reflecting the confines in which the industry operated. The development of television reflected the national stage on which it was presented, with a greater or lesser role played by national policy and government regulations (as was the case in China and to a lesser degree, in Japan) balanced with commercial considerations, which have long had the upper hand in the United States. One distinguishing feature of the impact of globalization is that the pendulum seems to have swung far in favor of commercial concerns, though I believe this apparent swing is less decisive than is often presented.

Starting in the 1960s a major element of the debate concerned the relative merits of commercial versus public television, with public television often winning the argument. In the United States the Johnson administration decision to create the Public Broadcasting Service (PBS) was in large part due to despair over the lack of "quality" programming on American television, which FCC commissioner Newton Minnow had memorably characterized as "a vast wasteland." The 1967 report of the Carnegie commission (*Public Television: A Program for Action*) which served as a blueprint for the establishment of PBS was explicit in arguing for television which would include "all that is of human interest and importance which is not at the moment appropriate or available for support by advertising" and in identifying commercial TV's competition for viewers as the key factor that limited what could be broadcast (Ledbetter, 1997: 20,1).

In fact the most popular operational model for television worldwide was to function as some kind of public agency, largely operating outside market economics (with the U.S. as an exception[12]). Up to the 1980s, the "types" of television were fairly limited. Negrine and Papathanassopoulos (1990) identified four basic models operational at that time: the American (competitive, commercially funded); the British (autonomous, publicly funded monopoly, later developed into a duopoly with a regionally based commercial sector); the European (hybrid finance, competitive within a state-directed monopoly) and the Japanese (similar to the British, only with the commercial sector in place from the outset, although in a weaker position). This schema is a simplification, ignoring for instance the case of China, which at that time still had a fundamental state monopoly, with some degree of provincial autonomy, albeit closely regulated, or those of Thailand or Indonesia, where in both cases the military acted as an alternative locus of power to the national government and operated its own television network.

The key characteristic was that television was national, and its effects, good or bad, largely confined to national boundaries.[13] This made it comparatively easy for government authorities to control and regulate, in turn making broadcasting policy fit with the political goals of the day. Even when faced with the reality of international broadcasting, the initial reaction was to try and put the transnational genie back in the national bottle. When Japan became the first nation to introduce operational DTH satellite broadcasting, for example, great efforts were made to ensure that the satellite beam was narrowed and the signals were limited to Japan, and when this proved impossible, to apologize profusely to the governments (of Taiwan and South Korea) which had to deal with "unauthorized" TV signals.

THE MODEL WAS PUBLIC SERVICE TV

Audiovisual services typically reflect the social and cultural characteristics of nations and their peoples, and are consequently regarded as being

> *of great social and political importance. For these reasons, government regulations and public support programmes play a major role* (WTO, 1998: I.2).

It is worthwhile examining briefly how it was that the idea of television as a public service was for so long the dominant model around the world.

The television broadcast industries in Europe, Japan and elsewhere developed in a quite different fashion to the United States. The early histories of all were very similar, based as they were on the development of radio, but the ways of handling that new medium diverged from the outset. Both the British and Japanese governments were disturbed by the unregulated chaos of radio in the United States—where 570 stations had been licensed by 1922—and quickly opted to license only one organization.

In Britain, the British Broadcasting Company started operations in 1922, transmitting "those education and information programs that they believed the public ought to have, eschewing the whims of mass public taste" (Madge, 1989: 105). From the beginning the BBC was intended to be a national organization, in contrast to the United States, where the first nationwide broadcasting network, the National Broadcasting Company (NBC), was not launched until 1926 . Although the BBC did in fact have commercial origins—effectively created by a consortium of radio receiver manufacturers intent on increasing the sales of their radio sets—it was closely supervised by the Post Office and other government organs. In 1926 it was reconstituted as the British Broadcasting Corporation, given the semi-autonomous basis it has to this day, and dedicated to the ideal of public broadcasting promulgated by its first Director General, John Reith (Thompson, 1990: 184). The BBC operates under a royal charter, and is financed primarily by a license fee collected through the Post Office, both of which help ensure some measure of political freedom from the government of the day.

The BBC launched the world's first continuous television service in 1936: commercial television did not appear until 1955, based on a network of regional companies. As these regional companies began broadcasting, the popularity of television grew apace: where in 1950 only ten percent of British homes had television sets, by 1963 only ten percent were without them (Ibid: 184).

Even with the advent of commercial television, the governing ethos for television in Britain long remained that of public service broadcasting, which Madge summarizes as follows:

1. Geographic universality—programs should be available to the wholepopulation.

2. Universality of appeal—features should cater to all interest and tastes.
3. Minorities, especially disadvantaged minorities, should receive particularattention.
4. Broadcasting should be structured so as to encourage competition in good programming rather than competition for audience numbers (Madge, 1989: 112).

The BBC model is, arguably, an idealistic one, and probably the best known among national public broadcast organizations. As an organization which has withstood numerous assaults from different British governments and politicians, it is also representative of a fact often overlooked in the American media context, that national public broadcast systems have proved remarkably resilient and still dominate the world of television. Of the over 190 countries that began television with a public broadcast system, none of them have gone out of business, and even where private competition has been introduced, the public channels still capture the majority of the viewing audience (Parker, 13).

The reasons why this should be so are complex. One important reason is the heavy financial burden of technical efficiency. Ensuring geographic universality in a poor, sprawling country like China is a major enterprise, and reaching even the remotest hamlet in mountainous Japan is both expensive and technically challenging. In neither case was achieving universal television coverage a commercial proposition.

Another major element has already been referred to: the role the national broadcast media grew into, as builders of the national community and even defenders of the national identity. Paddy Scannell describes how the BBC "became perhaps *the* central agent of the national culture,'" in particular through its role in setting the national calendar, presenting "an orderly and regular progression of festivities, rituals and celebrations—major and minor, civil and sacred—that marked the unfolding of the broadcast year" (Scannel, 1988: 17, 18). Hall sees more than agency, identifying an active role in an ongoing process, the creation of the nation.

> Far from the BBC merely 'reflecting' the complex make-up of a nation which pre-existed it, it was an instrument, an apparatus, a 'machine' through which the nation was constituted. It produced the nation which it addressed: it constructed its audience by the ways in which it represented them (Hall, 1993: 32).

This definition of its role is not an academic abstraction, but a mission recognized by those working for the BBC as informing their work. The consensus among the twenty-one senior BBC staff members interviewed by Küng-Shankleman for her comparison of the BBC and CNN was that the BBC was "part of the British way of life," succinctly summarized by one interviewee.

> "As everything else fragments around you and becomes multinational, international, satellite and all the rest of it, the BBC remains a sort of touchstone for the identity of the nation." (Küng-Shankleman, 2000: 142).

Anyone who has lived in Japan can attest to the similar role occupied by NHK. The most famous example of NHK "producing" the nation is provided by a live New Year's Eve show called *Kohaku Utagassen* (Red and White Song Contest), which is described by NHK itself as a "National Event."

> most Japanese are sitting in front of their TV set by 8:00 P.M. to watch a 3-hour-and-45-minute song festival, the grandest of all TV music programs in Japan. Family and friends gather around the "kotatsu," a low heated table, watching the song festival and eating little oranges. This has been the standard Japanese New Year's Eve for decades (NHK, 2002).

The contest is between teams of red (female) and male (white) singers, chosen for their popularity in the past year. The concept of the show has historical resonances familiar to all Japanese, referring to the struggle for control of the country in the 11th century between the eventually victorious Genji clan (whose symbol was white) and the Heike (who fought under a red banner). "Red and white" competitions are common in high school sports events in Japan, but what is novel about the NHK show is the division of the teams according to gender, with women always associated with the historical losers. The show invariably achieves a 50+% audience figure, helping justify NHK's description that it is "probably the greatest common TV experience shared by Japanese."

Defining and reinforcing the notion of a national culture is also plainly and deliberately a major role for CCTV, which can also be symbolized by a Chinese New Year show *Chunjie Wanhui*, loosely translated as the Spring Festival Party or Get-together. As in Japan, watching the show has become a family tradition. Starting at 8 pm. and running for four and a half hours, it is the world's longest live-broadcast show. It is relentlessly cheerful, optimistic and nationalistic. In fact Dru Gladney sees the emphatic depiction of minorities in the show (typically minority songs and dances take up more than half of the running time) as being part of the ongoing Chinese nationalization and modernization project: "the homogenization of the majority at the expense of the exoticization of the minority"(Gladney, 1994).

Both Gladney's description and that of *Kohaku Utagassen* given by NHK are strikingly close to Morely and Robins' characterization of national television as playing a key role in promoting national unity, giving the family in the home symbolic access to the nation as a knowable community (Morely and Robins, 1995: 67).

In its turn this concept is an elaboration of Benedict Anderson's "imagined communities" and his argument that nationality and nationalism are "cultural artefacts of a particular kind" (Anderson, 1991: 4). For Anderson, people imagine the nation into existence—"in the minds of each lives the image of their communion" (Ibid: 6). However, Anderson has little to say about the non-print media in the production of those images, aside from a tantalizing footnote referring to the key role radio played as a midwife to the birth of nationalist movements, in reaching illiterate populations in Vietnam and Indonesia (Ibid: 54). This is surely a role assumed by television, in particular as watching television has in many ways superseded the 'mass ceremony' of reading the newspaper, which Hegel saw as serving as the modern substitute for morning prayers (Ibid: 35). In the case of a country like Turkey, where in 1996 there were 16 national, 15 regional and some 300 local TV stations (and also including a Kurdish separatist channel broadcast by satellite from London), television was described as "drawing up the agenda of life"(The Economist, 1996 (3). Television has become the mirror of the nation.

This fundamentally benign view of broadcasting as a kind of national integrator has been challenged by Gerbner (1976) and Pilger (1998), who see television as an instrument of the powers that be, used by them to reinforce social norms, and by Kellner, who views broadcasters as promoting "the conservative interests of those who own and control them" (1990: 173), a viewpoint I shall return to below.

I would argue that at best such criticisms are oversimplifications. There are ample examples of television programming which have deliberately or incidentally challenged the status quo, including some on commercial television: "Roots" in the U.S. would be an obvious case, "Heinmat" in Germany another, as would the broadcast of "River Elegy" in China or the creation of the "News Station" program on Asahi Television in Japan (see relevant sections for detailed discussion of these latter two programs).

More recently, the impact of Al-Jazeera, the only foreign broadcaster permitted in Afghanistan while it was under Taleban control, has also been remarkable. Founded in 1996, with most of the staff BBC-trained, Al-Jazeera (The Peninsula) quickly developed a reputation for independent, outspoken reporting, a novelty in the heavily-controlled world of Arabic television. The big gap between the relatively aggressive approach taken by Al-Jazeera and the highly circumspect and routinized news on state-run networks in the Gulf region was closed by coverage of the Israeli offensive against the Palestinians in the spring of 2002, with state-controlled networks forced to follow the satellite channel's lead, or risk losing viewers (Golden, 2002). Al-Jazeera and other channels have broken the Western news monopoly in the region, and opened the eyes of Arab viewers to criticism of their own rulers and governments, an unthinkable notion until the 1990s (Saghieh, 2004). Quinn and Walters (2004: 57) quote the words of Al-Jazeera's media relations manager just before the 2003 Gulf War: "Al-Jazeera is a drop of fresh water that was dropped into a pool of stale water that stood still for decades . . . The more the water moves the fresher it gets, until such a time that we have really fresh water for the audience to take from."

THE WORLD OF TELEVISION HAS CHANGED

Regardless of its ongoing potential for social and political impact, the world of television has changed since the 1980s. Fundamental changes in the economic and technological underpinnings of broadcast television directly challenged the cultural rationale of public service television. Conceptions of the viewer as a consumer and of programs as commodities ran counter to the established model of reality in broadcasting, where public service television had mostly dominated the commercial alternative.

The technological advance that made possible 24 hour news broadcasting or the mushrooming of multiple channels each devoted to satisfying one narrow interest have rapidly subverted the whole idea of television as a regulator of the day (children's television in the late afternoon, evening news at six or seven, adult fare after nine, etc) or setter of the national calendar. The role of presenting an "orderly and regular progression of festivities, rituals and celebrations" so important to NHK, CCTV or the BBC is ignored or minimalized by the 'new' television.

Most tellingly, it is no longer possible to consider television simply as a local, national phenomenon. Globalization now provides the context of speeches, reports and academic analysis of the television industry. The view of that context may shift, from the cultural (the content of the programming, or the approach taken to production), the social (the impact upon viewers in society, and similarities or differences evident in comparison with other societies), the economic (the search for international markets, the growth of transnational media corporations) or the political (the complex interplay between policy and regulation development on the national, regional and international stages).

It is interesting to speculate how deep this challenge goes. Does it directly affect an invaluable cultural resource, one from which people construct and re-construct their sense of self-identity? At the very least, it is reasonable to suppose that the nature of that construction will change. The question them becomes, what effects on national cultures can we observe from the fragmentation of the broadcast world?

The Director-General of the Finnish Broadcasting Company sees this as a real issue:

> For audiences in Western societies, radio and television have become a value- and culture-specific arena which reinforces personal identity. Radio and television channels broadcast programmes with elements of familiarity, belonging and continuity. They provide their audiences with identifiable points to which they can relate personal memories, common experiences of delight and pleasure or of anguish and sorrow. The broadcasting media have thus become the single most important 'user interface' for personal identities and for experiencing what is perceived as being 'personal' in modern culture . . . Unless people find intellectual, community, environmental or material values with which they can identify in the networking and diversifying media, change is likely to lead to confusion and chaos rather than to the moral strengthening of the community (Wessberg, 2000: 86).

Such concerns carry little weight in the new world of television. The contrast with the views of the current chairman of the Federal Communications Commission, Michael Powell, could not be sharper. When asked at his first news conference as commissioner how he defined "public interest," Powell replied that he had "no idea" other than that "It's an empty vessel in which people pour in whatever their preconceived views or biases are" (Hickey, 2001).

It is instructive to recall that Newton Minow's famous "vast wasteland" speech was made a few months after President Kennedy's inaugural address, and was specifically connected to the "New Frontier" foreign policy initiatives. Both he and David Sarnoff, chairman of the communications leader of the day, RCA, talked about television as a global phenomenon, a point man in the ideological war against a monolithic communism (Curtin, 2001). Television was seen in political terms, not simply social. Powell is totally unabashed in his espousal of the free-market ideology and blunt in his determination to abrogate the commission's established limitations on media ownership.

THE DEBATE WAS ABOUT CONTENT

The debate about television, specifically about the public service model versus the commercial, has a history. Prior to the 1980s and the emergence of the neoliberal "globalism" discourse of global arenas which demanded global giants, the argument tended to focus on the nature of television, the programming it carried and its perceived effects. As with the different directions taken over the structure of broadcasting, the debate over content can be seen as following different paths in Europe or Japan, compared with the United States.

Giving the people what they should have

In the British media the BBC was often referred to as "Auntie," conjuring up images of an overly solicitous relative intent on making sure the children—the public—swallowed the unpopular medicine of "high" culture and education. The BBC was seen as part of a deeply embedded tradition of not giving the people what they want, but what they should have. This tone had been set by the BBC's founder, Lord Reith, who was general manager from 1922 to 1938, by which time television broadcasts had already began. It was Reith who mandated that BBC news announcers should wear formal evening dress when reading the news—on radio. "Our responsibility," he wrote, "is to carry into the greatest possible number of homes everything that is best in every department of human knowledge, endeavour or achievement"(Smith, 1995: 82.).

Both NHK and European public service broadcasters in general subscribed to this intention, to assist their audience in the arduous ascent of what another renowned Director General of the BBC, Haley, described as "the cultural pyramid" (Collins, 1998: 10). A mindset which identifies culture as having a pyramid structure is one that believes in hierarchy, perceives "good" public service broadcasting as requiring custodians to decide what that is, and is totally convinced of the ability of those custodians to act in the best interests of the public. Tracey describes how at the start of the BBC this notion was totally unproblematic for Reith and his successors:

> it was clear just who the custodians were, the characteristics they would possess, and the locations in which they would be found. Such presuppositions appeared only natural throughout the history of broadcasting because that history was embedded within a social order in which hierarchy was also assumed: hierarchies of social status and cultural judgement. And in a curious way the point of hierarchy is to reproduce itself since the fundamental belief of the hierarchical is, and has to be, that such arrangements have worth and merit (Tracey, 1998: 23).

For Reith and his immediate successors, there was no doubt that public service broadcasting was the only model worthy of consideration. Commercial broadcasting was anathema, and attempts to introduce it into Britain after World War 2 provoked a bitter debate, with Reith, speaking from the House of Lords, delivering a scathing attack:

> What grounds are there for jeopardising this heritage and tradition?. . . . Somebody introduced dog racing into this country . . . and somebody introduced smallpox, bubonic plague and the Black Death. Somebody is minded now to introduce sponsored broadcasting into this country (Franklin, 1997: 163).

In the event commercial broadcasting was introduced with the Television Act of 1954, but the ideal of public broadcasting lived on.[14] Even those who defended the consequent ascendancy of quiz and variety shows did so with reference to a Reithian education mission (see, for example, Arthur Clarke, 1984).

The BBC tradition came under strong attack in the 1980s and 90s. Partly this was a reflection of fundamental changes in British society, where the conventional notions of class which underpin any social hierarchy had come to be widely questioned, but in particular it was due to pressure from commercial competitors like Murdoch. Murdoch had built his media empire on the basis that there was no such thing as "bad" television or newspapers, and had no qualms about attacking a repository of the "good" like the BBC, especially when this was in accord with the political agenda of the prime minister of the time, Margaret Thatcher. The ideal of public service television was also weakened by the need for capital to finance global television operations such as BBC World Service Television, a news service, and to compete with commercial rivals in the endless battle for ever more costly film and sports rights.

Giving the people what they want

The debate about television's purpose and values had been short-lived in the United States, with commercialism triumphing, although McChesney shows the origins of this debate, over the nature and structure of American radio, were not so straightforward, with the broadcast reform movement in the early 1930s fighting a determined but unsuccessful battle against the commercial networks. Halberstam identifies the early 1950s as the period when the pattern was finally set, after CBS under Jack Paley began to aggressively lure away NBC's biggest stars like Jack Benny, Amos 'n Andy and Burns and Allen. By 1954 the takeover of the comedians was complete, and CBS, which had previously enjoyed a reputation as the "serious" alternative to NBC, saw its revenues double, making it "the single biggest advertising medium in the world" (Halberstam, 1979: 186). As the balance between entertainment and news programming swung decisively in favor of the former, the American TV companies were caught up in a spiral where programming based on the concept of mass entertainment became paramount.

Halberstam's book appeared in 1979, at a time when there was considerable concern in America about the huge and apparently uncontrollable power of television [see Jerry Mander's *Four Arguments for the Elimination of Television* (1978) and Robert Wicklein's *Electronic Nightmare* (1982)]. However, the proposition that television in America is simply a way of connecting potential consumers with goods or services for sale was not a fait accompli at the time Halberstam was writing. Another underlying notion was also there, what Croteau and Hoynes (2001) describe as the "public sphere model,' the concept that the media in general and television in particular should serve to give people the information they need to understand and deal with the issues of the society that surrounds them. This was in fact the view that informed the FCC for much of its history, in the sense that such access to information was best achieved by assuring diversity of choice. But this concept has largely been undercut in the twenty five years since Halberstam's book appeared by three trends.

One was the influence of the neoliberal ideology, typified by the remark made by Mark Fowler, FCC chairman during the Ronald Reagan administration, that "television is just another appliance. It's a toaster with pictures" (Croteau and Hoynes, 2001: 25). As demonstrated by the words and actions of the current FCC chairman Powell, this view has been normalized. McChesney demonstrates how in the contemporary debate "the laissez faire media ideology has been internalized to such an extent that it has become an article of faith for anyone committed to democracy" (McChesney, 1993: 266) .

The second trend was the overt introduction of corporate interest into the equation—from corporations often involved in areas of business quite different from the media. For them, the lesson learned by CBS in the 1950s is plain: entertainment is more profitable than information—and it is also less problematic for corporate interests, which frequently are complex, and increasingly are global. The third trend was represented by the technological advances which have apparently obviated the need to defend a public sphere, and is explained in more detail below.

PUSHED INTO THE ARMS OF THE MARKET

The mounting tensions between broadcasters and politicians in the 1970s and the 1980s gave an added dimension to the debate about how the media was developing, but the nature of the debate about television was transformed in the 1990s by technology. The swing factor was the expansion of information carrying capacity, whether by cable or satellite or, following digitalization, on conventional broadcast channels.

Factor 1: The Technology Effect

With some abruptness, two of the key rationales for the public service approach to television were undercut. It became difficult to justify government regulation when the spectrum scarcity which demanded its attention was no longer a factor. The consequences were spelt out by the WTO and the OECD.

> Governments . . . will probably need to modify regulatory structures to accommodate the new multimedia audiovisual services. As observed by the OECD, "Governments have traditionally used the licensing of broadcasting facilities to ensure the implementation of policy goals in respect to foreign and domestic content carriage. The restricted electromagnetic spectrum available for analogue transmission provided a technological rationale for the regulatory procedures which underpinned these policy goals . . . However with the greater number of channels available for broadcasting which digital terrestrial over-the-air, satellite and cable technologies allow, [the new environment] makes a restrictive approach increasingly difficult to justify" (WTO, 1998: IV, 21).

At the same time the notion of a broadcaster as being involved in a unique, elevating, nation-building mission was challenged by the opening up of multiple channels theoretically offering a diversity of opinions. Dyson points out that

> both cross-national satellite broadcasting and the international flow of programs to meet the needs of new channels constituted a particular threat to local, regional and national cultural identities. . . . Ideologically, national cultural sovereignty was under assault from proponents of "the free flow of information" (Dyson, 1988: 8).

Critics of public-service broadcasters, notably on the political right, were handed a useful lever by the new communications technologies. These technologies offered an easy way to remove 'bias' and 'arrogance' that were held to be a feature of the investigative journalism pursued by public service broadcasting. The answer lay in the greater diversity and hence balance of programming promised by the new media.

Television had moved or been pushed into the arms of the market, creating a new international broadcast industry, which sometimes seemed beyond the reach of national governments to control. The situation raised fundamental questions of political and cultural sovereignty, as, for example, the concept of "language-area" superseded the territorial state as the target audience for broadcasting. Again, the technology—in this case, that of satellites—had developed at such a pace that "rogue" commercial broadcasters (and even rogue commercial satellites) were in operation before international law was able to catch up (see the early history of Star TV, below). And while the new rhetoric implied a stepping away from traditional kinds of regulation, the actual result in Japan was effective re-regulation, while in China the intention was plainly to continue the center's attempts to exert control (see Chapter 3 on Japan and Chapter 4 on China). It remains open to question how successful such regulation or attempts to control will be.

What *has* happened is a change in the nature of the regulation, or at least of the imperatives which drive its formation. Under the old rules of the game, the broadcaster—whether public or commercial—was presented with an ideal of public service, providing a communication channel to the citizen viewer, in a "balanced" way, with the programming nodes to be balanced usually including education, information, entertainment and cultural programming. Now the first question is one of competitive position, whether within the national market, or (increasingly) in a regional market, with the overarching aim of satisfying the needs of consumers, whoever and wherever they may be.

Tracey points out that there is an element of serendipity involved here, as a market system that sees the television audience purely as consumers was matched by new technologies, in satellite and cable, which are 'narrow' in their casting, and thus allow for segmentation of the audience, in much the same way that specialist magazines target the readership specific advertisers may be interested in (Tracey, 1998: 41).

Factor 2: The Telecoms Effect

In addition to having to gauge the direction and effects of new technology like satellite broadcasting, from the 1980s on, national broadcast systems were swept up in a much broader debate about the liberalization of entrenched monopolies, especially in telecommunications.

From the beginning of the 1990s the attention of governments and interested international organizations swung to focus on the 'digital revolution' in communications, often in grandiose terms: Thomas et al (2000) mention Australia's *A Strategic Framework for the Information Economy* (1998), Denmark's *Info-Society 2000* (1994), the U.S. *National Information Infrastructure* and *Global Information Infrastructure* reports (1993), and Singapore's *IT 2000*(1992). In the early to mid-1990s China announced no fewer than 16 electronic information 'golden' projects, including 'Golden Bridge,' a backbone network for all the other projects; 'Golden Card,' a nationwide network to link ATMs; 'Golden Customs,' an information exchange project for customs offices around the country; and 'Golden Sea,' an information service linking top government leaders around the country.

In short, governments were concerned to promote the information technology revolution, and to build the infrastructure it required. Consequently, information policy became an important political policy objective, rather than a subset to a media policy (as in the U.K.) or a cultural policy (as in France). Television lost the privileged position it had held in a debate centered on culture, and became another item in the *international* market place, required to justify its existence in economic terms, deal with investment from abroad, and contemplate moves outside its traditional boundaries—indeed, outside the technological limits of its known world of the broadcast industry. More and more broadcasting came to be seen as an internationally tradable service (Dyson, Humphreys et al, 1988).

Factor 3: The Regulatory Effect

A new regulatory environment reflected attempts to keep up with the rapid and quite fundamental changes in the nature of television. In the United States and Britain regulation has tended to follow technological and market developments: in Europe, it has attempted to accommodate them, by gradually allowing increased competition; in China and Japan it has tended to react to them, often defensively.

In the American case, in order for television, in particular television news, to evolve into another item for sale in the market place, the definition of property had to be extended to include "public" airwaves, now for sale for "private" use. According to Mark Fowler, chairman of the Federal Communications Commission (FCC) from 1981 to 1987: 'instead of defining public demand and specifying categories of programming to service this demand, the Commission should rely on broadcasters' ability to determine the wants of their audiences through the normal mechanisms of the marketplace.' In this and other pivotal reports (cf. in Britain the 1986 Peacock Committee Report) the safeguarding of the public interest was explicitly ceded to the workings of the market (Negrine, R. and Papathanassopoulos, S., 1990).

There were clear ideological underpinnings to the American regulatory changes. President Reagan chose as FCC chairman Mark Fowler, a lawyer who had specialized in representing broadcasters, precisely because he was a strong proponent of the neoliberal viewpoint and an advocate of the premise that broadcasting should be seen as just another economic sector. Under Fowler, and subsequently under Powell, the FCC began to deregulate television in America, freeing it from restrictions on advertising, from limits on the number of stations that one company could own, from cross-ownership restrictions, and from public service requirements. These latter, though mild by international precepts, had had a wide-ranging effect on local television standards, as previously there had been a perception that being seen as a contributor to the local community would aid in securing relicensing from the FCC.

Parker supplies a context to these changes, pointing out that as early as the Nixon administration's "Open Skies" policy, which compelled a reluctant FCC to make way for a competitive domestic satellite industry, a 'deregulatory' trend was underway that accelerated under the Carter administration, effectively undermining the FCC's legitimacy. At the same time (i.e. from the 1970s) European governments began to break down the broadcast monopolies which had been the norm in continental Europe, with "swift and significant" consequences: from the mid-1970s to the mid-1980s, the number of channels in Western Europe more than doubled, to 75, then doubled again to pass 150 by the mid-1990s (Parker, 1995: 30).

Humphreys points out that government decisions to pursue deregulation were driven by a team of economic imperatives and lobbies, led by the engine of the information age. Another factor was the dawning awareness of the media's importance for inward investment (with the flip side of the coin being the threat of disinvestment). A third, often overlooked, was intensive lobbying by the advertising industry. Growth of broadcasting meant an expansion of advertising opportunities, and ultimately led to an improved trade balance (Humphreys, 1996: 171).

In summary, television has evolved from a model based on national systems, to one where international sales and exchanges of finished programming became more important, to one where every attempt is made to incorporate it into a "global" system. Global may refer to the delivery system (e.g. satellite); to the programming (e.g. CNN); to the production (e.g. where programs are planned for multiple language versioning from the outset); or to the method of financing (e.g. where revenues are derived from supply to a cable head).

It is useful here to introduce the distinction developed by Parker, between international, multinational and global television. *International* television refers to the sales of television programming and licenses across countries, which dates back to the mid-1950s, and still is the most significant in purely economic terms. *Multinational* television covers a wider range of programming transfer and co-productions, often carried out under the auspices of regional multi-lateral organizations such as the European Broadcasting Union (EBU) or the Asian Broadcasting Union (ABU), and also to the increase in transnational ownership of broadcast and production facilities that began in the 1980s, typified by the growth of a company like Canal Plus. The third term, global television, Parker sees as being typified by

> an expansive multinationalism that promises to make all, or at least a great portion, of the planet's television audiences available to a set of individual broadcasters. It certainly includes many of the features of multinational television, but in scope vastly transcends the regional ambitions of multinationalism (Parker, 1995: 37, 8).

The emergence of global television represents a process of change that is still unfinished, however. It is certainly too early to describe the triumph of the market ethos in television, or to write the obituary of public service television. Public television in one way or another either represents or is often equated with the nation-state, and the natural tendency of markets is either to ignore national boundaries, or find a way around them, as is clearly illustrated by the story of STAR TV.

In this regard it is instructive to look at the case histories which are at the center of this research, and note that in both China and Japan the legitimacy and the basic policy of public-service television remains largely untouched. In addition the threatened homogenizing impact arising from the internationalization of media markets, a bogey which figures prominently in the communications literature of the 1980s and early 1990s, is not reflected in the actual outcomes of multinational or potential global television. On the contrary, it is the multinational media corporations that have had to radically adapt their strategies to local realities, in particular cultural and social differences, again embodied in the history of STAR TV.[15]

The reasons for the persistence of public-service television in the face of constant pressure to embrace the market more firmly are multiple, but one can generalize from the situation of mass media in general, and then focused more narrowly on television in particular.

I follow Croteau and Hoynes (2001) in seeing the mass media as playing a central role—regardless of whether they do this well or not—in cultural, social and political life. The health of these different facets of society depend to a considerable degree on the quality of information circulated by the media. The media provide essential material for the processes of debate, education, social integration and, yes, entertainment that make up the tapestry of social meaning. Whether or not the media achieve all these lofty aims is beside the point. What is plain that the simple market model ignores, obscures or perverts this larger meaning, whereas the public service model at least acknowledges that there is a public to serve, not simple a consumer to satisfy.

As already indicated, the fact is that as home production capability grows, the share of locally made programs grows—regardless of whether these are made by a public or commercial broadcaster. According to the head of content at Canal Plus, which operates in 11 European countries: "The more the world becomes global, the more people want their own culture" (The Economist, 2002: 13).

NEWS AND BROADCASTING

"News is a commodity. It's information retrieval. It's not a matter of better or worse; you sell it at the market price. It's like wheat." Reuven Frank, former head of NBC News (Parker, 1995: 83).

"We were aware that we were in the money-making business. There was no point in running a news service if people weren't going to watch and pay for it. We had no government money at all. The BBC leans over backwards to avoid cross-subsidy, so we have to pay for everything we do." Interview with Alan MacDonald, Director, BBC Worldwide, June 20, 1997.

Frank's statement is a succinct summary of news as seen by an insider to a commercial television network, while MacDonald's comment indicates how far the market ethos has impacted a public service broadcaster.

In Frank's view, information is produced, packaged and marketed as a commodity. In their analysis of the important role of the primary producers of much of the news, the news agencies, Boyd-Barrett and Rantanen (1998) see this process as having three purposes: political communication, trade (including financial trade) and entertainment. It is steered by technology (for example television, or more recently, the web), by scientism (the belief in the value of the 'fact'), and by the development of mass media markets.

For the purposes of this research three additional characteristics of news can be noted: its significance to government; its role as the driver of the broadcast industry, in particular public service broadcasting; and its complex embeddedness in social process. In examining these last two characteristics, it quickly becomes apparent that news, especially broadcast news, also serves a larger function, as a social ritual. I shall briefly survey these three characteristics below, and then question one of the chief claims underlying news production, that it is objective. I shall then turn to an analysis of the stress lines that emerge in the production of news on a global scale.

GOVERNMENTS AND NEWS

When examining the histories of NHK in Japan and CCTV in China (see Chapters 3 and 4), the heavy involvement of the state in the distribution and even the production of news is apparent. This has been the case since news as understood today first emerged through the rise of the news agencies, which essentially underpin the world of news as known in the west.

The three principal news agencies in the 19th century were Havas, Reuters and Wolff/Continental. Although all three were independent organizations, each had strong links to their national governments: in fact the Bismark government subsidized Wolff/Continental to prevent it being taken over by the British Reuters. In addition the three agencies consciously concentrated their news gathering activities in the spheres of influence of the three major European economic powers of the nineteenth century, a policy which was formalized by the Agency Alliance Treaty of 1869. Reuters' territory was the British empire and the Far East; Havas took the French empire, Italy, Spain and Portugal; Wolff had Germany, Austria, Scandinavia and Russia. This cartel effectively controlled the news of the world until the First World War when the two American agencies appeared on the international scene, Associated Press (AP) and United Press Association, later changed to United Press International (UPI) (Thompson, 1990).

Much of the information used by the agencies originated from the major governments. They were important sources of revenue as well, as governments were for long major consumers of information[16], both directly and later indirectly, with the growth of public broadcasting, which through much of the world was owned by the state (Boyd-Barnett, 1998).

This brief history indicates how in a deep sense the relationship between the state and the media institution, like the news agency or the public broadcaster, is symbiotic. Usually, the media institution needs the state's approval, actively or passively, for its very existence, and it needs access to the organs of state in order to obtain the information it needs to 'create' news. The state also needs the media institution, however, so that it can disseminate information, and secure the support of society.

Today there are three major commercial news agencies: Reuters, AP and Agence France-Presse (AFP), the successor to Havas. Originally, the agencies concentrated on supplying news to newspapers, but today also feed news to radio and television networks, and most importantly have become key suppliers of financial news.

The influence of the news agencies in the creation of news is overwhelming. The extent to which the sourcing of the news makes a difference was demonstrated clearly by Li in his comparison of world news coverage by two Chinese newspapers, *The People's Daily* of Beijing and the *Oriental Daily News* of Hong Kong, at the outbreak of the Gulf War. There were major thematic differences: the *Oriental Daily* had more extensive coverage, and more negative themes, and relied very heavily on the big four news agencies, while *People's Daily* relied on its own efforts and the state news agency Xinhua. Correlation in coverage was close to negligible (Li, 1993). However Beverly Horvit's comparative study of news agency coverage of the international debate in the run up to the invasion of Iraq in March, 2003, indicated that four of the agencies coverage was not overly nationalistic (the exception was ITAR-TASS). AP and AFP were found to do a "remarkable job . . . of balancing positive and negative information" (Horvit, 2004:82). The surprise finding was that the Chinese Xinhua's coverage was the most positive towards the United States, using more Western sources and fewer Chinese sources than might have been predicted.

It is relevant to note here news has never existed in some kind of pristine vacuum, but has always had to deal with political and commercial pressures. The satellite television news channel Al-Jazeera was not only heavily criticized and even boycotted by the Bush administration for its coverage of the 2003 Iraq war, but was repeatedly banned by various Arab states, had regional offices closed and was denied membership of the Arab States Broadcasting Union, for refusing to accept a union precept not to broadcast material critical of any Arab head of state (Quinn and Walters, 2004: 67) .

Historically newspapers in both the United States and Britain tried hard to prevent radio from broadcasting the news, while in Japan until 1930, NHK radio news consisted of the reading of unedited newspaper or wire service reports (Krauss, 2000: 91). In its early years the BBC was prevented from running anything except a special bulletin prepared by the wire services, which was delivered at the end of the day, with a ban on reading it over the airwaves until after 7 P.M., by which time newspaper news was assumed read and over. The BBC was explicitly forbidden to collect its own news, or face the risk of having the wire services cut (Smith, 1973: 87,8).

While the commercial sector did its best to restrict what the BBC could say, and when, the government tried to go much further. Prior to the BBC becoming a corporation at the end of 1926, the Postmaster General (the senior government official responsible for broadcasting) had ordered it not to broadcast on "matters of political, industrial or religious controversy." This explicitly affirmed the control wielded by the government over the British Broadcasting Company a few months earlier during the bitterly fought General Strike that had divided the nation, and during which the Trade Union Congress had dismissed radio as "just another tool in the hands of the

Government" (Burns, 1977:16,7). The relative independence the BBC eventually attained was won only after a lengthy process, and in a way that still allowed for interference. By 1933 a House of Commons resolution was stating that

> it would be contrary to the public interest to subject the Corporation to any control by Government or by Parliament other than the control already provided for in the Charter and the License of the Corporation; that controversial matter is rightly not excluded from broadcast programmes, but that the governors should ensure the effective expression of all important opinion relating thereto . . .

However two paragraphs later the same resolution added

> Where the interests of the State appear to be at all closely involved, it is open to the Corporation to consult a Minister or Department informally and of its own accord (Ibid.: 12).

Although the BBC became a national institution due in no small part to the honesty and relative objectivity of its reporting during the Second World War, it in fact long continued to represent the establishment consensus implied in the Commons resolution, so that a Director General of the BBC could describe it in the mid-1950s as "a largely obsequious and deferential organisation" (Dyke, 2000).

NEWS IS THE DRIVER

News events drove the growth of broadcasting, and especially television. The original NHK radio network was rushed to completion in order to allow for nationwide coverage of the Emperor Hirohito's enthronement, which in turn resulted in a steep increase in the sales of radios (Krauss, 2000: 90). Similarly BBC television received its first major boost from its all-day, live coverage of the coronation of Queen Elizabeth in 1953, which won an unprecedented audience of 20 million, and caused sales of BBC television licenses to rise by 50 percent in the following year (whirligig-tv, 2001). In Japan, the electoral defeat of the Liberal Democratic Party (LDP) in 1993, after nearly four decades in power, was attributed by the LDP in part to television news coverage, leading one commentator to describe a political revolution:

> Political debate, which had been almost nonexistent in Japan, suddenly became popular through television as politics entered voters' living rooms. The television revolution accelerated Japan's long march toward increased democracy (Altman, 1996: 184).

The defining point for *international* broadcast television was a news story, the Kennedy assassination on November 22, 1963. An estimated 166 million Americans in 51 million homes tuned in at some point, beginning a change in their news reception habits. A Roper survey of American attitudes towards television from 1959 to 1976 showed that 1963 was the first year in which respondents cited TV as their number-one source of news, instead of newspapers. Internationally, the impact was equally dramatic. On that Friday night, NBC sent a fifteen-minute news program on the assassination by satellite relay to Japan. Ultimately all of Western Europe and parts of Asia, twenty-three countries in all, received the news by satellite from America (Goldberg, 1991: 219, 20). Abruptly, television was global.

The assassination brought the reality of satellite television to Japan. The following year the sales of color television receivers took off in Japan with the 1964 Tokyo Olympics, which was also called "the first major test of modern-day broadcasting," as satellites made the event literally international (Marr, 2000). The July 20, 1969, moon landing was watched by an estimated 600 million people—about one fifth of the planet's population.

CNN reached a new level of recognition through its coverage of the events unfolding in Tiananmen Square in 1989, which was also the first instance in which CNN was no longer just reporting events but shaping those events and even becoming part of them. It was also the first time a major breaking story was covered 24 hours a day for a worldwide television audience (Flournoy and Stewart, 1997: 100,1).

The ultimate news event is a war. CNN did not achieve its present international stature until its coverage of the Gulf War, when it not only was in the unique position of having a correspondent, Peter Arnett, in Baghdad for most of the war, but also had a telephone line open to Jordan so the story could be relayed. Murdoch's Fox News Channel increased its average audience by 43%, eventually passing CNN in the audience ratings, thanks in large part to its jingoistic coverage of President Bush's 'war' on terrorism.

Comparatively minor incidents make a difference, too. Both NBC, MSNBC and CNN celebrated the dramatic increase in their audience numbers at the time of the Littleton, Colorado school shootings in April, 1999, while the BBC reported that viewer figures more than doubled on the day that a popular local TV presenter was shot and killed outside her home in that same month. The examples are numerous.

It is therefore not surprising that the major public broadcasters typically describe news as their fundamental activity: for example TV Japan, the distributor of NHK programs on American cable and satellite, promotes NHK news above all else, because it is "well known for its promptness, accuracy and impartiality" (tvjapan, 2002), while for the BBC it is the "cornerstone" (Dyke, 2000).

THE SOCIAL PROCESS OF NEWS

Such powerful events as a war, the assassination of a president or the Olympics play an important ritual role. One essential feature of such events is that they are transmitted at length and covered simultaneously by different channels. Dyan and Katz see these news "stories" as having a much larger role in society, helping to integrate, to legitimate, to re-affirm values held in common, and, in some cases, to help bring together disparate elements through a kind of celebration of shared feelings (Dayan and Katz, 1992). Recent examples of this might include the death of Princess Diana, or the media coverage of the September 11, 2001 attacks on the World Trade Center towers.

What is different is the fact that the global news coverage of such events is now the norm. The unique precedent-setting aspects of the coverage of Kennedy's assassination have become absorbed into the modus operandi of the major broadcast media organizations. Indeed, because such events help boost audience numbers, there is a tendency for the media to try to build events of limited significance into something bigger. Arguably, this was the case with the O.J. Simpson trial. A clearer example was the disappearance of congressional intern Chandra Levy, where the extensive media interest was in distinct contrast to 'lukewarm' public interest (Pew Research Center: July, 2001).

It is also the case that governments attempt to use the same tendency for their own purposes. One example was the Chinese government's long drawn-out reaction to the incident of April 1, 2001, when a U.S. spy plane landed on Hainan island after colliding with a Chinese fighter jet. Another instance was the manner in which the Bush administration created the loosely defined "war on terrorism" and took advantage of the ensuing positive media reporting on the administration to push through a raft of legislation which in many instances had only tenuous connections to war or to terrorism.

Regardless of the parentage of the news, there is always a tendency to concentrate on the event as a thing in itself, rather than as being part of a process. But this does not lessen the importance of the legitimation effect. As Alexander and Jacobs point out, the effect is on societies, not necessarily states. Where the event becomes global, it becomes possible to speculate the event may be creating new communities of people who otherwise could not gather together or experience a common feeling of attachment: in effect, a new variant of Anderson's 'imagined communities.' An obvious example here would be the near universal television coverage of world cup soccer, and the huge global audiences that follow the event.[18]

The question then becomes whether these new communities have positive connotations, as Alexander and Jacobs argue—"the media create public narratives that emphasize not only the tragic distance between is and ought but the possibility of heroically overcoming it" (1998: 28), citing the televised Senate Watergate hearings in 1973 as an example—or negative, in so far as the events most likely reflect the broad interests of the powers that be, and can serve to depress and atomize as much as to uplift and unify. There are also important questions about who gets to frame those public narratives: when Shima came up with the idea of GNN he was at least in part reacting to the way coverage of the Gulf War had been dominated by the Western media.

We have to acknowledge that news itself does not exist in a vacuum, but is firmly located in a social process. I follow Lee and Chan in their identification and definition of a "journalistic paradigm" as a set of passively understood assumptions, the context in which decisions on what to report and what not to report are imbedded. Journalistic paradigms are both shaped by social formations, and also help to shape them. Mass media not only reflect the perspectives of the powerful but also relations of social power in flux.

> From an organizational perspective, a journalistic paradigm is imperative to the mapping of time and space and to the organizing of a glut of occurrences into news events. Paradigms acquire stability, tending to "normalize" anomalies and assimilate them into their explanatory framework. (Lee and Chan, 1990: 141)

Lee and Chan tracked how for Hong Kong journalists the result has been a kind of drift to the center in their coverage of relations with China, following the reversion to Chinese control. Ognianova and Endersby apply the spatial theory of political choice (based on theories of economic competition) to give a context to this paradigm.

> Mass media are economic institutions competing in the marketplace for audiences and advertisers. Like competing political candidates, the mass media must be perceived as ideologically centrist if they are to attract a majority . . . in order to be perceived as centrist, (mainstream media) must maintain a politically neutral position and imitate their competitors' structure and content (Ognianova and Endersby, 1996: 2).

One example of a consequence as applied to broadcast media, is the worldwide tendency for competing television stations to broadcast news at the same time. This can be seen with the early evening broadcasts of the three major networks in America and of the BBC and ITV in Britain, or the late night news of all the major Japanese commercial television stations, all of which go out simultaneously.

NOTHING BUT THE FACTS

Another strategy for capturing the mass audience is to lay claim to objectivity, described by Lippmann as the "central motive (for) the immediate satisfaction of the largest number of people" (1931: 436), and seen by Ognianova and Endersby as "a tactical process in news reporting intended . . . to create a perception of centrist ideology" (1996: 3).

The pervasiveness of this presentation of objectivity is only revealed when it is challenged. Following the September 11 attacks on the World Trade Center and the Pentagon, the Reuter's news service confirmed a long-standing policy decision not to use terms like 'terrorist' and 'freedom fighter' unless they were in a direct quote or are otherwise attributable to a third party. The agency insisted that it does not characterize the subjects of news stories but instead reports their actions, identity and background, allowing readers to make their own decisions based on the facts.

This was followed by a policy decision from the BBC World Service not to describe the attacks on the US as "terrorism." Mark Damazer, the BBC's deputy director of news, said the service would lose its reputation for impartiality around the world—IRA bomb attacks in Britain had usually not been described as acts of terrorism. "However appalling and disgusting it was, there will nevertheless be a constituency of your listeners who don't regard it as terrorism. Describing it as such could downgrade your status as an impartial and independent broadcaster" (Wells, 2001).

The reason this attracted controversy was not simply because of the emotional impact of the events of September 11th, but because American news outlets routinely define terrorism the same way U.S. government officials do. At the same time as the Reuters announcement, CNN's Web site was stating: "There have been false reports that CNN has not used the word "terrorist" to refer to those who attacked the World Trade Center and Pentagon. In fact, CNN has consistently and repeatedly referred to the attackers and hijackers as terrorists, and it will continue to do so."

The difference here seems to be that Reuters and the BBC take their audience to be truly international—Reuters claims business in 160 countries—and therefore are compelled to define 'objectivity' on a broader plane than the American news organizations.

Golding and Elliott identify objectivity as just one of the inherent contradictions which exist in the structure of news-making

> First, the news attempts to be a comprehensive account of significant events in the world. Yet also, being finite, it has to be selective. . . . The second dilemma derives from the commitment of news to convey objective, factual accounts of events, and at the same time to make them meaningful and comprehensible to audiences. But even the simplest of contexts or explanatory additions will compromise complete objectivity (1979: 17).

The ideal of objectivity is a tenuous one at best. American television coverage of September 11, 2001, and the aftermath was often jingoistic in the extreme, with the most 'global' of the news generators, CNN, immediately dubbing its coverage "America at War," a direct reflection of administration announcements rather than any legal reality. Most alarmingly, Miller has detailed the degree to which the media in the United States and Britain acted as a cheerleader for the war with Afghanistan. While the headlines consistently reported overwhelming support for the war, the reality according to polls was that a majority opposed bombing that would cause civilian casualties, while a Gallup International poll of opinion in 37 countries in late September 2001 found that apart from the United States, Israel and India a majority in every country preferred extradition and the trial of suspects to a U.S. attack (Miller, 2002).

STRESS LINES

The contradictions indicated above represent problems that exist inside the process of news production, the kinds of dilemma that any editor has to face on a daily basis, regardless of the medium. In addition, broadcasting compounds the dilemmas of news production along a number of specific stress lines:

- first, the fact that broadcasters are in the business of producing audiences (the need to cater to a massive audience, as already described);
- second, the inherently problematic relationship between broadcasters and the state;
- third, the unusual degree to which technical considerations drive television production in general, and news gathering in particular; and
- fourth, the economics of gathering and disseminating broadcast news.

Below I shall review briefly these four stress lines, in the context of globalization.

As market relationships have become increasingly important in the operation of television institutions around the world, the strain of the inherent contradictions imbedded in news production (such as the claims to objectivity, to comprehensiveness, or to being neutral or value-free) and in television's relations to its audience and to the state, grows ever heavier. Globalization has been midwife to the birth of giant media organizations like the Orwellian-sounding News Corporation, in which news production is just another business activity. Such organizations have developed a standardized approach to the gathering, reporting and marketing of news. In particular they are unabashed in acknowledging the priority for television as a business: to deliver an audience to the advertiser.[19]

As an integral part of the process of globalization, news also epitomizes many of the characteristics of globalization previously identified: it is forced to grapple with complexity; it is often self-referential (especially in international coverage); it is increasingly non-linear in its presentation of events; it deals on a minute-by-minute basis with a situation of flux; it is often driven by technology, but it always functions in very specific cultural, economic and social contexts.

Stress 1: "If we do not have a huge audience, we go out of business."

The media's need to attract the largest possible audience has been well documented in mass communication research (for example Ang, 1991; Gans, 1979; Ginsberg, 1986; Herman and Chomsky, 1988; Ledbetter, 1997). On television, news is subsumed into a milieu where the need to keep that "huge audience" is paramount, making entertainment the key factor. In congressional testimony Ted Koppel, the executive producer and anchorman for "Nightline," emphasized an overriding priority: " . . . the nature of commercial television is such that if we do not have a huge audience, we go out of business" (Committee on Foreign Affairs, 1994: 31). "Nightline" is one of the handful of daily national news analysis programs on American television, in successful competition with popular entertainment talk shows broadcast at the same time on the two major rival broadcasters. Koppel's statement was part of a defense of the choice of news stories on TV, such as the intense coverage given at that time to the story of the ice skater Tonya Harding, although the hearings were intended to examine the impact television had on U.S. foreign policy.

News "stories" are precisely that, stories with a propensity for drama and action reinforced by the need to be "new" all the time. The story-tellers, the journalists and editors involved in the production of news, not only naturally reflect the values of the popular culture which they are a part of, but in fact are compelled by the need to reach a mass audience to actively cater to it. This tendency has accelerated, with the increasing use of the focus groups long favored by entertainment producers to try and determine what kind of news viewers want to watch (Johnson, 2001: 181).

The advantages of a Tonya Harding story was that it was about right and wrong (bad girl versus good girl), basic if unattractive human emotions (jealousy, ambition, greed), transgressing the "norm." The disadvantage of, say, a Rwanda genocide story—which was happening at the same time as Tony Harding attacked her rival—was that it required extensive commentary, connections and interpretation, which American journalistic tradition shys away from, and demanded reference to a large and complex context.

In lieu of that context, the temptation is to default to a presentation of the news in terms already familiar to the media audience. Bennett cites a story from the Wall Street Journal on the "new" China under Deng Xiao Ping that used American stereotypes of progress and development to describe a 'typical' Chinese family:

> "They chatter in eager, sometimes mirthful, manner about the improvements in their lives since Mr. Deng has been in power. Their sofa, TV, a coat of blue paint on the walls and partitions separating the living room from the eating area are all post-Mao additions." . . . In short, the news takes us on a daily tour of the world-as-it-ought-to-be: a world filled with mainstream American values, and comforting images of authority and security (Bennett, 25).

The 'commodification' of broadcasting in the United States is near total, especially as PBS has become increasingly dependent on commercial sponsorship. Viewers are consumers, programs are products to be marketed, program libraries are commercial assets, and so on. The customer for a broadcaster funded through advertising is the advertiser—not the viewer. Broadcasting is an economic sector like any other, as recent FCC chairmen repeatedly inform us.

This is also the model which is presented as the alternative to public service broadcasting, and which national broadcasters like NHK or CCTV feel they have to respond to. In the words of a CCTV journalist : "it's just a matter of time before our national media will have to compete head-on with CNN, NHK, BBC and the rest for Chinese audiences. On or off the air, we've got to train for that day" (Kaye, 1997:58)

But the overriding need to attract and keep a mass audience has a direct effect on decisions regarding content, including news, with far-reaching consequences.

Ultimately the drive for high viewing figures can provide the rationale for major revisions of the journalistic paradigm. In Hong Kong, the reversion of the former colony to Chinese control led to a visible shift in media coverage of China, towards a pro-China stance. In the United States, the attacks on New York and the Pentagon on September 11, 2001, resulted in a visibly nationalistic presentation of the news. The most extreme example of this was provided by the Fox News Channel, part of Rupert Murdoch's News Corporation. Its reports referred to Osama bin Laden as "a dirtbag" and "a monster" overseeing a "web of hate." His followers in Al Qaeda were labeled "terror goons," and Taliban government fighters identified as "diabolical" and "henchmen." Reports on American Taliban member John Walker Lindh were labeled "Jihad Johnny." This extremism has been popular: Fox News' audience rose 43% compared with the same period in 2000, often passing CNN, which had much wider distribution. Roger Ailes, the Fox News chairman and formerly television consultant to Ronald Reagan and George Bush, was unabashed in making the connection:

> We don't sit around and get all gooey and wonder if these people have been misunderstood in their childhood. If they're trying to kill us, that's bad. . . . I don't believe that democracy and terrorism are relative things you can talk about, and I don't think there's any moral equivalence in those two positions. . . . If that makes me a bad guy, tough luck. I'm still getting the ratings (Rutenberg, 2001).

More generally there has been a discernable shift towards news as entertainment or 'newszak," a neologism invented by a renowned British journalist and editor, Malcolm Muggeridge. Franklin defines 'newszak' as "news as product designed and 'processed' for a particular market and delivered in increasingly homogenous 'snippets' which make only modest demands on the audience (Franklin, 1997: 4, 5). This is a trend which is very rapidly accelerating, as the media cultures of "entertainment, infotainment, argument, analysis, tabloid, and mainstream press not only work side by side but intermingle and merge" (Kovach and Rosenstiel, 1999: 4). The apotheosis may well have been the overtly salacious coverage of the Clinton/ Lewinsky affair. What is quickly lost is any attempt to provide serious contextualization for the news. Reeves and Campbell (1994), for example, have provided a detailed analysis of how the media was co-opted in the coverage of the crack "epidemic' in America, a coverage divorced from any description or analysis of the wider context.

'Newszak' has had its effect on public broadcasters as well, which are forced to defend their positions of financial privilege in a multi-channel world. When a former Director-General of the BBC gave a major speech on the institution he was careful to stress that "news is the cornerstone of public service broadcasting on the BBC" and then quickly relate it to the audience as consumers in the language of the marketplace: "(T)he BBC is now Britain's pre-eminent news supplier. Currently we have a 66% share of all network television news consumed in Britain"(Dyke, 2000).

Empirical studies show that there has been a discernible impact on content, particularly in coverage of international affairs. One of Britain's leading national daily news shows, "News at Ten," for example, recorded a 65 percent decline in international news coverage, while sports and entertainment doubled between the late 1980s and 1995 (Pilling cited in op.cit: 12). According to a 1997 Harvard University study international news coverage on American network television fell by more than 70% between the 1970s and 1995, with that trend accelerating according to a Tyndall report which indicated such coverage fell by more than 65% from 1989 through 2001 (both cited in Mediatenor, 2002).

As news content changes, and international news coverage declines in volume, the avenues of access to the news are narrowed. The executive vice president of CNN has acknowledged that in the process of news selection there is manipulation by both the government and the media, with outsiders to the process having great difficulty even getting on the agenda:

> During the Gulf war, I walked past the international desk and one of the younger assistants was just slamming down the phone and saying something like, "I wish this guy would leave us alone." And I said, "what is this all about?" And he said, "it is somebody claiming to be Muammar al-Qaddafi who wants to be interviewed on CNN." [Laughter.] And I said, "maybe it is Muammar al-Qaddafi." He said, "oh." I said, "call this number," and he did, and sure enough, it was. [Laughter.] And we put him on (Committee on Foreign Affairs, 1994: 26,7).

The question of access is in fact a double-edged sword. Peter Arnett, the Australian reporter who was renowned for his 'live' broadcasts from Baghdad as it was bombed during the Gulf war, said Iraqi authorities allowed CNN to stay in Iraq because of the network's willingness to give Iraqi President Saddam Hussein access to CNN (Flournoy and Stewart:34). CNN has a reputation for willingness to dilute its coverage in exchange for a different kind of access, that of entry to a 'difficult' markets. A senior BBC official interviewed for this research was adamant in his opinion that CNN was prepared to compromise its editorial integrity in order to ensure such access, citing the example of CNN being able to broadcast in Malaysia while the BBC was banned there.[20]

The consequences of loss of access to the news agenda can be grave. Christiane Amanpour, CNN's best known international reporter has acknowledged that some regions (especially Africa) and some cultures (in particular Arab/Islamic) have long been sidelined in international news coverage, to the extent that a murder story involving a minor celebrity in California supersedes coverage of genocide in Africa.

> In truth there are countries to which CNN returns time and time again and some countries to which we never go. African countries are examples.

> The most significant illustration of this was the Rwanda genocide in 1994. Everybody was late getting in there. For CNN, it was the year of O.J. and the attention of the company was focused elsewhere. Africa is a big continent. (Flournoy and Stewart, 1997: 67)

Stress 2: The inherently problematic relationship with the state

For a company like CNN, a national broadcaster like CCTV is a valued customer, and the Chinese government's wishes are to be respected. As a senior vice president for network distribution explains it:

> We fully understand that they do not want CNN International on a 24-hour basis to be distributed to every household in China. We respect that and will operate accordingly . . . We don't have the view that we will rain down on a country via satellite television whether we are welcome or unwelcome. We will work with the powers that be, the state broadcasters, the ministers of communication, and we will abide by the rules of their country . . . We do not want to force our products on them" (Flournoy, ibid: 7).

Television has always had a symbiotic relationship with government. The examples already cited in this section make this clear in the case of public service broadcasters, but the same applies to commercial television. In his description of the eclipse of an icon of American TV, Ed Murrow, Halberstam notes "an unwritten law of American journalism that states that the greater and more powerful the platform, the more carefully it must be used and the more closely it must adhere to the norms of American society, particularly the norms of the American government." (Halberstam, 1979: 198).

Halberstam also describes how American presidents gradually adapted to the possibilities of the new medium for eliciting a national and often emotional response: an evolution from Eisenhower, who scorned it, to Nixon, who initially underestimated it and always distrusted it, to Kennedy, who appreciated its potential and used it, helping launch the enormous increase in presidential power that took place in the late Sixties and Seventies (op.cit: 443)

Since the days of Kennedy and Nixon, television has become an intrinsic part of the business of politics. In fact, most of the huge budgets spent on political campaigns in the United States and other Western countries go to buying television time, and the "made-for-television candidate is packaged, marketed and sold like any other commodity, except, of course, that toothpaste does not determine foreign policy" (Parsons and Frieden, 1998: 342). One reason for this is that news coverage and analysis of political affairs is often skimpy at best, a news gap that is filled with paid commercials and other advocacy programming.

Bennett, Chomsky, Greider and others see television as part of a conditioning process, where our social and political worlds are constructed in such a way as to best serve the interests of those in power. In Bennett's view, political leaders no longer have to try and hide the truth, because they have gained control of the bureaucracies and intelligence organizations that manufacture the information on which the truth rests (1983: 134). The media in the West and in Japan are now part of a news/information dispersal business, in which, for example, the "game of politics" is often more important than the social issues which the politicians are supposed to be addressing.

The 1997 State of the Union address happened to coincide with the announcement of the verdict in the O.J. Simpson civil trial: one major network used split screens to cover both. By 2000, the trend had accelerated, with two of the four networks, NBC and Fox, dropping the broadcast of the first presidential debate in favor of a baseball game and an entertainment show (Johnson, 2001: 210).

The trend to trivialization in television coverage has considerable implications for future directions of globalization. As the description of Muammar al-Qaddafi 's attempts to get his views aired on CNN indicate, our understanding of the processes of globalization are often media-ated, as we become both observers and would-be participants in one another's affairs—or as we are denied the opportunity to be observers or participants, without our knowing.

Stress 3: The degree to which technical considerations drive television production in general, and news gathering in particular

Technological developments have had a major impact on the development of television, and underlie many of the forces for change to the status quo of public broadcasting in particular. One development is the huge expansion in carrying capacity, first with cable and satellite transmission of television signals, and now with digital television. Another is the great increase in reach of the television signal, especially with satellite transmissions. A third is the development of totally new ways of both capturing and delivering audiovisual news content, via the world wide web. A fourth will probably be the convergence of one or more of these developments, such that traditional means of distribution are liable to be replaced or marginalized.

The "grammar" of news delivery has changed radically in the past 20 years, thanks to new technology, such as satellites, and to the influence of the CNN model. MacGregor reminds us that the Vietnam war was shot on film, usually flown to Hong Kong where it was processed, and then beamed by satellite to New York for editing and broadcasting, an operation that typically took days. The introduction of broadcast quality video and portable editing equipment speeded the process up, but it was not until 1985 that the first "fly-away" satellite uplinks made today's norm possible—the reporting live from anywhere in the globe (MacGregor, 1995: 80).

Many of the journalists MacGregor spoke to expressed strong reservations about the superficiality of such coverage, and how misleading it can be. One noted that during the attempted coup d'etat in Russia in 1993: "Western governments, including certainly Mitterand and Major, were making very rapid assumptions based on a fixed camera on the CNN office overlooking Kutuzovsky Prospekt . . . that the coup had succeeded, Gorbachev was out and so on. Television is very dangerous" (Ibid.: 88).

In a very real sense, the technology changes the nature of how news is reported. According to MacGregor, "(t)he competitive, management-driven and often unthinking deployment of technical resources has changed location-based news reporting utterly," and in ways which are not widely realized (Ibid.: 92). The engineer with the ground station and the task of establishing a link has the priority, not the local correspondent with a knowledge of the background to what is happening, or even the journalist sent to dig out the story.

The consequences of this can be baleful. Calhoun describes how the reporters flown in to cover Tiananmen Square would often have extremely superficial knowledge of the situation, and would remain distant from the Chinese.

> The CBS crew stayed at one of Beijing's best joint-venture hotels, the Shangri-La, taking over the fifth floor. When they went to Tiananmen Square, they did so in a bus or a two-ton red truck, which they parked well away from the core of the protest and from which they only ventured out on specific forays for interviews or footage. They were able to arrange lots of interviews, including with key leaders, but they seemed to have little direct acquaintance with what was going on. . . . Many seemed more interested in the predigested accounts of other Westerners than in the first hand statements which Chinese students—many fluent in English—could provide for themselves (Calhoun, 1989: 60).

One result of the intermediation effect of the technology observed by Calhoun was that, while media sympathies might lie with students, their attention was on the government.

> The way it reported the story consistently gave the impression that the really interesting questions were what the official political leaders were up to and who would wind up on top . . . it was much weaker on the

> questions of what made this student movement happen and what the students wanted. Biases against this sort of background are built into the canonical style of most TV reporting. So the activities and especially the goals of the student protesters all but disappeared from view except as the occasion for the leadership struggle and authoritarian crackdown (ibid: 62).

There are several other consequences. The "visiting firemen" approach to journalism indicated in Calhoun's description goes hand-in-hand with an increasing reliance on television news agencies, a subject covered in more detail in the next section. The superficiality in the reporting observed by Calhoun also feeds into an observation from the previous section, concerning the rise of news as entertainment, where the objective is not to help the viewer understand a situation, but to involve them in an event.

Another result is an increase in the imbalance in the flow of news between the 'developed' world and the 'developing.' Use of satellite transponders for international television signal transmission is expensive, beyond the reach of poorer countries. In many countries television services rely entirely on global services such as CNN, Visnews, and WTN. Broadcasters in developing nations are forced to accept the fact that even news reports about matters of extreme relevance to their own country must be presented through the eyes of a commentator in London or New York (Wallis and Baran, 1990).

The difference a satellite link, or its lack, can make becomes clear in times of war. The image of a frustrated Qaddafi trying to persuade a desk editor at CNN to let his voice be heard is indicative of where this leads us: a major component of both the Gulf and the Falklands wars was the successful management of news about the conflicts by the victorious parties, a process made easier by technological changes.

This situation is changing. The success of Al-Jazeera, initially in its reporting on the Taliban and on Osama bin Laden's Al-Qaeda, which might well be indicative of a break in the power of the traditional international news providers, at least in terms of providing alternative viewpoints. Al-Jazeera's remarkable accomplishment led to a flourishing of broadcast media in the Arabic-speaking world, including Abu Dhabi television, Al-Arabiya from Dubai, and a joint venture between the Lebanese Broadcasting Corporation and the London-based newspaper Al-Hayat, all employing satellites. Another result was a major disconnect between coverage of the 2003 Iraq war in the Arab media and in the American media in particular.

Finally, one of the greatest pressures on news production created by the new technologies is the need for speed, which has become a constant with the "always on" aspect of the Internet and the "7x24" concept of the news popularized by CNN. The Internet in particular has had a deep impact on the way news is generated and distributed.

In 2000 The Pew Research Center for the People and the Press documented the rapid emergence of the Internet as a news source, as well as a significant decline in regular viewership of broadcast television news. While a third of Americans surveyed got their news from an online source at least once a week, compared to 20% in 1998, regular viewership of network news had fallen from 38% to 30% over this period, and local news viewership had fallen from 64% to 56% . The viewership figure of 38% in 1998 itself represented an even more steep decline over the previous five years, as viewership in 1993 had stood at 60%. Conversely, while only 6% had claimed to never watch network news in 1993, this figure had risen to 19% in 1998. Perhaps most ominously for the future of broadcast television in the United States was the finding that the younger and better educated were more inclined to use the Internet than watch one of the nightly network news broadcasts (Pew, 2000).

However, it is important to note that the decline is in network television: cable news (as represented by CNN, MSNBC, Fox , ESPN and the Weather Channel) has been rising in popularity, with a 1998 Pew survey reporting that 60% of Americans regularly watch one of the cable channels for news (Pew, 1998).

The key element for the relative success of both cable news and news carried on the Internet is immediacy. In a remarkably short period of time, the idea that news should always be available, literally on demand, has become a commonplace. This also has its consequences, notably regarding the lack of editorial time to check the information for accuracy, and a tendency to 'narrowcast' the news to appeal to the assumed preferences of an identified audience.

Stress 4: The economics of gathering and disseminating broadcast news

This section began with a blunt statement from the former head of NBC news that news is a commodity, produced and sold like any other. As market relationships become increasingly important in the operation of television institutions around the world, the stress on the inherent contradictions outlined above, and on television's relationships with its audience and the state, grow apace. We can discern three characteristics of this stress line: the size and wealth of the business, which tends to induce consolidation; the concomitant economic pressures on the production of news, and the consequences thereof; and the dubious economic logic that propelled news production and distribution onto a global stage, where commercial television organizations may find themselves dealing with a diverse world that demands to be taken into account, on its own terms.

TELEVISION IS VERY BIG BUSINESS

The unbridled commercialism of the American television market has its effects, including a direct influence on the content of what is broadcast. Epstein (1974) describes how the process or economic logic of television—the demands of audience maintenance, cost control and scheduling—overwhelm journalistic considerations. The imperative is to keep the audience watching, with an emphasis on presentation and packaging to achieve that end.

Historians of television, like Eric Barnouw and J. Fred McDonald have described how commercial logic pushed television to favor uniformity over diversity, replication over innovation, and the national over the local. As Curtin points out "the narrative trajectory in these histories is toward homogenization, nationalization, and ultimately transnationalization."(Curtin, 2001: 336).

Broadcasting empires

In the past the question of ownership has been complicated, involving not only issues of regulation and control (of the signal) and creation and editing (of the content) but also ownership of the means of distribution and of the means of production. Often the interests of these different parties overlap, but they may also be at odds with each other, especially when the signal is cast on as broad a scale as happens through satellite transmission. While one government agency may consider it has a mandate to restrict or ban a satellite transmission, for instance, another branch of the same government may be actively engaged in widening the possibility for the reception of such signals, as happened in China (see Chapter 4). But in America this kind of conflict may be disappearing, as what Tasini (1996) dubs the "Tele-Barons" consolidate in their hands a breathtaking amount of power, with overt support from politicians and from the bureaucrats charged with their regulation.

This power is a factor of the gigantic size of the media conglomerates. Bagdikian points out that Time Warner, for example, had more technical communication power than most governments, assets greater than the GDP of many small countries, control of the second largest cable system in the world and an aggregate worldwide readership exceeding 120 million (Bagdikian. 1992: 240). Following its merger with AOL, this power and wealth and reach expanded considerably, although it subsequently contracted following revelations that the value of AOL's stock had been artificially inflated.

A rational tendency of companies of this size seems to be to consolidate their positions by feeding "product" (a revealing term which ignores distinctions between news and entertainment, if indeed such distinctions any longer exist) up and down a vertically integrated structure.

The main functions in the chain of television production have been identified as those of originator, programmer, broadcaster, carrier and network operator (Logica cited in Morely and Robins, 1995: 32). What is remarkable is how many media corporations have now achieved vertical integration of all or most of those roles, notably the various parts of the Murdoch empire (Fox Broadcasting, 20th Century Fox, Sky, STAR and many others), Disney/ABC, AOL/Time-Warner and the Berlusconi octopus, which notably also includes effective control of RAI, the state broadcaster. However, it should also be noted that major public television broadcasters, including NHK, CCTV and the BBC combine many of these functions.

THE ECONOMICS OF TELEVISION NEWS

The economics of television news is a recurring sub-theme of this book. Ultimately cost was the rationale given for NHK's decision not to proceed with Shima's vision of GNN, rather than any question of technological feasibility or political appropriateness. And the revolution in the news information gathering and distribution business represented by CNN was as much a story of changes in the economics of news gathering and broadcasting as of the application of new technologies.

The way that economic imperatives may impact television news production was clearly illustrated in the mid-1990s when the great drama in American journalism revolved around coverage of the tobacco industry. A PBS documentary showed in considerable detail how both ABC and CBS were forced into what was effectively self-censorship in their reporting of the way the major tobacco companies manipulated nicotine levels in cigarettes, despite being aware of the health hazards posed (PBS, 1996). Eventually both broadcasters did report on the issue, but only after one of the tobacco companies, Brown & Williamson, had tried and failed to deny public access at the University of California, San Francisco (UCSF) library to documents which showed its culpability in nicotine manipulation (Wiener, 1996: 11)

What the PBS report showed was the news producers at CBS and ABC being forced to change their reports under pressure from the corporate lawyers, at a time when both corporations were involved in multi-billion dollar buy-out negotiations. It also pointed out that the successful defense employed by the UCSF lawyer, based on the university library's intent to publish the documents on the World Wide Web, was the same as one the TV companies could have used, but had decided against because of the financial implications.

As Halberstam makes clear in "The Powers That Be," corporate pressure on individual journalists or on particular programs is nothing new in the checkered history of American media conglomerates. What has changed is the degree of pressure, and also the nature of the conglomerates themselves which are now rarely managed by people with direct experience of the news production process.

CONSEQUENCES

Economic pressures have clear consequences for news production on television.

The news as a sausage

Epstein (1973) shows how the economic logic of American broadcasting—the problems of scheduling, audience maintenance and cost control—swamp journalistic needs, while organizational imperatives result in a sausage-factory approach to news, based on story models, presented by personalities, in a production environment entirely geared to pre-planned, digestible and limited packages. The consequence in the United States is the same, whether for news reporting in a four-network market, car production in a three-company industry, or political campaigning in a two-party system: employ production efficiencies and market techniques to standardize the product as much as possible, so as to minimize the risk of losing a minimally acceptable share of that market (Bennett, 1983).

Cost control

The imperative to control costs has become a mantra. This applies not only to staff salaries, but also to running costs, including the bills for hours of satellite time and other new technologies, increasing costs of travel, and expanding costs of maintaining foreign and domestic bureaux. One result has been a steep decline in the number of overseas bureaus—except for the international news agencies like Reuters, or the public broadcasters like NHK or the BBC.

As a second result, the news divisions of the major networks in the U.S. often find themselves at a disadvantage when dealing with big international stories.

A third consequence is a steep decline in foreign news appearing in American media in general, and on television in particular. A survey for the Joan Shorenstein Center on the Press, Politics and Public Policy at Harvard showed a steep decline in the time devoted to foreign news on American network TV from 45 percent in the 1970s to 13.5 percent by 1995. A 2001 Tyndall report showed that foreign news coverage on the evening news programs of the major U.S. networks in 2000 was one third the amount aired in 1989 (Mitchell, 2001: 2).

Advertising rules

Auletta (1992) has tracked in detail the closely symbiotic relationship between the advertising industry and the major American broadcasters. The problematic nature of this relationship, and the economic realities underpinning broadcast news, were revealed starkly by the impact of the events of September 11, 2001. Best estimates were that radio, television and television syndicators in the United States lost in the region of $1 billion in the first five days, due to lost advertising revenue and the cost of covering the news non-stop. For the executives of media corporations charged with making a profit, the logic would be to cut the costs associated with reporting, including lay-offs and early retirements—as had already happened earlier in 2001 when advertising revenues declined with the slowing of the U.S. economy. In other words, "the cost of covering a story aggressively could threaten the media's ability to continue to do so"(Schwanhausser, 2001).

Commercial news organizations are businesses; increasingly public news service organizations operate in the same way. At the time of Deng Xiao Ping's death a senior CCTV official openly complained to the author about the extent of advertising revenue CCTV had lost because of the mass cancellation of regular, advertising supported programming.[21]

The norm for the television industry has become huge companies catering to very large markets, facing a small number of competitors. There are two consequences in the news business: most editors find it expedient to take their story leads from the wire services, and editors tend to standardize their product further by bringing it in line with the competition (Bennett: 1983). Another consequence which is becoming more and more apparent is that news today may be produced in the context of a large corporation which may have no fundamental commitment to production of news, or may dismiss traditional claims to fairness or objectivity. Murdoch's Fox News, for example, has a clear conservative stance in its news presentation, which is explained as an attempt "to provide a little more balance to the news."

As already indicated, yet another consequence is that increasingly the production of raw news is 'outsourced.' The origins of world news are plain: increasingly, the 'wholesale' source is the news agencies, a business which is dominated by Britain (Reuters, Reuters Television, formerly Visnews), the

United States (AP, AP Television and WTN) and France (Agence France-Presse). Despite the NWICO controversy of the 1970s, it is a situation of global dominance that seems to be by and large accepted. The major national news broadcasters, especially NHK and the BBC, together with CNN, represent the major exceptions to the agencies' predominance, although all three take 'raw news product' from the agencies.

Agencies rule

The "sausage factory" aspect of modern news production has already been remarked on. The standardization of news is in part a result of economic pressures. It is also a consequence of people from similar backgrounds with similar values making similar choices (Wallis and Baran, 1990)—as can be witnessed in Japan with NHK and its commercial rivals, in Britain with the BBC and ITN, or with the half-hour national news broadcast that the three American majors run every evening at the same time.

But in television probably the key factor is the fact that there are now only two major video news 'wholesalers': the British Reuters TV News, with 184 bureaux in 163 countries, 76 of which are television equipped; and the American Associated Press Television News (APTN), with 83 bureaux in 67 countries. Between them they control "in excess of 90 percent" of the market, with the big international broadcasters typically taking news from both (Ritchie, 2001). Most of the material is basically 'raw,' though one of the Reuters services , "Reuters Reports,' promises "voiced, ready-to-air stories which are updated every six hours and provide the ideal finished solution for broadcasters and online users alike."

As Boyd-Barrett (1998) points out, the situation with regard to news agencies at the beginning of the 21st century is little changed from that at the beginning of the 20th. The major agencies are still to be found headquartered in London, Paris and New York. In terms of television news, the situation is even more limited: because London serves as the headquarters of both Reuters and APTN, and is also home to one of CNN's key offices, the British influence is especially heavy.

NEWS AND GLOBALIZATION

At the end of 1995 Microsoft and NBC reached an agreement to launch MSNBC, a round-the-clock cable news service to rival CNN's, and also to develop an interactive online news service. This brought to five the number of organizations proposing such a service at that time, the others being ABC, News Corp., CBS and the BBC. It had all the appearances of the apotheosis of Anglo-American domination of global information distribution, turbo capitalism applied to another aspect of the media.

But the strange feature of this flurry of announcements was that none of the organizations expected the business to be profitable. Almost 25 years after its launch in 1980, CNN's average audience still hovers around 500,000, compared with the average 12 million reached by the top nightly news shows of the major American networks. These comparatively low figures do not square with the fact that running a 24-hour news service is expensive. According to NBC's president, "News is a place for people who have an appetite for losses" (Auletta, 1996: 45).

International television news is equally problematic. Of the main English-language international news channels, it took CNN International six years to make money from its launch in 1985. BBC World and Euronews have yet to make a profit, and the major American broadcasters largely abandoned the international networks they had promised. The exception was CNBC, a joint venture between Dow Jones and NBC, which has had little success. Even Al-Jazeera, which has financial backing from the emir of Qatar and has been a runaway success in terms of building an audience, is reported to be unprofitable, due in large part to a regional advertising boycott in reaction to its independent stance (Wheeler, 2003)

According to one American television services provider quoted at the time the new networks were mooted, any plan for a 24-hour international news service had to include Asia: "When U.S. and other worldwide programmers look for new opportunity, Asia is where they look."(Cosper, 1996: 27) In the event, Asia's television market proved much harder to enter than the international conglomerates originally thought. In particular, the conventional wisdom has followed the lessons taught by the history of STAR TV and swung from the concept of a pan-Asian market, based on advertising revenue, and using English as a lingua franca, to clearly demarcated programming aimed at specific areas or sub-regions, using the language of that area, and preferably subscription based, with the signal scrambled. The experience of Murdoch's BSkyB in Britain had shown that such a pay-television system can be immensely profitable. But the lesson could not be simply applied to Asia, absent a reliable system for collecting the revenues, or the ability to stop pirating of the signals, or a stage of economic development and national income which made possible a high enough level of charges.

At the same time as the media conglomerates attempted to get their marketing strategies straight in Asia, they had to deal with widely differing local priorities, and, unusually, fierce competition. As revealed by the case histories that follow, it is inaccurate to see globalization in terms of the kind of straightforward process indicated by phrases like 'turbo capitalism.' It is an oversimplification to see attempts to build worldwide media empires as especially coherent. The apparent control is not exclusive, necessarily, nor is media domination assured.

I have already referred to the degree to which media institutions have a symbiotic relationship with the state. Traditionally the media institution required the state's approval, actively or passively, for its very existence, and it wants access to the organs of state in order to access the information it needs to 'create' news. The state also needs the media institution, however, so that it can disseminate information, and secure the support of society. When the media become global, this relationship is problematized, as the media institution needs to build connections on a much wider scale than previously, while the state has to become more sophisticated in trying to communicate through the media, over which it may have far less direct influence. Nevertheless, at some point, the 'global' media company like News Corporation has to become 'local'—or at least regional—at which time a state like China has the opportunity to compel the kind of relationship it is most comfortable with.

In addition to the commercial and political reasons why it may be difficult to make the distribution of global news into a successful business there are more existential factors as well. Satellite news can be measured in length of time, but exists outside of it. It occupies a space but has no location. It gives us information, but no substantial context. It may increase knowledge, but not necessarily raise understanding.

This represents a minefield for those charged with its creation and distribution, who function with no other reference point than that of an ill-defined international market place. In testimony before a congressional committee, Ed Turner, an Executive Vice President with CNN, explained that the word "foreign" is banned from the CNN lexicon.

> After all, if you live in Paris and you are watching CNN doing a story about a street demonstration outside your apartment building, it might be a bit insulting to hear the participants all described as foreigners. They are not foreigners to you, the consumer (Committee on Foreign Affairs, 1994: 8)

The comment is revealing in a number of ways. For CNN management news is a product, and it is fear of offending a consumer of the product that dictates an editorial decision on the use of language. It is also interesting that the example chosen was a street demonstration, with the implications that this is something "foreigners" are prone to do, that this is the kind of international event which is "news worthy" for an American audience,[22] and that the exemplar location is Paris, as the French remain some of the most vocal objectors to the Anglo-American status quo.

Thus it is appropriate that Régis Debray argues in favor of "mediodiversity" in the face of the increasing uniformity of content which he sees resulting from the spread of global networks. The alternative could be a revolt against those who control our dreams (Joscelyne,1995).

Tomlinson takes this debate a step further by distinguishing between the idea of cultural domination at the level of institutions, and the idea that

> Ultimately people must have both the desire and the institutional space to create narratives of cultural meaning . . . As global cultures fall into the conditions of modernity through the spread of the institutions of modernity, they all face the same problem of the failure of a collective will to generate shared narratives of meaning and orientation (Tomlinson, 1991: 165).

The notion of "generating shared narratives of meaning and orientation" is the first line of defense for the public service broadcaster. Dayan and Katz have made a strong argument that the great ceremonial media events already fulfill this function. They are equivalent to the live broadcasting of history (examples might be the funeral ceremonies of President Kennedy, Deng XiaoPing and Princess Diana, the Watergate hearings, the 1989 changes in Eastern Europe, the Olympics and World Cup Soccer). These broadcasts attract the largest audiences in the history of the world, measured in hundreds of millions. They go beyond conquering space and time to take on the power of a civil religion, interrupting daily routine, concentrating on experiences of communitas and integration—on a global scale (Dayan and Katz, 1992). Are these shared narratives best told by institutions informed by a mission to provide a forum for the public, or by commercial organizations whose primary raison d'etre is to make money?

The case histories which follow examine this debate in detail and in action, and reflect the complexity of the processes of globalization.

Chapter Three

Case History 1—Japan and NHK

BACKGROUND

Japan is a media dense society. There are five major national newspapers, whose combined daily circulations are 40 million.[1] In addition to the nationals there are major 'bloc' papers serving whole regions, prefectural newspapers, community newspapers and four English-language papers. The total daily circulation of newspapers in 2002 was calculated at almost 71 million, with 94% delivered direct to the home, resulting in the highest per capita circulation in the world. In 2003 there were 3,554 magazines on the market, with the total number of copies issued amounting to 4,679 million. Advertising revenue is huge, nearly ten percent of the worldwide total of advertising expenditures, and second only to the United States.

The largest newspapers serve as the flagships for diversified conglomerates. The largest in terms of circulation, the Yomiuri, has majority shareholding in a TV company, a travel agency, an amusement park and Japan's most popular professional baseball team, two junior colleges, two advertising agencies, a medical clinic and a symphony orchestra. Its major rival the Asahi publishes five weeklies, four monthlies, two quarterlies, nine annuals and an English-language evening paper, in addition to operating a national TV network and a culture center in Tokyo, and controlling six advertising agencies, two of which are in the top ten nationally. The newspapers are privately owned and consolidated accounts are not published, so it is difficult to get an accurate picture of the wealth of the groups.

According to the Japanese Statistics Bureau there are approximately 100 million televisions in Japan. They are serviced by 121 terrestrial television stations, two of which are run by the *Nippon Hoso Kyokai* (the Japan Broadcasting Corporation, popularly known as NHK), with national coverage.

The rest are commercial, most of them affiliated with one of five private networks. Because the commercial stations are by law restricted to serving one or two prefectures at most, these networks are informal alliances, designed to help share the cost of producing national news and other shows, and to offer advertisers national coverage. Each of the commercial television networks is built around a key station operating in Tokyo, and has a close connection to one of the five national newspapers already mentioned. The networks have widely differing histories and corporate cultures, but comparatively little variety in types of programming.

A 1987 NHK survey found that 94% of the population watched television daily, and in a typical household the TV set was on for eight hours a day (White, 1988: 32). According to 1998 estimates, there were 42.59 million sets in operation, representing a penetration rate of 86%. Access varies from four terrestrial channels in rural areas to eight or more in big cities. Satellite TV connections amount to almost 22% of households, while cable penetration is at just over one third (Asian Television, 2002).

With such exceptionally high levels of media conglomeration and penetration, it is surprising that the media are typically paid little attention in overviews of the Japanese social and political structure, either by Japanese or by respected foreign academics.[2] Most commentators who do refer to the media tend to concentrate on the press, especially the newspapers.

The limited mention of television which does appear swings from the wildly hostile to the embarrassingly uncritical, as illustrated by the two books which did much to fix foreign media perceptions of Japan in the years following their publication. At the end of the 1970s, a Harvard sociologist suggested that Japan offered "Lessons for America," including the media. Vogel (1979: 180–3) described in admiring tones an NHK which had "complete autonomy," with one channel dedicated to producing a "high-quality national (educational) service." A decade later, a Dutch newspaper correspondent, van Wolferen (1989: 177, 386), depicted a mass media which was "coordinated" by Japan's largest advertising agency, Dentsu, and singled out television as producing programs for an audience with "an average (mental) age of eight or nine."

More recent work, in particular by Krauss, has attempted to develop a more considered view. But, if Krauss is correct in his contention (1996: 359, 360) that the media in Japan have performed a vital role, both in representing and relaying public opinion to the governing elites, as well as serving to reinforce state bureaucratic power by legitimizing the elite's hold on that power, then the historical sidelining of the media in analyses of Japan represents a serious gap.

In general, as already described in Chapter 2, the media are often ignored or sidelined in political science analysis (Pharr, 1996). Taylor points out how rare it is to find a history of the twentieth century which embraces the mass media as an important theme, although the emergence of the mass media was one feature which made the twentieth distinct from all others (Taylor, 2001). This is a remarkable omission, especially when the media plays to the kind of huge—and well-educated—audience it does in Japan. The media affect the way people in a society see the world and how they understand it, and thereby affect their social and political behavior. In Japan the media also enjoys considerable prestige. A 2001 comparative survey showed that NHK was trusted more than the National Diet, the Courts of Law or, by a large margin, the government (NHK Broadcasting Culture Research Institute, 2002).

Thompson(1990) attributes this lacuna to the traditional division of labor in academia, especially in the United States, where mass communication studies have tended to be left to specialist research into media and communications, leaving them outside the mainstream of social and political theory. He also points out the degree to which the legacy of nineteenth and early twentieth century thought (Marx, Weber, Durkehim, Simmel, Mannheim and others) continues to "set the agenda for contemporary theoretical debates."

I can only propose several possible reasons relevant to the Japanese case. Taking a cue from Thompson, one seems to be the underlying influence of Marxist analysis, which has long tended to marginalize the media and see them as acting in tandem with the power structure and reflecting the views of the powers that be. Specific to the Japanese context is a certain political economy model of Japanese policy making, which concentrates on the power of the government bureaucracy, in particular in economic policy making, and effectively ignores the media.

A leading proponent of this view is Chalmers Johnson, who early set the tone with his classic work on MITI (1982), and who continued to argue in the 1990s that "bureaucracy . . . does hold an ascendant position (in Japan) and is likely to continue to do so" (Johnson, 1995: 140). The full title of the earlier work was "MITI and the Japanese Miracle," and the picture it painted of a central bureaucratic elite operating with near autonomy in developing national policy established an early reference point to explain the (then) unprecedented economic success of Japan. This view was further elaborated by Prestowitz in 1988 with another popular work "Trading Places," but the apotheosis was James Fallows' "Looking at the Sun," which described a country where most of the key political decisions were made by "highly skilled officials in Japan's central government ministries" (1994: 101), and suggested that the closer other Asian nations were to the Japanese model, the more likely their chance of emulating that "miracle." In this view, the media have essentially been co-opted into the power structure.

Johnson's book on MITI was to set the tone for a generation of popular writing about Japan by Western authors, much of it laudatory. Ultimately it produced a revisionist school, spearheaded by van Wolferen in 1989, which took a highly jaundiced view of an elite-led, secretive and highly undemocratic nation, where relationships supersede all other considerations. Both schools held out little hope for change in Japanese government or society, short of a revolution.

Fallows and van Wolferen were by no means the only writers to overestimate Japan's uniqueness, or its (and Asia's) success, or to have some of their contentions made to look hollow by the implosion of Asian economic growth since 1997. But at the same time there was a growing body of writing on Japan which has advanced a much more pluralistic view of the policy development and decision-making process in the Japanese polity, often by narrowing the focus to a particular industry or sector.[3]

Thayer (1975) was able to see both "competition and conformity" in his summary view of the Japanese press. Other examples include works on big business in general (Samuels, 1987), finance (Rosenbluth, 1989), foreign investment (Mason, 1992) and telecommunications (Yoshimatsu, 1998). Yoshimatsu, for instance, identifies not only NTT and MPT, the government bureaucracies specifically charged with NTT reform, but also politicians of the LDP and the Japan Socialist Party, trade unions, various *zaikai* (business interests) represented by Keidanren, and other administrative agencies, as all being intimately involved in the reform process (1998: 5). This attempt to capture the complexity of the policy process corresponds with my experience in looking at the impact of satellite technology on NHK and the broadcast industry in Japan, where the actors include not only NHK and the MPT, but also a host of others, international as well as national.

One key finding of this line of research is that interaction between state and society in Japan is a complex process, with business and government in particular engaged in a dance in which it is not always clear who is leading. In the case of the broadcast industry the complexity is deepened by the key role of NHK, which in law and in theory is independent of the government, while by tradition, by culture and in practice it tends to represent a consensus, status quo view of the world. Krauss points out that the traditional political science concentration on the formal process of policy formulation misses the interactive nature of the state-society relationship, and overlooks the more subtle ways in which the state may be influential, or the degree to which the actor may be able to modify the state's intent (2000: 18, 19). This is especially so when the actor is a powerful one, like a national broadcast organization, and when the effects of globalization are added to the mix.

At the same time, NHK was clearly a leading developer of policy in two key areas, of high definition television and satellite television, up to the point where it apparently "went too far" and had to be restrained. In many ways NHK (and CCTV) are in fact "front line" organizations forced to deal with globalization forces in the first instance, while the state may be slow to comprehend or react to the new realities which have swept in.

The second reason I can suggest why there is scant consideration of the media, especially broadcast, in overviews of the Japanese political and social system (and what little there is tends to be negative), lies in the checkered history of mass communications in Japan. In particular the history of NHK is a map of what Tracey (1998) calls the central problem for all publicly instituted broadcasters, the relationship with the state.

THE BIRTH OF PUBLIC BROADCASTING IN JAPAN

In the early 1920s the Ministry of Communications in Japan was considering various licensing options for radio. Reluctant to become heavily involved in the new medium at a time when it was preoccupied with expanding telephone and telegraph services, the ministry was initially in favor of private but non-commercial stations. A change of government in 1924 brought in a new Communications Minister, Inukai Tsuyoshi, a future Prime Minister and a Diet member since 1890. This latter date is important, as it links him with the hereditary elites that governed during the Meiji era (1868–1912), who in turn combined the authoritarian tradition which had characterized Japanese government practices for centuries, with a commitment to a powerful, centralized nation-state on the Western model.

Inukai's first decision was to license only non-profit, public interest broadcasting companies, despite considerable opposition from the Communications Ministry bureaucrats (Kasza, 1986: 751). This was a decision which echoed those made in a number of European countries, including Britain and Germany, and stood in contrast to the chaotic situation regarding the use of airwaves in the United States (Tracey, 1998: 99)

Three stations were initially authorized in 1925, in the major urban centers of Tokyo, Osaka and Nagoya. Japan's (and Asia's) first public broadcast was made from Tokyo in March 1925. The backers of each station represented an uneasy alliance of radio manufacturers and dealers and the press, who saw radio as an opportunity to promote themselves. One unusual feature was that the broadcasters were allowed to collect a 'receiving' fee themselves, unlike Britain for example, where a 'license' fee was paid to the post office, then later passed on to the broadcaster after the government had collected its percentage. This system continues today with NHK, and is the major reason why it is the richest public broadcaster in the world.

From the outset the government exercised tight control over the stations. Severe restrictions were placed on broadcast content, especially for anything with political connotations, enforced not only by the Ministry of Communications but also by a rival, the Japanese Home Ministry, through a 1925 Law for Maintenance of the Public Peace (Browne, 1989: 309). The degree of control over radio was at the time far greater than any of the other mass media, extending even to a stipulation that news, weather and practical knowledge programs must have precedence over music and entertainment (Kasza, 1986: 748).

However, the Ministry of Communications soon grew uneasy with the individualistic attitude of the stations, in particular Osaka, at the same time as it was facing unexpected demand for services in other regions. Within 18 months the ministry proposed and arranged a shotgun marriage between the stations, allocating to itself absolute power to appoint senior managers for the new system, dubbed the *Nippon Hoso Kyokai* (Japan Broadcasting Corporation). When NHK started operation in August, 1926, it had eight *riji* or board directors, all of whom were retiring Communications Ministry officials, despite vehement opposition to their appointment by the management of the local stations and criticism in the press. In addition, ministerial approval was now required on all business and budgetary plans.

The then Communications Minister made the thinking behind these moves clear in an address to the first general investors' meeting:

> It goes without saying that the broadcasting business exerts an enormous influence on the nation's general culture. Further, when necessary for the state (*kokka*), namely, when the state confronts an emergency, broadcasting is a great, unrivaled communications medium that can be used for state duties . . . I think, then, that it is proper to say that this undertaking for the most part is to be treated as an affair of state. (Kasza, 1986: 755)

Kasza points out one reason for this overtly political caste to the issue of broadcasting was the impact on Japanese officialdom of the British government's effective use of broadcasting during the general strike of May, 1926.

Through the following years the "politicization" of broadcasting was to proceed apace, with the Ministry of Communications under constant pressure from the Home Ministry to preview all broadcast content. This process was accelerated by Japan's successful invasion of Manchuria in 1931, which received extensive coverage on NHK, and helped boost the popularity of radio. In the same year a second service devoted to educational and cultural broadcasts was introduced by the Ministry of Communications, but only after beating off a challenge for control of the new service from the Ministry of Education. The separate educational and cultural broadcasts became a tradition which continues to this day, on television as well as on radio.

The government encouraged NHK's expansion. By 1934 there were two million license holders, and the Ministry introduced new rules of incorporation designed to further centralize control through Tokyo, and eradicate the remaining vestiges of regional autonomy. This removed the last obstacle to state mobilization of radio, which henceforth "would not simply flatter popular desires but would promote the 'Japanese spirit' and provide leadership."(Kasza, 1988: 154)

By 1935 the service was available from 27 stations across the country. As Krauss reports (2000: 90), by then NHK had established a policy of promoting a common, standardized language for all its announcers, built around a model based on the speech patterns of an educated Tokyo native (a Japanese version of what was to become known as "BBC English"). The measured, didactic tones of the NHK announcer were to become easily recognizable, in a paternalistic tradition which was to continue after the war.

In recognition of its increasingly important role in relaying the government viewpoint, NHK was a major investor in the newly created Domei News Agency "itself designed to disseminate the 'correct' interpretation of events in Japan to the Japanese and to the outside world"(Browne, 1989: 311). This aspect was of considerable concern to the Ministry of Foreign Affairs, which had proposed the creation of such an agency, as China was by this time waging a successful public relations campaign to accuse and isolate Japan for its aggression.

Domei was the progeny of another shotgun marriage, this time between the two competing domestic news agencies: Nippon Rengo (which had a relationship with AP, and which was close to the Foreign Ministry in pre-war Japan) and Nippon Denpo (which favored the military, was in alliance with UPI, and was also the forerunner of the powerful advertising agency Dentsu). NHK henceforth took all its news from Domei, and became the mouthpiece of the highly militaristic government.

In 1936 an Information Committee (later upgraded to a bureau) was created, which directly reported to the cabinet, and gave directives to NHK through the Ministry of Communications. The result was ever tighter controls over content all through the war years.

This brief account of the birth of broadcasting in Japan is revealing in a number of ways. The steady shift from what was at first a private sector industry with local autonomy to a centrally controlled organization for state mobilization parallels the rise to domination of the coalition of bureaucrats and militarists who led Japan's plunge into war in Asia. It shows how the attitudes of Ministry of Communications' bureaucrats towards the broadcast industry developed, to the point where NHK became a prize to be jealously guarded against incursions from other ministries.

It also reveals the special relationship developed between NHK as an organization and the politicians and bureaucrats, which continued in a straight line after the war. The meaning of this relationship was perhaps most notoriously typified by the decision by Prime Minister Sato (1964–1972) to banish all TV networks except NHK from his last press conference (Sato was a former administrative vice minister (*jimu jikan*) in the Ministry of Communications).

Krauss (2000) also points out how several "motifs" established before the war were to continue in the postwar NHK, including the concept that the corporation was the bearer of some kind of national cultural standard; a willingness to self-regulate; and a continued interest by politicians to influence the selection of NHK's leadership, and thereby its conception of its role. Indeed Shima, the former president of NHK, identified the need to break NHK of its habit of kowtowing to the politicians as the main driver behind his attempts to radically reform NHK, including a major push into satellite broadcasting (Shima, 1995: 81).

THE BEGINNINGS OF COMMERCIAL BROADCASTING

As described by Tracey (1998) and Krauss (2000), the policies of the Allied GHQ towards the media were riven with internal contradictions, most notably the desire to foster the independence of the press and radio as guard dogs for the democratic experiment in Japan, while at the same time wishing to control the same institutions, as a part of a carefully planned process of social reorientation, thus compromising the media's independence.

Broadcasting in particular was seen as having "served as a propaganda medium for the Japanese warlords" (Tracey: 128). As a consequence, up to 1949 program content was censored directly, and there was considerable debate over the future shape of the Japanese broadcasting system. The allied powers that ran the military occupation were initially in favor of retaining a monopoly public broadcaster, in part because two of them, Great Britain and the USSR, operated such a system, but also because it was easier to supervise (Browne, 1989: 314). The argument had been anticipated in a position paper prepared immediately before the occupation by the U.S. State, War, Navy, Coordinating Committee, on 'Control of Media of Public Information and Expression in Japan.' The dilemma of what to do with NHK was addressed directly, with an early reference to a favored model: the BBC.

> The question (of whether to permit monopoly broadcasting) should be examined in the light of the then existing conditions taking into account our general policies with respect to information policies, the practice in other countries, the desires of the Japanese and, in particular whether monopoly broadcasting could be developed in Japan along non-political lines as in England.[4]

But, as before the war, the Japanese press led a vigorous campaign for private commercial broadcasting, and by 1947, when development of legislation on broadcasting began, the principle of allowing private radio broadcasting together with broadcasting by a public authority had been accepted. The reference model was the Japanese national railway system, which featured privately-owned lines running on the same routes, and sometimes the same tracks, as the national carrier, JNR.

The major dispute between the office of the Supreme Commander Allied Powers (SCAP) and the various Japanese interested parties was over the question of control, with SCAP insisting that broadcasting be regulated by a genuinely autonomous organization, while the Ministry of Communications, which was charged with preparing the actual legislation for consideration by the Diet, repeatedly attempted to strengthen its supervisory role over broadcasting, at the same time as NHK fought to have its line of reporting go direct to the Prime Minister's office.

The question of regulation was to remain a sticking point: the legislation eventually enacted in 1950 (The Radio Regulatory Commission Establishment Law, #133) provided for the creation of a supervising agency modeled on the American Federal Communications Commission, but it was overturned within months of the end of the allied occupation, and supervision reverted to the Ministry of Communications. In this way, and with the Radio Law (#131, May 1950), which deals with technical aspects of broadcasting and which laid the framework for government licensing of new commercial stations, including the qualifications for radio operators, the Ministry succeeded in re-establishing its ultimate dominance over broadcasting. As a result, the MPT now reviews the budget and has considerable leverage over the choice of President of NHK (appointed by the NHK Board of Governors, who are in turn appointed by the Prime Minister, with advice from the MPT). However, the Broadcast Law (#132) which was also passed in 1950, helped bolster a reborn NHK's administrative independence from the government, with a specific guarantee of impartiality, integrity and autonomy of broadcasting (Tracey, 1998).

Although there had been some internal re-organization of NHK, reflecting pressure from inside the organization as well as from the occupation authorities, the structure and the personnel of NHK were little touched by the Allied occupation after the war. Indeed, in common with other Japanese ministries, the MPT had also remained largely unscathed. Writing about the political comeback of Kishi Nobosuke, a former Class A war criminal who became Prime Minister of Japan in the late 1950s (and who rammed through the Diet a hugely unpopular new security pact with the United States), Ian Buruma points out that

> Very few wartime bureaucrats had been purged. Most ministries remained intact. Instead it was the Communists, who had welcomed the Americans as liberators, who were purged after 1949, the year China was "lost." In June 1951, a West German diplomat returned from Tokyo and wrote the following letter to a Minister for Economic Affairs in Bonn: "All those who were purged from their jobs in 1945–46 for political or other reason have now resumed their work in complete freedom. In other words, everything in Japan that corresponded to what was done in Germany under the name of denazification has been laid aside. I have absolutely no doubt that in one year we will see a complete change of personnel in Japanese politics. Because of their superior discipline, a large number of our old friends will once again be taking up leading positions" (1994: 61, 2).

CONSEQUENCES

This history continues to provide the backdrop for the broadcast industry to this day. It was NHK and the commercial radio stations (supported by their press parents) which formed the television stations known today. The commercial television stations are still closely allied with the big press combines,[5] and NHK is still seen as being "establishment" and highly sensitive to government positions. The apotheosis of this sensitivity may have been reached in 1975 when the President of NHK was forced to resign for a "lack of political neutrality"—he had visited the home of Prime Minister Tanaka, at a time when the latter was under investigation for the Lockheed bribery scandal which eventually brought him down.

At the same time NHK is the wealthiest public broadcasting system in the world, and dominates the broadcast industry in Japan. NHK today is a massive organization, with some 13,000 employees, 54 domestic broadcasting stations and 35 overseas bureaus. Its revenues come direct from 38 million households, 11.58 million of which are also contracted for DBS services (2003 figures). Operating income for FY 2004 is budgeted at 678,5 billion yen (over $6 billion), tax free.[6] For the fiscal year ended March 31, 2004, NHK recorded an official "excess of revenue over expenses" of 11.5 billion yen ($104 million), putting it firmly in the black for the fifteenth consecutive year. It is the largest public service broadcaster in the world.

The 1950 broadcast law had guaranteed freedom of expression, as well as explicitly prohibiting government or other outside interference in its programming, and this coupled with its unusual financial independence has given NHK a uniquely autonomous status. However, theory and practice do not necessarily coincide. Burns' acerbic description of the real status of the BBC surely applies to NHK: "[the state] allows it all the liberty, independence, autonomy that can be hoped for, but which has proved, time and again, to be liberty on parole" (Burns, 1977: 21). When Shima attempted to break NHK of its habit of "kowtowing" to politicians, he was trying to change a history as well as a corporate culture.

Defining the status of commercial broadcasters took longer; in fact, throughout most of the 1950s, all commercial stations were operating under temporary licenses. In October 1957 the Ministry of Posts and Telecommunications (MPT) finally authorized NHK to operate nationally, while each of 36 private television licenses were awarded on a prefectural basis. In March 1959 the Broadcast Law was amended by the ministry to compel a theoretical balance during the broadcast day between news, entertainment, cultural and educational programming. As Kitatani points out (1988: 177), this amendment also effectively prohibited the development of the large centralized commercial networks which characterized American broadcasting. The networks which do exist, built around key stations in Tokyo, are in fact informal alliances, initially designed to provide national news coverage as well as meeting the needs of advertisers for one-stop national advertising.

The result is that the status quo of the commercial broadcasters was effectively frozen, and they have never been able to rival seriously the preeminence of NHK. There is a positive side to this: in Westney's view, fears about the growth of huge mass media conglomerates in Japan have been limited, because "the size of any single shareholding in media firms is limited by law, newspaper company shares can be held internally, and the creation of broadcasting networks is severely constrained by regulation"(1996: 49).

It was in this context that Rupert Murdoch's attempt to buy his way into Asahi TV in 1996 caused such alarm. Thanks to the laws and regulations imposed by the Allied occupation after the Second World War, outright media conglomeration had been effectively banned: the media groupings which did emerge were loosely organized and inward-looking, ill-prepared to deal with a predator like Murdoch. NHK is the only Japanese media organization currently able to be a "player" in the new world of global media (although arguably Sony has also positioned itself for that role).

In interviews with commercial broadcasters the MPT's buttressing of the television status quo in the 1950s was just one of many examples cited of the ministry's staunch championing of NHK at the expense of the commercial stations (although in fact the commercial stations did very well out of their own oligopolistic situation). The quid pro quo for NHK is that, as a bureaucratic organization supervised by a state organ, it participates in the development of government policy in its area of interest. It must follow those policies, as was the case with both satellite broadcasting, and ultimately with the development of high definition television.

In a very real sense, NHK was, and is, a part of the establishment.

> NHK's audience dominance in the news for the quarter century from the 1960s through the mid-1980s . . . exposed much of the Japanese public to a form of information that may well have served to legitimize and reinforce the cultural hegemony of the LDP-dominated postwar Japan state (Krauss, 1998: 688)

When a chairman comes along who is widely regarded as a maverick—who is reluctant to cooperate with government bureaucrats, who espouses a vastly more ambitious role for the organization he heads, and who actively seeks to introduce new ways of gathering and presenting the news—he is likely to be treated as the nail which sticks out, and which must be hammered flat: exactly what happened to Keiji Shima in 1991. Shima's hasty exit was widely interpreted as a victory for the powers-that-be. However, it remains to be seen whether his legacy is entirely dead: certainly the issues he was willing to confront—concerning the role of a national broadcaster forced to deal with fast-moving international developments—have not gone away.

Since the sixties, NHK has had to face two major challenges, both technological in origin and both international by nature: satellite television and high-definition TV (HDTV). They are heavily interlinked, but while one turned into a major success story, the other must be counted a dismal failure. Interestingly, while public organizations like the BBC have had to face similar dilemmas (in the British case, the challenges posed by rapid deregulation, leading to abrupt challenges to the status quo from cable and satellite), they have done so in an essential reactive manner, while NHK was, literally, a world leader in dealing with the changes sweeping through the broadcast communications industry.

DEVELOPMENT OF SATELLITE TV BROADCASTS IN JAPAN

On November 23, 1963, the first trans-Pacific images were to be transmitted from the United States to Japan on the first satellite to achieve geosynchronous orbit successfully, one which was owned and operated by the American company Hughes. A pre-recorded address by President Kennedy had been scheduled for the historic moment. Instead a shooting in Dallas intervened, and news of the president's assassination was sent.

In those days news events were still shot on 16-millimeter film. As it took days or even weeks for film from abroad to reach a place like Tokyo, typically the international news on NHK was presented by an announcer reading straight to camera, supported at best by a still photo, but more often by plain text. The effect of the "instant" footage from Dallas was amazing, and it is surely no hyperbole to mark it as the day "Japanese international television journalism took its first step" (Takashima, 1995: 22)

Just one year later, in 1964, coverage of the Tokyo Olympics was transmitted across the Pacific via Syncom 3, using American technology on an American satellite. The writing was on the wall, and read by NHK management. When President Yoshinori Maeda of NHK defended his 1968 budget, which had a substantial allocation for developing a broadcast satellite service, the justifications used were not only to ensure the 100% coverage of the mountainous Japanese land mass, which was part of NHK's legal mandate, but also to guarantee that Japan would have its own satellite television capability (Krauss, 2000: 178). This in turn neatly coincided with Japanese government policy, to develop its own satellite manufacture and launch capability.

The National Space Development Agency of Japan (NASDA) was established in 1969, charged with developing launching systems, deploying satellites into geosynchronous orbit, and testing and controlling the systems when in orbit (NASDA, 1978). In 1970 the Institute of Space and Aeronautical Science of the University of Tokyo launched Japan's first test satellite. The first experimental communication satellite, CS-1A, known as "Sakura" (Cherry blossom), was launched in 1977, in a collaborative effort between the Mitsubishi group and Ford Aerospace.

According to Gershon and Kanayama (1995: 220) NHK was the prime instigator of Japan's experiments with developing a DBS system,[7] as Maeda, the NHK president of the time, insisted on Japan's need for its own DBS satellite or risk being in a location "like a valley between two powerful waves" (of anticipated US and USSR broadcasts by satellite). After feasibility studies into satellite broadcast television were successfully completed, an experimental satellite, BS-1, was launched in April 1978, and demonstrated that Japan could be covered by the signals.[8]

NHK's satellite interests did not function in a vacuum. At the time Japanese government policy was to develop a domestic aerospace industry, and NHK was encouraged to be a part of a process designed to nurture a domestic satellite production capability. President Maeda was quoted as admitting as much: "The broadcast satellite concept is not at all being driven by the interests of NHK. I am acting on behalf of government policy" (Krauss, 2000: 179). This was a costly consensus, as the domestic rockets were vastly more expensive than foreign ones. They were also unreliable, which in turn drove up insurance costs. In fact Shima later claimed that NHK's decision under his leadership to save money and change to using foreign launchers was a key element in his downfall, as he made powerful establishment enemies in rejecting the MPT-led policy (Shima, 1995: 233).

The MPT was the lead government agency in developing direct broadcasting technology, eventually supervising (and, with NHK, jointly funding) the launch by NASDA of the "Yuri" (Lily) satellites, BS-2a in 1984 and BS-2b in 1986. Despite serious problems with its transponders, BS-2a was the world's first dedicated DBS satellite. Both BS-2 satellites were for the exclusive use of NHK and, due to a host of technical and engineering problems, were initially used for experiments, including broadcasts of the Japanese HDTV system (Hudson, 1990: 143). In July, 1987, following extensive rejigging of the BS-2b's channel configuration, NHK began 24 hour broadcasting of a dedicated DBS channel.

As Negrine points out (1988: 250), there was controversy surrounding the DBS service before it became fully operational, a capability eventually achieved in June 1989. The main criticism came from the commercial broadcasters, who saw the introduction of a government-supported advanced technology as a potential threat to their very lucrative monopoly on commercial broadcasting.

They were also unhappy that on BS-2b's eventual replacement, BS-3b, only four channels were available, of which NHK took three (including one for HDTV), forcing all the commercial forces which had vied for space on the satellite into an unwieldy consortium of 187 companies called Japan Satellite Broadcasting (JSB), a shotgun marriage arranged by *Keidanren* (the Federation of Economic Organizations). A former MPT bureaucrat was made president of JSB, which included all the commercial TV networks and newspaper conglomerates, in addition to Matsushita,

Sony and the Industrial Bank of Japan (Hamilton, 1993). In fact, the manufacturers and other commercial concerns held 60 percent of the shares in JSB, while the mass-media-related concerns were limited to less than 40 percent. Of this latter grouping the commercial broadcasters accounted for only 19%, compared with the 51% majority ownership they had hoped for (Gershon and Kanayama, 1995).

In fact the DBS services thus launched represented little change to the status quo of television in Japan. Rather they reflected a conscious policy to preserve the existing, highly lucrative broadcasting system. A strong indication that this was the MPT's intention was its directive to JSB not to run commercials for fear of "crowding out" the terrestrial private broadcasters. In the event JSB scrambled the signal for the service, named WOWOW, and made it entirely subscription based, which many suspected was the root cause of its near-disastrous early lack of popularity (Mainichi, 1993: 1).

Nakamura (1988) identified another important reason for the DBS service being configured in the way it was, the fact that broadcasting by satellite represented the only practical way of distributing the HDTV service which NHK had spent years developing. HDTV requires a much wider frequency bandwidth than a conventional TV signal, and constructing a new terrestrial system to relay the signal would have been prohibitively expensive. Nakamura also mentions in passing that, if the DBS service were a success (as indeed it later was), it would "encourage the development of a whole industry linked to the construction and marketing of receiving dishes," (1988: 253) which in view of the size and wealth of the Japanese consumer electronics industry doubtless was not a minor consideration.

Ironically, NHK's Executive Director-General of Engineering, Yuko Nakamura, took the notion that HDTV was dependent on satellites for distribution and turned it on its head, insisting in an article apparently written before 1988 that HDTV would be the "key to the future success of satellite broadcasting," and it would have to be introduced "to attract the public" (Nakamura, 1988: 264,5).

In fact, DBS was a success without HDTV, though it took time, especially for the commercial DBS service. WOWOW was launched in April 1991 (22 months after NHK's BS-1 and BS-2), as Japan sailed into recession. For years the encrypted service could not build up the subscriber base needed for profitability, especially as WOWOW was primarily a movie channel, so that JSB incurred massive debts as it became one of the largest buyers of American films in Japan. By the end of March, 1993, cumulative losses were over Y50 billion (approximately $400 million at then prevailing rates), which were projected to double in the following 18 months. The ex-MPT bureaucrat president was replaced by a businessmen seconded from Matsushita Electrical Industries in May, 1993 (Hamilton, 1993).

The contrast between NHK and the commercial consortium was striking: by January, 1993, NHK already had 4.6 million paying subscribers for its two broadcast channels (with an estimated additional two million non-payers), compared with 1.18 million for WOWOW, well below its breakeven point (Takashi, 1993). By September, 1996, NHK had a global figure of 7.8 million viewers for its satellite service which reached 10 million by 1997: in that same year WOWOW finally went into the black, when its numbers crept up to the 2.3 million mark.

But HDTV was never even in the game. By the end of 1997 a total of only 530,000 dedicated HDTV sets had been sold, with an additional 780,000 conventional sets fitted with a converter to allow the HDTV signal to be received (NHK Fact Sheets #6 and #7). At the same time NHK had contracted 8.8 million households for the satellite service (with the total number including 'illegal' viewers estimated at over 12 million), by March, 1998.

Nevertheless, the development of the two technologies did become heavily interlinked, as NHK used the heavy investment in the one to defend the giant investment in the other.[9] This strategy was no doubt made necessary by the fact that "they were developed for the technological innovations and commercial opportunities," rather than as a result of consumer demand (Kitatani, 1988: 184).

HI-VISION IN AND OUT OF FOCUS

The way in which NHK developed and promoted its HDTV system is not only illustrative of how complex the relationship between the various players in Japanese policy-making has become, but also clearly demonstrates how thoroughly it has become a part of the globalization process, where NHK effectively represents Japan in relevant international forums. Television broadcasting has become part of "very complex politico-economic systems comprised of hundred or even thousands of individual participants and the organizations they represent" (Dupagne and Seel, 1998: 294) and NHK is now a major player in the game. Indeed, in their diagrammatic "Global HDTV policy making model," Dupagne and Seel only identify one broadcaster by name—NHK (ibid:305).

Because of this, while it is possible to depict the development of the Japanese HDTV system as an embarrassing failure—the system not only failed to be adopted as a new international standard, but also never achieved any widespread popularity in Japan itself—it also showed that NHK had become an integral part of a much wider, complex process in which it could, because of its unity of purpose, sometimes take a lead, while its political master, the MPT, was left to react to developments.

In 1972 NHK informed the government and television manufacturers that its experiments to develop a high-definition alternative to the regular TV system (NTSC—the same as the U.S.) were working well, and that it believed HDTV would replace conventional TV broadcasting equipment in the future. NHK's enthusiasm was not shared by the manufacturers, who disliked the idea that the new system would be completely incompatible with existing equipment, nor by the Ministry of Posts and Telecommunications (MPT), which favored another system, EDTV (Enhanced Definition TV).

In the event it was to take another twelve plus years before MPT swung firmly behind the new system. For many years NHK kept the whole, very expensive project afloat by itself. Its reasons were twofold. First, the fee-dependent organization's need for more fees (resulting from new TV set purchases) and for higher fees (possible with the introduction of a new technology). Second, a desire to win back audience share, which had been steadily eroded by the commercial stations, a process which might be reversed by an impressive new technology in which NHK alone had developed the expertise.[10]

NHK arrived at the specifications of its HDTV system after extensive research and experimentation, with 35mm motion picture quality used as a goal and a technical reference point—the aspect ratio of 5:3 is the same as the film standard, for example (Dupagne and Seel, 1998: 72,3).

As a result of the MPT's lukewarm attitude, it was NHK that represented Japan at international meetings of engineers to explain their system, and which waged an intensive (and initially successful) campaign to appeal to the American entertainment industry, especially Hollywood. In fact, the U.S. Society of Motion Picture and Television Engineers (SMPTE), and other international technical bodies, provided valuable feedback that helped influence the final specifications for the system, both for the Hi-Vision production standard, and the MUSE transmission standard.[11] Both Hi-Vision and MUSE "were greatly influenced by international scientific and political considerations" (Dupagne and Seel: 77, 80).

Chief opposition to the HDTV system came from the Europeans, in a concerted effort by the major European electronics manufacturers and their national governments. Hi-Vision was seen as a Japanese attempt to effectively pre-empt the debate over standards for the next generation of television.[12] There was little doubt that this would be a new kind of *international* television, especially as the MUSE standard had been specifically developed to make satellite transmission possible.

Another reason for developing Hi-Vision as a specifically satellite-delivered system was to ensure the continuance of the terrestrial status quo, so that HDTV was a supplement rather than a substitute for the NTSC system (Schreiber, 1991: 268). As Dupagne and Seel point out, this decision also served both the purposes of NHK (in giving a rationale for an additional license fee charge) and of the consumer electronics industry (in necessitating new and expensive receiving equipment).

It was not until 1987 that the MPT became actively involved, after HDTV was accepted as the future standard for Japan by Japanese broadcasters and manufacturers, but long after Hi-Vision had emerged from the laboratory, and as a whole family of MUSE standards was being developed, "largely at the request of organizations in the United States" (Dupagne and Seel: 79). Krauss relates this decision to the ongoing competition between MPT and MITI.

> (MPT), in the postwar era considered a second-rank, politicized agency, during the 1980s was attempting to raise its status by assuming industrial policy strategies toward telecommunications, a course that was putting it in competition with (MITI), that considered industrial policy toward any industry under its jurisdiction . . . in the so-called "Telecom Wars" (MPT) had won more than it lost to the vaunted, powerful MITI. (MPT) now seized upon HDTV as its next area of industrial and telecommunications policy strategy (Krauss, 1992 : 11).

Nevertheless, (in Krauss' account and also in Brinkley's) it is made clear that the next round of the battle to get HDTV accepted as an *international* standard, a battle waged in the U.S., was fought by NHK and Japanese electronics manufacturers.[13]

HDTV also provided NHK with a convenient argument for hogging two of the three transponders available on BS-3b. By 1987 the Executive Director-General of Engineering at NHK was deliberately tying the fortunes of the soon-to-be-launched direct broadcasting satellite to HDTV, arguing that the new service would be essential for "satellite broadcasting to become a popular and successful medium in the future" (Nakamura, 1988: 264).

In the end HDTV suffered an ignominious defeat,[14] due to a mix of political reasons (in particular the intensive lobbying of the Europeans) and technical arguments (its lack of compatibility with existing systems, and its basically outdated, non-digital technology), but NHK waged a fierce rearguard action to defend its investment.

When, in February 1994, the director of the Broadcasting Bureau at the MPT, Akimasa Egawa, questioned the wisdom of continuing to invest in developing the analog system, when "the world is going digital," his remarks raised a storm of controversy, from NHK, the Electronics Industries Association of Japan, and from MPT's rival in this regulatory area, MITI. Egawa was forced to withdraw the statement, saying he would continue to promote Hi-Vision while studying the possibility of digital broadcasting. In his view, NHK was anxious to block even discussion of going digital, because of the immense sums it had invested in analog Hi-Vision (Fukuyama, 1997: 5). Together NHK (as it tried desperately to save its analog format Hi-Vision) and the commercial broadcasters (equally loathe to deal with the reality of a digital future) managed to stall a decision on whether the second BS-4 satellite should be analog or digital until February 1997 (Yomiuri Shimbun, 1997: 1).

OUT FLOW: PRESENTING JAPAN TO THE WORLD

A Belligerent Japanese

In April, 1989, Keiji Shima became chairman of NHK. His first official overseas visit was to the United States, where he proceeded to lobby vigorously, and unsuccessfully, to win acceptance for the Japanese HDTV system, to the extent of first offering free use of the MUSE distribution method, then topping that proposal with an offer to the NAB, to give them 50 percent of the worldwide licensing rights. He was desperate: NHK had already invested five hundred million dollars in developing the system, which was in the process of being cut out of the running for the new high definition system being considered in the United States (Brinkley, 1997)

On July 15, 1991, after little more than two years in office, Shima resigned. The reason given was that he was taking responsibility for having lied to a Diet committee on communications, which had been examining NHK's satellite business investments. He admitted having given a false statement about his whereabouts when a $88 million NHK satellite was destroyed in a failed launch of an American Atlas-Centaur in Florida in April of the same year. He had claimed to be at the New Jersey headquarters of the satellite's manufacturer, GE, when in fact he had been in Los Angeles, reportedly with an NHK female staff member.

The misdeed was plainly a minor one. Local press commentary emphasized that he had been the most belligerent head NHK had ever had, and that his enemies inside the government, the broadcast industry and NHK itself were the real cause of his downfall. Six out of the ten NHK chairmen from 1950 to 1991 had to resign without completing their terms in office, usually due to their involvement in political and bureaucratic power struggles. Shima's rise to power had been attributed to the close relationship he had developed with a former Prime Minister and LDP faction leader, Masayoshi Ohira, when Shima was a junior NHK reporter attached to Ohira's press club. His abrupt fall reflected the failure of Ohira's successor as faction leader, Kiichi Miyazawa, to protect him from the enemies he had made in the LDP, notably former Prime Minister Yasuhiro Nakasone and the party's "strongman," Shin Kanemaru (Asahi, 1991, July 23).

One of Shima's most controversial gambits had been to attempt to launch an international satellite news service, as part of an ambitious plan to make NHK a leading, internationally recognized broadcaster. Called Global News Network (GNN), the putative service would have teamed NHK with ABC and (initially) the BBC as potential partners, and would have competed directly with CNN, which Shima had accused of "forcing American news on the rest of the world." On the same trip to the United States that had stirred the satellite controversy, Shima had announced in Las Vegas a plan to establish the GNN headquarters in New York by the end of 1991, with a budget of $1 billion. The concept was to provide a 24-hour English-language news service, with eight hours emanating from each of the three partners. In an interview with the Asian Wall Street Journal, Shima had said "We want to put the actual true faces of Japan and Asia more into the international scene."

Five months after Shima's resignation, his successor announced that NHK was abandoning plans for GNN, explaining that as a business "it's not feasible," citing the cost of launching the project (100 billion yen, about $800 million), the impossibility of making a return on the investment, and the lack of qualified personnel (Schlesinger, 1991: 1).

SPEAKING FOR JAPAN

Shima's failed attempt to launch GNN had a context, in which NHK had progressively taken over the role of popular spokesman for Japan. In fact, the concept of GNN was a logical, if major, development from previous attempts to represent the Japanese view in the Western (primarily American) media situation. Since the early 1980s this had been done through a variety of news and information feature shows (see Table 2). Initially these had been coordinated or sponsored indirectly by the Foreign Ministry, and later by MITI (Ministry of International Trade and Industry) both of which were concerned with ever more vociferous complaints against and attacks on Japan, as it continued to run up huge trade surpluses with the United States. Their efforts may be seen as a reflection of the Foreign

Ministry's prewar attempts to co-opt the radio service for its own propaganda purposes.

The 1980s endeavors had little success. The programming approach seemed awkward and stilted to Western eyes, the distribution poor, and the presence of a Japanese government ministry in the background troubling enough to cause distribution deals to fall through and foreign advisors to resign (Judis, 1990). By the later 1980s NHK had effectively taken over the role of representing Japan on international television.

NHK's first venture (1989) into the field was "Today's Japan," which was basically NHK's domestic 7 P.M. news, translated and minimally repackaged, with the intention of showing the world the news which the Japanese themselves were looking at, in English. Although NHK had distributed its news abroad prior to this, it had always been in Japanese for Japanese audiences, in hotels and so on. This was NHK's first attempt to send regularly scheduled English-language programming abroad. In the U.S. it ran for over 5 years on the last late-night slot on PBS affiliates. However, the program was made to appear stiff and often irrelevant by the fact that not only was the script a straight translation, but also the content, editing and running order were directly carried over from the Japanese original, although the "pacing, style, writing and delivery of a Western news program is (sic) so different" (Sherman, 1994: 34).

"ASIA NOW" AND "JAPAN BUSINESS TODAY"

In 1990 NHK decided to try for broader distribution and developed the idea of a weekly magazine on different Asian topics from around the region, called "Asia Now." The checkered history of "Asia Now," an international co-production, and of "Japan Business Today," developed in-house by NHK, offer significant clues to why GNN as originally conceived stood little chance of success, and also serves as a moral story of how an overt attempt at creating a globalization artifact foundered on the shoals of cultural difference.

It was decided from the outset to make "Asia Now" more Western-oriented. Based on experience with "Today's Japan," and on studies done with WGBH Boston, NHK management realized that they would have to be more clearly international in approach. They took the big step of hiring the Western television journalist Bruce MacDonald, former NBC Bureau Chief for Asia, as producer/coordinator on the Japan end, and from the outset worked closely with the Seattle PBS station, KCTS. Later the Honolulu PBS station, KHET, was also involved.

Another ambitious program was launched at the same time, called "Japan Business Today." Unlike "Asia Now," this was entirely an NHK production, with a correspondent for PBS and NPR, Spencer Sherman, hired as Executive Producer. In a style that was typical of Shima's management, the program went from initial idea to proposal approval in 10 weeks, and then to regular broadcast in two months, with a production staff of 35, including 13 foreigners, many of whom had been recruited from outside Japan. The program was run by a triumvirate, with Sherman and Tatsu Miyoshi as co-Executive Producers, and Yoshinori Imai as Managing Editor. Both Miyoshi and Imai had held senior positions in the NHK bureaucracy, Miyoshi as an anchor for BS-1, Imai as Deputy Director of the Business News Department, but for "Japan Business Today" they were given specially developed titles more meaningful to Western television professionals. Decisions were made collectively, a system which was initially surprisingly effective, though not without problems.

> The reason it worked was, one, there was tremendous pressure from the chairman (Shima) to make it work; and two, Miyoshi and Imai realized, very shrewdly, that, in order for the program to function, not only internally, but externally, not only for the people who produced it but for the people who watched it, that a lot of decisions would have to be made that went against their sense of what journalism really was, that Western news judgement was going to have to prevail in a lot of circumstances. That doesn't mean that we didn't have arguments. We had a lot of them.[15]

According to Sherman, both he and the Japanese producers had their own, separate but similar concerns: he, to make sure the program had the kind of editorial legitimacy which he considered necessary for the program to be a success, and, more importantly, to give him some armor against criticism from his journalistic colleagues for what was perceived as a "crazy" move; Miyoshi and Imai, to handle the essential, ongoing *nemawashi* process inside NHK, especially difficult because of the skepticism with which the program was viewed internally, and because of the challenge of reconciling the NHK culture with these foreign demands, and also because of the unusual pressure from the top executive in the corporation.

The show debuted on October 8, 1990. It followed a conventional half-hour news broadcast formula, going out every weekday night, carried in the United States on CNBC, the cable network of NBC; on Super Channel across Europe and the Middle East, which was then owned by the Italian right-wing media magnate Berlusconi, and was later bought by NBC; and on Murdoch's Sky Channel in the U.K.

Table 2 Representing Japan Abroad: Major TV shows produced in Japan for international television distribution, 1980–1990

Name/type of show	Started	Distribution	Producer/ Sponsor
Various specials	1983	Christian Broadcasting Network	Telejapan/MITI
This Week in Japan Weekly Magazine	1984	CNN	Japan Center for Information and
Cultural Ministry			Affairs/Foreign
Japan Today/ Weekly News Show	1984	USA Cable	Telejapan/MITI
Faces of Japan (Various) *Feature Series*	1986	PBS	Telejapan/MITI
Today's Japan	1989 *Nightly News Show*	PBS	NHK/WGBH/ NEC
Electronics (Various)			
Asia Now Weekly Magazine	1990(?)	PBS	NHK/KCTS(Seattle)/ KHET(Hawaii)
Japan Business Today Business news and features	1990	FNN(later CNBC) Super Channel(European satellite)	NHK

"Japan Business Today" lasted for almost four years, with its last broadcast made in September, 1994. The foreign journalists associated with the program attributed its demise to internal tensions, usually depicted as between Western ideals of news reporting and Japanese social and political realities, with NHK management described as complaining about the program's "wayward independence," and continually trying to "quash politically sensitive stories" (Hadfield, 1994, 1). According to Hadfield, NHK's unsuccessful attempts to stop "Japan Business Today" reporting on the troubles facing HDTV—in other words, reporting a story about itself—was the final impetus behind the show's closure. Sherman took a more sanguine view of the situation:

> When I began analyzing the economic news being presented on NHK's general news, it was clear that our agenda was the same one being used for Japanese-language broadcasts. The real problem was a desire to shy away from controversial news for both audiences, Japanese and foreign alike (Sherman, 1994: 35).

Unsurprisingly, the Japanese participants have different memories. A staff member and former anchor of "Asia Now" recalls an endless series of examples of obduracy on the part of the Western staff, and an apparent inability to appreciate the seriousness with which NHK took its didactic role as teacher and reference point.

> I remember one of the examples (of cultural difficulties), was what name to use for the country which is now called Myanmar. He (the foreign anchor) stuck to calling it Burma, instead of Myanmar. And in Japanese news when we refer to North Korea, we say in Japanese "the People's Republic of Korea." We have to be very strict on this kind of international political issue. Or when we made a program about the 25th anniversary of the Vietnam war, we had the issue of how to name (the war). We always had that kind of problem.
>
> And there were things like, for the Japanese viewers it was not necessary to explain things Japanese, but for foreign viewers it was better to have some additional comment about Japanese culture or traditional things like the imperial palace and so forth. So we had many, many kinds of problems, even on how to translate, on whether to use American English or British English.[16]

THE FOREIGN MODEL

For the NHK staffers involved, the new programs were part of a raft of directives from the Shima management, which were explicit about the need to sell news and other programs to the rest of the world. To achieve this, to produce programs in English for international sale, it was necessary to borrow American know-how. Two ideas were at war here. One was the notion that NHK should continue in its traditional role, of presenting the (usually establishment) Japanese view, essentially the same in content and style as the Japanese domestic original, whether in English or in Japanese. The other was the precept that NHK should pay heed to the new model developed by CNN and Ted Turner, which meant international news being presented in a way that was attractive commercially—international news as a product.

In his autobiography, Shima makes it clear that he was inspired by the example of CNN when he developed the GNN concept.

> Mr. Turner had succeeded in distributing American-style news all over the world. But I came up with the idea of making allocations, dividing the 24 hours among three broadcasting centers, i.e. from America, an American broadcasting station, for example ABC; from Europe, Euro News of the EBU[17]; from Japan, NHK; each having eight hours each, distributing news together. My idea was that each station help each other and have access to what the others had to offer, as equal partners (Shima, 1995: 193).

According to Sherman and others who were involved in the planning for GNN, it was never explained what NHK's eight hours would actually consist of, other than a nucleus of existing English-language programming: "Today's Japan," "Japan Business Today" and "Asia Now." One programming notion Shima did have in mind was for NHK to act as a relay center for news from other Asian countries. In his first public announcement about GNN, given, significantly, at the Foreign Correspondents' Club of Japan, Shima had made the thinking behind this clear.

> I don't mean to bad mouth Mr. Turner, but CNN is trying to force U.S. news on the rest of the world . . . When Asian news is treated by Western broadcasters, it tends to be given a low priority . . . We, faced with a flood of information from the U.S., need to have a network that will pay more attention to reports from Asia (Sherman, 1994: 32).

Whether or not this was ever a practical idea is highly debatable: the Chinese, who would have been a key player in any such system, never thought the idea was feasible.[18] The "Global Satellite Transmission System" diagram (Figure 1), which was developed at the time, shows another problem, that metaphorically and possibly literally Tokyo was presented as the Asian hub for the system, a reality which many other Asian nations would have found unacceptable for political and cultural reasons.[19]

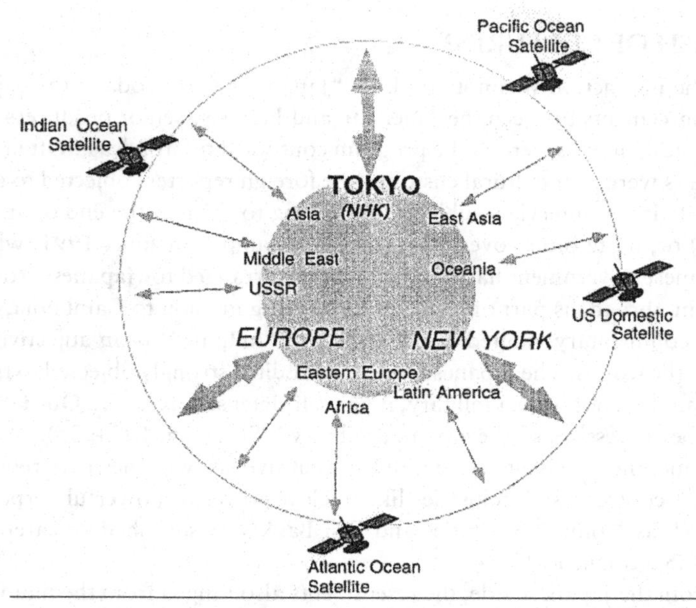

Figure 1: Global News Network—Global Satellite Transmission System (NHK)

It is also doubtful whether NHK would have been able to make the internal cultural transition that the foreign journalists involved thought would have been necessary to run an international 24-hour news service.

> Fundamental changes would have been required for this undertaking. Not in terms of budget, the money was there. But in terms of news gathering philosophy. NHK wanted basically to control the news flow out of Asia. But they realized there were going to be very strong editorial concerns from the GNN partners, that NHK would not be able to cover Asia in the way it currently does. There was a faction in NHK that for various reasons thought this was too dangerous.[20]

In Sherman's view, this potential for loss of control was real, as the actual network operating center would not have been in Tokyo. When Shima had announced plans to establish GNN by the end of 1991, the headquarters site chosen was in New York (Inoue, 1991).

> It would have meant that New York would in essence have handled the network, and that New York office would be filled with Japanese and Americans and Europeans. That's why the petri dish of "Japan Business Today" was interesting, because we could see what the interaction between those forces was (Ibid).

A CLASH OF CULTURES?

Often the interaction was not good. At "Japan Business Today" the editorial disagreements between the American and Japanese senior producers became steadily more severe as the program continued to broadcast. Often the arguments were over cultural customs (the foreign reporters objected to giving small gifts to interview subjects, or bowing to them at the end of an interview) or, more often, over language. For example, in June, 1991, when the Japanese government had for the first time arranged for Japanese troops to be sent abroad, as part of a UN peace-keeping mission to Cambodia, the English commentary wanted to use the word "military" as an adjective to describe the troops. The Japanese Managing Editor strongly objected to this, as "Japan does not have a military, it has self-defense forces. . . . Our forces cannot be aggressive, so they are not military" (Sherman, 1994: 35).

Sometimes the issues were more substantive, as when negative reporting about controversial industries like nuclear power or powerful corporations such as Nomura Securities and Fuji Bank was squashed or carefully avoided (Sherman, 1994: 36).[21]

From the Japanese side, the resentments also ranged from the minor—the fact that the foreign anchor of "Japan Business Today" had stayed in a five-star hotel during his time in Tokyo—to more substantive claims, such as (on "Asia Now") the insistence by Seattle PBS station KCTS that the editor-in-chief should be someone "who could understand what Americans wanted." NHK had reluctantly agreed, even though NHK was carrying 90% of the production cost at the beginning.[22]

In general the Japanese production staff felt that for the Americans everything should be American.

> KCTS always wanted it to be more American. Even if local people were speaking English, they should have subtitles. They used to complain constantly that NHK reporters had very poor English, therefore they wanted to use their own. If we insisted on using our own, what I hated was that they weren't content with just subtitles—they wanted to do voiceovers.[23]

Other problems were frankly acknowledged by the Japanese side to be political, but this did not have the negative connotation that the Americans gave the term.

> Japan recognizes China as the official government, and regards Taiwan as a region of China. That's how we see it. But the US (producers) always wanted to report from the Taiwan or South Korea point of view. They always wanted to talk about "brainwashed" North Koreans. We don't see it that way. We're very close to Korea. America isn't close to Asia at all.[24]

For the American journalists and producers, such disputes tended to be expressed in terms of theoretical professional ethics, while their Japanese counterparts saw things both in cultural terms (for example, their perception of the need for NHK as a major force in Japanese society to have perfectly legitimate working relationships with other major power brokers, such as the large trading companies) and also defensively, as the Westerners often seemed out to "get" Japan and trample on its own sense of identity in its own part of the world—a sense which was still extremely delicate, due to the legacy of imperial Japan's activities in Asia.[25]

The differences arose at least in part out of a fundamentally different conception of the role of the media, and of information. A journalist in Washington may like to describe her or himself as a knight errant, the professional role defined in terms of questioning, challenging and attacking, and by so doing helping ensure the health of government and society. A Tokyo journalist working for a large public corporation like NHK is likely to see himself as part of the existing structure of society, which translates into a role as an insider, as someone who should give measured consideration to the views of the powers-that-be.

> In Japan, I think there are some more a priori judgements that are made. How will this news story affect public opinion? Will it affect public opinion in a positive, nation-building way, or in a negative, chaotic way? You know, in Asia, the concept of "chaos" or "confusion" is one that's raised all the time. This question was asked to me so many times, that it couldn't have been an artificial question. Japanese producers would ask me "Would this cause confusion in the public?" At first I thought what they were talking about was whether the story was told clearly or not. No, what they meant was, was the story going to challenge the status quo? When you start there, a lot of your judgements are based on that notion, and lot of what's a good story is determined by whether it will cause confusion or chaos.[26]

Sherman also gradually became aware that what he understood to be the Japanese perception of "the news" could be quite different.

> I was bemused by NHK's news agenda, which was skewed by the unending calendar of seasonal festivals across the island nation, excruciating hours of talking heads, and soft documentaries about Japan's beautiful places. Because so many of NHK's resources were allocated to this kind of news, it was not easy to fill an all-business program in a country that prided itself on being the world's second-most powerful economic engine. That was the first hint that news agenda at NHK was being shaped in accordance with a set of standards not usually present in the newsrooms of America's television networks. (Sherman,1994: 33)

There seem to be two levels of understanding lacking here. One could place Sherman's statement side by side with Paddy Scannel's description of national broadcast media like NHK or BBC as central agents of the national culture, in particular through their roles in setting the national calendar, presenting "an orderly and regular progression of festivities, rituals and celebrations—major and minor, civil and sacred—that marked the unfolding of the broadcast year" (Scannel, 1988: 17, 18). What Sherman saw as "excruciating" or "soft" may have appeared to the NHK producers responsible as an integral part of their work.

Another refers to Hall's critique of the BBC as an active player in an ongoing process, the creation of the nation, a position very close to that taken by Krauss in his analysis of the role of NHK in Japanese society.

A PERCEPTION GAP

Comparing the two key interviews cited in the preceding section, with Noriyoshi Fujii and Spencer Sherman, is revealing. Both have an understanding of the other's viewpoint, but ultimately find the cultural differences to be too great for a middle ground to be established. Togo describes this difference as one between perception and reality, a "perception gap," where the media plays a major role in its creation (Togo, 1998: 110).

Togo's view was reinforced by the results of a nine-month intensive study of national television news reporting carried out in 1992/3 under the aegis of the Mansfield Center for Pacific Affairs and NHK Joho Network.[27] In Japan the research covered prime time news on NHK, NTV, TBS, Fuji, and TV Asahi, while in the United States it looked at ABC, CBS, CNN, NBC and PBS. The study used a codified system of questions covering 12 different aspects of the news, ranging from inquiries about presentation to content, allowance for differing viewpoints, portrayal of the government or political parties and so on.

The resulting report (*Creating Images*, 1997) gives insight into how television news helps build and reinforce stereotypes about "the other." For example, while American coverage tends to emphasize conflicts between nations, Japanese coverage is inclined to focus on scandal, crime and violence within other nations. One interesting finding was that, while Japanese television was judged to be more "balanced and objective," once it departed from those subjective ideals it was far more likely to show a negative bias. Also, it was found that the effect of coverage of similar content may be different in different countries. It was notable, for example, that when the story dealt with conflict, this might result in either an increased negative or positive image of Japan in the American assessment, while a focus on conflict involving the United States resulted in a sharp increase in a negative perception among Japanese reporters.

The tentative conclusion was that "people from different countries have different reactions to parallel news reports, possibly because cultural values may affect responses to the same phenomenon" (Mansfield: 10). Another was that "the way television news stories are presented seems to have a real effect on the image of the other country" (Krauss in Mansfield: 11).

WHY GNN?

Research such as the Mansfield Center report indicate that the philosophical basis for the GNN proposal had a basis in real need. But in strictly practical terms there is an open question why Shima chose to promote an idea which so many felt was at best vastly premature.

In his autobiography Shima is less than forthcoming about the genesis of GNN, making it sound like a logical but visionary extension of NHK's programming for its satellite channels, specifically referring to a successful (and remarkably innovative idea) to run the main news programs of the BBC, Gostelradio (USSR), CCTV (China) ABC (USA), and others (including Germany, France, South Korea, Thailand, the Philippines) as originally broadcast, with a straight Japanese translation (Shima, 1995: 192).

Underlying Shima's initiative was the perception that NHK had to extend its reach, in order to deal with new realities. In part the thinking can surely be attributed to the economic rationale that seems to have dominated Shima's thinking, finding a way for NHK to break out of the double bind of being forced to kowtow to the bureaucrats at the MPT and the politicians in the Diet in order to get its budget approved, at the same time as dealing with the basic conundrum NHK faced every fiscal year, of having to balance huge resource requirements with a fixed or declining revenue from license fees.

Value added broadcasting, including high-definition television and international satellite-based networks, was the way out of this bind. On at least one level, that of domestic satellite broadcasting, time has proved Shima right, as it soon became a major profit center for NHK, accounting for 26% of the corporation's profits by mid-1992 (Sato, 1992). This figure could have been much higher, as one report, based on figures from the Economic Planning Agency, suggested that almost 50% of DBS viewers were not paying the user fee which is NHK's lifeblood (Morikawa, 1992: 5).

An element of hubris also seems to have been present. Every foreigner who met Shima describes him as being an atypical Japanese, blunt and outspoken, while the Japanese press called him autocratic, even megalomaniacal (Brinkley, 1997: 128 and interviews). He appears to have been obsessed with Ted Turner, at least in part out of admiration for Turner's go-getting reputation. More importantly the achievement of CNN was enough to concern every top television executive, especially following the success of the 24-hour news channel in hogging coverage of the Persian Gulf war. By the time Shima tried to explain GNN to a Diet Lower House committee in April, 1991, all the major commercial broadcasters had announced plans to radically upgrade their news divisions, and establish deeper overseas connections (Asahi Evening News, 1991: 4).

However, Shima was not quite the maverick depicted in the media of the time: he was responding to real challenges, both internally and from outside NHK. Krauss points out that as far back as 1982 a "Long-term Vision Advisory Council" set up by NHK had recommended an activist role for NHK in developing new media services, and charging for them (Krauss, 2000: 183).

In addition, Shima had inherited an organization which had been under increasingly strong pressure from the government of Yasuhiro Nakasone (1982–1987) to reform itself, reflecting the strong neoconservative influence of Reagan in the United States and Thatcher in the U.K.[28] A specific focus for the Nakasone administration had been communications, as it pushed for the privatization of two of the biggest public corporations in the world, Nippon Telephone and Telegraph (NTT) and Japan National

Railways (JNR). Nakasone himself was known to dislike NHK, for reasons similar to Thatcher's antipathy towards the BBC: the belief that the national broadcaster was biased against the conservative viewpoint.[29]

THE FUTURE OF NHK

His autobiography also makes it clear that Shima was obsessed by one thing, the future of NHK. More clearly than others he saw that television, and especially television news was changing, like it or not.[30] The advent of STAR TV in particular sent a warning signal. One senior NHK producer involved in the planning of GNN recalls that "the impact of Star made us jealous." It was necessary to react, because "the borderless world was threatening (*ureimeshi koto*)."[31]

It is important to remember that the Gulf war was unpopular in Japan, but the Japanese networks, including NHK, had been forced to rely on the superior reporting resources of CNN, the other American networks, and the BBC. In effect, the American networks had been able to influence the reporting of the war on Japanese television screens (Brull, 1991). GNN was more than a challenge to CNN: it was also a call for a more pluralistic approach to international news gathering and distribution. Shima himself was characteristically blunt on the intention behind GNN: "We want to put the actual true faces of Japan and Asia more into the international scene." (Schlesinger, 1991: 1).

> I felt that the media in Japan were reaching only the domestic audience, while we were in an era when information could be moving across borders, as evident in the way news about the Persian Gulf war was shown around the world by CNN. Japanese media failed to serve the purpose of sending overseas the news about Japan and Asia. It also failed to carry to Japan the important news that was happening abroad. (Hara, 1995: 3)

The success of CNN was indicative of a larger trend, toward a "highly privatized, transnational media environment," where NHK might not be able to compete (Gershon and Kanayama, 1995: 222). This did not simply refer to news gathering, but also to the purchase of television and film programming. There were also numerous indications that non-broadcast corporate giants were investing in commercial media. Most notably, the year Shima became president, 1989, was also the year when Sony completed its purchase of Columbia Pictures and of CBS records, which was followed in 1991 by Matsushita buying MCA, which included Universal Studios. Sony later extended its investment into satellite television, to the extent that it is now seen as the lead company in the JSkyB consortium: Matsushita sold MCA/Universal to Seagram's in 1995.

At the same time, the commercial terrestrial stations had been relatively successful at increasing their operating revenues compared with NHK

(Krauss, 1998: 687), which was largely dependent on one stagnant source of income, the license fee. According to one analyst, "television advertising revenues for the five Tokyo channels grew by a compound annual rate of 10.1% over the past 28 Years" (up to 1996) (Smith, 1996: 16).

MICO AND TV JAPAN

NHK's heavy investments in satellite television and HDTV, while it remained tied to an essentially inflexible source of income (the license fee) making it constantly vulnerable to political pressure, represented a quandary that had long obsessed NHK management. According to the Broadcast Law, NHK was forbidden from taking the logical step taken by the BBC, and diversifying into commercial activities. After lobbying by NHK and the MPT, two revisions to the law were passed, in 1982 and 1988, which led to an enormous increase in NHK 'related organizations,' in particular the most powerful, NHK Enterprises, which had been directly modeled on BBC Enterprises, and Sogo Vision, a joint venture with Dentsu and others to sell programming abroad (Krauss, 2000: 198–202).

As revealed in his autobiography, Shima was an enthusiastic supporter of this development, especially the notion of selling NHK abroad. In 1989 he had supervised the setting up of the Kokusai Media Corporation (known as Media International Corp—MICO). The principal investor in the generously financed MICO was NHK Enterprises Inc., together with 47 other firms, including Dai-Ichi Kangyo Bank, Sumitomo Bank and the trading company Itochu. NHK Enterprises itself had been established in 1986 as a commercial corporation, charged with making a profit, and included investment from NEC, Sony, Matsushita and Toshiba. MICO was seen as emblematic of Shima's pushing NHK in a more commercial enterprises, a direct threat to the commercial broadcasters, and beyond the brief of a non-profit public broadcasting corporation (Gershon and Kanayama, 1995).

One of MICO's functions was to produce and acquire programming material worldwide, making it a rival of the commercial stations: as a direct result, it was effectively boycotted by all the commercial TV networks in Japan. MICO also acted as the umbrella for "TV Japan," which from April, 1991 served as the vehicle for broadcasting NHK Japanese language programming abroad. In the United States, it functioned under the Japan Network Group (JNG), a joint venture between MICO and the trading company Itochu. The principal investors in the European operation, known as Japan Satellite Television (JST) and based in London, were MICO and another trading company, Marubeni.

Contrary to the expressed purpose of helping generate side profits for NHK, both JNG and JST lost money, with accrued losses reaching around 25 million dollars by 1994. At that time revenues abruptly doubled, and the two joint ventures appeared to operate in the black, thanks to hidden subsidies from NHK amounting to over a billion yen a year, although neither firm has a direct relationship with NHK (Yamamoto in Schreiber, 2000). At the same time the rationale for their existence has been undercut by the emergence of NHK World TV, which is broadcast free to air.

NHK RETURNS TO OLD CERTAINTIES

Ultimately Shima was defeated by the bureaucrats and politicians who objected to his efforts to give NHK greater independence (Asahi, 1991, July 23) and by the organization he was supposed to be in charge of. In interviews carried out in 1998 among NHK staff, it was difficult to elicit many warm memories about his time as president. The most common assessment was that under Shima NHK had lost its way, and then after his departure found its way back to the path of old certainties: NHK was a Japanese broadcaster, and "international broadcasting" meant telling the world about Japan.

One Shima sympathizer in NHK attributed the failure of the GNN proposal to get off the ground to a fundamental difference between NHK and CNN, the former's lack of a "business mind."[32] There was a genuine and quite central issue here, whether or not you could use public money to develop a commercial enterprise. Faced with the same quandary, the BBC's answer was to develop a completely separate organization, BBC World, in order to keep commercialization safely corralled away from the mainstream organization.[33] NHK's ultimate response was to turn its back on the notion of making money from international sales. Even when it too created an organization called NHK World, and put it on satellite around the world, profit was not the main objective.

> NHK has a policy that they just want as many people as possible to watch NHK. So we are working with that policy, and trying to develop contracts with local stations in as many countries as possible. To make money is secondary . . . The principle of this business (of NHK World) is to make NHK available to expatriate Japanese. So we are not supposed to make so much money. We don't advertise.[34]

NHK WORLD

The fifth in a list of "Major Goals for Fiscal 1998" established as part of the operational plan for NHK was "Expand broadcasting to overseas audiences—

Start International TV Broadcasting Services to virtually all of the world" (NHK Factsheet #2, April 1998). In April 1998 NHK launched its World TV service, split into two tiers: NHK World TV, unscrambled, featuring news and information programs, and NHK World Premium, scrambled, providing NHK Japanese programming, mostly dramas, soap operas and entertainment shows, to cable stations and other distributors. The signal was digital, making these the first digital broadcasts distributed by NHK.

The rationale behind NHK World is vague in the extreme, officially an intent to "enhance the mutual contact and goodwill among countries, regions and people," and "to promote greater understanding of Japan and to provide informative, educational and entertaining programs to Japanese living or traveling abroad." The latter reason seems to be the priority: NHK reckons there are about 700,000 Japanese people living abroad, while between 16 to 17 million people travel abroad from Japan every year. The service is also a response to Article 33 of the Broadcast Law, which states that the MPT "may order NHK to conduct international broadcasting by designating Broadcast Service Area, broadcasting matters and other relevant matters." [MPT, 1998 (2): 26]

By the end of 1998 NHK World covered most of the world except the southern part of Africa, using a total of three satellites.[35] As presently constituted the service is basically a provider of programs to local TV stations and to cable heads, with the Premium service scrambled in order to facilitate copyright clearance.

Virtually all the programming is in Japanese, with English translation available on a subchannel for the 7 o'clock and the 9 o'clock news. Broadcasts last for 18 hours, and the aim in 1998 was eventually to make 30% available with English translation. Foreigners have no role in production of NHK World, other than to edit the English translations of the Japanese scripts.

In interviews NHK officials are candid about the difference in philosophy between the reality of NHK World and Shima's vision of GNN. Shima described his actions in terms of meeting a challenge, and anticipating future trends: NHK now talks of duty and obligation, and of going "back to the basics as a public broadcaster."

> We found his (Shima's) analysis of the market was not correct, because we found there was no such demand for NHK news, commercially. The reason why we strengthened our international broadcasting service this time is that there was a revision of the Broadcasting Law four years ago, in 1994. Due to that change it has become something like a duty, an obligation of NHK as the nation's sole public broadcaster to do international TV broadcasting, just like we have been doing with Radio Japan.[36]

It is also made clear that the intent is "not to make money, but to let the peoples of the world know about Japan." NHK World's primary purpose is to act as a start-of-the-art distribution network.

> We are just trying first to make contracts with local stations in each country. That is the main purpose. We just want to expand the number of countries to distribute our programs.[37]

And it appears that the experience of the foreigners who were engaged in trying to set up the putative precursors to GNN, that there was an institutional reluctance to tread on international toes, was reinforced by bureaucratic fiat from the MPT in 1998, the year NHK World was launched.

> In editing broadcasting programs of entrusted domestic and overseas broadcasting, program-supplying broadcasters must take into consideration the natural, economic, social and cultural conditions of the countries that are the target of said entrusted domestic and overseas broadcasting as much as possible, so that friendship and exchange with other countries are not impaired [MPT, 1998 (2): 49].

IN FLOW: THE WORLD COMES TO JAPAN

The Borderless TV World Arrives in Japan

Shima's perception that the world of television was changing in fundamental way has been proved largely correct. At home, NHK's long unchallenged position as *the* authoritative news source has been undermined by a new, longer, more personal style of news presentation pioneered by one of the commercial stations, Asahi Television, with a program called News Station. Less than three years after Shima's resignation, Asahi was pulling in the same audience ratings for its late night news show as NHK had for its long-established peak TV news show at 7 P.M. (Sender, 1994: 80). Younger Japanese in particular were showing a clear preference for commercial television: significantly, they are also the main target for the new cable and satellite TV services in Japan (Economist, July 1995: 49).

Another major concern of Shima and his supporters was also realized. The world of borderless TV arrived in Japan, courtesy of a radical revision in the regulations covering cable TV in Japan, and thanks to the Internet. This was an outcome which, after his resignation, Shima was in a position to welcome:

> TV has a terminal weakness . . . (it) is a one-way street. Broadcasters decide what to air; viewers fiddle with the dials to find the station they

> want to watch. That's not going to work anymore, as we can see by the decline of the large U.S. networks . . . the Internet and CATV are the media of the future . . . By 2001, anyone will be able to generate information and anyone will be able to access it. Our whole concept of information will undergo a mighty change. Some or much of the information will be inaccurate, so people will have to rely much more on their own judgement (Whipple, 1995: 7).

THE MPT REVERSES COURSE

Another indication that Shima had been fundamentally correct in his assessment of what the future held in store for television was when the MPT belatedly accepted the inevitable and abruptly changed the rules of the TV game in Japan. The first move was in December, 1993, when the regulations governing the cable TV industry were overhauled. The changes were radical, allowing firms to merge and permitting foreign investors to take up to a one-third shareholding in a joint venture (where previously they had been restricted to less than one-fifth). This made possible the advent of multiple system operators (MSOs), companies offering telephony and Internet access services through the same line used to deliver cable. They were inspired by successful experiments run by U.S. companies in Britain, and followed a pattern which is rapidly becoming popular in the United States (Muranaka, 1997: 3).[38]

Six months later, in June 1994, the MPT also opened up the satellite broadcast market, both for outgoing and incoming signals. The reasons why MPT so abruptly and so radically changed its regulations concerning broadcast satellites and cable TV are not completely clear, other than the realization that the significance of both technologies had been transformed, and that foreign expertise was needed for Japan to catch up with the new developments.

For years cable use had been tightly controlled by the MPT (which regulates entry to and rates for CATV), in an apparent attempt to defend the status quo of the broadcast companies. The primary rationale for cable had been to redistribute television signals (relayed via microwave or satellite to the local cable head) in areas where mountainous terrain or urban conglomeration resulted in poor reception.[39] As a result, most early cable TV systems were non-profit: in fact, in the early 1970s, sixty percent of CATV systems in Japan were part of the NHK network, as the corporation is required by Article 7 of the original Broadcasting Act to ensure clear reception throughout the country (Sugaya, 1995). By the mid-1990s 80% of the CATV companies were operating in the red, and there were no independent commercial cable companies of any significant size (Smith, 1996).

Similarly the spread of the Internet in Japan was initially severely limited, again in an apparent attempt to bolster the position of NTT, the former national monopoly telecoms company, and still by far the largest telecoms company in Japan. Attempts to set up commercial Internet nodes in the early 1990s were blocked, on the grounds that the Internet was primarily for academic use.[40] In the mid-1990s costs were extremely high, either for businesses leasing the high capacity lines required by Internet providers, or for individuals using the Internet through a commercial provider (typically Y30,000 for an initial connection, plus a monthly fee of Y2,000, and a per minute charge of Y30) (Economist, July 1995: 50).

At some point, the competitive cost of this became apparent. In the early to mid-1990s Japan clearly lagged behind other countries in the extent of its linkage to the Internet, and in its ability to exploit the potential high-carrying capacity of cable.

The cable situation was particularly anomalous. At the time of the November 1994 regulatory changes, the "penetration rate" of cable TV (number of total television households with access to cable) was very low: by the beginning of 1996 it was still only 7 percent[41] of the total 41 million households in Japan, compared with well over 60 percent in the U.S (Smith, 1997: 4). Throughout the 1980s, at the same time that the American cable TV industry had been growing very quickly, the MPT had deliberately blocked the development of American-style cable conglomerates like TCI and Time-Warner, by forbidding MSOs, limiting foreign investment to the point where it was uneconomic,[42] and holding fast to a policy which basically only permitted local ownership of comparatively small, local cable stations. For example the largest cable operation in Tokyo in 1994 was limited to serving just one of the city's 23 wards, with the remainder served by 19 other cable companies (Schilling, 1994: 14).

For foreign businessmen, the extent of regulatory change in late 1993 and early 1994 was remarkable:[43] effectively, it marked a 180 degree reversal, as the Time-Warner representative in Japan remembers:

> 1994. That was the watershed year. Prior to that MSOs were legally not allowed in Japan. *Yuseisho* (the MPT) changed the rules basically. What we had heard from them was that previously they had focused on DTH, on satellite provision of audio-visual services. And they suddenly had this realization they were being left behind in the Internet world, and they wanted to create an infrastructure that was capable of delivering Internet and was capable of competing in telephony, as well as cable television. So they did a very abrupt about face, and really reversed all their laws, to the point where they previously discouraged cable infrastructure, they now encouraged it[44]. . . . Not only did they see the success of

> the cable industry elsewhere in the world, they saw the development of the Internet and the fact the cable companies were picking up high-speed Internet and exploiting it, and they just didn't want to get left out. They didn't want the manufacturers left out.[45]

The most significant innovation was to allow cable companies to seek economies of scale by operating across several areas. The changes produced rapid results, the most obvious being the creation of two major multinational companies, specifically to bring new communication services to the Japanese market. By January 1995 two giant MSOs had been established: Jupiter Telecommunications (Sumitomo Corp. in a 60–40 partnership with Telecommunications Inc. (TCI)—then the largest American cable TV company); and Titus Communications Corp. (equal shareholding between Itochu, Toshiba, U.S. West and Time Warner).

While Jupiter immediately launched an ambitious expansion program by taking stakes in existing small cable operators, forecasting 10 million subscribers by 2000, Titus embarked on building "green field" cable operations from scratch, with a far more modest target of two million by 2000. One reason for the different strategies was that Titus concentrated on putting in the high-end cable needed for multiple applications, looking at an ideal mix of 40% cable television, 40% telephony services and 20% data transmission, mostly internet connections.[46]

The new ventures were seen as reflecting the growing interdependence of industries across national boundaries in developing the new multimedia businesses, which were both capital and expertise intensive (Nakamoto, 1995).[47] They also introduced foreign know-how to an area Japanese bureaucrats had difficulty in coming to grips with, developing the practical reality of a Japanese version of the information superhighway proposed by Vice President Gore, a proposal which had attracted considerable attention in Japan.

As one example, plans MITI had announced in March, 1994, to create "multimedia information centers" across Japan, had been delayed when the municipal officials charged with setting up the centers confessed they had no idea what to put in them. The old dirigiste economic planning that MITI was famous for and that had worked so well with such mass-produced technologies as automobiles and videocassette and fax machines had proved to be inimical to the information industries (Urakami, 1994). This and other clumsy attempts by MITI to assert its position in the development of telecommunications and information industries allowed the more nimble MPT to eventually win for itself the role of information industry arbiter, by building on the areas of its undoubted prerogative, such as cable television.

That the intention behind the changes was to shake up the telecommunications/ information status quo was made remarkably explicit by the MPT publication "Manual for Market Entry into Cable TV Business," published in both Japanese and English in March, 1998. In the section dealing with foreign ownership a paragraph makes it clear that, in order to promote "convergence of the cable TV and telecommunications business," businesses wishing to introduce telephony on cable are exempt from the restrictions on foreign ownership (which themselves were clearly relaxed compared with the old regulatory regime). To drive the point home the section ends with the bald statement that "regulations for terrestrial and satellite broadcasting are different from those for cable television" (Ministry of Post and Telecommunications, 1998). A note in parenthesis adds the final piece to the puzzle: the amendment was to become effective when the fourth protocol to the General Agreement on Trade in Services (GATS) was effective in Japan.

It did not take long for foreign corporations to take advantage of the new regulatory regime. By April 2000 the make-up of Titus Communications had changed dramatically, with Microsoft Corporation emerging as the majority shareholder, a prelude to a takeover of Titus by Jupiter Telecommunications in September 2000. J-Com Broadband, as it is now known, is Japan's largest cable system operator. Although Sumitomo remains the largest single shareholder (41%) two foreign corporations, Liberty Media (35%) and Microsoft (24%), together have majority control. The total number of households served had increased to 1.45 million by June 30, 2002, in the Hokkaido, Kanto, Kansai and Kyushu regions. The fastest growing services offered were telephony and internet access—by March 2004 it had 667,000 subscribers.

The MPT, now part of the Ministry of Public Management, Home Affairs, Posts and Telecommunications (MPHPT), can only regard with satisfaction the concrete results of its policies to shake up the industry. By FY 1999 over 50% of cable companies were operating in the black, and by 2002 cable penetration reportedly exceeded 20% of the country's 46 million TV households.

BROADCAST AND COMMUNICATIONS SATELLITES

The world of satellite TV had also changed in Japan. At the same time as the very expensive and exotic DBS technology was being developed and pushed into service a more seemingly mundane development was under way. In the mid-1980s, the MPT had opened up the domestic telecommunications sector to competition, and almost immediately two new satellite companies (see box), announced plans to launch multipurpose communication satellites.

The number later grew to three, in response to US pressure on the Japanese government to buy American high technology, in this case satellites (Hudson, 1990: 142). The facts that the new companies appeared so rapidly, and that their ownership reflected the interests of all the major trading companies indicated that the MPT's change of regulations had been prepared well in advance of execution.

Table 3: The Trading Houses Invest in Space

SCC (Space Communications Corporation)
Mitsubishi Heavy Engineering and 29 Mitsubishi companies
Established in March, 1985
Customers included the Defense Agency and Tokyo Electric

JCSAT (Japan Communications Satellite Co.)
C. Itoh, Mitsui, Hughes
Established in April 1985
Customers included NTT, Nomura and Daiwa Securities

SAJAC (Satellite Japan Corp)
Nissho Iwai, Sumitomo, Marubeni, Orix, Sony and three others
Established in April, 1985
In 1993 merged with JCSAT to form JSAT

Traditionally, the MPT had divided communications satellites into two kind, according to purpose: communications (*tsushin eisei*) and broadcasting (*hoso eisei*). In part this reflected the MPT's faithful following of the ITU's attempts to control the advent of satellites equipped with transponders powerful enough to broadcast direct to the home, by strictly allocating certain orbital slots for each nation dedicated to DBS satellites only.

However, the MPT took matters one step further, by treating DBS signals on DBS satellites in the same way as they did terrestrial broadcasters, i.e. requiring licenses, a privilege which the MPT guarded very carefully. The "other" category, CS satellites, were supposed to be limited to traditional telecommunications services, relaying voice, data and video. If a company used CS for "broadcasting" (transmission of programs from one point to many) a license from the MPT was required and foreign ownership was limited to 20%. However if the company wanted to deliver programming to a cable-head only (point to point transmission), this was considered to be acting as an "information provider," and thus was "communication," not broadcast, and no foreign equity restrictions applied. This hair-splitting policy was clearly in NHK's favor, and according to many Japanese analysts had been part of the MPT's attempt to protect Shima's flank while he was trying to salvage Hi-Vision.

> The purpose of dividing broadcast and communication satellites was to protect NHK against competition. It was a national policy decision. This was the time of Shima.[48]

In an interview conducted in 1998, ministry officials were still persisting in maintaining the anomalous position that communications and broadcasting could never be mixed, although the rationale had changed: to deny the possibility of using a broadcast satellite to relay the "receive" end of pages from the World Wide Web, and have one dish configured to receive both the TV signal and the data communications.

> We separate broadcasting and communications. They cannot be mixed. The Internet is communications. There's no such thing as broadcasting and communications mixed.[49]

In fact at the time of the interview this was a service already offered in the US by Hughes (under the name "DirecDuo"), while SCC had been offering at least one part of the service, the "DirecPC," under license from Hughes, since January 1997—albeit with very limited success (Kallender (2), 99: 15).

A SHAKY START FOR SATELLITE TV

In response to pressure from the operators of the new communications satellites, who had found it impossible to recoup their investment from voice and data communications services alone,[50] a 1989 revision to the Broadcast Act allowed communication satellites to deliver television programming direct to consumers. Both JCSAT and SCC satellites were designed for both telecommunications and television relay, and television was quickly identified as a primary potential source of revenue.[51]

In 1992, further amendments to the Broadcast Law and the Radio Law allowed the communication satellite operators to use six channels (on two satellites) for non-commercial scrambled programming delivered direct to home (Shimizu, 1993: 191)

Starting in mid-1992 six channels were on offer from the operators of two communications satellites, one service called CS-BAAN or Satellite Broadcast Center (offering music, sports and Japanese dramas) and the other called Sky Port, which featured CNN, MTV and the STAR channel out of Hong Kong. But by April 1993 there were only 47,500 subscribers, nowhere near the 300,000 which the operators had projected. At the same time in June 1993 two of the new satellite operators, JCSAT and Satellite Japan Corp., were forced into a merger, before SAJAC had even managed one successful satellite launch. The new company was Japan Satellite Systems (JSAT), which is now the largest satellite operator in the Asia-Pacific region, with eight communications satellites. Leading shareholders are the four major trading companies and NTT.

There were multiple reasons for the initial complete failure of the new services. The CS satellites used C-Band, requiring different, larger and more expensive receiving equipment, compared with the already existing NHK BS-1 and BS-2, and WOWOW (which shares the same satellite as the NHK services). Programming was either inappropriate (both CNN and MTV were in English) or inadequate, so that there was little incentive to take the services (Gershon and Kanayama, 1995: 227).

The success or failure of a new television service would not normally be a cause of much anxiety, but in this case the MPT was concerned enough to introduce a radical opening of the satellite broadcast market in June, 1994, which enabled Japanese broadcasters to send their programs abroad, while allowing foreign broadcasters to start services in Japan.[52]

As with the revision of regulations for cable, the reasons were multiple, including the necessity to acknowledge a fait accompli, that in fact international satellite TV signals were already accessible in Japan, and the sudden awareness that Japan was one of the few countries in the Asia region that denied its citizens legal, open access to international satellite programming (Mainichi, 1993: 5). The advisory panel which made the recommendations that allowed for the changes was also explicit in its acknowledgement of the philosophical reasoning behind its report, advising that the government

> should abolish or review restrictions on participation in the telecommunications and broadcasting fields, because curbs placed by the bureaucracy that forecasts the supply and demand situation contravene the principles of a market economy (Mainichi, 1994: 5).

But the most direct pressure for change seems to have come from the satellite operators, notably Mitsubishi and Mitsui, which were anxious to see some kind of return on their very expensive investments in communication satellites, and saw satellite TV as their one best hope. The trading companies were not so much interested in the TV channels (although all of the current commercial satellite TV companies do have substantial trading company shareholding), but in having more customers use the satellite transponders. The aim was to get the operating rates on the satellites themselves up, because of the severe losses the trading companies as operators were carrying from the satellite launch operation business.[53]

In short order the existing communication satellite TV service companies were reorganized or merged, major foreign players came and made alliances with Japanese parties, and digital broadcasting via CS satellite was introduced in Japan.

DIGITAL BROADCASTS, COMMUNICATIONS SATELLITES

There are two distinct satellite services offered in Japan. One is DBS, heavily regulated by the government. This began as an experimental analogue service in 1987, dominated by NHK, with a film channel called WOWOW as its eventual, not very successful competitor. In December 2000 a digital service was launched, which added channels offered by the five major terrestrial networks and some limited datacast services.

The other service, where competition was permitted, was the CS broadcasts. As described above, the early, analogue services were a failure, and quickly absorbed by digital CS platforms, which began operation well ahead of the digital DBS broadcasts.

In June 1996 PerfecTV started up, based on some of the JCSAT shareholders (four major trading companies) and others, including TBS (Tokyo Broadcasting System), Toyota, NTT and Sony. One of its first moves was to take over the analog CS-BAAN service. The actual service launched in October, 1996, using the JCSAT-3 satellite to broadcast a digital signal, and offering a theoretical 70 channels. Digital satellite broadcasting had begun.

Initially PerfecTV seemed to do well in terms of attracting subscribers, but only by heavily subsidizing the price of the receiving equipment, which at Y40,000 (approximately $350) still was not cheap. The result was heavy losses in the first two years of operation, at which point it was still far short of the number of subscribers needed for profitability. Apart from cost, a major reason for its lack of popularity was its lack of original programming: in fact, there was little to distinguish it from cable television service.[54]

The decision to merge with the third planned system, JSkyB, in May 1998, was no doubt inevitable, and probably made easier by the fact that from the outset it had planned on using the same satellite platform, the JCSAT series (though not the same satellite), and the same receiving equipment as PerfecTV.

In November 1997, DirecTV Japan was launched, four months after buying Skyport Center Corp, which had been broadcasting nine channels on analog communications satellites, but had only achieved about 80,000 subscribers. DirecTV Japan represented a link-up between Hughes Electronics (owned by General Motors), Culture Convenience Club (CCC), Japan's largest video rental chain, Matsushita Electric Industries and several Mitsubishi companies (Mitsubishi Corp., Mitsubishi Electric and Space Communications Corp (SCC—a satellite service provider[55]). In January 1999 CCC sold two-thirds of its stock, mostly to Hughes Electronics, which became the majority stockholder with about 43 percent of the stock, with the rest held by Matsushita Electric Industrial and others (Kallender, 1999: 10).

The third system, JSkyB, was planned to start operations in April, 1998. Originally, this was a joint venture between News Corp and SoftbankCorp, Japan's biggest computer-software distributor and computer magazine publisher. In May, 1997, Sony Corp. joined as an equal partner (together with Fuji TV), following a disastrous attempt by News Corp and Softbank to buy control of Asahi TV (see below).

Sony's announced aim was to test the potential of the satellite broadcasting business, and to explore the possibility of exploiting the Sony brand name in the broadcast market, including the idea of developing its own "narrowcast" TV channels, such as a music channel (Jiji Press Idei, Japan Times, 1997). The addition of Fuji TV was also significant: it was the first terrestrial broadcaster to actively join in the management of a new satellite broadcasting company.

One year later, in May 1998, JSkyB merged with PerfecTV to make SkyPerfecTV, with five major shareholders: Itochu, Sony, Softbank, News Corp., and Fuji TV. The motivations for the merger were concern over the large start-up losses already incurred by PerfecTV (running at $58 million per year) and the slow growth in subscribers (at the time of the merger, estimated at 672,000, roughly one third the number need for breakeven (Scott and Fukui, 1998: 12), and awareness by the CS satellite channel owners that they had very limited time to establish their market, before the launch of digital DBS services, planned for the year 2000 (Yanagisawa, 1998: 2). In view of the fact that Sony immediately filled a number of key positions with its own managers, and later emerged as the lead company in the group of shareholders, it seems that Sony, as a shareholder in both companies, was the principal instigator of the merger (Sasaki, 1998).

The one fact that clearly differentiated the two new services was technical: although the satellites used were communication satellites, their signals were all digital. In addition to exceptional picture and sound quality, the main advantage that digital offers is the ability to pack more into the same signal. At start up, PerfecTV was offering 70 channels: following the merger with JSkyB, as many as 171 channels were on offer, from two satellites.[56] This huge carrying capacity translates into a pressing need: more programming, which represents both a problem and an opportunity for foreign companies.

THE IMPORTANCE OF PROGRAMMING

For both cable and satellite television, the key is programming, especially in an environment like Japan's, where good quality broadcasting is universally available, and in the case of NHK is also advertising free. For both the MPT bureaucrats and for the trading companies that had invested so heavily in "new" media, this realization seems to have been slow in coming.

> No one wants to buy cable (services). They buy programs. The dearth of non-terrestrial and non-broadcast programming in Japan for a long time was a detriment to the development of cable. In the last year (1997) we've seen a lot of liberalization from the Yuseisho in terms of allowing foreign programmers to come in. There have been a lot of partnering with local Japanese companies to originate Japanese programming, a lot has happened in the last three to five years to enhance the amount of programming available, and that has been helping. There's still a way to go yet. But with a lot more good programming available, people are a lot more willing to pay for something which previously they didn't have to.[57]

No one understands this better than the Chairman of News Corp., Rupert Murdoch. When he first announced the establishment of JSkyB in Tokyo in June, 1996, he made it clear that "it is Japanese programmes that will be the true drivers . . . News Corporation accepts the importance of the Japanese terrestrial broadcasters and will, over all else, create an environment where the terrestrial broadcasters are able to provide programming" (Nakamoto, 1996 (1).

His idea of how to create such an environment was made clear later in the same month, when he announced that News Corp. was joining with Softbank Corp, its partner in JSkyB, to buy a 21.4 percent stake in Asahi National Broadcasting (ANB), operating as TV Asahi. This made them jointly the largest shareholder in one of the key Tokyo-based national commercial television networks, directly affiliated with arguably the most important national newspaper, the *Asahi Shimbun.* The partners announced their intention of posting a director to ANB, marking the first instance of a foreign company taking a management interest in a Japanese broadcasting company (Smith, 1996: 4). The apparent intention was to provide the Japanese programming needed to make their investment in JSkyB a success, as the digital satellite broadcasting service was due to start operation in April, 1997. Murdoch defined the investment as a strategic move to get "as close as possible to the terrestrial station" (Muranaka, 1996: 3)

The move was rejected. The *Asahi Shimbun* led the other established owners of TV Asahi (including three printing and publishing companies and two advertising agencies) in a rapid buy-back of outstanding shares, reducing News Corp/Softbank to the third largest shareholder. When the two outsider companies asked for representation on TV Asahi's board, they were requested to sign a written agreement preventing them from seeking more shares, from selling their existing shares to outside investors, and from any involvement in management (Yoshimi and Arai, and Sasaki, 1997). The result was stalemate.

Nine months later, in March 1997, Murdoch and Son (the owner of Softbank) sold their shares to Asahi Shimbun, the newspaper company behind TV Asahi, at the same price they had originally paid (Yoshimi and Arai, 1997: 17). The Asahi media group made a weak show of offering future cooperation with Murdoch, but in the end nothing resulted. At the same time it was announced that Sony Corp., which had acted as middleman in the arrangement to sell back the shares, would be taking a one third stake in JSkyB (Sasaki, 1997: 4).

As long as News Corp. and Softbank were in an antagonistic relationship with Asahi, the chances of getting access to TV Asahi's programming were nil. In fact, the need for programming was a double-edged sword, and may have been the decisive reason for Murdoch's abrupt about-face. In February the MPT had refused to grant licenses for three of the 12 channel operating licenses Murdoch had applied for to run his new satellite service, citing "a lack of ability to obtain software" (Yoshimi and Arai, 1997: 17). An MPT official was quoted as saying: "He will find it impossible to get programs from Japan's broadcasters if he keeps his TV Asahi shares. By selling them, he may find it easier to get what he wants" (Sato, 1997: 7). Significantly, one of the three channels denied permission was for Japanese-language TV dramas and cartoons (Kyodo News, 1997: 5).

CHALLENGES TO THE STATUS QUO

The apparent defeat of two outsiders, Murdoch and Son (of Korean ancestry), seemed to represent a victory for the Japanese broadcasting establishment, but this was only one battle in a much larger war. It was not only NHK that was threatened by challenges to the status quo, but also the five Tokyo-based terrestrial networks. Since the establishment of the commercial stations, the MPT had protected them from competition. By 1996, the MPT reckoned they together had 89 percent of a market worth Y2,800 billion ($25.2 billion) by sales (Nakamoto, 1996).

The key element in reaching a settlement had been the direct intervention of the chairman of Sony, Nobuyuki Idei, who had not only arranged for Sony to take a shareholding in JSkyB, but also contrived for an invitation to Fuji TV, an arch rival of TV Asahi's and then the most successful commercial

TV company in Japan (in terms of sales), to take an equal stake in JSkyB. This was the first time a commercial Japanese TV network had moved into satellite broadcasting (Sasaki (2), 1997).

It was left to a large electronics manufacturer like Sony, with its ambitions to become a multimedia giant, to make the running, while the TV companies were left in an essentially defensive posture. This seems to be the downside of belonging to a large media grouping, with a powerful and essentially conservative newspaper calling the management shots, despite the fact that the television operations provide major shares of the revenues of the two biggest groupings—*Yomiuri Shimbun* with Nippon Television (NTV), and *Asahi Shimbun* with Asahi National Broadcasting (TV Asahi).

In part the defensiveness was due to uncertainly about the future: by 1994 both *Asahi Shimbun* and *Yomiuri Shimbun* had seen major drops in net profit, while overall television ad spending fell every year from 1992 to 1994. An *Asahi Shimbun* general director described the decline in newspaper advertising revenues as "shaking all of us to our foundations" (Friedland, 1994: 45).

Ironically, the discovery that "content is king" was not such a boon to the commercial TV broadcasters as (unlike NHK) much of their programming was made by outside production companies. Clearing copyright for rebroadcast on another delivery system or in another media is immensely complicated.[58]

In an interview, Idei was forthright about Sony's reasons for involvement in SkyPerfecTV: to test the waters of the satellite TV business, and to see whether Sony can create a global broadcasting brand of its own, specifically mentioning the possibility of Sony launching a music channel, eventually for a worldwide market. With this rationale he was interested in 'narrowcasting' via specialty channels on CS satellites, rather then the mass audience which BS satellites were aimed at (Jiji Press, 1997: 12). These were waters Sony had been testing for some time, as it had invested in cable and satellite in Germany, Latin America and East Asia, and operates Sony Entertainment Television, the second-ranked Hindi language cable channel in India.

Sony's interest in distribution is fueled by its heavy investment in production, which it has taken global to a degree unmatched by any of its Hollywood rivals. In 1999 it was scheduled to make 4,000 hours of foreign (i.e. non-English) TV programs, compared with 1,700 hours in English, much of which is shown on a growing network of 'branded' channels around the world [Economist, 1999 (4): 56].

A DIGITAL WORLD

Ultimately it is the commercial potential of digital TV which drives a company like Sony, and the notion that Japan must "keep up" with the rest of the developed world which caused the MPT to advance its target dates for the introduction of digital terrestrial broadcasting by five years, as both the U.S. and Britain introduced digital on an experimental basis in 1998 (Pollack, 1997: 11).

The commercial stations feel the same pressures, and react to them in a similar fashion, but often with open feelings of regret for the way things were.

> Next year (1999) will be 40 years since we (Fuji TV) started broadcasting, and now we have to change our thinking about what will be the next era of broadcasting. Our idea of making programmes was one set or stereotype of what the TV industry is. CS will change the face of the TV industry. We have to make programs at a very cheap cost, but acceptable to people . . . In every sense it is a trial . . . but we have to do it. This generation is changing rapidly. The technical breakthroughs are unimaginable. Anything could happen. We must be in the race.[59]

There is a sense of inevitability about this statement, but little enthusiasm. For decades the Japanese broadcasting industry had enjoyed superior returns on equity thanks to the virtual absence of competition, which allowed it to capitalize on its role of delivering an audience to the advertiser.[60] The sudden arrival of new competitors—who did not necessarily have to compete for advertising at all, as both cable and satellite are subscription driven—plus the demand to prepare for digitalization marked an abrupt change to the status quo. The abruptness was remarkable: in March, 1997, the MPT had moved forward by a full five years the target date for starting digital terrestrial broadcasting, to 2000, while simultaneously deciding that Japan's next broadcast satellite, BS-4B, would be digital—the final nail in the coffin of Hi-Vision.

Digitalization is extraordinarily expensive: one commentator interviewed for this research calculated that each media grouping would have to spend upwards of Yen 100 billion (approximately $833 million), beyond the means of the commercial TV stations to do on their own.[61] In fact the smallest and weakest of the commercial networks, TV Tokyo, openly criticized the Japanese government's decision to advance the date for the introduction of digital terrestrial television, saying it was financially impossible to handle both terrestrial and satellite digital broadcasts (Japan Times, 1997). For terrestrial relay the digital TV signals will need TV towers (like the existing Tokyo tower, jointly owned by the terrestrial stations) throughout the country in major provincial capitals. One proposal is to turn this into a national capital works project, using taxpayer's money. The thinking is that this digitalization will create a new TV market, and the government would get the investment back from increased tax revenue from new equipment sales.[62]

One possible consequence of the gigantic investments in plant and equipment that will be required may be a weakening of the control exerted by the major newspapers over commercial television. The last time the TV stations had had to invest heavily in equipment, in the 1960s and 1970s, the two stations with a stock market listing, TBS and NTV, had seen a heavy reduction in the percentage of ownership by the newspaper parent. In particular, Mainichi Newspaper's stockholding in TBS had dropped from 8.16 percent in 1970 to 0.81 percent in 1977, making TBS the most autonomous commercial station.

As with cable the pressure to change is coming directly from the MPT, now known as MPHPT. In July 2001 the ministry ruled that analogue broadcasting should be terminated completely by 2011, with an initial launch of digital terrestrial broadcasting in 2003, scheduled to go nationwide by 2006 (Asia Pacific Satellite 2002). The burden on the terrestrial broadcasters—already investing heavily in satellite and cable channels, in addition to expensive digital facilities such as studios—is heavy, resulting in unprecedented losses (Forrester, 2001).

A key characteristic of digitalization is a leap in information-carrying capacity, and for television the ultimate challenge is likely to be represented by the need for content to fill that capacity.[63] With the commercial stations currently controlling only 20–25% of the dramas they produce, it seems inevitable that Japanese TV will head in the same direction as the US networks, and invest more in news and current affairs programming: in fact, this was a trend which started in Japan well before American TV.

CONTENT: THE TV NEWS BUSINESS IN JAPAN

Television news in Japan has long been dominated by NHK. The reasons are multiple, including considerations of history,[64] of resources,[65] and of the sheer number of hours which NHK as a public broadcaster unworried by commercial considerations could devote to news. Traditionally, the only commercial network which could lay claim to compete with NHK was TBS (Tokyo Broadcasting System), in part due to the fact that TBS is by far the most independent of its newspaper parent, the *Mainichi Shimbun* (Kitatani, 1988: 182).

Accordingly there was considerable impact when TV Asahi succeeded in breaking into the sacred territory of NHK with a magazine format news show called "News Station," which was launched in 1985. The show followed an American format, building around a popular anchor, Kume Hiroshi, who freely (and often critically) commented on the news items, a format which was immensely successful, and quickly copied by all the other commercial TV channels. The contrast with the plain, descriptive approach that was the hallmark of NHK's orthodoxy was clear, most especially in the willingness of the commercial news presenters to question the social status quo:

> the approach taken to subjects involving political authority is different. The state here becomes personalized: political figures are treated as individuals and the consequences of their decisions for the average citizen are emphasized. This personalized state may try to portray itself as paternal guardian of the people's interests, but this claim is treated warily if not with cynicism. Scandals and mistakes are often the focus of stories on the bureaucracy. The state—not only in Japan but also in foreign countries—as often as not, is portrayed as creating problems through its actions or inactions . . . (Krauss, 1998: 678)

There is an implicit (and unfavorable) comparison made here with NHK's blandness and shyness of controversy: however, NHK has little leeway in this respect. Article 3–2 of the Broadcast Law is clear that NHK

> i) Shall not disturb public security, good morals and manners;
> ii) Shall be politically impartial;
> iii) Shall broadcast news without distorting facts;
> iv) As regards controversial issues, shall clarify the point of issue from as many angles as possible (MPT, 1998 (2): 8).

News Station reached a position of remarkable stature in a relatively short space of time. Ikeda cites a 1993 survey, designed to find out which newspaper or television program people had relied on most heavily for information during a election. Predictably, NHK news was top in the television rating (with 65.8%) , but Kume Hiroshi News Station also achieved a comparable rating (52.8%), way ahead of the next-ranked source (Chikushi Tetsuya News 23 (23.3%)—a show closely modeled on News Station) (Ikeda, 2001). The same survey found that while there was one grouping of television viewers who only watched NHK News for information on the election (34%), there was an equal number who watched both NHK and News Station to the exclusion of other sources.

As with CNN's coverage of the Gulf War, News Station was early on given a boost by its coverage of key news events, the 'Challenger' disaster and the 'citizen's revolution' against the Marcos regime, both in 1986. Ratings came close to 20%, at that time an unprecedented achievement for a commercial TV station. Significantly, both events were international. Krauss' comparative analysis of the content of coverage from two weeks of weeknight news programs in 1996 shows that the trend continued, as TV

Asahi News Station had 20% more coverage of foreign news than did NHK's flagship 7 P.M. News (Krauss, 1998: 671). Foreign news coverage had been a traditional NHK preserve, thanks to the public corporations superior resources: one reason why TV Asahi in particular was able to upset this balance was the long-standing relationship they had with CNN, including housing its first office in Tokyo, which gave the station unique access to immediate coverage of major breaking news stories and experience of handling the problem of speedy translation.

The unusual emphasis on news from abroad reflected in part an awareness of the differences in demographics between the audiences for NHK's 7 P.M. News and News Station, which was broadcast at 10. The time difference was significant. While NHK was aiming for a larger, national audience, much of it provincial if not rural, News Station appealed to an urban audience, younger and more cosmopolitan.[66] Typically they were more interested in international affairs and openly cynical about domestic politics, at the same time as being attracted to 'soft' news subjects, such as sports and entertainment (Krauss, 1998: 685). It was no coincidence that this was exactly the same audience that the new delivery systems like satellite and high-end cable were most successful in appealing to.

An argument could be made that the battle of cultures fought by the participants in Japan Business Today may have been lost by the foreigners, but they won the war, at least in the sense that it is their model of news production and presentation that is now clearly ascendant in Japan. This is one in which the values of entertainment have won out. The currently most successful network in the U.S. is NBC, as it has succeeded in getting all three contemporary TV news outlets—network, cable, Internet—working together. But its critics charge it has done this by perfecting news-by-marketing: "figure out what people want to see and tailor the news to suit their tastes, whether or not the story is really important, and even if real news gets short thrift" (Pogrebin, 1999: 93). In cable the success story is Fox News, which presents its news with as much visual and aural drama as possible.

This trend is a long way from the dry and didactic approach that has long characterized the NHK 7:00pm news. Krauss has described how in the 1950s, when NHK was looking for a model of how to develop itself as a news organization, it adhered closely to the organization and mindset of the national newspapers, in part out of the necessity of having to fit in with the organization of the powerful press clubs (Krauss, 2000: 54), but also because the reporters themselves were consciously trained in the newspaper tradition. In fact when the commercial television stations were starting up in the 1950s and 1960s, news programs were produced by special TV news departments set up inside the parent newspaper organizations, and the TV news programs still often mention their connection with a famous newspaper (Kitatani, 1988: 182).

One consequence of this was that NHK, like the major newspaper groupings, developed a tendency to focus on predictable stories about government, in particular the bureaucracy of the state at work (Krauss, 2000). The ultimate result was a reporting system whose "operative organization, process, and norms make it highly unlikely that anything critical about a particular party, politician, or bureaucrat would ever make it on to the 7:00 pm news" (Krauss, op.cit.: 83).[67] Under the influence of News Station and other commercial TV news programs NHK's top 7:00 pm and other news programs have become noticeably more lively and visual, but they remain comparatively sober: for legal, bureaucratic and institutional reasons it seems unable to respond to the competition that now characterizes news making and distribution in Japan, and that Shima had clearly anticipated.

The impact of News Station and its cousins is much debated, ranging from laying the blame[68] (or feting the achievement) of the eclipse of the ruling LDP at their door, to dismissing them as a cheapening of Japanese culture and an attack on the social compact that undergirds the society. Krauss' assessment seems fair:

> For the first time since the polarized politics of the late 1940s and early 1950s, a major source of information offers a critique of those in power to a significant segment of the Japanese public . . . the news source assumes the legitimacy of the democratic state, criticizes its incumbents in an ad hoc manner for not living up to its principles, and is delivered by a skillful entertainer and aimed at a younger audience . . . the information pluralism provided now by these more free-wheeling news programs may be functional for Japanese democracy. (Krauss, op. cit, 237–8)

The explanations Krauss offer for the emergence of such a new major source of information are multiple. The most important is probably commercial: News Station was conceived as a package aimed at advertisers by Dentsu, Japan's biggest advertising and marketing company, and Asahi Television, a perennial loser in the ratings wars with the other commercial TV companies, was desperate enough to take what was regarded as a very risky move. Digitalization, and the need for new content was no doubt an added incentive.

But an additional element seems to be missing: the influence of other models of television production, in particular in Asahi TV's case that of CNN, with which it had a close corporate relationship, and of other examples of the arrival of the borderless world in Asia symbolized by STAR TV and then embodied in Rupert Murdoch. Ultimately that influence seems to be heavier on a commercial entity, like Asahi TV, than it does on the national broadcaster NHK.

THE SHIMA BALANCE SHEET

With the benefit of considerable amounts of hindsight, it is possible to re-examine Shima's legacy as president of NHK, and relate to larger processes in the television industry, in Japan and internationally.

Plus

Some of his perceptions have stood well the test of time. It is difficult, for example to deny the accuracy of Shima's criticisms of CNN. Until quite recently—the pivotal year was probably 1996, when CNN recruited a BBC news veteran called Chris Cramer to be president of CNN International (CNNI)—CNN was basically a relayer of American news. Certainly in Shima's day CNN was American, provincial and narrow in its focus.

> CNN International did little more than borrow the feed from CNN's domestic service—60 percent of CNNI's programming was American—and beam that around the globe, typically to hotels. The prototypical CNNI viewer was a weary American businessman, unwinding after a long day in a distant foreign capital, searching for a lifeline to home—a dollop of news about the stock market, say, or the score of a hometown ballgame (Varchaver, 1999: 104).

CNNI in particular has changed, and become vastly more cosmopolitan in audience as well as in approach. At the time of the Gulf War CNN's international audience was estimated at 10 million households: by 1999 that figure had jumped to 150 million (ibid: 104). Reportedly only 10% of the programming on CNNI is "U.S. oriented," and the programming focus is also varied according to four mega-regions: Europe, the Middle East and Africa; Asia; Central and South America; and the U.S (ibid: 105).

Shima's analysis of how to transform the financial base of NHK operations has proved correct. The corporation operated comfortably in the black for the nine years following his departure (Yomiuri Shimbun, 1999:3).

He also seems prescient in his insight into how technologies like satellites and the Internet were transforming the business of television, worldwide. In Japan the television industry has been forced to change, as have the government officials charged with regulating it, as delivery systems like cable and satellite have been transformed into interactive information conduits.

Minus

But at the same time the fundamentals appear unchanged. The most obvious is that NHK remains firmly aligned with the Japanese establishment, including direct support for the ambitions of the MPT regulators.[69] The most blatant example of this occurred in 1998. When Yoshio Utsumi won the election for the highly prestigious post of secretary-general of the ITU in October of that year, it was attributed to lavish spending on an ITU conference held in Kyoto in September 1994, and subsequent parties and gift giving. NHK and the National Association of Commercial Broadcasters jointly contributed 105 million yen to the campaign (Mainichi Shimbun, 1999: 12).

While television has changed, the players remain the same. Despite dire warnings about the fiscal disaster that the move to digital portends, none of the commercial broadcasters seems to be in danger of collapse, thanks in no small part to substantial government support for investment in the new plant and equipment required. The rivals from abroad, who were early touted as western robber barons come to pillage Japan's broadcasting heritage have either effectively withdrawn (like Hughes) or been co-opted (like Time Warner) or had their swashbuckling ways severely curtailed (like News Corporation).

All the while, NHK sails on. Prime minister Junichiro Koizumi came to office on the promise of scrapping or restructuring some of the 163 special public corporations. NHK was almost immediately removed from consideration, although the Regulatory Reform Committee had earlier targeted the information technology field as a key area for review, with special mention of the status of NHK and NTT Corp. A proposal to turn NHK into an "independent administrative corporation" was shelved after the MPHPT specifically opposed it, claiming that the move would compromise NHK's mission to provide neutral public-interest broadcasting (Nikkei Weekly 2001 and Yomiuri Shimbun, 2000).

NHK today still represents a Japanese social constant, and is deliberately reflective of mainstream values.[70] These includes a sense of separation from the world outside Japan, so that communication resembles that between two villages separated by a raging river, who must shout to communicate, and often suffer misinterpretation or misconstruction of the message delivered. NHK World is not a serious attempt to present Japan in a way meaningful to those not familiar with Japanese social norms, but basically a relay of existing Japanese views. It is as if satellites did not exist.

Chapter Four

Case History 2—China and CCTV

In the course of researching this book in Japan it became plain that the trigger for action by Shima and others was the literal and metaphorical advent of "the borderless world" in Asia, heralded by the abrupt arrival of STAR TV. The strange history of STAR TV constitutes a reference point for the second case history I shall examine, as it not only serves to show how globalization can impact a whole continent, but also casts a light on the other major player in international television in Asia, China.

As with Japan, the background to the development of the modern media in China is complex. The complexity is increased by the intense battles which continue to be fought over control of information flows in China, battles involving competing cultural, political and economic interests.

The narrative history of broadcast media in China is more straightforward than Japan, at least for the early history, when policy followed a single-minded purpose, to consolidate and extend Chinese Communist Party control. For the past two decades, however, the media has wriggled away from that control, at the same time as it has experienced exponential growth. China, which until the 1980s did not even have a true national television network, now has the largest TV audience in the world. Most urban areas are heavily cabled, so that the average city dweller has at least 20 channels at home. These facts, to which might be added advances in the applications of satellite broadcasting technology, in which Asian countries have long taken leads, have tended to be ignored, downplayed or appear as minor sections in longer works on telecommunications.[1]

As with my look at the media in Japan, it would be interesting to examine in detail why the media in China does not receive more serious analysis. An investigation of why this gap exists is beyond the scope of this work, although as Zhao points out, the media in China tended to be studied with reference only to its propaganda and persuasion role, a model which is simply inadequate to explain the situation that has arisen since the reform movement got underway in the late 1970s (Zhao, 1998:4).[2] However the key factor seems to be akin to that underlying the lack of studies in Japan: that the media is often ignored or sidelined in conventional political science and sociological analysis.

BACKGROUND

In China, the media has a purpose: it was ever so. Up to the nineteenth century, journalism served a tiny minority of the population: basically the emperor, the nobility, and the landlords, the only ones with education who had access to the official "papers with news" of that time, the Beijing Gazettes (*Jing Bao*) (Chang, 1989: 27). The gazettes contained official documents released by the Imperial Grand council in the Qing dynasty, under the supervision of the Communications Department of the Board of War. The gazettes were copied and circulated in the provinces, providing "a valuable means of horizontal communication in an empire where vertical communication was generally emphasized" (Smith, 1994: 57). The distinction between communication to the "public" and to a highly privileged elite was to extend into the era of the CCP, where the unalloyed propaganda was for the common man, while the "real" media (*neibu*) were reserved for cadre study. This is a history and a tradition that the public service television broadcaster, CCTV, has to struggle with.

Newspapers in the modern sense were introduced in the nineteenth century, under the direct influence of Western missionaries and merchants.[3] Lin points out that many missionaries took a broad interpretation of their mission, to include "the general awakening of the Chinese people," with the introduction of modern scientific knowledge as a key element. One tool was the Christian hospitals; another was the publication of modern periodicals as "a very important and influential branch of missionary work" (Lin, 1936: 78).

The first major Chinese language daily, *Shen Bao,* was founded by a British merchant in Shanghai in 1872. According to Lin, general newspapers were not popular with the Chinese public,[4] but were primarily intended for the foreign firms and the Chinese concerns that had dealings with them (Lin, 1936: 90). Foreign ownership also offered the advantage of relative independence and freedom from imperial censorship, thanks to the autonomy of the foreign concessions in the treaty ports (Womack, 1986: 16). This autonomy was, of course, to continue until 1997 in the ultimate treaty port, Hong Kong, as was the tradition of a relatively free and outspoken media, which provided the context for the emergence of the Hong Kong-based STAR TV.

One consequence of the Opium Wars was an increase in Western influence, especially in metropolitan areas, and the numerous newspapers which appeared were an important conduit for that influence. As China struggled to free itself from its imperial legacy, the media took on the role of agents of modernity.

> Because of its function of providing nonofficial communication and its Western orientation, modern Chinese journalism was in a position to take a leading role in Chinese politics in the period of compressed intellectual modernization from 1900 to 1927. . . . The western-oriented press in the big cities were the forefront of China's modern culture, the mouthpiece of the young China, the China with a future (Womack in Lee, 1990: 236).

Journalism as constituted in the republic often referred to the Western norms of professionalism and objectivity, with journalism education directly inspired by the University of Missouri and Columbia University models. This liberal American practice was often at odds with the Chinese tradition that saw the media as an instrument for social influence or control rather than a simple transmitter of information (Chan, Lee and Lee 1996: 126).

When the Guomindang took control of the national government in 1927, regulation of the media was an immediate priority, through censorship and the establishment of official journals, notably the *Zhongyang Ribao* (Central Daily News), which continues to be the official Guomindang newspaper on Taiwan to this day (Womack, 1986: 16).

Despite increasing Guomindang controls, the number of Chinese-language newspapers grew apace in the years following the establishment of the Republic (see chart). But the numbers did not equate with quality: writing in 1936 Lin denounced the commercialism ruling in Chinese newspapers, and regretted that "the power of the press in the last four or five years has dwindled almost to nothing, and there is less freedom of speech or publication than in any period from 1900 . . . thought and information are more rigidly controlled today in China than in any period after 1900." This was a censorship which specifically targeted all Communist writing, while also allowing anti-Japanese material to be suppressed (Lin, 1936: 172).

Table 4: Number of Chinese-language Newspapers, and Circulations, 1921–1982

Year	Number of Chinese-language Newspapers	Circulations
1921	550	NA
1926	628	NA
1935	910	3,000,000
1948	1,372	4,500,000
1953	265	29,400,000
1966	227	131,800,000
1975	180	177,900,000
1982	822	180,200,000

Sources: Womack (1986) and Lin (1936)

The Communist Party of China paid great attention to the role of media in the revolutionary cause. By the later 1930s the CCP had developed an elaborate system of propaganda, modeled on the Soviet scheme, which viewed propaganda as a function of education. The system was dedicated to propagation of the Mass Line, the CCP's set of ideological pronouncements, policies and administrative procedures designed to strengthen the CCP and its revolutionary goals in local society (Cheek, 1997: 68).

In 1943 Mao himself provided a clear definition of what political communication was to mean under the Chinese Communist Party (CCP); that is, how the "mass line" was to be developed in action:

> In all the practical work of our Party, all correct leadership is necessarily "from the masses, to the masses." This means: take the ideas of the masses (scattered and unsystematic ideas) and concentrate them (through study turn them into concentrated and systematic ideas), then go to the masses and propagate and explain these ideas until the masses embrace them as their own, hold fast to them and translate them into action, and test the correctness of these ideas in such action. Then once again concentrate ideas from the masses and once again go to the masses so that the ideas are persevered in and carried though. And so on, over and over again in an endless spiral, with the ideas becoming more correct, more vital and richer each time. Such is the Marxist theory of knowledge. (Zhao, 1998: 24)

In practice this provided the rationale for a massive apparatus of thought control, with all the forces of CCP propaganda and education dedicated to producing "a uniform normative framework in an effort to create a unified national will and objective" (Ogden, 1989: 213). One of the very few Western journalists who was allowed to travel around China in the mid-1950s thought the effort was a success, as he reported the surreal feeling induced by seeing "600 million Chinese all dressed in the same uniform" of heavy blue cotton, resulting in a "terrifying uniformity" (Guillain, 1957: 121).

> The head of a good Chinese citizen today functions like a sort of radio receiving set. Somewhere in Peiping buzzes the great transmitting station which broadcasts the right thought and the words to be repeated. Millions of heads faithfully pick them up, and millions of mouths repeat them like loud-speakers. (ibid: 137)

As revealed in the box above, one consequence of this was clear. Once the CCP had control of the central government, the number of newspapers in China shrank, while the circulations of those remaining expanded exponentially, a reflection both of heavy state investment and of highly effective literacy campaigns (Womack, 1986: 18).

Ironically, the party's monopolization of the media effectively resulted in destruction of Mao's endless spiral: the mass line became a megaphone, incapable of hearing any messages except its own. Without an independent media to give widely available, relatively objective and accurate reports on what was going on, a highly unreliable system of bureaucratic reporting developed, where junior officials stifled voices of discontent and only relayed positive information. It was a process in which the distortion got worse the higher it rose. The ultimate result was the tragic disaster of the Great Leap Forward, where the leadership in Beijing was unable to get an accurate picture of what the situation in the countryside was, including the size of the harvest, leading to the death through starvation of an estimated thirty million (Lieberthal, 1995: 65).

Throughout his long career, Mao made repeated use of the media for his own political ends,[5] notably in the carefully orchestrated backlash to the "Let a Hundred School of Thoughts Contend" campaign of 1956–7, and in the launch of the Cultural Revolution (1966–76). In fact, Mulligan goes so far as to describe Mao's battle with Liu Shaoqi for control of the Chinese Communist Party in terms of a contest between the view that the media should be an educational and propaganda tool, and Western notions of a modern media, unafraid to criticize and aware of a responsibility to its readers and audience (Mulligan, 1992). Hood describes the former view as "waging political warfare" and discerns four such techniques: the use of historical analogies; the manipulation of foreign news; the manipulation of foreign news about China; and competing attempts to reorientate and restructure the media itself (Hood, 1994: 44).

As Cheek explains the notion of "propaganda" was not weighted with the entirely negative connotations that go with the word in the west. Especially in the early days of the People's Republic, it was seen as an honorable vocation, with a broad social function.

> The newspaper network was the blood-circulation system of the body politic: it carried essential information everywhere rapidly . . . The average citizen learned what were the legitimate public issues as defined by the leaders and learned the verbiage of political discourse. For the activist and for the Party functionary, reading the newspaper diligently was even more important. They found out how they had to act in small and large matters and learned how to discuss political and even nonpolitical issues with their fellow citizens (Cheek, 1997: 14).

The propaganda system itself was not an original Chinese development, but largely an import from the Soviet Union. The emphasis was on the notion that it was a part of education (Cheek, 1997: 68), in the wider sense used by the Soviet people's commissar for enlightenment in 1919: "the dissemination of ideas among minds that would otherwise remain a stranger to them" (Chang, 1997 : 77). Propaganda was also designed to constantly reinforce the legitimacy of the CCP, a role it still serves, though with ever diminishing success.[6]

In his profile of Deng Tuo, one of the intellectuals most closely involved in setting up the Chinese communist media apparatus, Cheek also describes how the role of propaganda was an honorable vocation in which ideology was a method, a tool, to be used in a discriminating fashion by an educated elite.

> [Tuo's] exhortations and popularizations call to mind similar efforts by Confucian literati who tried to reform local society through community compacts . . . Both believed they were bringing morality and civilized life to the untutored masses. (Cheek, 1997: 99).

Eventually the inevitable contradictions in this conceptualization were to make themselves apparent, as the tension between the social roles of the intellectuals—as Party functionaries and as political theorists—and the ideological stances of what Cheek calls "faith Maoism" grew to be unbearable. The latter won its grim triumph in the Cultural Revolution, with disastrous consequences for the intellectuals, which continue to this day. As Cheek points out:

> Problems for China's intellectuals do not stem only from the very real abuses of the CCP. The approach to public life and the priestly presumptions to minister to the public which China's educated elite have inherited and which enlivened Deng Tuo's career actually support the authority patterns which maintain the now-troubled CCP in power (Cheek, 1997: 317).

THE INTERNAL RIGHT TO KNOW

As already mentioned, a distinguishing feature of the media in China was and to as degree still is "the distinction between the commoner and the highly educated elite, resulting in two communications universes: one internal (*neibu*), the other materials for the general public (*gongkai*). (Townsend and Womack, 1986)

One consequence noted by Hood is the anomalous situation where Chinese journalism can not be judged based on what is openly available, which is likely to be inaccurate, unreliable and distorted for ideological reasons (or nowadays for commercial reasons), but instead must refer to the elaborate parallel structure of restricted media. One of these, *Reference News (Cankao Xiaoxi),* is in fact probably the most widely read newspaper in China, with a circulation of approximately seven to eight million and simultaneous printing in 25 cities (Hood, 1994: 40). Circulation is supposedly restricted to CCP members, but in fact it is far more widely available: for example, my Chinese father-in-law receives it purely on the basis of being a Korean War veteran.

The next level up is *Reference Materials (Cankao Ziliao),* which is at once more comprehensive in scope and more restricted in circulation. The top tier of information is even more secretive, represented by a daily report called *Internal Reference* (*Neibu Cankao*) which is limited to the ministerial (*bu*) level, and contains sensitive stories, some translated from the foreign press and others written expressly for internal publication by domestic and international Xinhua journalists. Finally, there are the *Hand-copied Documents* (*Shouchao Jian*), produced by the *People's Daily* staff for the top elite (Hood, 1994: 40 and Keng, 1994: 158).

According to Lu Keng, this situation, with the higher the privilege the richer the news, also applies to television. Guests at Zhongnanhai, the closely guarded compound in Beijing where the top leadership lives, find themselves watching a plethora of channels officially unavailable to the general public. Most are from abroad, including international news translated and commented on by a special television unit (Keng, 1994: 158).[7]

This inverted information pyramid—where more information, of better quality and higher reliability is available to an increasingly select number of government and party leaders—is also inherently unstable, as the media are frequently used as weapons in political battles. Indeed, one of the main reasons to follow the mainstream media in China is to look for signs of debate or struggle between different factions over policy, power or ideology. One of the biggest changes that occurred in the post reform period was that these battles became at once more overt, and more open in scope, and spilt into the general media. The most famous example was probably the battle over the TV series *River Elegy,* broadcast on CCTV in 1989, which called for a fundamental reconceptualisation of Chinese culture, implicitly questioning the direction in which the winds of globalization were blowing China (see section below).

But even those excluded from the inner circles of power, where information is allowed to flow more freely, are able to extract a picture of what is going on in society, mainly by adopting the accept-it-for-what-it-really-is philosophy of Alice in Wonderland.

> There is truth in Chinese newspapers, but you have to know how to find it. This often means reading upside down. If they say great strides have

> been made against corruption in Henan, you know that corruption is especially bad in Henan. If they say dozens of police were hurt in a clash with students, you know hundreds of students were injured or killed (Link, 1992: 86).

Finally there is a recognized place for rumor. The Barone Center report on the U.S. media coverage of the Beijing Spring of 1989 points out that, as the events in Tiananmen were reaching their climax, and the behind the scenes story became more difficult to decipher, rumor took on a special significance. In a totalitarian society like China's rumor may be the only way of circulating information, especially at a time of crisis. It cannot be ignored, but it must be treated with skepticism, something CNN in particular was criticized for not doing enough (Barone Center, 1992: 16). In the Tiananmen case, the result was a misreading of the situation in favor of the reformist side of the political spectrum in Beijing, and the mistaken impression that they were winning the power struggle in the party, at the same time as underestimating the internecine squabbles inside the student leadership.

THE BROADCAST MEDIA IN CHINA

Radio

As with newspapers, radio broadcasting got its initial impetus from a foreigner, when an American reporter set up a radio station in Shanghai in January 1923. Official Chinese government broadcasting did not start until October 1926, in Harbin, while a Shanghai department store sponsored the first commercial broadcasting service in the spring of 1927 (Zou et al, 1988: 69).

When the Guomindang took control of the national government in 1927, control of the media was an immediate priority, through censorship and the establishment of official journals, notably the *Zhongyang Ribao* (Central Daily News), which continues to be the official Guomindang newspaper on Taiwan to this day (Womack, 1986: 16). In August 1928 the Guomindang government set up the Central Broadcasting Station in Nanjing, which also moved to Taiwan after 1949 (Zou et al, 1988: 69).

The first radio station under Communist control began broadcasting in December, 1940, in Yanan, under the control of *Xinhua* (New China News Agency), the official news agency. The station was moved to Beijing in March, 1949, and eventually, after the founding of the People's Republic, became the Central People's Broadcasting Station in December of that year. It soon began national broadcasts, relayed through an ad hoc network of former Kuomintang local stations which had been take over by the People's Liberation Army (Zou et al, 1988: 70). At that time there were only some one million radio receivers in the country, however, mostly concentrated in the Shanghai and Nanjing areas (Womack, 1986: 25).

According to Guillain's first-hand observations, radio and television were in fact still very little used five years later, as the government preferred to rely on word of mouth—through work unit meetings, study sessions and conferences (Guillain, 1957: 146). The Chinese general population was simply too poor to afford radio receivers: one solution was to establish broadcast monitoring networks (*guangbo shouyin wang*) in the early 1950s, with rooms in villages or urban districts set up with reception equipment, later used as the hubs for wired-speaker networks, in inescapable "collective listening"(Chang, 1997: 87).

At the peak of the system in 1965 there were some 2,365 'rediffusion' stations broadcasting through 87 million loudspeakers, which Womack calculates was sufficient to ensure that every citizen in China was covered (Womack, 1986: 26). Although the wired broadcast system has remained an intrinsic part of rural life, its use has faded in urban areas. However, thanks to lengthy stays in two work units, belonging to Kunming Medical College and to the University of Pekin,the author can attest to the fact that the loudspeakers are still in regular use, with notices of events, advice and exhortations from work unit leadership interspersed with out-of-date pop music, all relayed just below distortion level.

Television

For reasons of cost, the establishment of television in China was slow. The large investments required for a national television service resulted in very limited penetration prior to the reform period, which meant that post-reform the huge gap between existing infrastructure and demand could only be closed by local development. This came to mean both commercial and, to a degree, operational self-sufficiency, in turn resulting in big challenges to central control when international satellite television made its presence felt.

Experimental broadcasts began on May 1, 1958, on one channel in Beijing, which started regular broadcasts in September of the same year operating as Peking (Beijing) Television. According to Womack, at that time there were only twenty television sets in China.[8] In the following two years provincial stations were set up in Shanghai, Tianjin and 12 provinces, including Yunnan. Initially broadcasts were for only two or three hours a day (Yu, 1990: 70).

The break with the Soviet Union at the end of 1960 greatly hampered development. The number of stations, which had grown to 23, was abruptly cut back to five. The second blow was the Cultural Revolution, which led to

Beijing TV going off the air in January, 1967, followed by all the local stations. When they resumed broadcasts consisted exclusively of political slogans (Yu, 1990: 70).

Despite these setbacks by 1970 there were 30 urban stations, with the four largest (Beijing, Tianjin, Shanghai, Guangzhou) connected by microwave, and by 1971–72 broadcasts with something approaching "national" coverage could begin (Chang, 1989: 218). However, by Womack's estimate (based on Howkins) there were only 50,000 TV sets in China in 1970, one for every 16,400 people (Womack, 1986: 27).

Throughout the decade, television was a luxury—by the end of the 1970s a set still cost more than a year's wages—and during the Cultural Revolution the content was entirely turned over to propaganda, with the only entertainment provided by song and dance performances of the "Mao Zedong Thought Propaganda Teams" (Yu, 1990 : 71). The result was small audiences: in 1978 there were 3.04 million television sets for a population of one billion (Yu, 1990: 71).

By 1976 the Cultural Revolution was over, and for the first time Chinese TV began to broadcast world news. On May 1, 1978 Beijing TV was renamed China Central TV (CCTV),[9] and became the core of the nation's television network, broadcasting color programs on two channels since the previous year (Zou et al, 1988: 70). In April, 1980, CCTV began to broadcast international satellite feeds. At the beginning of 1980 there were already 3.5 million television sets: by the end of that year, the number had doubled.[10] A reasonable explanation for this remarkable increase seems to be that 1980 was the year of the trial of the Gang of Four, which won an audience estimated at times at 300 million. This was the first big TV news story in China—and was also the first time a Chinese TV broadcast went abroad via satellite (Womack, 1986: 28).

Television had arrived. At the start of the 1980s radio was still probably the most widely used media in China (Townsend and Womack, 1986: 234), but at the same time a basic national television network of relay, transmission and channel switching stations was finally in place (Yu, 1990: 71). During the decade television overtook newspapers and radio in importance. The number of relay stations grew by almost 40-fold between 1983 and 1986 (Yu, 1990: 72). Official estimates put the TV audience at 350 million by 1982 (Womack, 1986: 27). In 1984 China launched an experimental communications satellite, followed in February 1986 by its first fully operational telecommunications and broadcast satellite, DFH-2. Chinese satellite television had also arrived.

MEDIA IN THE POST-REFORM ERA

The post-Mao reform era in China was a remarkable time. This applied to the media, too, which went through a period of extraordinary growth. As described above, TV ownership was capable of doubling in a single year. In the first five years of the 1980s, White reports a new paper started every two days: by the beginning of 1986 more than half the newspapers in China were less than five years old (White, 1990: 90).

The growth in TV penetration was due in large part to government policy, which had been fundamentally redirected towards modernization and away from class struggle by the Central Committee's Third Plenum in December, 1978. In order to win acceptance for his reform program, and to introduce a genuine review and overhaul of the CCP's problems and options, Deng Xiaoping targeted the ideological straightjacket on thought and information from the outset (Hamrin, 1994).

In television the winds of change were symbolized by the upgrading of the Broadcasting Bureau to the Ministry of Radio and Television in 1982, then to the Ministry of Radio, Film and Television (MRFT) in 1985. However, expansion was only possible by a devolution of authority to the local level: previously the central government had shouldered all the operating costs, and the revenues were not available for an ambitious development program. Under a policy implemented in 1983, new stations were to be set up at four levels (national, provincial, prefectural and county), with a particular emphasis on extending coverage to remote and rural areas (Yu, 1990). This policy was to have fateful consequences for central control of television in China.

The expansion of television was also driven by viewer demand, as their numbers climbed exponentially, quickly leading to more channels, and to the extension of broadcasting hours. The state—which simultaneously was seeing its income shrink—was barely able to fund minimal operations, let alone upgrade equipment, introduce new technologies and expand services. According to Zhao government finance could only cover 50 to 70 percent of regular broadcast operations during the 1980s: "to end complete dependence on state subsidies and to find other sources of financing was thus more an economic necessity than an espoused political principle" (Zhao, 1998: 53).

In 1983 the CCP came out with a statement encouraging broadcast organizations to look for other sources of income; by 1988, multiple channels of financing became party and government policy (ibid: 54). Again the consequences were a diminution of central control, and the growth of broadcast organizations as institutions with considerable financial autonomy and, therefore, independence (see The Media in China Now, p.150).

"INVIGORATE THE ECONOMY"

"Multiple channels of financing" had in fact been in place for ten years before the policy became official. The first appearance of advertising on Shanghai Television[11] and a four-day series of advertisements in the Shanghai *Liberation Daily* in February 1979 (Chinese New Year) are generally reckoned as the beginning of media commercialization in China (Zhao, op.cit and Stross, 1990). Media "recommercialization" might be a more appropriate phrase, as advertising had been pervasive in the Guomindang period, and the Chinese government had tolerated extensive advertising in Hong Kong on behalf of PRC enterprises, even at the height of the Cultural Revolution (Stross, op.cit.).

Stross describes the contortions party theoreticians initially had to adopt in the late 1970s in order to justify the introduction of such an unalloyed symbol of capitalism, eventually hitting on the formula that advertising helped link producers and consumers by supplying important economic information, and providing "scientific guidance" (ibid: 229, 230). By 1982, the State Council had lost any sense of embarrassment about advertising, enumerating its ability to "promote production, increase commodity circulation, guide consumption, invigorate the economy, increase consumer convenience, develop international economic activities, serve the needs of socialist construction and promote socialist moral standards" (Zhao, 1998).

Once again, the growth figures were phenomenal. Advertising for a time was China's fastest growing industry, with sales volume expanding at an annual growth rate of 41 percent between 1981 and 1992. By 1992, television was accounting for 30.2 percent of total advertising income, or 2.05 billion yuan. This was almost equivalent to the 2.38 billion yuan provided for broadcast operations by governments at all levels in China (ibid: 55). In the case of one particularly successful station, Shanghai TV, advertising revenue zoomed from 0.49 million RMB in 1979 to 170 million RMB in 1992, obviating the need for financial support from the state (Weber, 2002).

Advertising was embraced, as was the growth in all sources of information, as a necessary adjunct to the CCP's new commitment to high economic performance, measured by indices imported from the capitalist west. To transform the governing elite, to open their imaginations and give them new skills, information was essential. But as Hamrin notes, "these steps amounted to an undeclared but profound political reform in the relationship between state and society" (Hamrin, 1994: 60).

Such reform was radical, in form, content and scope. Writing in 1986, Townsend and Womack could still describe a public communications network whose content and management were subject to central political control, and whose nature was ideological in character and pedagogical in style.

> Virtually all information disseminated through the network is that which central leadership or subordinates acting on their perceptions of central intent have approved for public release. The public is told what the leadership wants to know; competing or contradictory messages have no organized vehicle for response. Thus almost every news item in the Chinese press has a quasi-official quality; it is there because it relates positively to current policy. Politically neutral news, such as accidents and minor disasters, are ignored, and published news that conflicts with current policy is usually a sign of dissension or of impending policy change . . . a clear sense of hierarchical authority permeates the system and is in fact essential to its effective operation (Townsend and Womack, 1986: 230).

Even as their work was published, this status quo was in the process of imploding,[12] under internal pressure for change, for debate and for variety, and from external pressure for new markets. The proliferation of mass media in China in the 1980s effectively undermined the apparatus of central control, by making it irrelevant. The normative framework of information dissemination lingers on in the 2000s, in compulsory political study groups in the work place, in the Beijing media, and so on—all now regarded with deep cynicism. STAR TV was, inadvertently, a leader in this remarkable transformation.

"RIVER ELEGY"

Moves to loosen central control did not go unchallenged. At the beginning of 1987, the secretary-general of the CCP, Hu Yaobang, was purged, and leading intellectuals were expelled from the party, as a campaign to "oppose bourgeois liberalization" got underway, part of a conservative reaction to the scope and pace of change, triggered by student demonstrations in December, 1986. As the CCP pendulum swung from openness to oppression and back again, there was considerable discussion among intellectuals, about a question underlying modernization reform: what does it mean to be Chinese? The debate went under the rubric of "culture fever" or "searching-for-roots fever" (*wenhua re*). It culminated in the television documentary *He Shang* (River Elegy) in June 1988 (Kim and Dittmer, 1993).

The six-part series was broadcast on national TV, and came as a shock not only to the TV audience in China, but to the Chinese-speaking world in Asia.[13] Within two months it was rebroadcast on CCTV, by popular demand. Its content, the fact of its broadcasts, and its various impacts showed the extent to which media had changed in China, especially television, demonstrating its ability to "bridge the great chasm between elite and mass culture." While the series plainly had a political agenda (it was explicit in its support of the leaders of economic reform), it also called for a major transformation of the civilization identity

> Arguably, River Elegy comes close . . . to being the functional equivalent of a national referendum on the symbol system of Chinese identity . . . omnipresent symbols, so beloved by Western tourists, were dramatized as symbolizing China's conservatism, backwardness, tyrannical rule, and impotent national defense as well as smothering the gentler, kinder, and more humane aspects of the national spirit. (Kim and Dittmer, 1993: 265)

The overall theme was that China is shackled by what Jenner calls "the tyranny of history," as represented by the Yellow River, a traditional symbol for China. The final episode was entitled "Azure" (*Weilan se*) and contrasts the outgoing Western "maritime culture" with the Chinese inward-looking yellow "river culture." This was illustrated by some striking aerial photography showing the muddy, salty Yellow River meeting the clean-looking blue sea. The implication was that China must open up to the outside world, and embrace the deep blue yonder (Rosen and Zou, 1991). Drawing on documentary footage shot for a Japanese TV series, the show was technically surprising, with fast, sometimes impressionistic MTV-style editing which let the visuals drive the show, and with an often elliptical narration that allowed the viewer to fill in the blanks (Calhoun, 1989).

Due to popular demand CCTV ran it again over the national network in August, after stations in Shanghai and Shenzhen had already taken the initiative in rebroadcasting (Kim and Dittmer, 1993). While the series was attacked by Vice President Wang Zhen as serving the interests of the Guomindang, it was defended by secretary-general Zhao Ziyang, and became a cause célèbre before and after Tianenmen Square (Rosen and Zou, 1991).

The significance of "River Elegy" was its attempt to present a genuinely critical approach to China's history. This was incendiary stuff: Jenner points out that the Chinese communists had a fascination for ancient emperors, especially the more powerful and expansionist ones, and had co-opted traditional histories and ancient imperial symbols for their own ends, "as if the French revolutionaries had taken Versailles as the symbol of their republic. . . . (Following "River Elegy") one of the messages of those who sent the troops into Peking (to Tiananmen) was that China's imperial past was not to be maligned" (Jenner, 1992 : 16).

"River Elegy" can also be seen as an early attempt to assess the implications of globalization, positive as well as negative, for China and its people. It served as a critical analysis of the tension built into the official Chinese government stance of encouraging economic liberalization, while keeping strict political control, and ignoring the implications for Chinese culture.

TIANANMEN

As "River Elegy" showed, there is always the possibility that some sectors in Chinese society may actively welcome the weakening of their own cultural tradition. Tu argues that for some

> a total transformation of Chineseness is a precondition of China's modernization. Strategically, the most painful and yet effective method of this total transformation is to invite the modern West with all of its fruitful ambiguities to "decenter" the Chinese mentality (Tu, 1991: 5).

This concept was clearly understood by the students in Tiananmen Square, when they appealed directly to the western media, through numerous interviews and such devices as the erection of a fiberglass statue of the Goddess of Liberty directly facing the gigantic portrait of Mao that dominates the plaza.

> There's never been a generation like ours, one that mocked the state, mocked the government, mocked the leaders. And there's never been a generation that has seen that the outside world is so beautiful . . . We don't have the goals our parents had. We don't have the fanatical idealism our older brothers and sisters once had. So what do we want? Nike shoes. Lots of free time to take our girlfriends to a bar. Freedom to discuss an issue with someone, and to get a little respect (Interview with WuerKaixi in Benzakin, 1989).

The use of brute force by the Chinese government against its own population in Beijing on the night of June 3, 1989, had multiple, complex reasons, beyond the scope of this research to examine. It is clear there was one key element, however: the role played by the media.

The events in Tiananmen Square represented a challenge to internal, central control of information flows. In the early days of the student occupation of the square not only did the media report on events, but journalists actually marched in support: there was even a banner on the square declaring the support of the Ministry of Radio, Film and Television for the student hunger-strikers (Hopkins, 1989).

Tiananmen also became the biggest international news story ever reported from China, in large part because the foreign media were in China at the time to report on the Sino-Soviet summit. When the Chinese government eventually imposed martial law it did not anticipate how the simple television image of a man with a small case blocking the way of a column of tanks would overnight come to stand as a metaphor for real politik Chinese-style: after all, the image was not shown in China itself (Hopkins, ibid).

Unfortunately for the Chinese government, Tiananmen was also the news story that transformed international television news coverage, and began the elevation of CNN to the status it holds today. It was the first time a major breaking story was covered 24 hours a day for a worldwide television audience. Specifically it was the first instance in which CNN was no longer just reporting events but also helping shape them and even becoming part of them (Flournoy and Stewart, 1997). This was not an outcome the Chinese authorities had anticipated—but neither had the media.

> "The only reason we were able to provide the scale of live coverage we had is because we had prior permission from the Chinese government to bring in our own satellite up-links for Gorbachev's visit," said Mike Chinoy, the CNN bureau chief in Beijing. "We set up to broadcast live from the rostrum at Tiananmen Square in anticipation of Gorbachev's arrival. But by the time his plane touched down, the students had that area occupied, so his arrival ceremony was canceled. We were still there, though, so we shot the scene and sent it off to the satellite. And later that week, when the crowds swelled to more than a million people, we were in a position to cover it live again. Neither we nor the Chinese counted on that happening" (Hertsgaard, 2002).

The fact that television was there, ready to broadcast live around the globe, did little to raise the accuracy of the reporting. Hertsgaard, Barone Center and others have commented on the lack of depth in American media reports in particular, which tended to characterize the protesters as "pro-democracy," with no analysis of what that might mean in the Chinese context, but rather an assumption that the desire was for something approaching American ideals or ideas about itself.

What television did do, by its presence, its immediacy and its instantaneous global reach was help shape perceptions of what was happening. The students were adept at staging events for the cameras, notably by the creation of their "Goddess of Liberty," by preparing signs and giving interviews in English and other Western languages, and for the American media quoting the Declaration of Independence, Patrick Henry and Abraham Lincoln, including the Gettysburg address (Barone Center on the Press, 1992). The Western media were highly receptive to the students' messages, to the point that claims to professional objectivity were compromised. The Barone Center's exhaustive survey of coverage of Tiananmen by the Western media is clear on this point.[14] A Canadian Television (CTV) correspondent summarized the common standpoint:

> "We were totally involved . . . with the students," he said. "We lost our objectivity for a while. I certainly did. It was hard to be objective with a

government that seemed . . . run by a group of thugs who had no real right to kill their children. . . . I found my anti-government rhetoric rather shrill on occasion. And you could see it in copy. And I think the responsibility lies with the reporter . . . to sit back and say 'Hold on just a second. Is this the way I normally cover stories elsewhere?' I'm not holding any guilt about that, by the way, because I think it was one of those rare occasions in history that maybe it wasn't so bad to lose your objectivity. . . . But I sometimes wonder whether we built peoples' expectations up too much" (Barone Center, op.cit.: 11).

All this helped create immense public sympathy for the protesters. Tom Brokaw, the NBC news anchor who became famous for his fury with the Chinese government spokesman Yuan Ma when he denied after the event that any protesters had been killed and charged NBC with doctoring the tapes that showed killing, saw the story as one that had "penetrated the American consciousness. People everywhere I went were talking about it. I was doing a story about street gangs in Los Angeles, and one member of the Crips wanted to talk to me about what was going on in China" (Hertsgaard, op.cit.). This popular awareness impacted official American reactions to what was happening, compelling the administration of President Bush to ratchet up its criticism over the course of events.

The upper echelons of the Chinese bureaucracy were at the beginning of a learning process about the growing power of the media that had happened in the U.S. decades before, and which in its day also caused a sea change in the American political status quo, a loss of control by an entrenched governing elite.

In the sixties events suddenly moved with their own energy, for with television an event was electric and explosive. Television could reach the nation (not just the elite, but the nation) so much more quickly than the normal political system that events could sweep past politicians, sweep past their calculations and scenarios. Nothing could control this. . . . There were times when events simply outstripped everyone (Halberstam, 1977: 677, 678).

This idea, of events sweeping past those charged with their control, is precisely what the Chinese authorities saw happening with Tiananmen Square. Control, in particular control of information, was (and still is) vitally important, for the whole edifice of one-party rule rests on one essential foundation: secrecy. However, the corollary pointed out by Ogden is that this creates a situation where policies which are objectionable can only be objected to by mass resistance, as happened in Tiananmen, which was much more than a student protest movement.

> Secrecy makes it difficult to carry out political reforms aimed at eliminating the power of officials over the people, assigning individuals responsibility for their acts, or ending corruption. Shielding the policy making process from public debate and scrutiny allows the leadership to make decisions based on power, bureaucratic struggles over turf, or factional ties. It need not reveal its information base, nor what alternatives it rejected. The real reasons for official attacks on a individual leader or for policy reversals can be carefully disguised. . . . the problem that secrecy creates for the Chinese leadership is this: policies that the people played no role in formulating receive feedback in a form detrimental to the leadership's objective—mass resistance to the policies. (Ogden, 1989: 100,1)

But while the Chinese government periodically attempts to stuff the genie of political discussion back in the bottle labeled "information access," the reassertion of ideological controls fails to check this force on other fronts, as entertainment and advertising, broadcasting outlets and publication outlets continue to increase at a rapid rate, and the distinction between overtly political and non-political information is increasingly obscure (Man Chan, 1995).

The ghosts of Tiananmen haunt foreign views of China, and the policies of governments towards it. In 1993 President Clinton issued an executive order which made further renewal of China's "most favored nation" trading status conditional on "progress" in seven areas falling under the rubric of human rights. These included adherence to the universal declaration of human rights, and "allowing freedom of international broadcasting into China" (Alagappa, 1994: 18).

POST TIANANMEN

In the immediate aftermath of June 4, 1989, the Chinese media was literally in denial, reporting the fact of martial law, without mentioning any of the deaths which had occurred (Mulligan, 1989).

The contrast with the same media before the crackdown in Beijing could not have been starker. Not only had the media reported on the events in Tiananmen with increasing frankness, but many of the media work units had joined the demonstrations, and many journalists had signed an open letter to the CCP Central Committee openly supporting the students. On June 30, the mayor of Beijing gave a speech to the People's Congress, giving the official report on the "Counter-revolutionary Rebellion." The media's role—and in particular, Secretary Zhao Ziyang's encouragement of its increased openness—was singled out for criticism (ibid.).

In fact, the media had plainly supported Zhao, and were apparently manipulated by him, in what was seen as a political showdown between

Zhao and Deng Xiaoping (Hood, 1994). As soon as he was elected CCP secretary general Zhao Ziyang had shown a full awareneness of the media, and how to use it, when he answered questions from several hundred foreign correspondents at a press conference in November 1987. Less than two years later, on May 1989, the cameras were there again, as Zhao made a tearful plea to the students to end their hunger strike (Hopkins, 1989).

There was an element of theater to all this. Ming makes a strong case that the reform movement's ideological bankruptcy (and strategic incompetence) was clearly demonstrated by its inability to promote the notion of free and open communications more aggressively—in the event, all the media freedom and protests were in fact limited to three days, from May 17—19 (Ming, 127, 8).

Nevertheless, the theater was in its own way revolutionary. It would be a mistake to belittle the significance of those three days on national television, which included reports on the scenes in Tiananmen Square, presented so as to make clear how widespread the support for the students was, culminating in the scene in the Great Hall of the People on May 19, when the student leaders lectured the visibly annoyed Prime Minister, Li Peng (Hopkins, 1989: 37). Words fail to convey the impact of this scene, except maybe Wuer Kaixi's, that this was the first Chinese generation to mock the state, mock the government, mock the leaders.

After the event, the government went to extraordinary lengths to rewrite television history. Throughout the month of June, CCTV was dominated by special programming from the army and the internal security police, presenting carefully edited video designed to prove the official story, that they had been required to put down a counterrevolutionary rebellion (Hopkins, 1989: 38,9).

At the same time the Western media went through some self-reflection of its own. As already mentioned the reporting on Tiananmen was frequently marred by a tendency to equate what was happening to ideals recognizable in a Western context (a struggle for democratic reform) rather than a recognition of Chinese realities (initially a limited protest reflecting among other things disgust with the extensive corruption and blatant nepotism that characterized the regime and calling for limited political reform, rather than a total change to the status quo). This preconception led to reporting that was openly biased against the government, and also made it comparatively easy for the 'liberal' faction supporting Communist Party Secretary Zhao Ziyang to persuade the western media that their faction was winning the power struggle inside the Politburo. It contributed to some of the wild estimates about the number of people killed on the night of June

3–4, and most egregiously, to the reporting as fact of near civil war conditions between June 5 and 8, rumors apparently spread by Western diplomats(Barone Center, op.cit: 21).

A key element here was the new role of CNN, which became in effect a video wire service, watched avidly by members of the administration and of the Congress in Washington, as well as by other governments and, importantly, by other media. The need to feed pictures of events as they happened left little or no time for reflection or analysis, and was seen as one reason for the extent to which rumors, such as that of fighting between different units of the military, became part of 'the story,' while other important elements, such as the key role played by Hong Kong in providing money and materiel to the protesters was largely ignored.

THE MEDIA IN CHINA NOW: 1991—2002

Overview

The mainstream media in China today remain part of the power structure, with the CCP insisting they are instruments for its use. At times of direct national need, this is plainly still true: before his death there were no stories about the state of Deng Xiaoping's health, for example, while his death and funeral were uniformly reported as a time for national mourning.

The changes in media in the 1990s and 2000s have continued in the direction set in the 1980s, but these are changes in presentation and focus, rather than in nature or purpose. One way or another, the media is controlled. Zhao has a trenchant critique of the notion that Chinese media is moving through stages to become a "liberal free press" in the Western pattern,[15] which she points out is in reality a "press market model of editorial freedom. . . . The public's right to free speech is typically equated to the property right of media owners" (Zhao, 1998: 9).

Those media owners have little concern with challenging the government's editorial control. This certainly applies to foreign media concerns that have an interest in China, notably Rupert Murdoch's News Corporation. In fact, in June 1995, two years after Murdoch took over STAR TV, he signed an agreement with the Chinese government's major propaganda organ, the People's Daily, "to develop a range of opportunities in China's information technology sector," stating with an on-line data service, and contemplating electronic publishing, data transmission networks and digital mapping (Clari. Reuters, 1995). This followed a deal Murdoch made in February of the same year with Deng Xiaoping's youngest daughter, Maomao, to publish her hagiography "Deng Xiaoping: My father" through HarperCollins, part of his publishing empire.

For the rest of the 1990s up to the present Murdoch has continued his active courtship of the Chinese leadership (see STAR TV section below). In March, 2001, James Murdoch, Murdoch's son and CEO of News Corporation in Asia was reported by the New York Times as "stunning" listeners at a business conference by disparaging the Falun Gong, the religious group that has been banned by Chinese government, and criticizing Western news organizations for "portraying China in a harsh light"(New York Times, March 26, 2001, Business P.1)

In terms of international media, the Chinese government's success in presenting a coherent and positive picture of China may owe much to complicity by foreign media in that presentation. This is not simply a question of a company like News Corporation putting its business interests first, but also can be traced to superficial reporting as much as to any skilled presentation of an ideological argument.

In fact one of the conclusions drawn from Tiananmen is that the foreign media (defined as media operating outside the direct control of the People's Republic, by which I include the Hong Kong media) often have been remarkably complicit in bolstering the CCP status quo, to the extent that Long, a former BBC correspondent in China remarks on a "curious phenomenon":

> that the foreign media, regarded by Chinese leaders as the advance guard of an imperialist plot to topple them from power, are in fact fostering some of the very myths that the party generates to help it cling to power (Long, 1992: 107).

He enumerates five of those "central myths" about contemporary China: that China is a socialist country; that the CCP is a strong central government; that the present leadership is stable and united; that economic growth is conducive to political stability; and that China never compromises in issues affecting its internal affairs (ibid: 99).

For domestic media, government policy remains conservative, which in the Chinese context means constant reiteration of standpoints already taken. The media constitute a highly sensitive area for the government. Attempts at reform are regularly squashed, and even acknowledgement of existing realities is difficult. For long the CCP was unable to accept the near universal commercialization of the media as official policy, and instead ruled by denial:

> In late 1994, the Propaganda Department's six no's were circulated in top journals and news media research circles: no private media ownership, no shareholding of media organizations, no joint ventures with foreign companies, no discussion of the commodity nature of news, no discussion of a press law, and no openness for foreign satellite television. This is by far the most important media statement made by the party in the 1990s. Its negative and colloquial formulation are illustrative of the ad hoc, informal, and reactive nature of media policy-making by the Party (Zhao, 1998: 176).

Even though today the commercial media in China appears unshackled, those prohibitions remain in force. In fact, success in enforcement of regulations governing the media is in direct relation to the degree to which the interests of the government and the commercial sector go hand in hand. Nowhere is this seen more clearly than in the attempts to control content on the Internet.

> In the short to medium term . . . the multifarious close partnerships between the regime and the commercial Internet sector, institutionalized in a complex web of regulations and fiscal relationships, imply that the government will not lose the upper hand soon. The government's strategy is also aided by the current economic environment in China, which encourages the commercialization of the Internet, not its politicization. As one Internet executive put it, for Chinese and foreign companies, "the point is to make profits, not political statements" (Chase and Mulvenon, 2002:90).

REALITY BITES

What is suggested here is that while the Chinese government may have had some success in defending its traditional hold on media and information, that success should not be equated with a coherent policy or even a consistent implementation of the laws and regulations which have been introduced to deal with the new world of information.

Indeed, attempts to actually implement such policies—whether by regulating satellite TV dishes or attempting to "control" the Internet—are met with highly varied success. Three broad categories of explanations why this should be so can be identified immediately. One is the extremely rapid developments in the technologies of gathering and distributing information, including satellites, cable and the Internet. The second is the anomalous situation of Hong Kong, and to a lesser degree, Taiwan. Third, and the most important, is the hard reality that the central government has to contend with on a daily basis: it does not have the funds to develop, modernize and control the media all at the same time.

In short there are multiple reasons why fiats from the center do not necessarily work, even when they are aimed at thwarting an avowed enemy of the state like the Falun Gong. In the next section I shall be examining each of these reasons in some detail. This analysis will serve as the context for the case history of "globalization in action"—the ongoing saga of STAR TV.

REALITY BITES 1: TECHNOLOGICAL DEVELOPMENTS

1.A. The Arrival of Regional Satellite Television

Satellites over Asia

On April 24, 1970, China launched its first satellite, China 1 (aka Mao 1), which orbited the earth transmitting the tune *Dong Fang Hong* ("The East is Red"). It was later confirmed that both this satellite and its successor were in fact communications test satellites, and were modeled closely on the original Telstar satellite (Grahn, 2001). They were the outriders of a comprehensive experimental program which was to continue throughout the 1970s. At a time when the Chinese government saw itself as surrounded by enemies, the driver behind the Chinese satellite program was military, coupled with a desire to boost national prestige on the international stage. In 1990 Deng Xiaoping was to recall that "if China had not exploded atom and hydrogen bombs in the 1960s and launched satellites, it would not have been considered one of the three big powers and would not occupy such a position in the world" (Hong, 1995: 121,122).

In a sense, Richard Nixon brought international satellite communications to China. According to Slack, when the then president visited China to open relations in February, 1972, the U.S. government installed three satellite antenna stations in different locations, both for government communications and to facilitate media coverage of the historic trip. These were left behind, connecting China to the world through the Intelsat (International Telecommunications Satellite Organization) system (Slack, 2001: 13). For over a decade, China was to rely on Intelsat and Intersputnik satellites for its domestic and international communications.

The primary usage was for television signal broadcast and relay, to cover remote areas where terrestrial microwave relay would be too expensive (Sun, 1999: 1). This was a serious challenge: Hong describes how CCTV used to have send tapes of its programs by air to the more remote and mountainous regions, where they would be eventually broadcast three to five days late, or in the not uncommon case of places with no airport, as many as 15 days late (Hong, 1995: 128).

In the 1980s China developed its own *Dong Fang Hong* (DFH) series of communications satellites, with the first experimental geosynchronous communication satellite successfully launched in 1984. However their limited transmission capacity contributed little to the major overhaul of the telecommunications infrastructure that was becoming a national priority. That need was answered by a new generation of regional satellites, which dramatically increased the availability of transponders.

In 1984 a Western Union Westar 6 satellite was carried to orbit by the space shuttle Challenger, but failed to reach the planned orbital height. In November that year the satellite was retrieved by astronauts spacewalking from the shuttle Discovery, and returned to earth. After refurbishing the satellite was sold to the Asiasat consortium, renamed AsiaSat-1 and launched on a Chinese Long March 3 rocket on April 7, 1990. It was the first American satellite sent to orbit by a non-Western country, Asia's first privately-owned satellite, and the first to offer pan-Asian coverage, with its footprint extending from Japan in the east to Egypt in the west, and from Russia in the north to New Zealand in the South (ibid: 120).

AsiaSat-1 had 24 transponders, each capable of carrying one analog television channel or the equivalent of 1,200 telephone calls. Voice and data transmission users of the satellite included the PRC, South Korea, Mongolia, Myanmar, Taiwan and Thailand.

Asiasat's most prominent television client was CCTV, which primarily used the satellite to get its expanded menu of programs to the fast-growing number of cable head operators across the nation. STAR TV used the same satellite: with one extra twist of the tuning dial, the operator suddenly had STAR TV available—modern, popular and free. In addition, Asiasat-1 transponders transmitted TV services for Myanmar TV, Pakistan, Mongolia, and two Chinese provincial stations, Guizhou and Yunnan.

The impact of Asiasat-1 was immense. In part this was due to the fact that it carried the first regional television service, the heavily-publicized STAR TV. But it also served as a wake-up call to governments in Asia. Up to the 1990s, there was effectively only one satellite system with regional reach, the Indonesian Palapa, which was never fully booked. By 1995 Lovelock could identify 685 transponders available on 13 different satellite systems, all powerful enough to offer some degree of regional coverage. This extraordinary expansion (the number of transponders had tripled in the three years from 1992 to 1995, for example) was not driven by simple demand or economic forecasts alone.

> The proliferation of satellites has to do with issues of national status, strategic bargaining over satellite slots, overspill and transborder information

> flows, and positioning for, and posturing over, regional hubbing and sub-regional hubbing. Thus, we find Thailand targeting to be the gateway to Indochina; Malaysia and the Philippines wanting to loosen their dependency upon Indonesia's Palapa system; Singapore wishing to persuade ASEAN and China to hub a regional mobile network through a Singapore satellite; South Korea wanting to be independent of Japan's broadcast satellites (and perhaps gain a strategic advantage over the peninsula); and Taiwan, which is unable to have satellite of its own (since the ITU does not recognize it as an independent nation), looking for a partner to share with, despite China's objections. (Lovelock, 1995: 133,4)

SUDDENLY A CHOICE OF CONTENT

Another consequence of the launch of Asiasat was a rapid growth in the number and variety of program suppliers, in particular suppliers of information and entertainment. This, coupled with the fact that the satellite signals did not fit neatly into national boundaries—in fact, in the case of Asiasat-1 were specifically designed to offer as wide a regional coverage as technically feasible—had serious implications for the national authorities charged with regulating broadcasting, who were abruptly faced with television content over which they had no effective control, emanating from international media conglomerates rather than from domestic government-related organizations.

Thus one year after the launch of Asiasat-1, in 1991, Asian viewers had the choice of potential access to the BBC's World Television Service, developed specifically for launch on STAR TV, and CNN International, broadcast from one of the Palapa satellites. As Lovelock and Shoenfeld (1995) point out, this was a radically new situation, as with few exceptions Asia had never been seen as a major media market.

Strong government control over broadcast television was very much the Asian tradition—in fact, government monopoly of the television industry was also common, even in places where other media were comparatively free of restrictions (such as India). Program content was also heavily regulated, under the general rubric of safeguarding cultural integrity and/or social stability. Lee and Wang identified a list of sensitive "content elements" in Asia, including obscenity, violence, religious beliefs, ethnic relations, national security, and cultural and family values (Lee and Wang, 1995: 138).

Consequently the advent of satellite television seemed to pose a significant challenge to the television status quo. By 1994 viewers in Asia had the choice of over 40 channels of satellite television programs—in theory, and if dish size was not a consideration—including ESPN, Turner, Viacom (MTV), Discovery, CNN International, HBO, Australian Broadcast Corporation

(ABC), Deutsche Welle TV, and TVB from Hong Kong, in addition to the STAR TV channels.

THE GOVERNMENT REACTS

It was against this background that State Council Decree No. 129 (*Provisions on the Control of Ground Receiving Installations for Satellite Television*) was promulgated on October 5, 1993.[16] Article 1 of the decree was forthright in its intention of "strengthening the control of ground receiving installations" (aka satellite dishes), through "a system of granting licenses in respect to the production, import, sale, installation and use of satellite ground receiving installations" (Article 3). Work units wishing to receive satellite signals were required to apply for a license to the radio and television administration in their local government (Article 8).

Article 9 began with the bald statement that "No individuals shall be allowed to install or use the satellite ground receiving installations." This edict became the focus of media reports on the decree, which uniformly reported that private ownership of satellite dishes was henceforth illegal. However, the same article went on to declare that "If an individual has a real need to install or use satellite ground receiving installations under special circumstances which are in accordance with licensed conditions," then an application for a license was permitted. When the Ministry of Radio, Film and Television subsequently issued its *Detailed Rules for Implementation of the Provisions,* it specified that the 'real need' would be related to problems in receiving broadcast or cable television signals.

The Detailed Rules stated that satellite installations in use prior to the decree "may be dismantled if they are not in conformity with the (new) conditions for application," which again led to media coverage predicting the forcible removal of hundreds of the dishes already installed, despite the highly conditional language ("*may be* dismantled *if*") used in the Detailed Rules. The MRFT's Detailed Rules also contained a number of restrictions nowhere mentioned in the Decree, in particular detailed prohibitions on the "broadcast or relay by other means (of) TV programmes produced outside the Chinese territory transmitted by satellite," whether in "public places" such as stations, shops or cinemas, or through any kind of television distribution channel.

Four months after Decree No. 129, on February 3, 1994, the *Regulations of the PRC on the Administration of Cable Television* were issued, which were considerably more explicit than the decree. The subordination of cable TV to broadcast TV was stated clearly, as was an assertion of the MRFT's authority in "the administration and development planning of cable television for the PRC as a whole" (Article 4). Foreign investment in cable systems, in whole or in part, was banned. Detailed rules were laid down on what content was permitted, with specific bans on "television programmes originating from Hong Kong, Taiwan and Macao" and on "foreign television programmes delivered via satellite" (Article 25), with a detailed listing of the penalties involved, including the rescinding of license to operate (Article 28).

At the time Decree No. 129 was introduced official figures were that there were an estimated 11 million satellite dishes installed in China, and it can be questioned whether it was ever practical to track them all down, identify ownership, and enforce a retroactive licensing scheme. In the event, six months later reports were appearing that there was no attempt to even begin to enforce the ban (Karp, 1994: 69). The MRFT's restrictions on television distribution did have an effect, however, although not the total ban implied by the Detailed Rules. The U.S. sports network ESPN, for example, was temporarily removed from Beijing Cable Television, but returned after a two-month hiatus as a recorded, edited program (ibid: 68). The problem it seemed had not been the fact it was a satellite program, but that it had been relayed direct, making it impossible to check the content.

THE GAP BETWEEN POLICY AND ENFORCEMENT

There are patterns which seem to recur in the handling of satellite TV news by the Chinese authorities. Referencing the history of the media in China we can quickly identify one, the Chinese bureaucratic tradition of restricting access to information; another revolves around the deep concern about external opinion, especially as it impacts internal views.

For the Chinese government, the Internet and the international TV signal, which speak directly to the individual without intermediaries, may seem to represent a fundamental threat to the way Chinese society had grown to be constituted. This is a construct where the values of Confucianism have been distorted out of their original context of "a discourse of self-mastery . . . to one which demanded the detailed specification, classification and surveillance of family and community"(Dutton, 1992: 350). In this paradigm, the loss of control which is implied by open communication, the sudden inability of the center to filter information flows, is equated with a threat to the rightful authority of a collective leadership. It has encouraged an ongoing fear in Chinese administrators, one with long historical roots, concerning the consequences of a loss of central control. When the edict banning satellite dishes in 1994 was actually implemented, it soon became clear that the overriding concern was to control, rather than to ban.

In addition, there was a commercial incentive at work, as the ongoing overhaul of the Chinese telecommunications system makes accessible the biggest multimedia audience in the world. The ambivalence which surrounded both the rationale behind the original government directive and its actual implementation in part reflect a constant dilemma facing modern Chinese leadership, how much slack to cut in a system that has relied on central control to maintain order and restrict political change.

Part of what must be controlled, but which becomes problematic, is views and information from the outside. In China news from abroad has a peculiar charge to it, not least because it represents a direct threat to a process which, until very recently, was hidden from view, and in which control of access to information was central. One of the fascinating strands running through the memoirs of Mao's doctor is precisely this, the degree to which the top leadership relied on restricting access to accurate information, a policy which could badly misfire when even news digests produced for "internal reference" became corrupted by the need to fit in with one of the succession of "rectification" campaigns (Li, 1994).

At the time, Decree No. 129 was frequently depicted as a panicked reaction by the Chinese government to Rupert Murdoch's purchase of STAR TV in July, 1993 (see Star TV section below), and this view has crept into the media history of the period. Despite the unlikelihood of the State Council bureaucracy being able to develop and promulgate a major decree in just over two months, a detailed analysis of the language of the Decree, the Detailed Rules and the Cable Television Regulations suggests that what was involved was, first, an attempt by the MRFT to establish absolute authority over satellite and cable TV, and, second, a concerted drive to set up a legal template and a technical structure which would allow the state to continue to control the content of what was being broadcast, regardless of the medium of transmission. To achieve this, cable television played a key role (see below). It allowed a way for the populace to receive satellite television signals, but through the filter of the cable operator, thus giving the government the time and the means to control the content.[17] The new regulations were an attempt to deal with a general situation of change—the arrival of "the borderless world"—rather than a reaction to a particular event.

The reality was that Decree No. 129, and subsequent reinforcing regulations, were quite ineffective. In 1997, when the bulk of the field research for this dissertation was carried out, I visited a number of satellite equipment shops in Kunming, and found there was literally no difficulty in buying any equipment I wanted, with no question of a license arising. The following exchange with a manager of the "Shenzhen China-Taiwan-Economic Cooperation Electrical Equipment Company " was quite typical:[18]

> Q. *I have a new apartment: is it possible to set up a satellite dish to receive TV?*
>
> Of course. Everyone can get one for themselves.
>
> Q. *Do I need a license or a certificate from the shop or from some official place?*
>
> No, you don't need one now. Even though officially there is a government regulation controlling the setting up of a satellite dish on a building, no one pays any attention to that. If you can pay, everything is OK.
>
> Q. *How much would I have to pay?*
>
> There are two sizes of dishes for private apartment, 1.5m and 2m. They are made in Shenzhen, but the material is high-quality, imported. The best one is made by Toshiba, "West 4." It's two meters in diameter. That is Yuen 2,800.
>
> Q. *Who can help me set it up and get the signal?*
>
> The shop does that.
>
> Q. *If I had a Toshiba W4 what kind of channel s would I be able to get?*
>
> You can get StarTV, four different Hong Kong channels, Tibet and Guizhou, and a music channel and a sports channel.
>
> Q. *Can I get CNN?*
>
> No. CNN is for "star" hotels, it's for foreigners.
>
> Q. *Do you need special technical knowledge to set up a dish?*
>
> The shop staff know what direction to point the dish, to get Asiasat 1 in the south.
>
> You know, what some private apartment owners do, several families make an agreement to own a dish, because if someday the government cracks down, if several families are involved, numbers are strength.
>
> Q. *If it breaks down, what do I do?*
>
> Bring it back here, we'll fix it.
>
> Do you work here? No? That's good. The government cannot control you. If you want to come back tomorrow morning, we have a car, we can take you and the dish and set it up for you.

Although this particular shop apparently did not have the equipment to pick up the CNN signal, at least one other claimed to be able to do so. The price quoted in this interview was very high: by the early 2000s the price was down to about 800 yuen in southern China, the best market for the equipment.

By the end of 2001 estimates were that about 45 million people were able to view foreign channels picked by such satellite dishes. The government's reaction was ill-fated. In February, 2002, China International Television Corporation (CITV), the government agency that administers foreign broadcasts, brought in a regulation requiring all foreign broadcasters wishing to send signals into China to use a "re-broadcast platform." The order apparently was initiated by the SARFT, which wanted to place all foreign satellite TV channels under its administration. The SARFT proposed to charge each of the estimated 27 foreign broadcasters $100,000 to intercept the signals from their satellites, encrypt and retransmit them on the state-owned Sinosat-1. However the encryption technology used was outdated, and in short order cheap pirate decoders appeared. This had the effect of boosting the audience for foreign channels—as they were all now available on the same satellite—at the same time as HBO, Cinemax, CNN and the BBC all found that orders for new licenses declined steeply. To make matters worse, this was also the satellite that had its signal hijacked by the Falun Gong, in June and July 2002 (Murphy, 2002 and Satnews Asia: November 2001, January 2002, September 2002).

There are a number of interesting aspects to the story. One is that Sinosat (Sino Satellite Communications) was formed in 1994 with partners that included the People's Bank of China and the Government of Shanghai, with the avowed purpose of breaking the domination that ChinaSat (China Telecommunications Broadcast Satellite Corporation) had over the Chinese satellite communications market (FAS, 1998). In January, 2002, Chinasat and several other satellite communication had been forcibly merged into a new giant conglomerate, the China Telecommunications Satellite Group, controlled directly by the MII. Sinosat, closely linked with the SARFT, was pointedly able to avoid the merger.

Apart from boosting the SARFT in its ongoing battle to maintain operational independence despite its shotgun marriage into MII, the move also allowed the government to achieve its aim of controlling satellite transmissions. On July 1, 2002, CITC abruptly suspended BBC satellite transmission only six months after the BBC had been granted a license to broadcast into China, after the station had aired "some content that is not allowed." The cut off came after a program covering the fifth anniversary of Hong Kong's 1997 handover, a news item that included coverage of the Falun Gong protests. Apart from the irony that Falun Gong had just a few days before managed to take over broadcasts by CCTV on the same satellite, the BBC signal was still theoretically available on other PanAmSat satellites operating over Asia (AFP, 2002).

Reality Bites 1: Technological developments

1.B. The Growth of Cable

As was the case in Japan, cable TV started in China as a supplement to the existing broadcast system, a way to extend the broadcast service area. Also as in Japan cable usually took the form of community antenna TV (CATV) systems. In the United States cable television had developed in parallel with the spread of broadcast TV stations in the 1950s (Parson and Frieden, 1998: 33); in Japan, the spread of CATV had largely been fostered by NHK, as part of its remit to provide a national service. In China the service was initiated by work units, although it quickly expanded beyond them.

The Chinese word *danwei* is translated as "work unit," English terminology which does little to convey the size and complexity of most of these institutional employment organizations. For example, my Chinese in-laws belong to the Kunming Medical College work unit, which is responsible for every aspect of the living and working conditions of those attached to the college, in any capacity. In addition to all the educational facilities (lecture halls, laboratories, offices, sports grounds, library, cafeterias, clinics, dormitories, gardens and more) all the faculty and administration staff have their own apartments and support facilities, including a preschool and a clinic. In short the larger work units each constitute the work place, the home and the social base for hundreds or even thousands of people.

Not only did CATV make sense in order to improve reception among these conglomerations of people, where apartment tower blocks often lead to antenna sitting problems, but also such systems became part of a 'benefit package' designed to attract and keep residents in the unit.[19] According to Liu, these systems were initially offered free.

In the early 1980s certain municipal and district government began developing their own cable systems, again largely in an effort to improve reception in built-up areas. In the late 1980s these two systems, the systems developed by government administrators and those established by enterprises, began to link up, as did systems in counties and small towns with larger urban conurbations (Liu, 1994: 218). Cable TV, which had basically been offered free in the start-up stages by the work units, now came with an installation fee and a small monthly payment.[20]

The result was what came to be known as "urban networks," in effect cable TV operations. In theory these networks are state-controlled, and with the *Regulations of the PRC on the Administration of Cable Television*

(February 3, 1994) the MRFT attempted to map out its vision of how the mushrooming cable industry should be run. The Regulations divided stations into two types: Administrative Region Cable Television Stations (ARCTVS) and Non-Administrative Region Cable Television Stations (NARCTVS). ARCTVS referred to "stations established under local government and which cover the administrative region of the said local government" (Article 7), while NARCTVS covered all the *danwei* cable networks. The regulations mandated "only one ARCTVS may be established within each city or administrative region" (Article 8) and further urged that work unit cable systems should be integrated into the local ARCTVS "at an appropriate time" (Article 9).

The MRFT also went out of its way to make the complementary aspect of cable TV explicit. The 1994 regulations are explicit in stating that "cable television in the PRC . . . is an extension of and supplement to television broadcasting" (Article 3). Liu quotes an early 1990s directive from the Shashi Bureau of Radio and Television in Hubei province which instructed Shashi Cable Television to "not compete in news, not engage in advertisement, yield precedence in conflict, and relay completely." (ibid: 219). The last two provisos, to "yield precedence" and to "relay completely" in effect are instructions to give broadcast television the lead in everything, specifically not putting on a program before it has been aired by a broadcaster, national or local, and to ensure the right of CCTV or local broadcast stations to preempt air time, especially when important programming is scheduled.

In reality, this system works only partially at best. Even at the time of Deng Xiaoping's death, when I was in China, there was an obvious contrast between the amount of time the cable stations were willing to devote to the mourning period and the much longer coverage given by CCTV. This was confirmed by a senior CCTV official, who openly complained about the extent of advertising revenue CCTV had lost because of the mass cancellation of regular, advertising supported programming and an effective ban on advertising for 24 days.[21]

Further, the regulation insisting on only one 'authorized' cable TV station per city or local government administrative area seemed to be honored mostly in the breech, while the ideal of incorporating NARCTVS into ARCTVS may have been a non-starter. There were and are formidable technical obstacles to getting the hundreds or even thousands of CATV systems in any one city to link up: the two systems I was able to inspect, at Kunming Medical College and at the University of Peking, were basic in the extreme, and signal reception even in a relatively new building varied greatly.[22]

There were other reasons, economic and political, why the number of cable stations mushroomed in such an uncontrolled fashion in the late 1980s and early 1990s. When the head of the Yunnan Cable TV Association was asked to explain why in 1996 Kunming had five cable operators, to serve some 18,000 households,[23] the answer was because each operator had his 'territory,' and each area wanted to "achieve its own economic growth." This even extended to trying to produce their own programs separately. "Economic growth" seemed to mean the opportunity to make a profit—through advertising, rather than through the rock bottom monthly reception charges. In addition, each area represented a traditional political division in the city, with its own history of rivalry with other areas.[24]

The concept of each station having its own territory also has other implications than the historical, as cable TV became the site of numerous power struggles of different organs of the state. The players in this struggle varied from location to location, but could include the provincial government and the city government and their respective MRFT bureaus, the local bureaus of the Ministry of Posts and Telecommunications and the Ministry of Electronic Industries, the city construction bureaus, and local business forces, including the CCP and the PLA. Local conflicts over control mirrored the fights for regulatory control at the national level, in particular between the MPT and the MRFT, as government agencies battled for the spoils of the newly emerged information world. These fights were at a peak at the time when I was doing the bulk of my field research for this book, and were supposed to end with the forceful merger of all the departments into a new Ministry of Information Industries. The fights apparently still go on, however (see section on "Convergence," p.165).

In 1990, the MRFT tried to introduce unified planning for cable television systems, which it split into three categories, according to degree of ability to produce original programming. Cable TV was regulated in a four-tier system—the central government, the provinces, the cities and the counties—with a top-down hierarchy of authority and a bottom-up reporting structure (Liu, 1994: 221).

All operators were required to re-apply for a franchise agreement from the ministry. Part of the agreement required the operators to follow MRFT regulations, and to conform to service limits (ibid: 218). According to the director of cable TV within the MRFT at the time, the reasons were two-fold: the need to stop the airing of smuggled video showing violence or pornography, and the desire to achieve control of the cable systems by forcing them to merge.[25]

The regulations seemed to have had little effect. Apart from the situation I observed in Kunming, I heard numerous accounts of similar circumstances in other cities. It is a safe conclusion that official figures regularly underestimate the number of cable stations and the degree of penetration, but to what extent is a matter of speculation. Accurate and reliable statistics are always hard to come by in China, and this certainly applies to the world of Chinese television.

A clear example of the confusion over statistics was provided by the China Cable and Satellite Television Summit '96, held in Beijing in 1996, which featured speeches from a number of senior officials from various relevant government ministries. Most of them mentioned cable TV as an example of extraordinary growth in television in China, but there was little consensus about how to measure that growth. Estimates for the number of cable TV subscribers—a figure which in theory should be fairly 'hard,' as by definition each subscriber is registered—in fact changed from 20 to 40 to 50 million in different speeches over the course of the three-day event, while the mentions of the number of cable TV stations ranged between 1,200, 1,285 and 1,300.[26] Again in theory the number of cable TV stations should be comparatively straightforward to ascertain, as each one requires a government license to operate. But in fact a considerable number operate without such permission: of the two cities which served as bases for my field research, both had stations operating openly without official license.[27] MRFT officials expressed little surprise when told of this situation as observed in Kunming, but were visibly disconcerted to find out that there was an "unofficial" station in Beijing.[28]

The somewhat chaotic situation regarding cable TV in the 1990s reflects the lack of overall planning or even regulation at its birth, and the subsequent inability of any one government body to assert control—and despite the repeated attempts by the MRFT and its successor the SARFT to do so. The underlying reason is straightforward: at the local level, cable TV is seen as a money maker, with a future potential for growth. Local operators control all the personnel and financial aspects of their stations, with the SARFT only able to offer "administrative guidance." This makes cable TV highly attractive to local governments, all of which are faced with budgetary constraints. As already indicated it also lends itself to traditional rivalries, between provincial level and municipal level government, a situation familiar to followers of the endless bickering between different levels of local government in the United States.

CABLE CONTENT

One of the functions of the MRFT (and now the SARFT) is propaganda, relaying the view from Beijing to the nation. Programming carried by cable TV stations is required to follow the same laws and observe the same restrictions as apply to broadcast TV, in particular regarding national security and the stability of society. However, these regulations were created and amended with one model in mind, that of a national broadcast monopoly, with local provincial TV supporting and mirroring the monopoly, initially with only one or two channels on offer.

Cable television exploded that model. The whole rationale behind paying for a cable TV subscription is to be able to watch a wider variety of programming, specifically programming *not* available on regular broadcast TV. This puts immense pressure on cable system operators to offer something different. This pressure, coupled with the fact that cable has a vociferous appetite for programming, pushes the operators to engage in an endless search for new material. When the material is both free and very attractive—as is the case with programs from Hong Kong in Guangzhou and was the case with STAR TV in various areas, including Beijing—the temptation to use the programming is irresistible, especially when the local government is itself comparatively laid back in its enforcement of central government edicts.[29]

In addition, cable can do much more than carry television channels. In the late 1990s government regulators found themselves in a very similar situation to that of the Ministry of Posts and Telecommunications in Japan (see Chapter 3), in having to balance the need for greater information carrying capacity nationwide with the official demand that the content of that information should be closely monitored. An additional layer of complexity was added by the infighting and widely differing views on how to manage this change.

TO CONVERGE OR NOT TO CONVERGE

The anomalies that characterize these bureaucratic fights are striking. According to the 1997 *Measures for the Administration of Radio and Television,* SARFT had been clearly awarded overall jurisdiction over the networks as well as over programming. This apparently clear legislation was almost immediately overshadowed in 1998 by the merger which created the Ministry of Information Industry (MII), with a seeming resolution of the dispute in the former MPT's favor, as MII was plainly put in charge of all transmission networks. This was eventually codified in 2000 by a new set of Telecommunications Regulations, putting MII in charge of all telecommunications activities, including, explicitly, television and radio transmission.

At the same time, in late October 1999, the State Council promulgated the *Notice of the General Office of the State Council Concerning the Strengthening of Administration over the Construction of Television Transmission Networks*. The edict banned telecom departments from entering the radio and television transmission business, and likewise forbad cable television operators from competing with the telephone service providers, China Telecom and China Unicom, by offering internet protocol telephony or internet access over cable lines.

The following month, China and the U.S. reached agreement over China's future entry into the World Trade Organization. Some—including the U.S. Trade Representative Charlene Barshefsky—"claimed that the deal would open the door for foreign investment in China's Internet and telecom sector," an opinion soon rebutted by the MII Minister Wu Jichuan (Chang and Dorn, February 2, 2000).

The controversy deepened when the MII and the State Administration of Radio, Film and Television (SARFT) quickly issued a joint document (#82), the *Opinions on Strengthening Administration of Cable Television Networks*, an attempt to clarify how the State Council notice would be implemented. The Opinions were shot through with contradictions and ambiguities, reflecting the different goals and standpoints of the MII and SARFT, an ongoing rivalry that predates their forcible merger, and which has plainly not died down.

Notably, while Article 1 charges the MII with the overall regulation of companies transmitting commercial television broadcasts, Article 2 gives the local SARFT bureaus effective control over setting up cable head ends, establishing new channels, and the actual broadcasting of television programs.

Article 1A charges SARFT with using existing national communications networks, and with linking existing cable television networks into an "integrated network" dedicated to cable TV. It does not say anything about the carrying capacity of such networks, however. Any modern integrated cable TV network is almost certain to be broadband, with the concomitant ability to service internet and telephony needs as well as television, and thus begging the question of how to stop the MII and SARFT from trying to poach on each other's turf. As Chang and Dorn describe it, this kind of bureaucratic in-fighting in the face of technological change is very similar to the situation in Japan.

> In many ways, the Opinions are typical of the overall legislative framework for China's cable television, telecom and Internet industries: they attempt to compartmentalize administrative and operational responsibilities in industries where technological innovations have resulted in a convergence of media. The Opinion's vague provisions illustrate the internal conflict within the Chinese government on how the Internet and related sectors should be governed (op.cit.)

This conflict is no minor matter. In Hunan province, with a population of 64 million, the provincial cable television company has literally battled representatives of China Telecom in order to prevent them from offering television services, with reports of officials shot at, lines cut, and many injured in brawls. When the local telecoms bureau was eventually forced to accept a ban on broadcasting, in line with the 1999 State Council notice, the bureau rented its lines to Xinhua, the official news agency, which has its own commercial interests. Xinhua began immediate broadcast of the same programming, but with subtitles reading "Xinhua Information Reference" or "Testing Signal" (McGregor, 2000: 5).

The inconsistencies and equivocations that characterize document #82 reflect a long-running battle between the former MPT and the former MRFT over a rich prize—the regulation of China's radio and television networks—that seems not to have been ameliorated at all by their forcible merger into the MII. The battle reached new levels of acrimony at the turn of the century as the technology for convergence—whereby a telecoms provider can also supply television services, and vice versa—is already well developed. By December, 2000, China's first large-scale (10,000 viewers) interactive TV system had already begun trials in Beijing, offering digital film storage, video on demand and modem access (Interactive TV, China Online, December, 2000) .

In November, 2000, a senior MII official—the Director of Policy, Law and Regulation—indicated that the 1999 State Council notice was likely to be reversed, just one year after it had been promulgated, and that the government would "allow cable TV and landline telephone companies to compete after all" (ChinaOnline, November 9, 2000). This was followed by a speech given by MII Vice Minister Zhang Chunjiang in July, 2001, in which he explicitly proposed that the telecommunications and radio/television markets by opened on a reciprocal basis, allowing each to 'participate' in the other's area of interest. The SARFT immediately responded, by telling reporters: "What the vice-minister said is just a request. It is not a result . . . The idea of both sides opening up is not going to be possible for another couple of years" (Kynge, 2001).

The plain contradictions between the Telecommunications Regulations and Document #82 remain unresolved. There is an interesting ideological basis for the argument, which may give a clue as to why it remains unresolved. This sees broadcasting in its traditional role, as part of the CCP's and the government's propaganda effort: an information 'tool' too valuable to risk losing. While China has committed to opening up its telecommunications services as part of the agreement to win WTO membership, it has made no such commitment for opening radio and television, including cable television (Perkins Cole, 2002).

Meanwhile, the SARFT continues with its attempts to integrate all the Chinese cable local operators into one vast cable monopoly. The first step taken in 1999 was to establish provincial level network corporations, composed of all local stations, and controlled by the provincial TV stations. Predictably, this met with heavy opposition from local operators, and in two provinces, Guangdong and Hubei, resulted in network corporations financed by compulsory "contributions" from local stations, but without any networks to operate (ChinaOnline: December 11, 2000).

The ultimate goal of the SARFT is the creation of a nationwide radio and television network transmission company, referred to as China Cable Network, that would bring cable, wireless and satellite transmission under its control. The rationale behind such a network would be to offer expanded value-added services, such as pay-TV, video on demand, and broadband Internet access, in addition to television program distribution—in apparent conflict with State Council edicts already described (ChinaOnline, May 21, 2001). This plan was described in detail by Haito Zhang, a deputy minister of SARFT, in March, 2001, including a full description of the planned transition from analog to digital by 2015. This transition would also provide the opportunity for creating a digital cable network, unifying all of China's estimated 90 million cable subscribers, covering 20 provinces, and expecting to reach an estimated 200 million users with "full service" (i.e. including two-way communication) by 2010 (Liu, 2001).

Zhang chose to make his speech announcing the plan at the "China Cable Broadcasting Network 2001" show, which was heavily attended by international companies, lured by the prospect of huge sales and key decision being made in the still unresolved competition to set digital TV standards. As always, China's ability to influence the direction of international decisions lies in the numbers: at the time of the speech, there were an estimated 350 million TV sets in China, 293 radio stations, 653 TV stations and the aforementioned 90 million cable TV subscribers, the largest cable television market in the world (ibid).

Reality Bites 1: Technological developments

1.C. The Growth of the Internet

In August, 2000, the Chinese President Jiang Zemin gave a speech reflecting the deep ambivalence underlying Chinese government's attempts to come to terms with the growth of the Internet. He acknowledged "the tremendous power of information technology" and described how "the melding of the traditional economy and information technology will provide the engine for the development of the economy and society in the 21st century." But he warned of " a flood of trash" that comes with the Internet. "The Internet also brings problems that make people uneasy: anti-science, false science and information that is unhealthy to the point of being downright harmful" (BBC News, August 21, 2000).

In the same month as the president's speech, a People's Daily commentary raised the level of discussion on the Internet to new symbolic heights. The spread of the internet around the globe was described as *da, kuai, guang*(great, rapid, widespread), the same adjectives once used in official descriptions of the Great Leap Forward. It was also a "new phenomenon" (*xin shiwu*), the term used at the time of the Cultural Revolution to describe its achievements. According to the People's Daily:

> The Internet . . . has become a new arena for struggle between the "correct propaganda" of the government and the "reactionary, superstitious and pornographic" content of China's enemies. Party authorities all over China should form crack units of web fighters who understand politics and news management, and have a good command of foreign languages, to wage battle with the enemy "at home and abroad" (Gittings, 2000: 2).

One reason for the Internet to be seen as a new "arena for struggle" is its phenomenal growth. The Chinese are now the second largest Internet users in the world. As of July 2002, there were 45 million according to CNNIC, a number growing by 6% every month.

It is beyond the scope of this work to examine the growth of the Internet in China in general. One key feature, the prospects of convergence with other technologies, in particular cable, has been examined above. I would like briefly to look at another important aspect: the attempt to control information on the Internet, and the development of bureaucratic understanding of it as just another media, to be regulated in a fashion similar to print or television.

ATTEMPTS TO CONTROL INFORMATION ON THE INTERNET

At its inception the Internet posed a fundamental challenge to national governments: what was it? Was it another kind of telecommunications service, and therefore to be regulated in the traditional way, with a focus on who provided the service (access to a telecommunications network), how, at what price? Or was it an information delivery service, requiring oversight of content, and concerned with the end users?

Like the slow development of awareness by the MPT in Japan, the initial reaction of the Chinese authorities was to see the Internet as another plank in the platform of infrastructural development. At first the Internet was conceived of as a part of telecommunications development in general; by the 1990s it was more specifically focused on information exchanges, with an assumption that this would be largely devoted to scientific and educational communications. What was not foreseen was the rocketing figures of Internet users (Table 5), or that the most popular application would be e-mail correspondence (Table 6), or that the most popular usage would be news retrieval (Table 7).

By June 2002 the number of internet users in China had reached 45.8 million, an increase of 72.8% over the same period in 2001; similarly, the figure of 26.5 million Internet users at the end of June, 2001, represented a 56.8% increase over the same period the previous year. At the same time Internet access is spreading into different strata of Chinese society, away from an initial focus in the most highly educated segments (although students remain the heaviest users), and the number of people using the Internet at home is increasing steeply (CNNIC, 2002).

Table 5. Increasing Internet Users in China 1997–2002

Time	Number
June 1998	1,175,000
December 1998	2,100,000
June 1999	4,000,000
December 1999	8,900,000
June 2000	16,900,000
December 2000	22,500,000
June 2001	26,500,000
June 2002	45,800,000

Source: CNNIC

Table 6. Most Frequently Used Network Services in China 2000–2001

Used network service	Percentage
E-mail	92.9
Search engine	63.8
Software downloading and uploading	51.0
Online chatting	45.5
Information acquiring	40.3

Source: CNNIC: multiple responses allowed

Table 7. Most Desired Information in China 2000–2001

Desired information	Percentage
News	75.8
Computer hardware and software	60.3
Entertainment	41.3
E-books	28.8
Living services	24.9

Source: CNNIC: multiple responses allowed

The Chinese government, like many other, has been severely challenged in adapting to explosive growth on this scale, and in trying to develop a regulatory framework which accommodates the dichotomy reflected in President Zemin's speech, the potential (economic and social) and the threat (political, cultural and ideological) of the Internet. In his description of one unanticipated spin-off development, IP telephony, Lovelock has shown the remarkable bureaucratic contortions that result, with the MII and China Telecom first attempting to ban the service outright and initiating prosecutions of those who offered the service, then "almost overnight" reversing policy and "driving (IP telephony) out as a central plank of their emerging telephony, data and Internet agendas" (Lovelock, 2000).

The flurry of regulations on the Internet that have appeared in China since the mid-1990s fall into two broad categories, those with a focus on security issues and those dealing with technical and organizational matters. The former tend to be painted with a very broad brush (wielded by the Ministry of Public Security), and are frequently undermined by the latter.

In 1994 the State Council promulgated Order No. 147, *Security Regulations for Computer Information Systems in the PRC,* which put the Ministry of Public Security (MPS) in charge of ensuring that such systems should not endanger national security.

The *Interim Regulations for Connecting Computer Networks to International Networks* (Order No. 195) issued in February 1996 was the first attempt to bring order to the chaos of the Internet itself. This limited international access to four "interconnecting networks (INs)," which in turn were required to use the Ministry of Posts and Telecommunications (MPT) portal for the actual connection. Local access could be achieved by "access networks (ANs)," but these could only make their links indirectly, via the INs. ANs are in effect Internet service providers (ISPs).

The following year, the MPS introduced the first comprehensive attempt to regulate content, wading in with *Computer Information Network and Internet Security, Protection and Management Regulations* (December, 1997). This drew together a number of previously issued orders on users and content, and added new requirements. The regulations attempted to meet national security concerns by requiring all users to register with the local public security office, and banning a long list of activities, from the specific (pornography, incitement to violence) to the general (destroying the order of society, challenging existing laws, threatening national unity). The onus was on the INs and ANs to do the actual policing.

Lovelock points out that these regulations represented a victory of the Ministry of Public Security over the MRFT, which had been slow to react to the Internet in general, or to see its potential as another delivery device for the mass media which are the MRFT's supposed domain. In fact the MRFT's stage had become crowded with competitors: Lovelock lists no fewer than 14 "Internet-interested actors" in 1997 (2000: 8).[30] He also argues that, despite measures which in any other context would surely be seen as draconian, the government's primary objective was growth rather than control.[31]

However, it could equally be argued that the regulations were by their nature unenforceable, except in particular cases where the whole national security apparatus is brought to bear, as has happened with the concerted attempts to squash the Falun Gong's Internet activity. Control of unwelcome content is a major concern of the CCP ideologues, and this is clearly indicated by numerous case histories (see below). But the Chinese officials charged with steering the country onto the information superhighway are realists. Yu Renlin, Deputy Secretary General of the State Council Steering Committee of National Information Infrastructure, said that the Internet policy makers recognized the impossibility of blocking all objectionable sites, and added, remarkably, that in fact "the new regulation was related to a relaxation of controls over Internet usage intended to encourage more widespread Internet usage." (U.S. Embassy China: 1998)

In addition, Tan, Mueller and Foster make the case that, in the inverted way common with Chinese laws, the new regulations also took some important positive steps. First, they offered official recognition of the Internet, and of the notion of making the necessary international connections, albeit in a carefully controlled way. Second, the regulations recognized the diversity intrinsic to the Internet, and thus opened the door to legislation in 1999 which actively encouraged competition in the new arena (see below) (Tan, Mueller, Foster: 1997).

And at the same time, other pressures were building, most noticeably those caused by the need to prepare for joining the WTO. On October 29, 1999, the MII announced the *Interim Regulations on the Administration of Telecommunication Network Interconnection,* obliging the leading Chinese telecom companies to connect their own telecom networks with those of other licensed telecom companies within seven months of receipt of an interconnection request. This was the first major regulation promulgated by the MII since its establishment in March 1998, and was described by the U.S. Embassy in Beijing as intending "to create a competitive market environment in China's telecom services sector and help domestic telecom operators familiarize themselves with a competitive environment before China opens its telecom services market to foreign participation" (U.S. Embassy China, 2000).

Immediately after the new regulation came into effect the U.S. and China signed a bilateral agreement on China's accession to the World Trade Organization (November 15, 1999). This was followed in September, 2000, by the first comprehensive regulatory framework for telecommunications, the "Regulations of the PRC on Telecommunications." Issues covered included operational licensing, interconnection, charges and standards, in apparent adherence to the Basic Telecommunication Agreement, which covers the liberalization of basic telecommunication services among WTO member states (Xu and Yip, 2001).

None of this diminished the ongoing concern with content, in particular news. In April 2000 a new 'Internet Information Management Bureau' was set up, with a mandate which included countering "the infiltration of harmful information on the Internet" (BBC News, May 15, 2000). This was a prelude to the *Measures for Managing Internet Information Services* (October 1, 2000), drafted jointly by the MII and the Information Office of the State Council, that charged the Information Office with managing all web sites providing news in China. The measures limited Internet news publishing to the web sites of official media organizations at the national and provincial government levels. Other media organizations could only set up pages on these sites. Commercial non-news organizations wishing to publish news had to apply for a license to do so, and were banned from carrying original news.

An absolute ban was declared on linking to foreign news sites, without the express approval of the Information Office. In addition, Article 15 carried explicit bans on any information that "goes against the basic principles set in the constitution," and which endangered national security, was detrimental to the "honor and interest of the state," that encouraged ethnic division, that "preaches the teaching of evil cults or that promotes feudalistic and superstitious beliefs," that undermines social stability, that spreads pornography or encourages crime, that "insults or slanders other people," or "other information prohibited by the law or administrative regulations."

In January 2002 the MII promulgated new regulations requiring ISPs to keep detailed records about their users, install e-mail tracking software, and notify the authorities of any violations of PRC laws. The intention was plain, to shift the initial responsibility for policing the Internet on to the companies servicing it (Chase And Mulvenon, 2002: 61). The trend towards self-regulation has been reinforced by a news set of MII regulations that came into effect on August 1, 2002, *Provisional Regulations for the Management and Control of Internet Publications.* These stipulate that any 'online publisher' must introduce an editorial system, just as in other media, and establish clear lines of responsibility in the system of production (CMI, 2002).

Impressive as this regulatory edifice may appear, the key question, as always in China, will revolve around implementation. As such the regulations serve to bolster the reserve of possible control mechanisms available to the authorities, rather than necessarily indicating how or to what extent they will actually be used. As it is, there is a considerable gap between the Chinese government's constant issuing of warnings and bans, and the reality on the ground. The limited empirical evidence available indicates that even the most 'sensitive' sites on the web, such as human rights and Tibet-related sites, remain available through proxy servers or even directly (op.cit.: 67). Another problem, as indicated by some examples below, is that the real rationale behind declaring a story to be in violation of the myriad laws applicable may in fact be quite different to the declared aim. One example was the mining disaster in July, 2001, in Guanxi province in south-west China in which 81 tin miners were killed. Mine owners and local government officials went out of their way to try and keep the story out of the media and off the Internet, but eventually failed because journalists from the local Communist party daily e-mailed the story to colleagues around the country (Wingfield-Hayes, 2002).

In view of the exponential increase in the number of Internet users in China, the Chinese government's attempts to control unwelcome information access or delivery on the Internet resemble nothing more than the fairground game in which the aim is to guess where the next object is going to pop out of a hole, and bonk it before it disappears. Although Chase and Mulvenon see these attempts as surprisingly successful so far, they also conclude that the presence of the Internet in China "has altered the dynamic between the Beijing regime and the dissident community. It has enabled local dissident efforts to become issues of national and even global discussion" (op.cit: 3). No example makes this more apparent than the remarkable resilience of the Falun Gong protesters, who have made extensive use of the Internet and other media, culminating in taking over national satellite television transmissions.

The Chinese government is totalitarian by nature and by deed, however, and its attempts to exert control are never-ending. In the 1990s the government began to introduce a raft of so-called "golden projects," designed to build a modern telecommunication and information infrastructure. The latest off these is called the "Golden Shield," launched in November 2000, and tantamount to a comprehensive surveillance network that makes the efforts of the Department of Homeland Security in the U.S. look modest by comparison. The "golden shield" refers to the badge worn on dress uniform by the Chinese police, who are not noted for their sensitivity to human rights. It incorporates speech and face recognition, closed circuit television, smart cards, credit records—and internet surveillance technologies—all tied in to a gigantic database for use by the security authorities (Walton, 2001).

CENSORSHIP CASE HISTORIES

Article 15 of the October 2000 Information Services Management Law serves as a list of all the concerns the Chinese administration has about the population having unlimited access to news and information. Commenting on the new regulations in *Renmin Ribao* (People's Daily), a State Council Information Office representative explained that "some web sites publish hearsay, recarry or quote false and harmful news that mislead the public and cause confusion and thus harm the interests of the public as well as the legitimate rights and interests of the victims. (This is) a measure to ensure that Web sites publish news in a way responsible for the public and the society"[ChinaOnline, November, 2000 (2)].

A scan of some of the items which were considered misleading and likely to cause confusion in the year the law was promulgated is revealing. In April 2000 local authorities in Nanjing closed the *Jiangnan Times* for three days after it broke the story of the murder of a German DaimlerChrysler executive and his wife and two children, apparently because of "reporting the incident too actively and in too much detail" (Kynge, 2000:3).

In May 2000 China Finance Information Network was fined for spreading rumors that "damaged the government's image," by reprinting a Hong Kong newspaper article about corruption by a provincial official. "An investigation by government authorities showed the news article was untrue and the website had trespassed on the person's reputation and affected foreign investment" (BBC News, May 15, 2000).

In June 2000 Huang Qi, who had launched China's first human rights website was arrested and accused of attempting to overthrow the state, after articles commemorating the 1989 Tiananmen protests were published on the website (BBC News, June 7, 2000). In August a pro-democracy site, the New Culture Forum, was closed down and a police hunt begun for its organizers (BBC News, August 9, 2000).

One interesting aspect of the Huang Qi and the New Culture Forum cases was how small the sites were (the New Culture Forum reportedly had only registered 2,200 hits before being closed down) and how easily they were re-opened, in both cases on the Human Rights in China website (www.hrichina. org) (Gittings, 2000: 2).

Symbolically, perhaps the most striking example in 2000 was one of an unsuccessful attempt at control. In May, 2000, students at Peking University organized two days of mass protests against the university administration, over its inaction when a young female student was raped and murdered. The students accused university officials of trying to suppress news of the slaying, including closing computer bulletin boards. The actions were ineffectual—in fact the Western media used accounts on local web sites to report on the protests—and the administration was forced to take responsibility, organize a memorial service and pressure police to solve the killing. Peking University is a traditional center for and instigator of protests against the government, including those that led to Tiananmen square in 1989, and the protests, which reportedly included more than1,500 students in candlelit marches, were the biggest since Tiananmen (Leicester, 2000 and news agency reports).

FALUN GONG

On the weekend of April 24th, 1999, between ten and 15 thousand people gathered in front of *Zhongnanhai* , the government leadership compound in the center of Beijing, standing or sitting four deep for over a kilometer along the street. They were all followers of the Falun Gong spiritual movement, protesting government criticism and ill-treatment and the banning of Falun Gong materials. The apparent intention was to petition the government and the CCP for official recognition. The protest was entirely peaceful, but nevertheless came as a powerful shock to the government, which was caught completely unawares by a demonstration coordinated through the use of the Internet and wireless telephones (Chase and Mulvenon, 2002: 10 and BBC News reports).

By the end of July the group had been officially outlawed, mass arrests of Falun Gong of key members had taken place and an arrest warrant issued for the founder Li Hongzhi, a former government clerk. By August the government was issuing assurances that the sect had been virtually wiped out (BBC News, 1999). In reality protests by the group have continued, marked by a sophisticated use of modern communications technology which has repeatedly caught the Chinese authorities by surprise.

In March 2002 cable television services were interrupted in the cities of Chnagchun and Songyuan in north-east China. Two videos, one praising Li Hongzhi and the other accusing the authorities of staging the self-immolation of two alleged Falun Gong members in Tiananmen Square the previous year, replaced state television for up to four hours on as many as eight of the 32 channels on Changchun cable (BBC News reports).

The most dramatic incidents took place from June 23 and June 25, when pro-Falun Gong messages briefly cut into transmissions from a Sinosat satellite, during broadcasts of the World Cup, coverage of the celebrations around the fifth anniversary of Hong Kong's return to China and other news. All ten CCTV channels and 10 provincial TV channels were hijacked, apparently from overseas. Unlike the Changchun cable TV incident, the official "Falun Dafa Information Center" did not claim credit for the incident, and in fact suggested it may have been a hoax (Space Daily, July). However the fact the interruptions took place was confirmed, though not apparently how it was done. One result was live coverage of President Jiang Zemin's speech at the swearing-in ceremony for Hong Kong leader Tung Chee-hwa and his new cabinet were scrapped out of fear of interruption (Wang, 2002).

REALITY BITES 2: THE ANOMALOUS SITUATION OF HONG KONG

In October 2000 China's president Jiang Zemin lost his temper before a photo call with Hong Kong's chief executive Tung Chee-hwa at the leadership compound in Beijing, *Zhongnanhai*. The reporters present insisted on asking if Beijing had issued an "imperial edict" prior to Chee-hwa's running for a second term in 2002, making the outcome pre-determined. The problem was that the reporters were from Hong Kong, and did not act with proper deference. Unfortunately for Jiang Zemin the whole scene—of him leaping up and marching towards the cameras, shouting in a confusion of Mandarin, Cantonese and English that the reporters' questions were "naive" and "simplistic"—was broadcast on Hong Kong and Taiwan TV, carried on the front page of Hong Kong newspapers and zipped around the Internet (Gittings, 2000; Gilley, 2000).

Although the scene was not reported in China, it epitomized the anomalous role of Hong Kong, which has continued despite the many predictions prior to the 1997 reversion that Hong Kong would lose any sense of independence or separateness. This is due in no small part to the truth embedded in a persistent traditional Chinese cultural cliché, that refers to the decrease in effective imperial influence the further the distance from the throne. As White and Cheng point out, a corollary to this was the concept that buffer areas, notably Guangdong, allowed the state to absorb ideas from across the ocean while keeping potential interlopers far from the center of power. In that sense Cantonese-speaking China has long served the Chinese state as a place for dealing safely with problems of interface (White and Cheng, 1993). This is a role that Hong Kong has come to epitomize. For the West, it has functioned as a convenient entry point for China, literally and metaphorically, a place where the inexplicable might be understood. As witnessed first hand during this research, while for the Chinese state it may have served as gatekeeper, for the Chinese public Hong Kong is the source of modern design, of high technology, of Western standards of quality, and of comparatively free expression of ideas.

At the same time Hong Kong serves as the lead actor in the play that underlies and constantly counterpoints the official Chinese national drama, the assertion of a regional, Cantonese identity, with the media often providing the stage. A 1985 survey in Guangzhou showed that 85 percent of the city's radios, when turned on, were listening to Hong Kong stations (White and Cheng, ibid: 170). A May 1994 survey of the percentage of TV homes in Guangzhou reached by the major broadcasters was startling, showing for example that the three major Hong Kong channels—including one in English—exceeded the penetration of the national broadcaster CCTV by 24% or more (Goll, 1994: 5).

An AC Nielsen/SRG audience survey at the end of 1995 showed that the top five television programs in Guangzhou were Hong Kong TV broadcasts, with four of the five produced by Television Broadcasts (TVB) (cited in AIM, 1998: 54). Estimates in 1998 were that some 75% (approximately 45 million people) of southern China's Cantonese speakers watched TVB.[32] The programs are popular because of what Hong Kong represents—modern, high tech, prosperous, "free"—and also because they are in Cantonese, the language of the region, not in Mandarin, the language of central control.

Hong Kong was and remains a major irritant in the Chinese government's attempts to control, for example, the media representations of the events in Tiananmen Square. Hong Kong television ran the same images that were shown everywhere in the world—except China—and Hong Kong citizens reacted to those events with a series of giant protest rallies, the biggest in the city's history (White and Cheng, op.cit.: 180). Lee and Chan describe how the Hong Kong press reacted to the unfolding events in Tiananmen, slowly moving from a basically pro-China stance which it had adopted following the Sino-British Joint Declaration in 1984 back to the anti-Communist stance which had typified the Hong Kong media prior to the Joint Declaration, but in an atypically unified fashion. Subsequent attempts by Xinhua to rebuild relationships with the Hong Kong media and refurbish the Beijing government's reputation met with limited success (Lee and Man Chan, 1990: 160,1). As a result the Chinese government became distrustful of the Hong Kong media, seeing the press as a "'rumor mill' conspiring to subvert the socialist system in the motherland" (Chan, Lee and Lee, 1996: 134), and this attitude has persisted in some degree to the present.

At the same time Hong Kong's raison d'etre is to function as a business, finance and trading hub, a role which extends to the media. The reversion of Hong Kong to China in 1997 has accelerated a trend already evident, of a shift in the local economy towards a heavy dependence on the service sector, the category into which the media fall. The manufacturing sector's share of GDP fell precipitously from 24.3% in 1984 to 5.7% in 1999, while services had risen to 85.4% in the same year. Hong Kong was increasingly identified—by transnationals and their advertising agencies—as a part of "Greater China" (Hong Kong, Taiwan and the mainland), a nomenclature and a way of thinking grown more common following China's entry into the WTO, and potentially a boost to Hong Kong's role as a gateway to China (Kim, 2002).

Hong Kong is a natural base for media with an interest in China. STAR TV was made possible by the deep pockets of a Hong Kong billionaire and the ambitions of his son, and continues to be based in Hong Kong, even though the recent achievement of the company in turning a profit is due to its success in India. The most influential television company in southern China is Television Broadcasts (TVB), Hong Kong's leading terrestrial broadcaster, whose signals have long been openly stolen by cable and even broadcast stations throughout Cantonese-speaking China, "topped and tailed" with new advertisements spliced in, and immediately relayed around the region.[33]

The broadcast media business in Hong Kong has been dependent on the policies of the mainland government, which in some respects has limited its growth. China has traditionally banned foreign (including Hong Kong) involvement in its media, and been extremely wary of foreign television content. Accordingly TVB had to sit quietly for years while its broadcast signals were blatantly pirated, with its official protests all made behind the scenes.[34]

This situation changed with China's entry into the WTO in October 2001. Within a month an AOL Time Warner subsidiary, China Entertainment Network (CETV), and Phoenix TV, in which News Corp. had a 38.25 shareholding, signed deals with the SARFT. They both obtained access to channels on the largest cable system in Guangdong province, in exchange for agreeing to carry CCTV's English-language service by cable (AOL) and satellite (News Corp). This was not quite the breakthrough that was heralded in the media: in fact, both channels had been carried on Guangdong cable channels since 1997, in a classic example of the lack of efficacy of television regulation in China. The move did mark a major departure in one important respect, however. Although foreign channels had been carried on Chinese cable before, in a variety of formats, they all had been heavily vetted, while the new permissions allowed for "an unrestricted 24-hour feed" (Howorth, 2001).

News of these agreements overshadowed probably more significant moves by TVB and CCTV. At the end of 2000 TVB obtained an official license from SARFT to downlink its two TVB Mandarin-language satellite channels, TVB8 and *Xing He*, both aimed initially at viewers in Guangdong. This was followed by a "cooperation agreement" with CCTV, whereby the two channels would be accessible via CCTV channels throughout China, in exchange for carrying CCTV channels on TVB DTH platforms in North America, Europe, Australia and Southeast Asia. The Hong Kong company was going national, while CCTV was going global (Stockhouse, 2001).

REALITY BITES 3: BETWEEN A POLICY ROCK AND A FINANCIAL HARD PLACE

The popularity of Hong Kong television programming is also indicative of another challenge to the government: the public's growing demand for more media services. With increasing prosperity, people have more money to spend on culture and entertainment. Indeed, one of the first things many Chinese families, urban and rural alike, buy with their savings is a television set.

As a result television has become big business, on every level. There were only 3.4 million television sets in China in 1978. By 1987, less than ten years later, the number of sets had reached 116 million, with about 20 million produced domestically every year (Hopkins, 1989: 35). By 1992, the number had reached 230 million. By 1994 China was producing 143 million sets a year, of which 4.6 million were for export (Reuters).

By 1998 official estimates for television ownership were set at 317 million, roughly equivalent to one set for every family in China, and the number of regular television viewers was reckoned at 1.1 billion (Chan, 2002). By 2000 national television coverage was estimated at 92% of the total population, equivalent to a potential audience of 1.19 billion (Li, 2002).

The television industry infrastructure grew to match these figures. In 1981 there were 15 television stations in China; in 1982, the figure had doubled, 32 stations reaching an estimated 78 million viewers. By 1994 there were over 700 stations, and television coverage was reaching almost 80 percent of the population: an estimated 948 million people (Gordon, 1995).

Viewing figures are correspondingly impressive. According to audience research by CSM, China's largest audience survey firm, published at the beginning of 2001, TV reaches 95% of all household; urban Chinese watch an average of three hours of TV a day, while 77% of all Chinese watch TV daily; 425 million people, or 37% of the population, watch primetime TV and 163 million viewers watch the CCTV evening news (Deloitte & Touche 2001).

At the same time the government suffers from an increasing inability to invest in the media. Because of the huge costs involved—which are certain to grow vastly more onerous with the advent of digital TV—the government has long had to look for other sources of funding. In 1988, the Party and the government for the first time clearly stated that broadcasting should depend on multiple channels of financing (Zhao, 54).

The result is that today media organizations function like business conglomerates. Externally they invest willy nilly: Beijing TV has majority shareholding in a taxi company and a hotel, for example. Internally, departments are frequently required to generate their own income, and run their own budgets, which in turn are tied in with larger organizational financial objectives.

What this means for lower and middle range staff was spelled out in a 1997 interview with a reporter working for Beijing TV,[35] working on a popular local events program called "City Life." According to her there are three categories of employment at Beijing TV:

*Permanent full-time employees, salaries paid by the MRFT—the holders of the iron rice bowls. No new employees have been hired in this category since 1993.
*Fixed staff, employees working on one-year fixed renewable contracts. Salaries are paid by the department. Employees hold a "blue card," allowing them free access anywhere in the station.
*Assignment staff. This is a category for freelancers, usually hired for a specific production, and paid by the production department responsible. Such workers have restricted access to the station's facilities.

Each department is regarded as self-supporting. Her show is 15 minutes long. She is obliged to "attract" a quota of five 15 second advertisements per show, towards a total target income for the program of Y170,000. Only after the target is attained does the station contribute to the costs of the program.

Media organizations are in the same situation as other work units. In Pekin University, the most prestigious university in the country, the government supplies less than 20% of the funds needed to run it. Salary levels are so low that each department is compelled to make a major effort to find additional, external sources of funding. One professor interviewed for this book said the international politics department to which he belonged had two full-time faculty who did nothing except try to raise funds, with sometimes disastrous results. In the early 1990s the department had set up a Chinese traditional medicine shop, which went bankrupt.[36] Anecdotal evidence from a number of different sources, including two hospitals and a building construction company, supported this picture.

These examples were from work units whose major source of capital is intellectual, the professional skills of its employees. For them, a corollary for having to scramble to keep their income at a reasonable level is an increasing sense of independence from any kind of central control. If the central government does not have the wherewithal to pay the piper, it does not have the right to call the tune.

Ways of measuring the extent of this change are difficult, in particular as applied to the content of what is aired, though there can be little doubt about the nature of the transformation. Hunan is one of China's poorest provinces, but also home to one of its most successful TV stations, including a highly popular variety show called "Happy Camp," and a talk show called "Talk It Easy," which looked at subjects sufficiently controversial in the Chinese context—such as homosexuality and the rapidly widening gap between the new rich and the poor—that the government had it pulled off the air. In an interview with a BBC reporter the station chief explained his success:

> Thirty years ago we only aired government propaganda and old movies. . . . Now we actually have to entertain people. Otherwise, advertisers don't buy space and we don't make money . . . It's very competitive, but much better these days. We decide what we want to air. Our programmes are popular so we're doing quite well (Williams, 2002).

In sum, while the CCP is able to intimidate or quarantine intellectuals and journalists, as described by Link (1992), attempts to manage the media structure itself are a lot less successful, thanks to its complexity and diversity. Enforcement of policies made in Beijing in distant places like Yunnan or poor places like Changsha, Hunan TV's base, has always been a challenge. After almost 15 years of commercialization and decentralization, both made necessary by the financial constraints on the central government, the challenge is greater and the obstacles to successful control much higher. This is a situation of flux, and provides the backdrop to the current circumstance of CCTV in China.

CCTV

The theoretical task of CCTV, as indicated clearly by the Chinese Communist Party Central Committee, is "to agitate and educate the whole Party, the whole army, and the people of all nationalities in the country to contribute to the socialist construction and to build socialist spiritual and material civilizations" (218: from China Journalism Yearbook, 1982).

Until the 1980s CCTV could follow such directives without much attention to whether the TV audience had any interest in "socialist spiritual and material civilizations." All revenues came from the public purse, which was controlled by the government, through the MRFT, with the CCP's

Propaganda Department given oversight of matters of content. Simply put, CCTV was a state institution charged with a clear ideological mission.

By the mid 1990s, that situation had changed out of recognition, as indicated above. One estimate for 1996 arrived at an average 50% of national television revenue as derived from advertising, and the percentage has certainly risen since. In the case of commercial stations like Beijing TV, direct income from the government is close to zero: at any rate, far less than the 5.7% broadcast advertising tax that the station has to pay to the national government (EIU, 1996: 6).[37] CCTV has been similarly impacted, to the point now where it is almost totally dependent on revenues from commercials, and pays far more to the government than it receives in subsidies.[38]

> In the year 2000, CCTV was able to raise 5.5 billion yuan or US$662.5 million while the government contribution was a mere 30 million yuan or US$ 3.61 million. Indeed, CCTV has been paying more in taxes and for philanthropic efforts than it used to receive from the government in income. Today government sources supply only 0.5% of total CCTV funds (Li, 2002: 18.9)

This radical change in the financial base of CCTV has caused an equally basic shift in employment practices. Li Xiaoping, who is a former executive producer and program director with CCTV explains that the famous "iron rice bowl," known to academics as the tenure system, has disappeared.

> The majority of lower and middle range staff are employed on short-term contracts with no tenure. Their income is primarily pegged to the quantity and quality of their output. They have to work hard to achieve their program quotas (ibid: 19).

Another major change to the status quo of CCTV that has occurred since the 1980s is the loss of its privileged status as the station that all local broadcast stations and cable systems *had* to carry. In particular there was an absolute obligation to give a prime position to CCTV-1, the oldest channel, and the main conduit for news broadcasts, which remain in effect the CCP's most important distribution conduit for propaganda. In theory therefore CCTV-1 should reach all television households, but survey results published in 1998 showed that this was not the case even in Beijing(where it was 97%) or Shanghai (91%),while in Guangzhou the percentage of viewers able to see CCTV-1 was a low as 60%, an apparent reflection of the preference for Cantonese-language programming.[39]

This situation is a matter of ongoing concern to the MRFT and its successor the SARFT, not only because of the key role that CCTV-1 plays in relaying the government's views and priorities, but also because of the threat it poses to CCTV's position as a cash cow, precisely because of its unique ability to deliver to advertisers a huge, stable, national audience (see below). Lynch cites the MRFT minister's blaming county-level stations and small-scale work-unit stations (the lowest levels in rural and urban areas respectively) for the problem. The reason is that most of these systems have very limited carrying capacity, and prefer to carry more entertaining fare, often pirated videos and usually ones of a pornographic nature (Lynch, 1999: 143,4). However, it does appear that the problem is frequently at a higher level than this: the stations that are periodically fined for carrying satellite transmissions without authorization, for example, seem to be mainstream urban systems.

CCTV has attempted to diversify its offerings in order to make them more attractive. There is another free-to-air channel, CCTV-2, a hybrid offering business, cultural and educational programming. A satellite-distributed pay-TV package provides one free-to-air channel CCTV-3 and four pay channels (5, 6, 7 and 8) which have been offered since January, 1996. The 'magnet' in the package is CCTV-5, a sports channel. CCTV-6 is a movie channel, 7 is a hybrid science/military/agricultural and children's channel, 8 is an arts and entertainment channel: only 5, sports, and 6, movies, have been able to build good-sized audiences. CCTV-4 and 9 are aimed at international audiences, the former broadcasting primarily in Chinese, the latter primarily in English.

Because CCTV controls programming and production, it has financial power and has long been closely guarded by the MRFT/SARFT, in a relationship that bears direct comparison with that between NHK and the former Communications Ministry. The president of CCTV is traditionally also a Vice Minister in the ministry, and the symbiotic relationship is a cause of resentment by Chinese terrestrial and cable operators, typified by the manner in which the then-MRFT made it mandatory for cable operators to offer the CCTV pay-TV package when it was introduced at the end of 1995. These operators, some of whom are very large, are in direct competition with CCTV not only for advertising but also for programming.

It is this context that attempts by foreign media interests to enter the Chinese market must be seen. While limited access to select regional markets may be permitted, there is nothing in China's WTO agreement that requires the opening of the media to foreign competition, and it seems plain that CCTV's monopoly on national broadcasting is inviolable.[40] Again, this is not simply because of CCTV's propaganda role, but also due to its revenue-generating—and tax paying—capacity. In 2000 CCTV earned $640 million in advertising revenue, a 16% increase over 1999. This business is so profitable that the rights to the most desirable advertising slots are auctioned off every November. The 2001 auction for the 230 most attractive slots in the 2002 broadcast year pulled in $317 million, a 20% increase over the previous year. The highest bidders were drug companies and liquor firms (Mo, 2001).

The overwhelming priority for CCTV, and presumably for its political masters, is to maintain its position as the only channel able to reach a national audience, a vital capacity for the government to have at its disposal. Chan describes the government as having moved from notions of propaganda to a more sophisticated concept of hegemony in its attitude towards the media, partly as a result of lessons learned from Tiananmen Square in 1989, which if nothing else was a public relations debacle on an international scale. In his view the priorities shifted throughout the 1990s, as

> the Party became more skilled at manufacturing consent through the official media, like CCTV (Chan, 2002). This view is given some reinforcement by Li Xiaoping, a former executive producer and program director in the Current Affairs Department of CCTV, who is frank in acknowledging that the media in China see their role as helping the government secure "a stable social order" (2002: 29).

At the same time Zhao describes a CCTV forced to meet the challenge posed by local television stations, in particular local news broadcasts, in addition to satellite, cable, and commercial interests moving into the national market. The result can be akin to horse trading: apparently the Shanghai Broadcasting Bureau was allowed to establish two "Shangahi East" stations as a trade-off for not putting Shanghai Television programs on a satellite, which would have posed a greater threat to the national monopoly of CCTV than any other provincial station, a prospect that was mentioned in several interviews for this book (Zhao, 165).

Chapter Five

Case History 3—Hong Kong and STAR TV

> The conflicting desire of satellite-based television—on the one hand, to maximize audiences, and at the same time to be paid for the audience it reaches . . . (Parker, 63)

ESTABLISHMENT

In February, 1984 Hughes Aircraft used the space shuttle to attempt to launch a giant Westar VI satellite, but failed to get it into the correct orbit. In November, 1984 the crew of the space shuttle Discovery successfully salvaged the satellite, which was then reconditioned and sold at a remarkably low price to Michael Johnson, an entrepreneur who proposed selling transponder space on the satellite to small countries unable to afford their own satellite programs.

In the event the satellite was sold on to a Hong Kong consortium consisting of Hutchison Telecommunications (controlled by Hong Kong's richest tycoon, Li Ka-shing); the British telecommunications company Cable & Wireless; and the foremost foreign investment institution of the PRC government, China International Trust and Investment Corporation (CITIC). Each took equal shareholding in a new project called AsiaSat.

The reason for this unusual assortment of partners seems to reflect the fact that all had been looking at starting a satellite communications company in Asia. In this view CITIC was the lead partner, representing the interests of the Chinese State Council, Hutchison represented access to Hong Kong finance and entrepreneurship, and Cable & Wireless provided the technical expertise. The idea of refurbishing Westar VI and then using it for a pan-Asia television concept seems to have originated with Johnson, who worked as a senior advisor to Hutchison Telecommunications at the time of Asiasat's launch.[1]

AsiaSat proposed to use a relatively cheap Chinese Long March 3 launcher to return the satellite to space, but immediately run afoul of sanctions imposed by the U.S. Government after Tiananmen Square, that effectively barred the transfer of high-tech equipment or know-how to the PRC. It took a presidential waiver of the sanctions to enable the launch to take place, from a Chinese military base in Sichuan in April, 1990 (Riley, 1990: 1).

Following the launch the billionaire owner of Hutchison Whampoa, Li Ka-shing, booked 12 of the satellites 24 C-Band transponders for the exclusive use of another branch of his empire, HutchVision, which controlled a newly created satellite broadcasting company, STAR (Satellite Television Asia Region) TV. STAR TV was run by Li Kashing's youngest son, Richard Li, at that time 24 years old. As part of its booking HutchVision obtained exclusive rights to use the satellite for international broadcasts. This was a major coup because at that time Asiasat-1, as it came to be known, was the only satellite with the power and the positioning to offer true pan-Asian coverage (South China Morning Post, 1991). It also secured profitability for Asiasat, which at the time of its launch apparently had no customers.[2]

Asiasat-1's signals had twin orientations: a northern footprint centered on China, but also covering Taiwan, all of Korea, and most of Japan; and a southern footprint focusing on Thailand but covering most of South Asia, including Singapore, Malaysia, Vietnam, India, Pakistan, Afghanistan, Iran and the Arab countries of the Gulf region. Altogether 38 countries were covered by the Asiasat-1 signals, from the Russian Far East to Indonesia, and from Egypt to Japan. An estimated three billion people lived in the area of coverage.

Asiasat-1 was not intended for the broadcast of signals for general reception, but for point-to-point transmission, in particular to cable head ends for redistribution. Because of the comparative weakness of its signal, receiving dishes were large, from 2.4 to 8 meters in diameter (Kishore, 1994), and expensive, beyond the economic reach of most Asian households.[3] This point is key, as the major initial impact of STAR TV was on countries with advanced cable systems, such as Taiwan and mainland China, or on places like India where the "cable wallahs" took the signal and created neighborhood systems by stringing their own cable from street utility pole to house to tree to house. The signal was unscrambled and "free to air," a key point in the early history of STAR TV.[4]

EARLY DAYS

The business plan for STAR TV was simple, and built on some untested assumptions. The concept was to use satellite to broadcast English-language channels across Asia, thus creating a regional audience of affluent, well-educated consumers, for which advertisers would pay handsomely.

The untested assumptions included the notion that Asian consumers were discontented with the usually very limited viewing choices on offer at the time, coupled with the supposition that "there is a strong link between the number of dissatisfied TV viewers who purchase VCRs and the number of potential subscribers to satellite TV and/or cable services" (Kishore, op.cit: 16). As VCR penetration was very high in Asia—reckoned at 70% in Hong Kong for example—this was a reassuring supposition.

Another notion was the belief in a new, "stateless" middle class in Asia, an international elite who would represent the perfect arranged marriage to build up an advertiser base for a commercial television operation, introducing a select audience to advertisers looking for a group of rich consumers. STAR's vice president for marketing and distribution specifically identified the top 5% of Asians. STAR's estimate was that there would be 400 million middle class consumers by 2001, a simple straight line projection made from the limited data available on Asian income levels in the early 1990s, but given credibility by the economic boom which had started to spread across Asia in the 1980s.

The STAR TV signals were "free-to-air," in other words they were not encrypted and were available for anyone with a satellite dish to receive. STAR's revenue was based on advertising, which in turn required a belief in that supra-national pan-Asian market. This proved a difficult sell and STAR ended up offering huge package discounts, while offering a share of future revenues from the company in order to secure programming. Effectively, it was running on barter.

> On the advertising side, they got this founder viewer thing going. I think we sold over 70 founder/viewer packages. The basic package was, you pay US$2 million now, up front, and we give you two years of cheap advertising, on all these channels, with all these spots, and companies bought that. That provided a good cash flow for the initial couple of years. At the same time the deal on the programming side was largely, hey, we can't pay you now, because we're not making any money, we'll share revenue with you up to this point, and from this point on we'll guarantee you these revenues from the business.[5]

The initial lack of a subscriber base and therefore any kind of guaranteed income also made it difficult to attract program suppliers, in particular news. CNN refused to join the service for that reason. In desperation Richard Li personally approached the BBC, and persuaded them to put forward their plans for a global TV service, BBC Worldwide, by, in effect, subsidizing its launch. Although the BBC broadcasts were initially only in English and never built a big audience, they lent the fledgling service a level of prestige which was needed, especially in what eventually turned out to be STAR's best market—India. Again, there was no elaborate planning involved.

> We were looking for opportunities, we were looking for partners, and we found STAR TV, and made a news channel for them. It was something that gave us a kick start because it worked, particularly worked in Southeast Asia and in India. We didn't have a business plan. We were presented with a STAR TV business plan, and that seemed like a good starting point. We were aware that we were in the money-making business. There was no point in running a news service if people weren't going to watch and pay for it. We had no government money at all. The BBC leans over backwards to avoid cross-subsidy, so we have to pay for everything we do.[6]

STAR TV was launched with remarkable speed. The first successful satellite uplink was on April 2, 1991, from an improvised studio, using a temporary uplink facility. On May 15 a preview channel was launched, and used as a regional sales tool. On August 26 the first regular broadcast channel started up, a sports channel, followed by MTV, Star Plus (a movie channel), the BBC in November and a Chinese Mandarin channel.

Former STAR TV employees who had played key roles in those early days all agreed that there was no plan: "we were making it up as we went along." They were also aware that they were skating the borders of illegality. David Manion, STAR TV's distribution manager, recalls how he got the job.

> I presented to them (the senior management) for an hour, a distribution plan. And Robert Chan, then Vice-President said, "Is this legal in any of these countries?" I said "Very unlikely." He said, "How are we going to deal with that?" I said, "We're not." So there was this pregnant pause. I said, "Frankly, if you want to deal with that, you'd better hire 50 lawyers and prepare for a siege, you know, it'll be ten years before you get anything." So they said, oh, OK then, and I got the job.[7]

Immediately after the preview channel was available for downloading, Manion toured Asia trying to build interest in the STAR channels.

> My strategy was still evolving as we went along, but what it turned into was you go there, you put the business proposition to the guy—it was a

> wonderful business proposition for the cable operator, it's all free, take it for as long as you want, you don't have to pay me anything, I'm your friend, call me when you need me, you need equipment, sure we'll give you equipment (Ibid.)

For the most part Manion and his colleagues ignored government channels, and went straight to the cable system operators. In many cases, these were shadowy operations in the extreme, as illustrated in the first country he visited, Taiwan.

> We'd arranged for a meeting with the illegal operators of cable systems in Taiwan—who were the mafia—and the equipment suppliers. We were presenting at a hotel, explaining the technology of STAR TV, to encourage the export of technology from Taiwan—this was the cover story—and all of the operators turned up at my suite at the hotel instead of downstairs. I arrived at 8 o'clock in the evening, we'd booked the Presidential suite, got one of these guys to put a dish on the roof, and make an illegal feed into the TV there . . . There was this knock on the door, there were four guys outside, they looked like the only thing missing was the violin case, broad shoulders, pin-striped suits, and they said "Mr. Manion?" and I said yes, and they shouldered their way into the room, and I thought what have I got into this time? In Taiwan, they were going to take it anyway. They were stealing everything in the sky, and they weren't going to pay for anything, so I said, please, be my guest—what else are you going to do? (Ibid.)

It was a formula that was very well received, especially in India, where most of the cable operators were in the cities, and the majority had a maximum of 100 households connected. These were the cable wallahs, whose technology was basic in the extreme: at the end of the cable was a VCR running movies. When STAR TV came in, they simply had to obtain some equipment, connect it to the head ends, advertise this new access to the modern world, and expand. STAR TV raised their credibility, and their revenues.[8] In exchange STAR was able to achieve its first aim, to rapidly build up the number of "able-to-view" homes.

The exceptional speed with which STAR was able to launch and have programs to offer was a key to its initial success in building viewership. The opposition when it came was from other vested interests. In Hong Kong for example TVB lobbied hard to have STAR TV banned from providing Cantonese-language programming for local cable distribution, while in India the cinema owners vigorously fought back and succeeded having STAR banned in effect in Bengal, and came close to stopping it in Madras. This opposition compelled Manion to curtail his first, highly successful tour of India.

> I got a phone call from Calcutta, saying that if we went there we were likely to be arrested, because the cinema association in that area, in Bengal, had seen the threat to their business and had decided to take it up with the government, and had got the police on their side, and there was all sorts of nasty stuff going on.

With the exception of Singapore, and later Malaysia, the STAR team was able to avoid having to deal with actions by the local government to block the reception of their signal, in part because the STAR channels were subject to heavy self-censorship, to anticipate objections of cultural insensitivity. According to Manion and Sahai, the problem was not the BBC and its news. The key concerns were mainly sex, violence, culture.[9]

STAR IN CHINA

The speed with which STAR was introduced had negative consequences as well, as the small staff had difficulty checking on how the new channels were being received. In China Ringo Leung, a senior engineer in charge of the technical support team, dealing with questions such as how to pick up the signal, where to buy equipment, etc., found that only the equipment sellers really knew the market.

It is important to note that Asiasat-1's other major customers were all Chinese. Following its launch in 1989, AsiaSat-1 biggest client was CCTV, which primarily used the satellite to get its expanded menu of programs to cable head operators across the nation. STARTV used the same satellite: so one extra twist of the tuning dial, and the operator suddenly had STAR TV available—modern, popular and free. In addition to CCTV, Yunnan TV and GuizhouTV were already using the satellite before STAR launched its actual programming. When the STAR Chinese channel launched in October, 1991, it was easy for the local cable operators to find it, without even knowing where it was coming from.

Two months after the Chinese channel launch Ringo Leung went to a home electronics exhibition in Chengdu, in Sichuan province, to promote the new service. He was amazed to find the square outside the exhibition hall full of dish antennas, all switched to STAR channels received from Asiasat-1. Everyone he met was very impressed by STAR—even by the promotional material.

Working from installation data he learnt that equipment manufacturers could not keep up with demand for reception equipment, all of which was being run through SMATV systems. Local work units were using the availability of STAR as a way of improving their appeal, as they felt under constant pressure to upgrade their entertainment offerings, and STAR was an easy answer. The primary interest was in the Chinese channel (mostly old dramas from the ATV channel in Hong Kong) followed by Sports and MTV. Few were interested in the BBC or Star Plus (the movie channel). They were both in English, and it was assumed they were not intended for China. Leung's best estimate from that experience was that there were probably already one million viewer homes in China, only a matter of months after STAR's launch.

Largely by luck, STAR's timing was perfect. 1992 is generally taken as the take-off year for the phenomenal growth of cable in China. The cable operators were avid for new channels, and STAR TV was the perfect bait to attract new subscribers.

For STAR, Sichuan and Yunnan in southwest China were to prove the best start-up markets. Both had large-scale, wealthy industries (for example, Yunnan is the home to China's highly lucrative tobacco industry), which can be equated with large-scale work units—and cable systems. According to Leung, in 1991 one enterprise alone in Sichuan already had a 500,000 subscriber-strong cable network. In particular Sichuan was also the center for the biggest military bases in China, all of which offered cable, and was traditionally one of the most politically independent provinces. It was a place that payed little attention to Beijing edicts.

Interestingly Leung found that Guangdong at that time was not good for STAR. Generally the south was poorer in cable installation, and was already openly pirating terrestrial signals from Hong Kong. Many of the factories in the area were joint ventures, run on the cheap and averse to offering the workers extra benefits like cable systems.[10]

STAR IN INDIA

For the Hong Kong entrepreneurs behind STAR TV, the rich Chinese middle class to be found throughout Asia always represented their dream audience. Describing the original target market, STAR's executive vice president for marketing and distribution alluded to an audience for whom a satellite dish would be another kind of status symbol. "We are talking about the top 5% of Asians, who travel frequently and have in common their money, their Mercedes and the English language" (Burton, 1991: 50). This was the 'Amex market,' the rich middle class. In Leung's view, the dream was precisely that: the reality was that STAR appealed to the lower middle class, by offering them a cheaper entertainment source. A satellite TV system cost about the same as a VCR, but there was no need to buy cassettes, it was free and available around the clock.

Partly because of this basic error in attempting to define their audience, STAR's management was very slow to recognize what in fact was (and still is) STAR's best market: India. According to Manion and Sahai, it took many months to win the argument to invest resources in developing a Hindi channel, in collaboration with Shubash Chandra, a well-connected entrepreneur. The result was the Zee channel, an immediate success and a door opener for other STAR channels.

> The impact of STAR was heaviest in India. Initially the most popular of the STAR channels was Star Plus, consisting mostly of soap operas from the U.S., and then came World Cup cricket in February of 1992. That's what really got it going. You have to realize, there all the movies were already MTV, you could see how that would fit perfectly. The excitement level was 100 times what it was in any other market.[11]

ENTER MURDOCH

In July 1993, Richard Li and Rupert Murdoch reached an agreement whereby Murdoch's News Corporation bought 63.6% of STAR TV for $525 million. The deal was remarkable for several reasons: STAR TV had never made a profit, and there was little ground for optimism that any would emerge soon; and just two years before Murdoch had been effectively bankrupt. In a sense the deal was a precursor to the kind of sale that was to become commonplace in the "new" economy of the late 1990s, where economic fundamentals seemed to lose their importance.

Following near collapse in early 1991, Murdoch had been able to remake News Corporation as a blue chip company by selling some stock and assets and by the expedient of retiring his high interest bank debt (variously estimated at £4 billion, $7.6 billion and $9.5 billion) for bond covenants, effectively substituting long-term debt for short-term, and building a buffer between himself and discontented shareholders (Davis, 1995: 25). Once this operation was complete he was able in remarkably short order to embark on expanding his empire again.[12]

The rationale for the purchase of STAR TV was at once simple and complex. The simple explanation was that Murdoch avowedly intended to build a global TV network, and to do this he needed a means of reaching an Asian television audience (Greenwald,1993: 64). In Murdoch's view there was a straightforward economic logic underlying this.

> "We're not going global because we want to or because of any megalomania, but because it's really necessary. . . . The costs are so enormous

> today that you really need to have worldwide revenues to cover them. If you're making films or making television programs, you've really got very little chance of making your money back just in the United States" (Davis, op.cit.: 23).

Purchasing STAR TV, in other words, would offer a guaranteed platform for the product of his Fox Broadcasting network and for 20th Century Fox films. In addition, controlling a satellite platform with a major hold on a market results in leverage, the power to extract favors from a programmer who wants to use the satellite. By being a gatekeeper on a major information distribution system in Asia, Murdoch could get advantages in the United States and elsewhere (Auletta,1995(2): 82). Finally, the acquisition of Star was part of News Corporation's long-term plans to build a global satellite television network.[13] The exact nature of that network has changed with time, currently illustrated by the lengthy and ultimately successful purchase of DirecTV, the satellite broadcaster unit of Hughes Electronics (owned by General Motors), in 2003.[14]

The model remains the same, however, and seems to be one of 'gatekeeper.' Rather than attempt to create one unified 'brand,' like CNN, the aim is to position News Corp or a subsidiary like STAR TV as the inevitable gate for information to flow through, regardless of its content. And as it flows, revenue is earned.

There was also an element of hubris in the purchase of STAR, the belief that News Corp had the management expertise and the programming resources needed to have STAR TV follow the course of British Sky Broadcasting (BSkyB) and, ultimately, of Murdoch's investments in the United States. Murdoch had invested heavily in developing BSkyB, which did not make a profit for years, only to become eventually one of the major sources of cash flow in the News Corporation. In 1986 he had paid $1.6 billion for the Metromedia group of television stations at a time when the conventional wisdom was that broadcast television was in terminal decline. He had then gone on and developed the stations into the Fox network, the first successful challenge ever to the monopoly of NBC, CBS and ABC (Farhi, 1995).

At the same time, STAR TV had been only one entry point to Asian television targeted by Murdoch, and in fact was his second choice. In June 1993, News Corp had reached an agreement to buy 22% of Television Broadcasts (TVB), the premier broadcaster not only in Hong Kong but in the surrounding region. This was seen as a direct challenge to STAR TV's ambitions in China. TVB regularly captured 80% of the TV audience in Hong Kong, was conservatively estimated to reach an additional 20 million Cantonese-speaking viewers in southern China, had ambitions plans to start broadcasting in Mandarin in Taiwan, and was part of a consortium with CNN, ESPN (Capital Cities/ABC), HBO (Time Warner) and the Australian Broadcasting Corporation, which had tentative plans for satellite broadcasting on Apstar, a Chinese rival to Asiasat (Twiston Davies, 1993: 7).

But TVB's biggest asset was generally seen to be its ownership of the world's largest library of Chinese-language television programs, reputedly over 100,000 hours. In the event the investment in TVB was thwarted by Hong Kong's television authority, which refused to allow Murdoch an exemption to a regulation barring foreigners from owning more than 10% of any Hong Kong station. One month later Murdoch bought a controlling interest in STAR TV.

At the time Murdoch's move was pictured as being part of a rush among the world largest media powers to grab pieces of the massive Asian market. The deal represented the first major investment by a western media conglomerate into the non-western market (outside Japan). Murdoch and Ted Turner were the most famous of the new breed of international media moguls, riding a wave of multinational capital which was focused on Asia. They were drawn to markets which until the early 1990s were regarded as impregnable (China, Japan) or lacking in the level of income to justify the investment (Malaysia, Thailand).

The purchase of STAR TV thus represented a move that had been anticipated, if not coming from Murdoch and News Corp., then from some of the other contenders. Those most often cited were Time Warner, Turner Broadcasting (CNN), Capital Cities/ABC, Dow Jones (Wall Street Journal), Tele-Communications Inc. (TCI—at that time the largest cable TV company in the United States) and GE (NBC). There was a perception that the time was right, the television audience fruit ripe for the picking. And what a fruit: a market of up to three billion people, over half the world's population.

The extremely rapid spread of cable systems in some parts of the region, and the runaway success (in terms of viewership) of STAR TV gave some credence to the mantra, often to be found in the reporting of the period, that Asia represented a marketplace starved for innovative television programming. According to STAR TV's original marketing plan there were 2.4 channels per country in Asia, and most of them were government-owned and boring. There was a sense that Murdoch had seized the moment, encapsulated in an interview given shortly after the acquisition, when he said: "The regulators are getting more and more powerless in every country as a satellite comes in, as cable comes. They just have more choices for everybody. The regulators who used to say only one program could be seen by their people are just being swamped by technology" (Mermigas, 1993: 1).

The regulators were not unaware of what was going on. By 1994 both Singapore and Malaysia had bans on the private ownership of satellite dishes, while the Japanese government kept heavily regulatory restrictions on the domestic cable industry, effectively making it impossible for local cable stations to rebroadcast the STAR TV signals. Prime Minister Mahathir Mohammed of Malaysia explicitly questioned why Murdoch had paid "such a fantastic price for a network that has never shown any profit" and wondered whether this was from a desire "to control the news that we are going to receive" in Asia. News Corp's official response was that the intention was to make STAR TV a service that "Asian families can enjoy in their homes" and one that Asian governments would consider both "friendly and useful" (Shenon, 1993: D1).

POLITICAL DIMENSIONS

In fact Murdoch had long been acutely aware of the political dimensions of the media, and of how to use the power they represent to advance his commercial ends. He used his popular working-class newspaper, the *Sun,* to support Prime Minister Margaret Thatcher, in the 1979 British general election, for example. In return the Conservative government overruled a recommendation of a referral to the Monopolies and Mergers Commission when he moved to purchase the *Times* and the *Sunday Tines* in 1981, and gave him massive police protection when he successfully broke the power of the British newspaper print unions in 1986 [Auletta, 1995(2)].

At the same time, in the course of building up his UK press and television holdings he was never referred to the Monopolies and Mergers Commission, a fate which happened to many of his rivals. The 1990 UK Broadcasting Bill introduced the concept of a 'non-domestic satellite service,' apparently designed to free him from restrictions on media cross-ownership. He avoided US laws which prohibit foreign nationals from controlling American TV stations by becoming a US citizen immediately before closing the deal to buy Metromedia, the foundation of Fox TV. This should have put him at odds with similar Australian legislation restricting holdings in media by foreign nationals, but an amendment was introduced applying the law only to future foreign investors, neatly excluding Murdoch, but including the Canadian Conrad Black when he subsequently tried to buy the Fairfax newspaper group (Davis, 1993: 5).

In addition to this long history of avoiding regulatory hurdles, Murdoch used to go on record acknowledging the great influence the media can have over politics and society. In 1988, two years before the fall of the Berlin wall, Murdoch had predicted that television would help open up

Eastern Europe. In June 1989 he had watched the events of Tiananmen Square on television, calling it "an extraordinary moment in history, to know what was happening in China was happening in part because we were all watching it" (Shawcross, 1994).

THE SPEECH

In this context, the speech he gave in London, in September, 1993, three months after he had taken control of STAR TV, was not unusual.[15] He recalled that George Orwell's *1984* had depicted a world where technology, in particular television, had been used by an all-powerful government to control the people. In fact, he said, the opposite was true. Fax machines, direct dial telephones and satellite broadcasting were examples of how people could bypass state control. The consequences were clear:

> Advances in the technology of telecommunications have proved an unambiguous threat to totalitarian regimes everywhere. Fax machines enable dissidents to bypass state-controlled print media; direct-dial telephony makes it difficult for a state to control interpersonal voice communications. And satellite broadcasting makes it possible for information-hungry residents of many closed societies to bypass state controlled television. In short, the march of telecommunications technology has been a key factor in the enormous spread of freedom that is the major distinguishing characteristic of recent years [Auletta 1995 (2), and Shawcross 1994].

The speech had immediate repercussions, as it drew fresh attention to the political dimensions of satellite TV. In early October of the same year, the Chinese government took action, introducing State Council Decree No. 129 ("Provisions on the Control of Ground Receiving Installations for Satellite Television"), which effectively introduced a licensing system for the operation of satellite signal receiving equipment, and had the theoretical effect of banning private ownership of satellite dishes.

The media at the time depicted the action as a direct reaction to Murdoch's speech, a near impossible feat in light of the extreme slowness with which the Chinese government usually proceeds in developing new legislation. It seems more likely that the law was a reaction to the known impact of STAR in China. One of the many unexpected consequences of the establishment of STAR TV was the application for the first time of Western market measuring approaches to the Chinese television audiences, so that by 1993 STAR was already claiming that almost five million "information-hungry" Chinese households could receive its five channels.

It also seems unlikely that the speech was specifically intended as a challenge to the Chinese authorities. On the contrary, at the same time as the Chinese government ban was introduced, Murdoch was selling most of his half share in the immensely profitable *South China Morning Post,* which was a firm supporter of the last British governor of Hong Kong, Chris Patten. Murdoch explained the reasons frankly "We don't want to find ourselves in conflict with Beijing unnecessarily. We certainly don't want STAR to be shut down because of the opinions of some of our newspaper editors" (Shawcross, op.cit.).

In April 1994, the BBC was removed from the northern beam of STAR TV, that covering China. At the time, there was again much media speculation that Murdoch was reacting to Chinese pressure. This story has taken on a life it its own, always referred to as fact in any description of Murdoch's dealings with the Chinese government. The actual reasons are less clear. The senior BBC executive in charge of developing BBC Worldwide flatly denied in an interview for this research that the BBC was aware of any pressure from the Chinese government to "get rid" of the BBC.

> On April 1st, 1994, after Rupert Murdoch had taken over from Li Ka Shing, he moved us from the northern beam. Why he did this is very interesting: I hope you don't fall into the trap of saying that he did so because the Chinese government put him under pressure. Because it's not true. Up to that point there had been no complaint by the Chinese about the BBC news channel. No public complaint at all.[16]

What does seem to have been the case was that Murdoch had not carried out due diligence before buying STAR TV, and once in control of the company found the possibility of profitability to be a lot more distant than his early predictions had indicated. One result was a series of changes in top management. Another was an attempt to start scrambling some of the STAR TV signals and promote them as subscription channels, to offer a mix of free-to-air and PAY-TV services, a model that had worked well in Britain, but which quickly proved unpopular in Asia (Twiston Davies, 1994). A third was a rigorous attempt to air broadcasting that would literally pay. The BBC signal, for example was replaced by Chinese-language films. In the view of the BBC official, the BBC was removed for strictly commercial reasons, and "Chinese pressure" used as a convenient excuse for STAR TV to break its contract with the BBC.

Murdoch himself presented the decision to remove the BBC in terms of a need to placate the Chinese authorities, which detested the BBC for its independence and refusal to cater to local "sensitivities." In an interview given the year after removing the BBC, Murdoch tried to explain his decision.

> "The BBC was driving them nuts," Murdoch says. "It's not worth it." The Chinese government is "scared to death of what happened in Tiananmen Square. . . . The truth is—and we Americans don't like to admit it—that authoritarian countries can work. . . . The best thing you can do in China is engage the Chinese and wait. . . . I'm not saying they're right. . . . We're not proud of (the BBC) decision. It was the only way." (Auletta, 1995(2): 84–5)

The BBC had previously been attacked by the then Ministry of Radio, Film and TV for showing library footage of the 1989 Tiananmen Square massacre around the time of its anniversary in June, but the specific reason the BBC was driving them nuts was a documentary on Chairman Mao Zedong which had been shown in Britain.[17] This is a wide-ranging critique of the Mao era, and features interviews with a number of his entourage, including Mao's personal physician, Dr. Li Zhisui, who described Mao's prodigious appetite for sex with young women. The documentary depicted the atmosphere of vicious intrigue and rampant paranoia which reigned among his entourage, "where great visions became father to great crimes"(Li, 1994: xiv). At the time the field research for this book was carried out there was a common rumor that Sir Run Run Shaw, owner of TVB and well connected in Beijing, had bought up the Asian rights to the documentary to forestall the possibility of the program being shown in Asia.

For Murdoch, there was a straight commercial logic behind the removal of the BBC—the need to pull STAR TV out of the red. It had become clear that programming had to be localized. The original rationale behind STAR had been that the new, rich Asia was spearheaded by a cosmopolitan elite prepared to watch English-language programming. Being wealthy and well educated, they would constitute a very desirable market for advertisers. But Murdoch soon abandoned the idea of a pan-Asia channel, first by clearly splitting the content of the northern beam (aimed at China) and the southern (focused on India). Localization became the new gospel, as explained by one of a succession of new chief executives of STAR TV appointed by Murdoch.

> We are customising our programming into local languages. . . . We now see ourselves as a mass-market communicator rather than a network targeting the top 5 percent of the population. (Twiston Davies, 1994)

As a business strategy, entry to the Chinese market was essential, as it had been in Richard Li's original planning for STAR TV. The BBC was dropped in order to make room for more commercial programming. It may also have been jettisoned as part of a general attempt to win favor with the Chinese authorities, but not in response to any direct pressure from them.[18] Murdoch told his biographer William Shawcross as much: "There is no answer to it. They say it's a cowardly way. But we said in order to get in there and get accepted, we'll cut the BBC out" (Higgins, 1998: 5).

PHOENIX TV

The controversy generated by the removal of the BBC, the enactment of State Council Decree No. 129 and moves by other governments in the region to control satellite TV, and the numerous difficulties encountered in trying to introduce subscription charges to a service whose major selling point had been the fact that is was "free to air" and had been earning 95% of its revenues from advertising, all contributed to a difficult transition for Murdoch's new acquisition. While audience figures continued to grow, revenues did not match the investment. By the end of 1996 estimates were that News Corp. had invested about $1.5 billion in STAR, including buying out the remainder of the shares from the original investors (Warner and Witcher, 1996: 9).

For China a new policy was developed, which involved working closely with Chinese partners carefully chosen for their political connection, with the overarching goal of winning back the access to cable TV viewers that STAR TV had initially won, by accident as much as by design. The first move in the new direction did not involved television, but was a small joint venture agreement with the Communist Party's flagship newspaper, People's Daily in June 1995, to develop online information services.

In March 1996 News Corporation announced another new venture called Phoenix Satellite Television, a Chinese-language network and a successor to STAR's Chinese Channel. The largest shareholder (45%) was Star TV Holdings, with two Hong Kong-registered companies, Today's Asia (45%) and China Wise (10%), as partners. Today's Asia is 93.3% owned by Liu Changle, with links to the PLA, and a partner, Chan Wing Kee (6.7%): Liu also serves as Chairman and CEO. Liu and Chan are major shareholders (18% and 14% respectively) in Hong Kong's second-ranked terrestrial broadcaster, ATV, which provides much of the drama and soap opera fare that is the base of Phoenix.

The "beneficial owner" of China Wise International is the Bank of China, a major advertiser on Phoenix. The ultimate owner of China Wise is Shanghai Alliance Investment, a state-owned investment company affiliated with Shanghai's Municipal Government and chaired by Jiang Mianheng, son of China's then-President Jiang Zemin. China Wise was described as an international sales and advertising agent for China's TV stations, and was supposedly linked to the Ministry of Radio, Film and Television.

At its launch, the Phoenix Chinese Channel, and other services planned, were in direct competition with new services then being introduced by the state broadcaster, China Central Television, an apparent tribute to the unique clout of the Chinese shareholders. The announcement itself followed a flurry of media rumors about the possible involvement of CCTV or the MRFT, including possible carriage agreements with CCTV, which were angrily denied.[19] In the event it was not until over a year later that Phoenix obtained its first official permission to broadcast in Guangdong on the area's cable television network, the first non-mainland satellite television operator to receive such approval (South China, 1997). The reasons for this remarkable reversal of the new channel's fortunes seemed to have everything to do with overt efforts by Murdoch to ingratiate himself with Chinese government leaders (see below).

At the Phoenix IPO on the Growth Enterprise Market (GEM) of the Hong Kong Stock Exchange in 2000, Liu Changle announced lofty aims: "Our vision is to become a dominant content provider of Chinese television programmes through satellite, cable redistribution and the internet targeting the Greater China area, and Chinese speaking communities around the world" (Chan, 2000).

Phoenix's main channel, the Phoenix Chinese Channel is, like STAR TV, unencrypted, and in 2000 was claiming 42 million television households "able to receive and view" (roughly equated to 130 million people).[20] Its major rival is TVB Galaxy, which broadcasts TVB content to the Cantonese population in the Cantonese-speaking hinterland around Hong Kong. However, TVB Galaxy has never been able to show a profit, thanks to the practice of local cable operators of recording the TVB programming, stripping off the Hong Kong advertisements and replacing them with their own. Phoenix claims to avoid this thanks to its good relationships with local cable operators and provincial broadcasting authorities, and was thus able to declare a doubling of advertising revenues from FY 1997 to FY 1999.

Phoenix also has an encrypted Phoenix Movies Channel. In 1999, Phoenix launched Phoenix Chinese News and Entertainment (CNE) Channel, a European version of its service via Murdoch's BSkyB platform, as a digital, free-to-air service, and followed by a North American version, the Phoenix North America Chinese Channel, a subscription-based DTH service. In the winter of 2000 Phoenix launched a 24-hour Chinese-language regional news channel, called InfoNews Channel.

At July, 2000, Phoenix Satellite Television was reportedly $53 million in the red, with no prospect of real profits in the future. In fact, its biggest regular advertiser was the state-owned Bank of China, which is a minority share holder (Gilley, 2000). Losses continued in 2001, attributed to the high start-up costs of Phoenix InfoNews and the North America Channel, and despite rises in advertising revenue.[21]

MURDOCH IN CHINA

Phoenix TV broadcasts in Mandarin a mix of popular entertainment, sports, soap operas and talk shows. Any reference to politics is entirely supportive of the CCP, to the extent of using party slogans as the studio backdrop to a pop video program. The company management includes a number of "parachutists" from CCTV, part of a clear policy to cultivate links with the state broadcaster. Phoenix linked up with CCTV to provide 60 hours live coverage of the handover of Hong Kong in 1997, reportedly mostly at News Corp's expense (Higgins, 1998: 5).

Phoenix has succeeded in attracting an audience for its news programming, notably thanks to coverage of September 11, 2001. Phoenix had live coverage within minutes of the attacks, and remained live for 37 hours, while it took CCTV three hours to run recorded footage. However it is careful to steer clear of controversial issues such as the Falun Gong protests. At the time of the 1999 NATO bombing of the Chinese embassy in Yugoslavia, on the other hand, it was even more shrilly nationalistic than the state media, and organized and repeatedly broadcast a concert denouncing the action (Bodeen, 2001). One result has been an increasingly close relationship with CCTV. In October, 2001 Phoenix formed a joint venture with CCTV to jointly bring Chinese-language programs to foreign markets, with the endorsement of the SARFT (China Online, October 2001).

The history of Phoenix is a clear example of the policy developed by Murdoch following his purchase of STAR, to do whatever appears necessary to win favor with the Chinese authorities. The list of actions taken is long and revealing.

Following the breaking of STAR TV's contract with BBC, he arranged for his publishing group, Harper Collins, to publish "Deng Xiaoping, My Father," a hagiography written by Deng's daughter, in early 1995.[22] In June, 1995, News Corporation formed a joint venture with the People's Daily, Beijing PDN Xinren Information Technology, to exploit information technology.

But this was still not enough. In August 1996, the deputy director of the MRFT said it was "not possible" that Phoenix was reaching as many viewers as claimed, and "described Murdoch's television ambitions in China as 'beautiful dreams'"(Vines and Poole, 1997:10). To realize his dreams, Murdoch had to raise the stakes, which he proceeded to do in 1997. In January 1997, Phoenix TV took an official CCTV documentary on Deng Xiaoping, and ran the 12 one-hour episodes on consecutive nights.

In May 1997 Murdoch gave the keynote address to a meeting of the International Federation of the Periodical Press in Tokyo, in which he effectively recanted his 1993 London speech. Contrary to his comments at that time, which had described technology as a threat to governments like China's, he reported that

> The Chinese leadership has proved the skeptics, including myself, wrong by not shunning the new information technologies but actively encouraging their use . . . China has embraced the Internet, the information superhighway and the digital age as a means of strengthening its culture and spreading economic development.

Significantly, he went on to comment that

> We recognize that China is a distinctive market with distinctive social and moral values that western companies like News Corporation must learn to abide by.

This was followed by a wish, as he claimed that China was probably more suitable for the development of digital satellite technology than any other country because of its vast size, huge urban centers and scattered communities (Walker and Snoddy, 1997: 4).

In July, 1997, while on a trip to Beijing to meet Zhu Rongji, the future Prime Minister, he learnt that HarperCollins had paid a £150,000 advance on "East and West," a book by the last governor of Hong Kong, Chris Patten. Murdoch had long been a critic of Patten,[23] and over the next months pressure was exerted on Patten and the HarperCollins editorial staff to water down the book. In February, the senior editor working on Patten's book resigned, Patten took his book to Macmillan's, and both sued HarperCollins (Gapper, 1998 and Cooper, 1998).

The incident was heavily criticized in the Western media, but praised in a report by the official New China News Agency, which suggested that Murdoch had acted correctly "after learning the book had much anti-Chinese content." And as an apparent consequence of the meeting with Zhu Rongji (who was confirmed as Prime Minister shortly after the Patten book furor), cable operators in Guangdong "suddenly let it be known that they would start downloading Murdoch's Hong Kong-based Phoenix satellite channel and relay it to subscribers across China's richest region" (Higgins, 1998: 5).

In December, 1998, Murdoch's efforts began to pay off on a higher level. The official English-language newspaper, the *China Daily* published a front-page photograph of Murdoch and Chinese President Jiang Zemin smiling and shaking hands, and the official news agency Xinhua followed up with a report on their meeting in which Jiang Zemin "expressed appreciation for the efforts made by the world media mogul Rupert Murdoch in presenting China objectively, and co-operating with the Chinese press over the years" (Kynge and Gapper, 1998: 20).

Subsequently, Murdoch continued to develop his view of globalization. Addressing the Entertainment and Media in Asia conference in May, 2000, he insisted that cultural sensitivity was a corporate responsibility.

> We in the entertainment and media industries must realize that, unlike many other industries, what we do has important consequences for the political, social and cultural life of the other nations in which we operate. . . . We can strike a balance by deferring to our host's views into what we may broadcast in countries in which we are guests, while refusing to distort what we are able to broadcast. If a film is unacceptable in a country in which we operate, we don't show it. If a TV program covers forbidden ground, we will have no choice but to delete it from our broadcast (Plate, 2000: A8).

This remarkable confession of self-censorship from the "world media mogul" apparently presaged a new phase in Murdoch's relationship with the Chinese government, where News Corp seems ready to act as a mouthpiece for official Chinese views. In 2000 he gave an interview to *Vanity Fair* in which he described the Dalai Lama as "a very political old monk shuffling around in Gucci shoes."

This was followed in March 2001 by an even more startling speech given by Murdoch's youngest son, James Murdoch, in the role of chairman and chief executive of STAR TV, positions he has held since May, 2000. With his father in the audience, the younger Murdoch condemned the Falun Gong as "dangerous," "an apocalyptic cult . . . (that) clearly does not have the success of China at heart," and criticized Western reporters for their "unfair and harsh" coverage of China, in particular human rights issues. "These destabilizing forces today are very, very dangerous for the Chinese government," the younger Murdoch said, and went on to recommend that democracy advocates in Hong Kong accept the reality of rule by an "absolutist" government (Iritani, 2001; Boehlert, 2001; Varadarajan, 2001).

The storm of media criticism which ensued included headlines like "Pimping for the People's Republic" (Boehlert, 2001) and descriptions of Rupert Murdoch as "master practitioner of the corporate kowtow" who "instructed his son James perfectly in the craft of craven submission" and who is "repeating (Chinese propaganda) word for word" (Varadarajan, 2001).

The main reason why the Murdoch family is willing to go so far in defense of Chinese policies seems directly connected with internal corporate maneuverings and with a desire to position New Corp to take maximum advantage of the anticipated liberalization of the information industry in China now that China has joined the WTO.

At the same time as the Entertainment and Media in Asia conference (May, 2000) News Corp was developing what was variously described as a "satellite internet concern," an "umbrella company showcasing its broad satellite holdings" and a "digital distributions company." Basically this was an attempt to bundle all News Corp.'s satellite holdings (including 100% of Star TV and 10% of SKY PerfecTV) into a new unit and float it on the stock market. The eventual name chosen was Sky Global Networks Inc. The float was delayed, however, for various reasons including the stock market decline and the delay in completing a key element in the News Corp international satellite network, the purchase of DirecTV in the United States.

The policy in China seems to be paying off. In February 2001 News Corp joined a group of investors in taking 12 percent of the equity in China Netcom, the third largest of China's six major telecommunications companies, providing broadband data and voice-over-IP services via a national fiber optic network (Backman, 2001). Theoretically, an investment by a foreign concern like New Corp. is illegal, but this was circumvented through purchasing the shares via a Hong Kong-based subsidiary (Lawson, 2001).

The deal was interesting for several reasons. One was the fact of investment in a broadband service provider, with all that implies for the future. Two was the fact that one of the original shareholders of China Netcom is the SARFT. And three was the presence of the chief backer of China Netcom, Jiang Mianheng, eldest son of President Jiang Zemin, described as "the most influential force shaping technology in China today" (Lee-Young), and clearly involved in the rising of Phoenix TV from the ashes of its near-disastrous launch.

The policy seems to be earning rewards in another sense. In 2002 STAR began to make a profit—after 10 years and the investment of an estimated $2 billion (Granitsas, 2002).

POSTSCRIPT: STAR IN INDIA REVISITED

STAR TV's slow climb to profitability is based on success in one market: India. Its operations in India account for about 70% of total revenues, equivalent to about $200 million.[24] STAR has more than 30 of India's top 50 most popular show and is now the second most watched channel after the national broadcaster Doordarshan, which has far deeper penetration than STAR (ibid).

The original rationale behind Star had been that the new, rich Asia was spearheaded by a cosmopolitan elite prepared to watch English-language programming. Being wealthy and well educated, they would constitute a very desirable market for advertisers. It was also assumed that they were dissatisfied both with the lack of choice available, at a time when national broadcasters dominated most Asian television systems, and with the often stultifying content of what was presented. The Chinese entrepreneurs behind STAR had the eyes on an imaginary market: the Chinese business elite, to be found throughout east Asia. In reality India was the only one place which actually seemed to fit this description.

Like China, the population of India is huge, approaching one billion. There are an estimated 70 million television owning homes, 30 million of which are estimated to have cable connections (Times of India, 2001). At the same time there has long been widespread dissatisfaction with Doordarshan, the Indian national television organization, which had a policy of allowing limited commercial sponsorship of some of its immensely popular serials, but had continued its public service programming, with such fare as panel discussions on national integration and local folk music shows (Pathania, 1994: 2).

The impact of STAR TV was almost as fast as it had been in China, aided by the fact that English-language programming was not the automatic liability it was in China. The addition of BBC News, for example, was well received, albeit not a commercial success.

> In India most people were listening to BBC News on the radio. So when it (BBC World) did come up it added a lot of credibility to the platform. In India they were watching, because there hardly any choice, in terms of news coming in from abroad. We only had one state broadcaster, which used to put the news on once a day in the evening at 7 o'clock. Suddenly you could switch on your TV any time of the day, and get international news. And credible.[25]

Overall the early impact of STAR was heaviest in India. The most popular programming was Star Plus—mostly American soap operas—and coverage of World Cup cricket in February of 1992.

Soon after buying STAR TV, and following the new controls on ownership of satellite dishes in China, Murdoch abandoned the idea of a pan-Asia regional network, and began developing several networks tailored for specific markets. His first move was to clearly split the content of the northern beam (largely aimed at China) and the southern (focused on India). In December 1993 he moved to bolster the availability of content for the southern beam, by buying 49.9 per cent of Asia Today, the holding company for Zee TV, which had become the anchor channel for Star's Indian operations in the 14 months since its satellite broadcasting launch in October 1992. At that time 50 per cent of STAR TV's viewers were claimed to be in India. At the time of the purchase Zee TV was seen in more than seven million Indian homes, as well as claiming "significant viewership" in the United Arab Emirates, Oman, Kuwait, Saudi Arabia and Pakistan (SCMP, 1993). The dramatic build up in audience had been achieved at the direct expense of Doordarshan, both in terms of subverting the "nation-building" propaganda element of its programming, and perhaps more importantly in its impact on advertising revenues. In 1993 STAR TV and Zee TV were already accounting for some 20 per cent of the advertising pie (Pathania, 1994: 2).

By 1996, the Indian side of the business was claimed to be near breakeven, although overall STAR continued to lose money at the rate of $100 million a year (The Economist, 1996 (2). In 1997 the Indian government moved to block Murdoch's further expansion into the Indian market, when he proposed ISkyB, an Indian version of his highly profitable BSkyB. A temporary ban was imposed on ownership of DTH hardware, until a new comprehensive broadcast bill could be approved by parliament, and justified because of the unregulated nature of DTH programming (Lall, 1997: 5). It was also seen as necessary as the whole arena of broadcasting was basically governed by legislation passed in the 19th century.

In the event a draft bill was introduced in the Indian parliament in 1997, but never passed into law. At the same time an even older bill, the Prasar Bharati Act, was passed. This brought Doordashan and All India Radio under a holding company called Prasar Bharati (Indian Broadcasting Corporation), and served to give the state broadcasters BBC-like autonomy, as their management now reported to an independent supervisory board. The fact that the act was passed so abruptly, after a seven-year wait, was seen as a direct reaction to the impact of satellite television. By 1997 more than 20 independent channels had begun broadcasting in Hindi, Tamil and Telugu, with all the services uplinked from locations outside India (Long, 1997).[26]

In fact it was language localization which had at long last enabled STAR TV in India to begin to head for profit in 2001, ten years after starting operations. Following the conversion of its flagship Indian channel, Star Plus, from a bilingual format to Hindi only in 2000, the channel had 38 of the top 50 programs on Indian television, and was anticipating a 50 percent growth in revenue.[27]Although only about 30 per cent of Indians have Hindi as their mother tongue, at least double that proportion understands the language (Times of India, 2001). This, coupled with STAR TV buying a 26 percent stake in India's second-largest cable network, Hathway Cable & Datacom, in September 2000, indicated that STAR TV had at last developed a strategy that worked and was capable of dealing with local rivals (Lee-Young, 2000 and Merchant and Harding, 2000).

Chapter Six

Conclusions—Meanwhile, Back in the Future

UNEXPECTED WAVES

One of the goals of this book has been to describe the actual situation concerning information flows as revealed through a comparative study of three television case histories in Asia. These case histories also illustrate the three different approaches to providing television services: public service, state and commercial.

By looking at these case histories in some detail, my intent has been to depict some of the workings of political power and the media in a global world. By delineating the pattern, or structure, of specific examples of the processes of globalization, and attempting to describe their impact, I have tried to suggest ways in which such patterns might change in the future, by following paths that might have been taken in the past.

As explained in the introduction, one strategy I have adopted to approach this problem is to see global forces as constituted at a distance, and thereby to focus on the ways in which they are resisted or negotiated. I hope this has been amply illustrated by the examination of NHK and CCTV. One of my contentions is that NHK (and potentially CCTV) are in fact "front line" organizations that are forced to deal with globalization forces as they first become apparent, while the state may be slow to comprehend or react to the new realities which are sweeping in. Another strategy is to see those forces themselves as the product of flows of people, things and ideas, the actual global connections between sites, as indicated by the case history of STAR TV.

In this concluding chapter I want to look at those forces and connections as imaginative constructs, and speculate on different ways in which the processes of globalization could or might develop, and at the possibilities of engaging with a no longer distant world.

In many ways the changes that have engulfed television around the world are emblematic of globalization at work. Television—not only the industry but also the device that sits in the living room—serves as a useful stage on which the tensions between the local and the global are played out at the levels of the political, the economic and the cultural. The importance of this last can not be denied, as culture provides the backdrop for the play. Global information systems circulate global media, offering images, ideas, music, fashion, and news. Local society and local culture can take or break those global artefacts, based on concepts as diverse as race, ethnicity, religion or even the construct that stubbornly refuses to be diminished—nationalism.

Resistance to globalization is commonly posited in terms of protesters and protest movements, who may wave banners or fight the police over abstract concepts. But there is also resistance aplenty from defenders of a different status quo, who tend to be reacting to a specific aspect or process of globalization—such as information flows. As revealed through the case histories, the Japanese approach has been to attempt to *use* information, in the service of bureaucratically-decided national aims, while the Chinese administrators remain fixated on trying to *control* information, as a defensive reaction to a perceived threat to authority over the polis. In this narrative the Hong Kong approach may be depicted as attempting to simply *profit from* information.

The checkered history of STAR TV tells us that such embedded resistance as epitomized by the case histories of Japan and China is enough to alter the nature of one aspect of globalization—the notion that globalization acts as an enervating, homogenizing blanket covering the vitality of the local—in dramatic and fundamental ways. STAR TV's pretensions to be a regional broadcaster covering one third of the world's population are reduced to becoming "a conglomeration of half a dozen local broadcasters slugging it out market by market"(Granitsas, 2000). STAR TV's business model, which had its eye on the wealthy audience represented by the Chinese diaspora in Asia, was exploded by local realities: STAR TV's biggest success to date is in India, a fact that its owners, Chinese and Australian/American, had difficult adjusting to. At least in its potential, globalization can be about de-centering. The waves of transformation can break in unexpected ways.

CAUSAL LAYERED ANALYSIS

One method to analyze these transformations is through a causal layered analysis. This is a critical futures research tool developed by Sohail Inayatullah, an attempt to use poststructuralism as a research method.

> The goal of critical research is thus to disturb present power relations through making problematic our categories and evoking other places or scenarios of the future. Through this historical, future and civilizational distance, the present becomes less rigid, indeed, it becomes remarkable. This allows the spaces of reality to loosen and the new possibilities, ideas and structures, to emerge. The issue is less what is the truth but how truth functions in particular policy settings, how truth is evoked, who evokes it, how it circulates, and who gains and loses by particular nominations of what is true, real and significant (Inayatullah, 2002).

Crucially, Inayatullah argues that the way in which one frames a problem potentially changes the solution and the actors responsible for creating transformation. This calls to mind Umberto Eco's (1991) arguing that the culture that provides the context for our lives also prioritizes the information we are able to digest.

The attraction of this method is that it allows room in analysis to accommodate some of the key characteristics of globalization already identified, viz. the overweening notion of complexity; the self-referential interdependent, and non-linear qualities; the idea of constant, necessary flux; the pivotal role of technological take-off points; and the assumption that culture counts.

The layers of analysis employed are a) the litany—quantitive trends, events, issues; b) social causes, including economic, cultural, political and historical factors; c) structure—the discourse and worldview that supports and legitimates the issues; and d) myth and metaphor, where an attempt is made to dig up the unconscious and paradoxical dimensions of the problem, the collective archetypes. Scenarios can be developed from any of these levels; however, the quality of the futures thus derived differ, depending on which level one focuses on. For example, quantitive scenarios (level 1) tend to be in-the-box futures, focused on extrapolations which usually point to low or high growth rates.

LEVEL 1 : THE LITANY—GLOBALIZATION AS LEVIATHAN

A major preoccupation of this research has been the national public broadcaster. Typically these are major institutions in the local society, distinguished by size and reach. Prasar Bharati, for example, has two components: AIR (radio) broadcasts from 208 stations, in 21 regional languages, covering 98% of the Indian population; Doordarshan (television) telecasts its programs from 52 stations over 21 channels in all the major regional languages. It has nearly 40,000 employees (Gill, 2001).

One of the public service broadcasters looked at in this research, NHK, is probably the wealthiest public broadcasting system in the world, with effectively total coverage of the Japanese population. Because of its wealth and its close ties with the government bureaucracy, it is the only Japanese media concern currently able to be a player in the new world of global media.

This is a world in which media organizations have grown and expanded abroad, as represented in this research by News Corporation. According to its 2003 annual report, News Corporation had major investments around the world in newspapers (111+ titles), magazines (8 major units or divisions listed), television (50), cable (16), direct broadcast satellite television (17), filmed entertainment (14), book publishing (1), and 'other' (including radio and music) (11).

On the surface, much can be revealed about global media, as the trend towards the creation of a global oligopoly has been well documented. Writing in 1999 McChesney identified nine transnationals that dominated the global media market: General Electric/NBC, AT&T/Liberty Media, Disney, TimeWarner, Sony, News Corporation, Viacom, Seagram and Bertelsmann. The result was a global media system that he saw as

> fundamentally noncompetitive in any meaningful economic sense of the term. Many of the largest media firms have some of the major shareholders, own pieces of one another or have interlocking boards of directors . . . The global market strongly encourages corporations to establish equity joint ventures in which the media giants all own a part of an enterprise. This way firms reduce competition and increase the chance of profitability. (McChesney, 1999: 13).

Such a bald description of trends in the media can all to easily lead to a feeling of helplessness in the face of what seems like an inexorable force, globalization as leviathan. As the transnational media conglomerates grow ever larger, and the connections between them ever stronger as described by McChesney, it is easy to follow the critiques of Schiller and Bagdikian, who see avenues of expression being narrowed, difference being ignored, and the commercial reigning supreme. Ultimately, as Dirlik and Said would see it, the power of the global media is used to implement a new colonialization of the mind, a homogenization of culture.

Futures visioning based on such descriptions of quantitive trends is likely to result in a doomsday scenario in which a few megalomaniac media moguls control all we see, read and hear through the media, while the public service broadcasters fight a doomed rearguard defense against an all-conquering wave of commercialism, with success or failure measured in terms of audience share.

LEVEL 2: SOCIAL CAUSES—THE SURVIVAL OF THE PUBLIC BROADCASTER

The picture of global media is by no means static, however. In the few years since McChesney wrote his article two of his dominant nine companies, AT&T and Seagram, have largely divested their media interests; only News Corporation has kept the same senior management, while all the others have seen dramatic changes, usually with concomitant policy reversals; and most have seen equally abrupt changes to their financial fortunes, as share prices have see-sawed.

It is also worth looking more closely at the data. IDATE (2000, 2001) ranks media groups on the basis of audiovisual revenue (derived from the operation of broadcast channels and cable networks and from film, video and related activities). This method makes it apparent that for a company like General Electric, audiovisual revenue is quite unimportant, accounting for only 5% of its total in the 2000 ranking. This helps explain why AT&T was quick to divest itself of its cable TV investment, as it represented a low 12% of the total. Even for Disney, almost 40% of its revenue stream comes from sources other than audio-visual.

Table 8. World Ranking of Media Groups, 2000.

Rank	Company	Country	Revenue latest fiscal year ($ million)	Audiovisual revenue latest fiscal year ($ million)	Audiovisual revenue share of total	Audiovisual revenue growth rate 00/99
1	AOL Time Warner	USA	36,213.0	20,975.0	58%	6.8%
2	Viacom	USA	20,043.7	19,759.9	99%	62.5%
3	Walt Disney	USA	25,402.0	15,609.0	61%	11.0%
4	News Corporation	Australia	14,895.2	9,509.1	64%	16.9%
5	AT&T	USA	65,981.0	8,217.0	12%	68.7%
6	Vivendi-Universal	France	22,410.4	8,103.5	36%	3.6%
7	Comcast Corporation	USA	8,218.6	7,187.0	87%	24.4%
8	General Electric/ NBC	USA	129,853.0	6,797.0	5%	17.4%
9	ARD	Germany	6,229.4	6,229.4	100%	-1.6%
10	NHK	Japan	6,183.4	6,183.4	100%	1.6%
11	Hughes Electronic	USA DirecTV	7,287.6	5,238.0	72%	38.4%
12	Sony	Japan	67,877.3	5,152.0	8%	12.3%
13	BBC	UK	4,797.7	4,797.7	100%	-1.3%
14	Cablevision Systems	USA	4,411.0	4,411.0	100%	11.9%
15	Cox Enterprises	USA	7,787.0	4,208.0	54%	43.1%
16	Fuji Television Network	Japan	4,081.1	4,081.1	100%	6.7%

Table 8. World Ranking of Media Groups, 2000 (continued)

Rank	Company	Country	Revenue latest fiscal year ($ million)	Audiovisual revenue latest fiscal year ($ million)	Audiovisual revenue share of total	Audiovisual revenue growth rate 00/99
17	RTL Group	Luxembourg	3,725.8	3,641.1	98%	-0.4%
18	BSkyB	UK	3,496.1	3,496.1	100%	24.9%
19	USA Networks	USA	4,601.5	3,415.9	74%	25.9%
20	Carlton Communications	UK	3,153.5	3,153.5	100%	0.5%
21	Nippon Television Network	Japan	3,270.1	3,139.5	96%	7.4%
22	Kirch Gruppe	Germany	3,065.7	3,065.7	100%	42.0%
23	Charter Communications	USA	3,249.2	2,826.8	87%	128.8%
24	Adelphia	USA	2,909.3	2,502.0	86%	120.8%
25	RAI	Italy	2,432.7	2,432.7	100%	-10.0%

Source: IDATE 2001

Looking at the top 20 groups, the big contrast is with the national broadcasters, whether public (ARD, NHK, BBC) or commercial (Fuji Television, BSkyB, Carlton Communications), all of which attribute most or all of their revenue to audiovisual activities. The difference here may be one of attitude: it is difficult to imagine NHK or the BBC changing their basic focus from broadcasting, regardless of how technology causes that term to be redefined. Part of that basic focus is an insistence on the importance of producing news, as an obligation to the public served, and of disseminating information that directly or indirectly functions to represent the nation with which they are associated.

At the same time an organization like NHK is a bureaucracy supervised by a state organ, and one that participates in the development and implementation of government policy in its area of interest. It is rooted.

The position and policy of News Corporation could not be more different: it is quite easy to imagine that company deciding to sell or even abandon STAR TV, should economics or politics so dictate. And while news has become an important part of, for example, the Fox cable operation, Fox News is avowedly about entertainment and about a deliberate presentation of the news for a certain effect. Any claim to objectivity or delivering news as a kind of public service has been consciously abandoned. News Corporation is a gadfly; STAR TV is based in Hong Kong, but at various times has been rumored considering moving to Singapore or India. If it did it would probably make little difference to the company or its policy.

Picard (2001) also demonstrates that rumors of the death of public service broadcasting may have been greatly exaggerated. The commonest evidence offered to bolster such a claim is the decline in audience share that has affected most of the public service broadcasters around the world. By carefully analyzing the reasons for a decline in market share—usually, increases in the number of competitors, the number of channels and the hours of programming, Picard is able to make comparable national evaluations in Europe. Using methodology based on current market conditions (rather than comparison with a historical situation before competition was introduced), he finds that

> as a whole public service broadcasters are performing better than statistical expectations and that public service broadcasting is maintaining market leadership in nearly all EU nations, with the exception of Greece and Portugal (Picard 2001).

This is not to deny that the public service broadcasters have been forced to change. The waves of transformation that have swept over CCTV, for example, are extraordinary. While it continues to fulfill its original mandate as a propaganda machine, it is no longer beholden to the center for finance. It has two masters, one political, one commercial, and today the former is treated with grudging deference at best. Similarly NHK's former position of security has been severely impacted by internal problems—such as the expensive failure of HDTV and the rocky development of satellite TV—and external challenges, like the advent of News Station and its ilk, the radical reforms of the cable television industry, and the challenges of digital TV.

Finally, it is necessary to query the notion that the integrative aspect of globalization described by Harvey, Giddings, Soja, Wallerstein and many others, can be equated with a process of cultural homogenization. Again television serves as a useful test bed to query such a conclusion. Curtin argues that, even if the villain of the piece is capitalism, it is an oversimplification to assume that the world of no difference depicted by Naomi Klein is necessarily in the best of corporate interest.

> Here television histories are particularly important, because they can offer richly detailed accounts of the actual strategies of cultural institutions, which have aimed not at producing global similarity, but instead at organizing local differences toward profitable ends under a global regime of consumer capitalism. Although it is true that huge media conglomerates attempt to shape and delimit the range of ideas in circulation at any given time, one must be careful not to fall into the trap of believing that the purpose of corporate television is to erase difference and create a dull homogeneity of thought, experience and lifestyle (Curtin, 2001: 337).

Appadurai (1990) argues that complexity, disjuncture and difference are the outcome of the flows that characterize globalization, rather than homogenization, a conclusion supported by the research in this book. The founders of STAR TV had in mind the idea that their programming would appeal to a new pan-Asian middle class, ready made global consumers with only shallow local roots. The reality was vastly more complicated, offering support for the view that encounters between the global and the local are more likely to lead to something hybrid, something "in-between" as Mignolo would have it, a goulash of the modern and the traditional. Culture is intricate, and endlessly mutable.

The scenarios that might emerge from this, the second tier, are notably different to the first. A focus on the state and corporate actors, and an analysis of what drives them, might lead to a description of possible policy outcomes. In this case the conclusion might be that the public service broadcaster is not out, not even down, but about to come back into the fight with surprising reserves of strength. The commercial players, by contrast, live in a world of uncertainty where nimbleness of action may in the end reflect little more than a desperation to survive.

LEVEL 3: STRUCTURE—POWER AND CONTROL

The third level is concerned with structure, and the worldview that supports and legitimates it. As Inayatullah describes this level:

> The task is to find deeper social, linguistic, cultural structures that are actor-invariant . . . At this stage one can explore how different discourses (the economic, the religious, the cultural, for example) do more than cause or mediate the issue but constitute it, how the discourse we use to understand is complicit in our framing of the issue (Inayatullah, 2002).

I have chosen to continue to focus on the political and economic discourses of the globalization of communication, but with a conclusion that points towards the cultural aspect.

The underlying structure that informs this research is that of the world of communication (in the sense of the transmission of information). Deutsch (1963) saw the state as defined by its information flows, as political legitimacy is affected by the amount, type, and source of information accessible to a country's inhabitants. This view has become commonplace, as there is little argument about the prime role communication technology now plays in policy development in modern society.

Communications today ignore time and space, worldwide. There is even a global industry based on the buying of time and the booking of space: advertising. As revealed through the case histories already described, the recent history of television shows us how its global growth is directly tied with its reconceptualisation as part of a commercial process—whether actively embraced by Rupert Murdoch and confreres, or gingerly accepted by the CCP as part of its ongoing endeavor to maintain its grip on power, or endlessly worried over by the mandarins of NHK, like a dog with a dubious bone.

Curtin sees television as one among many communication technologies employed by businesses in their never-ending quest for new sites of production and distribution, and thereby complicit in the management of communication. He inverts one standard claim against globalization—that global television leads to a homogenization of local cultures—and argues that the 'central mission' of television is to help organize and reorganize popular perceptions of difference within a global economic order. This is the way the world is, and this is the way the world should be.

> The medium is a tool for localizing and naturalizing a hierarchy of values and attitudes about places. It repeatedly works to anchor and orient one's perception of how power and wealth should be distributed. In this way it helps to manage the process of uneven development—one of capitalism's defining features—primarily under the banners of modernization and global citizenship (Curtin, 2001: 338,9).

This is a challenging concept. It would, for example, render hollow the claims of Shima that he was seeking to redress a perceived imbalance in information flows: rather, his mission can be seen as attempting to put the hands of the nation-state that NHK represented on the levers of power through which globalization is run, to ensure Japan a higher place in the 'hierarchy of values and attitudes' that underpin the globalization construct.

In a sense this view is in accord with at least one definition of the role and function of a public service broadcaster, as a builder of the national community and defender of the national identity. This is a general role description that seems to fit NHK quite well, as revealed through the history of the organization, and as symbolized by its heavy involvement in national projects such as the development of the Japanese satellite industry, and in the way it took on the function of representing Japan abroad.

However, what is depicted is essentially a passive or reactive role, and the case history of Shima indicates that this may be an oversimplification. Under his leadership, NHK was a world leader in dealing with changes sweeping through the broadcast communications industry, and in Japanese terms served as the watchdog that barked to alert the national community that the borderless world had arrived. Similarly, the broadcasts of "River Elegy" in China were a clarion call to the local society that times were changing. In this context, Turner's speech—"We're gonna take the news and put it on the satellite, and then we're gonna beam it down into Russia, and we're gonna bring world peace, and we're gonna get rich in the process!" (Whittemore, 1990: 124)—changes its character and import. Both Shima and Turner emerge as corporate leaders in the role of trickster or joker, always posing the uncomfortable questions, and intent on making the institutions they ran agents of change.

Both Shima and Turner fell from power, in part because the role of the institutions they were in charge of was too important or too valuable. Ultimately established government or corporate interests exerted their influence to take power away from them. But the hold on power held by this establishment is not consistent: on the contrary, it is constantly shifting, as the world in which it functions changes, with the rapid deployment of new technologies, with the financial base continually shifting and with unforeseen pressures emerging from near and afar. The discourse is under threat.

In sum, one side of the story presented here is about power and control. Communications and broadcasting in particular are intrinsic parts of political and economic power structures. This is a traditional way of looking at the media in the social sciences. Weber saw the control of knowledge as a fundamental means by which the bureaucratic administration of society maintains its domination, logically leading to the uncomfortable conclusion that the science of which he is one of the fathers is also complicit in the maintenance of that domination. For Adorno, this also resulted in the "industry" of popular culture, a means to conserve and control. Curtin develops a riff on this theme, to show how the media are used to win acceptance of globalization's weakest point, its tendency to foster gross inequality.

As such broadcasting reflects the thinking of those power structures: this was quite self-evident in the way news on Iraq was presented and packaged before, during and after the 2003 Gulf War. Driven by the need to fill the huge amount of time that "24x7 news" actually represents, the current fashion in news presentation in the United States is to tie stories into a theme, complete with special graphics and carefully chosen music. Prior to the war CNN ran news under the theme "Strike on Iraq"; for CBS, it was "Saddam Showdown"; for MSNBC it was "Conflict with Iraq," itself a subset of a broader post-September 11 theme, entitled "America At War."

A scenario is likely to reflect such trends, including (in America) a plainly discernible shift towards a more conservative posture in the broadcast industry. A simple extrapolation of this shift would be a mistake, however. 'Jokers' like Ted Turner or Shima can crop up at any time, in any organization, and have a major impact on developments.

The scenario may therefore choose as its a launching pad the argument of Poster, through examination of the linguistic dimension of culture, that we may be dealing with what he sees as a new social phenomenon,

> The extent to which communication is restricted by time and space governs, with striking force, the shape society may take. . . . What is at stake are new language formations that alter significantly the network of social relations, that restructure those relations and the subjects they constitute (Poster, 1990).

LEVEL 4: MYTH AND METAPHOR

The fourth layer of analysis is at the level of metaphor or myth, which Inayatullah describes as the deep stories, the collective archetypes, the unconscious dimensions of the problem or the paradox. What needs to be imaginatively grasped here are the issues of control and freedom, and of the meaning of community. A sub-theme of this book is an examination of the phenomena of globalization, so the questions revolve around global community. Does such a concept have any meaning? If it does, how to communicate across barriers of language and culture? And—returning to the starting point of this research—is there any possibility that the flow of communication may achieve balance?

In this case I would like to propose two 'dreams,' both grounded in the discussion outlined in Level 3. One is to speculate on the 'positive' aspects of the media, as represented by the public service broadcaster, and building on the work of Paddy Scannel to suggest that it be seen as a social resource, a public good. The second is to briefly re-examine the problems encountered by Japanese broadcasters in working together with their American counterparts, and from there query whether in fact working together has a global meaning.

Broadcasting: Brave lion or cowardly courtier?

For a romantic like Williams communication was part of an essential process of comparison and interaction, the process by which community in society is sustained. His writings maintain a guarded optimism that popular culture offers a mode of enlightenment as well as being a social soporific. This is a view I am in sympathy with. To claim that the media are part of a mechanism of ideology as Stuart Hall and others have argued seems to me reductionist in the extreme, ignoring the richness of the history of broadcasting, for example, or the complexity of the production process of television, as I have tried to illustrate in this research. The idea that broadcasters themselves are consciously or unconsciously complicit in the production of a dominant discourse may seem to fit in the case of the shameless commercialism of News Corporation in China, but does not accord with the thoughtful and self-aware discussions I had in the course of interviews with media professionals in the field.

This is not to deny that the mass media surely work in many ways to sustain the power and status of public institutions in society, in particular by the way in which they prioritizes certain news stories over others, or "frame" stories in a manner that often obfuscates or ignores inconvenient information or alternative interpretations. Taylor points out that nowadays the process by which programs are developed or even news stories are selected is carefully controlled, with input from market research and so on. The way the news is presented,

> may tell us as much, if not more, about the nature of our societies than it does about the contemporary media. What is not being reported upon,

> or how two or three out of twenty or so current conflicts around the world are decided upon as being news worthy, is an important element in understanding not so much this particular "window on the world' but upon the smaller number of panes of glass that the media chooses to let us see through. (Taylor, 2001: 255).

One recurring criticism of the present day BBC is precisely that it has learnt the lessons of the market place too well, reveling in its triumphs in rating wars with commercial rivals, at the expense of any idea of a more exalted mission for a public service broadcaster.

It is my belief that broadcasting can be, in Scannel's phrase, a public good that enhances "the reasonable character and conduct of . . . life by augmenting claims to communicative entitlements," which presuppose communicative rights.

> It does this . . . through asserting a right of access to public life; through extending its universe of discourse and entitling previously excluded voices to be heard: through questioning those in power, on behalf of viewers and listeners, and trying to get them to answer. More generally . . . The fact that the broadcasters do not control the communicative context means that they must take into account the conditions for reception for their utterances. As such they have learned to treat the communicative process not simply as the transmission of a content, but a relational process in which how things are said is as important as what is said (Scannel, 1992:342,3).

For Scannel public service television in particular represents a vital channel for the circulation of common understandings in a shared public life. It is literally a social good.

To anticipate the criticism that this is the mere sophistry of an innumerate social scientist who is ignoring the hard realities of 21st century market-driven societies, it is worth citing briefly the conclusions about the role of the market place in the 1999 Davies committee report "Review of the Future Funding of the BBC," which drew heavily on the work of an Oxford University economist, Andrew Graham. The conclusions appeared in an annex entitled "Market Failure in Broadcasting," which interpreted the notion that broadcasting is a public good in a strict economic framework.

Davies/Graham remind us that once a program has been produced for one person, there is no additional cost for producing it for any other. This brings with it the problems of non-exclusivity (people are reluctant to pay for something they do not have exclusive right to) and non-rivalry (the act of consumption does not affect the good itself). The social value of non-rivalrous goods is based on the consensus value—the total everyone is willing to pay—

not on the individual's valuation. The potential social value of a TV program is the aggregated value of all those who might watch the program, not just those who do.

Broadcasting is also a "merit good"—something whose value exceeds the estimation an individual in society might place on it. While television has the capacity to expand (or restrict) the imagination and the knowledge of the individual, if left to the free market that capacity may be under-developed as the individual may only be aware in retrospect of the benefit of developing such capacities.

This ruthless logic is also applied to one of the key assumptions of 'pure' market economics, that a competitive market place consists of fully informed consumers. But as the report points out:

> In general, markets do not always work well where what is being sold is information or experience. This is because consumers do not know what they are buying until they have experienced it, but once they have they no longer need to buy it. (BBC, 1999: 203)

Other factors in favor of public service television identified in the report were the production of externalities, the things extra to the market, which may be negative as well as positive (for example, a broadcaster does not have to face the wider social consequences of programming output, so may default to 'negative' externalities, such as screen violence, if operating without any wider social remit); and the likely concentration of ownership, thanks to the economies of scale that operate in broadcasting, thereby replacing one source of monopoly—spectrum scarcity—with another commercially-created monopoly.

At the same time the increase in distribution channels that accompanies digitalization leads to audience fragmentation; production costs will remain high, increasing average cost, reinforcing the 'natural monopoly' created through economies of scale. Rather than promoting free competition, there is a risk that the digital era will foster high concentration in private broadcasting, a tendency that already seems to be in place.

> Economic theory suggests that, rather than removing the case for public service broadcasting, the commercial pressures and globalisation that are reinforced by digital technology, could increase the need for such a (public service) broadcaster (Ibid: 205)

The divergent views portrayed by Taylor and Scannel, can be taken as two contrasting representations of public service broadcasting, as the brave lion and as the cowardly courtier.

If those in the television industry have the courage to believe in their own public service origins, the model offered is a powerful one: an agent of diversity in the broadest sense of the term. This is the power of the general broadcaster, as well, that catholic programming allows for the serendipity factor, the unexpected program encountered next to the familiar. The logic of commercial broadcasting, in particular as represented by the cable TV model, is the opposite: it is *narrow* casting, one channel catering to one interest. Whether it is golf for golfers, history for the history buffs or news for those who have a need to check the latest information feed, the aim is specifically to compartmentalize, in part to pre-define the nature of the audience being delivered to advertisers.

Only connect

Shima was fairly straightforward about what he thought the problem of global broadcasting was: control.

> CNN is trying to force U.S. news on the rest of the world . . . When Asian news is treated by Western broadcasters, it tends to be given a low priority . . . We, faced with a flood of information from the U.S., need to have a network that will pay more attention to reports from Asia (Sherman, 1994: 32).

As described in the case history, the real reasons for the sudden push to create GNN are murky. The planning behind the development of the concept was hurried, almost slapdash, and none of the practical details had been worked out before it was abruptly announced, and then unceremoniously abandoned. Based on the experience of the staff who had worked on "Japan Business Today" there would certainly have been countless problems and disagreements, some of them acrimonious, in trying to produce 'global' news.

But a closer look at the interviews conducted with former Japanese and American staff people shows how petty many of the disagreements were, and leads one to wonder whether these in fact were truly insolvable. And the beauty of the GNN proposal was that in fact the news would have been 'local,' in so far as each 8-hour segment would have been sourced out of a different center according to the earth's revolution, first Asian, then European and lastly North American. In this way GNN would have had the capacity to anticipate the learning curve that STAR TV was to go through, and gone immediately to the 'regional in the global' model. Potentially it would also have gone to the 'local in the regional,' as one of Shima's most successful innovations in broadcasting had been to use satellite technology to capture local national news broadcasts from around the world and run them direct, with fascinating results (and good viewing figures). This is the basic approach behind an already existing and highly regarded "World News," that run by the Australian alternate public broadcaster, SBS (Special Broadcasting Service).

No matter how feasible the concept was, or how problematic the execution might have been, the key question is whether GNN or anything similar would have done anything to address the issues of imbalance identified by Shima, or on a larger canvas, would have represented any advance in creating a global community.

The underlying issue here seems to center on the function, actual or potential, of a public service broadcaster. Is the role of broadcasting to participate in the spread of knowledge and the development of understanding, or is it a device designed to reinforce and support existing structures in society?

There may be two possible answers, for both of which I will reference the work of two scholars of globalization. Ashis Nandy has advanced the idea that the world is increasingly organized by categories—of work, of place in society, of ethnicity, or whatever.[1] Walter Mignolo has a different view of the same phenomenon, the need to resist against a perceived Anglo-Saxon hegemony. His argument is that, while it is not reasonable or necessarily desirable to try to eliminate the influence of Western thinking, we can see a choice between an acceptance of the milieus constructed in the past two centuries, where the choice is strictly limited. On the one hand is the world of Christianity, liberalism, conservatism or Marxism; fundamentally, a homogenized world, expressed through a common understanding of approaches to the law, the economy, the self, etc. Or there is an alternative construction, where the majority can see that the post-war American dream world constructed in the 1950s is finally revealed for what it is—a Hollywood movie—and we look for a different road to the future, which he characterizes with the phrase 'border' or 'in-between' thinking. This is a place where the local meets the global, accepts or rejects it, and goes on from there, celebrating 'in-betweenness,' with no resource to preserving an artificial construction of 'authenticity.'

Mignolo's proposal is for a "critical cosmopolitanism,' a political project involving people from different cultures and different languages who can work in the space 'in between.' He also makes a special plea for breaking out of the constraints of what he calls the 'languages of knowledge' (English, French and German), and broadening the pool of learning.

His approach offers a second answer to the question about the role of broadcasting: it can indeed participate in the spread of knowledge and the development of understanding, by celebrating diversity. It could be the brave lion. Again, Australia's SBS offers a functioning, successful reference point, as its mandate as a broadcaster is to reflect the multilingual, multicultural nature of Australian society, "to inform, educate and entertain all Australians."

In his discussion of the "Zapatista's theoretical revolution" Mignolo has advanced some terms which are useful in trying to construct a theoretical basis for re-imagining the role of a television broadcaster. One is the idea of "connectors," an attempt to allow for different understandings attached to the same words or ideas as used by people in different parts of the world, in different positions in hierarchies or on the social scale. Connectors are "the places of encounters of diverse epistemic principles underlining rules for social organization and moral codes for collective behavior" (Mignolo, 2002: 257).

The need is to see beyond "the limits imposed by two hegemonic abstract universals, (neo) liberalism and (neo) Marxism" (ibid: 249) . The theoretical revolution that he is describing is built around the concept of "double translation" that occurred when a group of Marxist-Leninist urban intellectuals joined with a group of indigenous leaders and intellectuals in Mexico, and ended up acknowledging the merging of Amerindian and Marxist cosmology, rather than simply insisting on a Marxist perspective, which would have been tantamount to an extension of the colonial and missionary history of the Americas. The voice of the indigenous community and the wealth of its history is given the respect that has been denied it through the silence of 500 years of the "coloniality of power." An epistemic framework emerges that indigenous communities were unable to find either in the liberal or the Marxist European legacies ultimately grounded in ancient Greek political and constitutional thought.

It seems to me that the idea of the broadcaster as a "connector" and as a "double translator" is a valuable one. If applied to Shima's proposal for GNN it helps push the concept beyond the confines that always threatened to cripple the idea from the outset, that it would simply be a reflection of Japanese attitudes and Japanese wealth. It would also offer a raison d'etre for such a service, without which access to public finance is unlikely to be available.

In what follows I shall offer very brief scenarios that attempt to illustrate some of the ideas discussed above at each layer of analysis. Rather than presenting conventional scenarios of possible futures, these are presented as speculations on what might have happened if Shima had in fact been able to get the Global News Network off the ground.

THE FOUR HISTORIES OF GNN

Keiji Shima was chairman of NHK from April, 1989 to June, 2000, an unprecedented eleven-year tenure of the position. In that time NHK was transformed as an institution. At various times in those eleven years NHK had come to a cross-roads, each offering the option of different ways of developing.

Road 1: The TANC

Following its unsuccessful attempt to purchase a major shareholding in the holding company of Asahi Television, News Corporation had developed a deep alliance with one of Asahi's rivals, Fuji Television. For some years the alliance was more symbolic than real, but in 1997 all the commercial broadcasters in Japan had come under heavy pressure from the MPT to perform the switch to digital broadcasting within the very short time period of three years. The announced policy was to foster the emergence of a "Digital Japan" by the end of 2000, with the television industry chosen as a guinea pig for the new direction; the hidden intent was to ensure that Japanese electronics manufacturers maintained their preeminent position as suppliers for the new technology. The extraordinary costs associated with the conversion to digital compelled the Japanese commercial broadcasters to seek agreements wherever finance seemed available. Inevitably, Fuji decided to deepen its connection with News Corporation, which in 1998 took a 33⅓% shareholding and a position on the board, held by James Murdoch. In response Fuji's commercial rivals also looked to deepen or develop relationships with foreign media conglomerates.

NHK paid especially close attention to the moves by News Corporation, as it had done ever since the launch of STAR TV. Not only was NHK also faced with the challenge of conversion to digital, but it was required to supervise the erection of ground and satellite relays sufficient to ensure complete coverage of the Japanese islands. In addition Prime Minister Koizumi, dissatisfied with the work of the Regulatory Reform Committee, had replaced it with a Government Restructuring Panel, with a much border remit and more extensive powers. The panel had rapidly reviewed the situation, and recommended that NHK be, at least in part, privatized.

In the aggressive manner for which he was known, Shima moved quickly. He turned to the American media mogul he had long admired, Ted Turner. There was also a structural reason for this approach: the launch of GNN in 1995 had been nearly disastrous, as the American partner, CBS News, had been notably unenthusiastic about promoting the new channel, not even succeeding in getting it on the major American cable channels. In desperation Shima had done a deal with CNN, whereby CNN took a one third shareholding, in exchange for which it ensured GNN's carriage on the Time Warner cable network.

Now, faced with an urgent need to shore up NHK'S financial position, Shima reached a new agreement. NHK became part of the soon-to-be-announced merger with AOL, creating the world's first true broadcasting multinational, known by the acronym TANC (Time-Warner/AOL/NHK/CNN), which proceeded to roll over commercial rivals.

*Road 2: **Birth of a Public Broadcasting Conglomerate***

Historically the ties between NHK and CCTV had always been close. NHK had, for example, provided the funding for the CCTV hotel which adjoined the CCTV headquarters building, and there were numerous co-production deals, including, perhaps most famously, the footage supplied by NHK for the production of "River Elegy" which had been reciprocated by the production support given by CCTV for the renowned "Silk Road" series which had had such an impact in Japan.

Following the successful launch of GNN President Shima had gone out of his way to court Chinese participation. Eventually agreement was reached when he promised to move the Asian headquarters from Hong Kong to Shanghai, a move regarded as politically astute, as the majority of the senior members of the Politburo had Shanghai connections. From that time on cooperation between CCTV and NHK became ever closer. There was a noticeable increase in the amount of time devoted to Chinese subjects on the GNN Asian newsfeed, and although the new National Reform Government took a vastly more relaxed view of controlling information than had its predecessor, there remained a tendency to gloss over problems or failings, and emphasize the positive side of government activities.

The link between NHK and CCTV went beyond GNN. There was a rapid increase in the extent of co-production activity, including investment in film production and web site development, and other activities that had the potential to earn revenue. NHK satellite launches were switched to Chinese rockets, a harbinger of the slimming down of the over-expensive Japanese satellite program. Both organizations were immensely wealthy, and began to look around for other investment opportunities. Talks were under way with Doordashan, with the hope of creating an Asian public broadcasting giant, the biggest in the world.

The final irony was a proposal from NHK that the Japanese broadcaster and CCTV should jointly fund a new Hong Kong-based venture, with the express purpose of buying STAR TV from News Corporation, which following an accounting scandal was in bankruptcy proceedings.

*Road 3: **The Road to Baghdad***

The success of President Shima in launching GNN had unintended consequences. One was that NHK had begun to shed its staid, establishment image, thanks to its vicarious connection with the news station. GNN was immensely popular among young people. Its announcers were much-admired celebrities, and the world news had become fashionable, with knowledge-testing contests and reprises of the "top ten news stories" every month serving to reinforce its appeal, and numerous borrowed words from other languages feeding youthful Japanese slang.

GNN also rapidly became influential, on a global scale, superseding CNN, which was more and more seen as parochial and superficial. The contrast between the two news networks was made more apparent by the fact that CNN had joined the shift in American broadcasting towards an openly conservative posture in the face of ongoing terrorist attacks on famous American cultural icons, notably the gassing of Disneyworld which had killed 268 children and parents. Ted Turner's attempts to reclaim control of CNN, avowedly to help recapture its editorial independence, were easily defeated by the board of TimeWarner. At the same time GNN had secured long-term carriage contracts with all the major cable and satellite networks, so almost by default it had become the major alternative media in the United States.

Somewhat to the surprise of those involved in its early creation and development GNN had developed as a successful example of journalists from different cultures working together. This had been achieved in part by an early employment qualification requirement, that all employees had to be able to communicate effectively in at least three languages, one of which had to be from another continent. Staff members were well-trained and well-rewarded, and aware of their position as an international media elite, charged with living up to the GNN slogan "We are the World of News." The slogan was given reality by the fact that, from 2000, all broadcasts were simultaneously multicast in all the major languages of the United Nations, a remarkable achievement of computer translation.

The ubiquity and accessibility of GNN had come to be seen by many as a symbol of the positive side of globalization, a beacon of intellectual hope that reinforced the idea of similarities across cultures. But to a degree this was superficial: the similarities tended to be between the middle class and financially secure. The attitudes that underpinned GNN still reflected its birth as the offspring of the rich societies of Asia, Europe and North America. Africa continued to receive scant coverage, while the Arab nations had effectively set up their own rival network, called Baghdad, in memory of the city that had been so crudely devastated in the bombings of 2003.

*Road 4: **Only Connect***

When President Shima of NHK had first advanced the concept of GNN few had anticipated that it would develop in the way that it did. His initial attempts to attract the interest of the BBC and ABC had failed. As a compromise NHK staff had turned to 'alternate' public service broadcasters and teamed up with Channel 4 of the UK and the Special Broadcasting Service (SBS) of Australia.

Both SBS and Channel 4 brought with them a commitment to adventurous programming: in fact, both were specifically mandated to provide alternatives to the mainstream television fare. They were both comparatively young and lean, a stark contrast to the huge NHK bureaucracy. They also took the role of the broadcaster as educator seriously, albeit not in a didactic manner. SBS had developed a remarkably successful formula of showing the best programming from literally anywhere, in a deliberate attempt to foster the idea of Australia as a multicultural society.

Thus it was that the GNN that was eventually launched at the beginning of 1995 was a variation of world news that had originally been offered on NHK satellite, and subsequently emulated by SBS. The morning news broadcast was taken direct from different public broadcasters in succession and rebroadcast over GNN, translated into the language of the nation receiving the signal, but otherwise unmediated. At three-quarters past the hour there was 15 minutes of commentary, in which a deliberate attempt was made to introduce the voices of smaller nations, and indeed ethnic groupings that did not fit the container of the nation-state, such as Basques, Kurds, Amerindians and the many voices of Africa.

By 2000 the GNN had evolved into a broadcasting bazaar, where every kind of and approach to information was at least potentially available. In addition to the straight news channel there was a global broadcast legislature channel, carrying debates from parliaments and congresses around the world; a united nations channel, reflecting not just the political UN, but also the work of its many agencies in education, health, humanitarian assistance and more; a popular children's channel, which featured reports made by children from all over, explaining their lives, and which featured a call-in facility so other children could ask questions; and a world culture channel, showing the best each society had to offer, whether films, musicals, dramas, comedies or whatever. For the first time television had slipped its national moorings, and had set sail on the sea of diversity.

Appendix: The GNN Planning Documents

Global News Network—Global Satellite Transmission System (NHK)

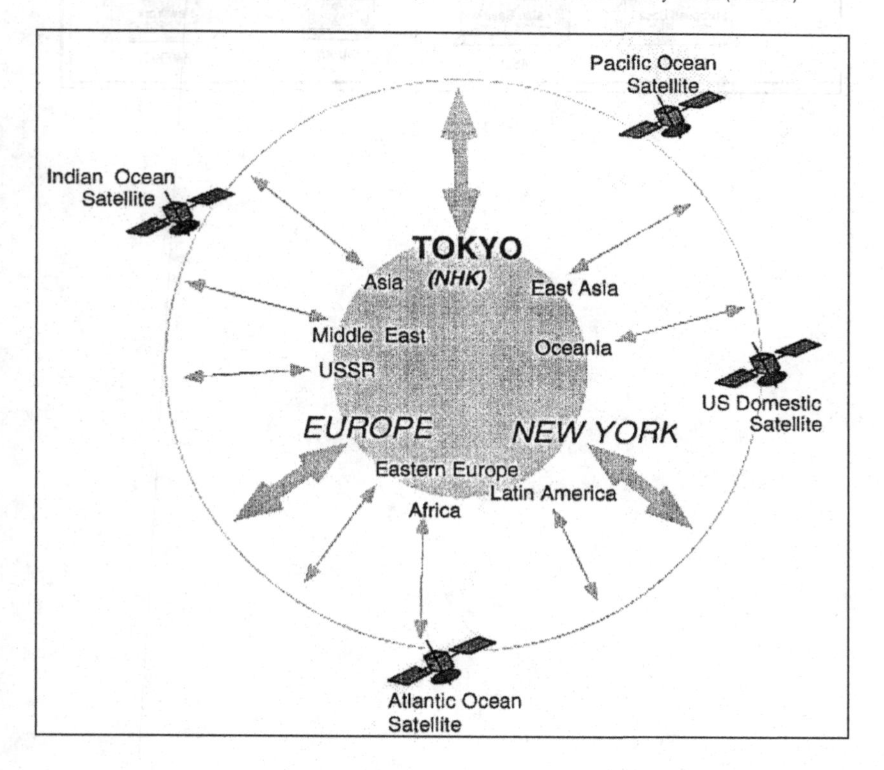

Figure 1

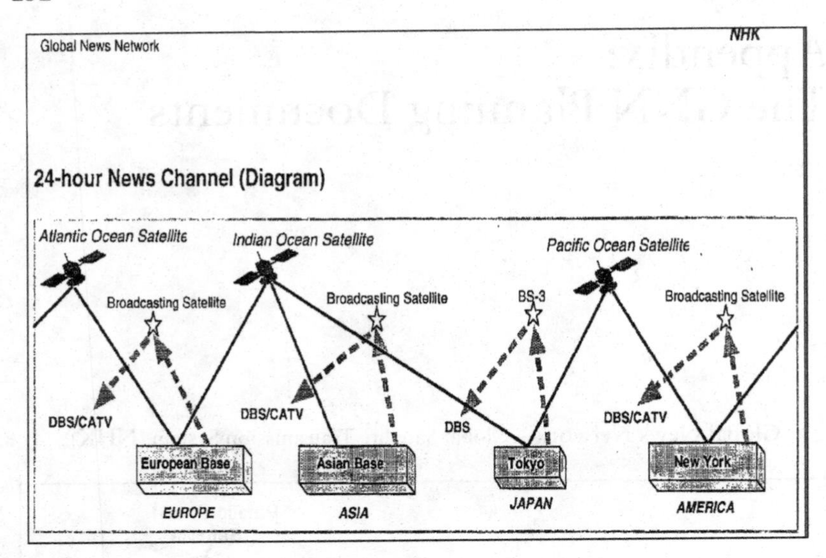
Global News Network
NHK
24-hour News Channel (Diagram)
Atlantic Ocean Satellite
Indian Ocean Satellite
Pacific Ocean Satellite
Broadcasting Satellite
Broadcasting Satellite
BS-3
Broadcasting Satellite
DBS/CATV
DBS/CATV
DBS
DBS/CATV
European Base
Asian Base
Tokyo
New York
EUROPE
ASIA
JAPAN
AMERICA

Figure 2

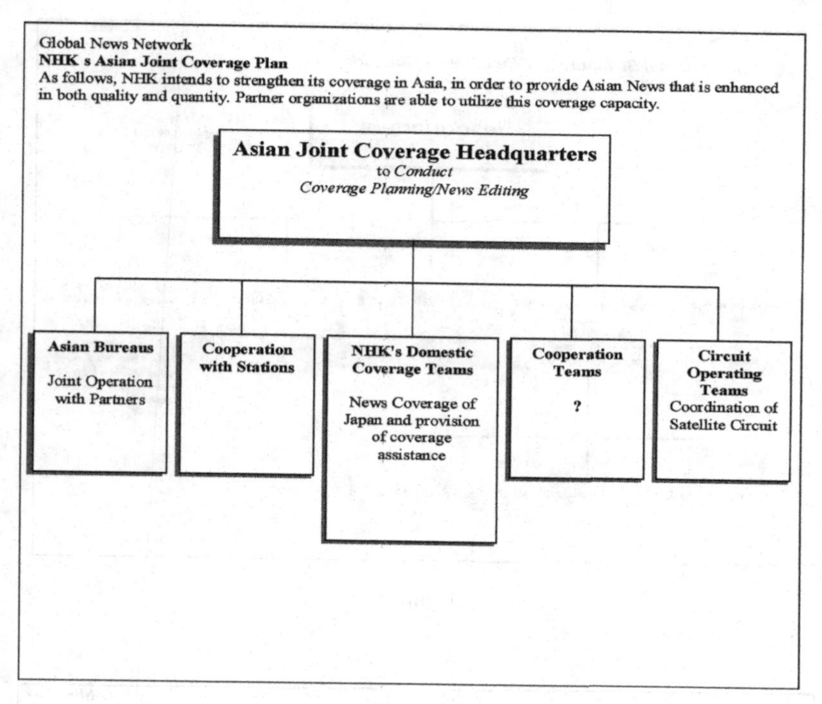
Global News Network
NHK s Asian Joint Coverage Plan
As follows, NHK intends to strengthen its coverage in Asia, in order to provide Asian News that is enhanced in both quality and quantity. Partner organizations are able to utilize this coverage capacity.
Asian Joint Coverage Headquarters
to Conduct
Coverage Planning/News Editing
Asian Bureaus
Joint Operation with Partners
Cooperation with Stations
NHK's Domestic Coverage Teams
News Coverage of Japan and provision of coverage assistance
Cooperation Teams
?
Circuit Operating Teams
Coordination of Satellite Circuit

Figure 3

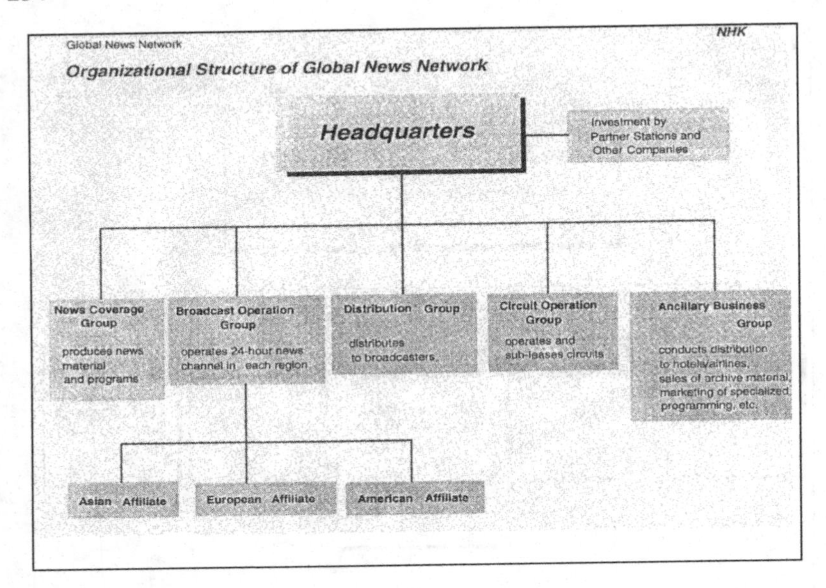

Figure 4

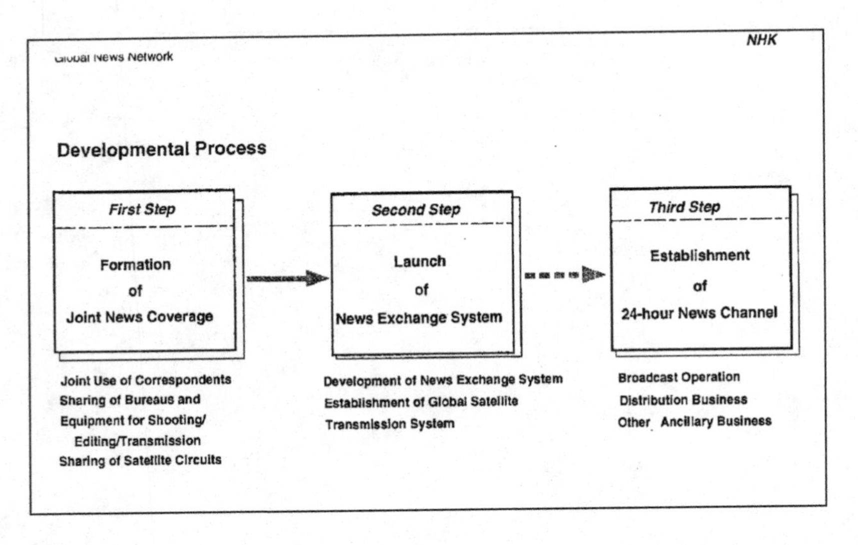

Figure 5

Glossary

ABU Asian Broadcasting Union.

Al-Jazeera First independent Arabic news channel, broadcast on satellite. Based in Doha, the capital of Qatar, and funded by the Emir of Qatar. Launched in November, 1996, had an audience estimated at 35 million in 2003.

Asiasat World's first relaunched satellite went up on Long March 3 on April 7, 1990 . Formerly was Westar 6, retrieved by the Space Shuttle in 1984.

Asiavision An Asian version of the Eurovision news exchange system. Asia is divided into two zones. Zone A includes the official ("State") broadcasters from China, Iran, South Korea, Japan, and Indonesia. Countries in Zone B are Bangladesh, India, Pakistan, Brunei, Malaysia, Sri Lanka, and Indonesia—the latter being the only country in both zones. The operation is run under the auspices of the ABU.

Astra The first European satellite launched and operated by a private company, the Société Européene des Satellites (SES) in December, 1988. Operates under a franchise from the Government of Luxembourg. Shareholders include Luxembourg, Belgian and German banks and British and Scandinavian TV interests. A medium-powered satellite (transmitting at a power of 47 dBW), and therefore officially designated as a telecommunications satellite, but used for direct-to-home television services.

BBC British Broadcasting Corporation. The BBC began radio transmissions in 1922. BBC Television was re-introduced after World War II in 1946. The first commercial TV channel was introduced in 1955, BBC 2 began in 1964, Channel 4 in 1982.

BBC World Formerly BBC World Service Television. Launched in 1995, this is the BBC's first foray into satellite television, a 24-hour, international news and information television channel built around comprehensive half-hour global news programs. Claims to reach 200 million homes in 200 countries and territories worldwide. It is a commercial service, run by BBC Worldwide and funded by advertising and subscription.

BBC World Service External radio broadcasting services of the BBC. Claims an audience of 125 million listeners at least once a week. This figure does not include countries where statistics are regarded as too uncertain, notably China.

BSkyB British Sky Broadcasting. The UK's largest satellite broadcaster, launched in 1994. Owned by News International (Rupert Murdoch), Granada TV and Pearson (owner of Financial Times, Economist, others). Its predecessor was Sky Television, the first commercial DBS service launched in 1989. Sky TV originated as a four-channel service on the Astra satellite. Sky TV is a European DBS service and is now owned by News Corporation.

Cable In the U.S cable is by far the most popular way to redistribute a television signal, often received from a satellite.

CATV Community Antenna Television. The most basic form of cable TV, based on radio frequency transmission though 75-ohms coaxial cable. The U.S. had an early start with cable TV in part because of its early adoption of CATV systems, which appeared as early as 1950: by 1953 there were more CATV systems than there were broadcast stations (see Parsons and Frieden, 1998). One of these systems grew to become Tele Communications, Inc., the largest American cable system, later bought and sold by AT&T.

CCTV China Central Television. China's national broadcasting network, claims to reach more than 240 million television households across China.

Communications satellites (CS) (aka geostationary communications satellites)Communications satellites are launched into a special orbit, called a 'geostationary orbit,' first theorized by Arthur C. Clarke. An unpowered satellite takes longer to orbit the Earth the further away it is, and in the "Clarke belt" 35 700km above the Earth, the time to complete an orbit is exactly one day. If a satellite is positioned directly over the equator, in this orbit, then it will seem to be stationary in the sky. A communications satellite is a spacecraft that orbits the Earth and relays messages, radio, telephone and television signals. Stations on the ground, called earth stations, transmit signals to the satellite, which then relays the signal to other earth stations. Modern satellites are 'active,' meaning they strengthen the signal before relaying it through a transponder. Broadcasts from a satellite in geostationary or synchronous orbit can cover only about one third of the Earth's surface. To send signals anywhere in the world, three communications satellites in geostationary orbit are needed. Broadcasts are in the C-band frequency range.Traditionally communication satellites were regarded as "medium-power" satellites. As non-DBS satellite systems they were seen as primarily commercial ventures, and therefore not as heavily regulated by international institutions. Examples were Astra and PanAmSat.

Compression Most forms of communication include a lot of repetition in the information sent. With a digital TV signal, it is possible to simply repeat those parts of the image information which are unchanged, rather than recreating the image in its entirety. This allows for the transmitted signal to be greatly reduced in size, using a compression algorithm.

DBS Direct Broadcasting by Satellite, or Direct Broadcast Satellite. The transmission of high-power TV signals for reception directly by individual viewers. DBS satellites are more powerful and usually heavier than 'telecommunication' satellites, therefore require a more powerful rocket and are more expensive. Frequencies and orbital slots are controlled by the ITU. Each country is assigned a fixed orbital position for DBS satellites, and frequencies for five channels. DBS uses special high powered Ku-Band satellites that send digitally compressed television and audio signals to 18- to 24-inch (45 to 60 cm) fixed satellite dishes. DBS systems transmit signals to Earth in what is called the Broadcast Satellite Service (BSS) portion of the Ku-Band between 12.2 and 12.7 GHz. Thanks to digital compression technologies, DBS systems can deliver hundreds of cable TV-style programming channels, as well as local network television affiliates. DBS systems have traditionally been subject to heavy governmental involvement, thanks to their uniquely (and purposely) domestic configurations. The definition of DBS has become confused due to the increased power of communications satellite, which may also be sufficiently strong to relay signals directly to terrestrial receivers.

DTH Direct-To-Home transmission. A DTH signal goes direct to each dwelling place via an individual dish. Generally refers to services using Ku-band frequencies for DBS-like applications in the all-purpose fixed satellite service.

Eurovision A pan-European program exchange system.

Footprint The geographical area inside which the signals from a satellite are designed to be received.

Frequency bands In the US, certain frequency bands are allocated for fixed satellite service by the FCC, viz.

C-band 3700–4200 MHz (space-to-Earth) and 5925–6425 MHz (Earth-to-space)

Ku-band 11.2–11.7 GHz (space-to-Earth) and 14.0–14.5 GHz (Earth-to-space)

HDTV High Definition Television. First commercial system was developed by NHK, an analog system based on 1125 lines and 60 fields (frames) per second. Needed a 18 MHz channel (compare with a 6 MHz channel for a regular TV channel)

HFC Hybrid Fiber/Coaxial (cable). HFC is essentially a local loop technology. The basic concept is to use fiber optic cable for trunk transmission (FTTC) and coaxial cable as a distribution network. In an HFC network, information requiring high bandwidth is digitized and multiplexed, then distributed to endusers to maximize bandwidth load on coaxial cable.

INN Independent News Network. An American news "packager," owned by Tribune Broadcasting, with close links to Visnews. Supplies a nightly half-hour news package, "USA Tonight," to 115 American TV stations.

Intelsat International Telecommunications Satellite Organization. Established in 1964 by 11 members of the ITU, with headquarters in Washington, D.C. By 1999 Intelsat had 143 members, each member state nominating a telecommunications operator as its representative, and each member having a share of ownership in proportion to the extent of usage of Intelsat's services. The result is that the U.S. and the U.K. have traditionally dominated the organization (25% and 14% shareholding respectively in the 1980s). At present Intelsat deploys 20 satellites, servicing a claimed 18,000 earth stations. Television services are now a major source of revenue.

Interlaced In effect, an early form of TV signal compression. In order to fit the 60 frame-per-second TV signal into the 6-megahertz channels, the NTSC engineers cut the signal in half, by sending half the frame every thirtieth of a second, followed immediately by the second half. In fact the frame is sliced into strips, with the even number strips sent first, followed by the odd-numbered; the strips are then "interlaced" together by the TV receiving set. Problems are picture shimmer (visible if you sit close to an old TV) and lack of a perfect match between the interlaced strips, often making text difficult to read. For both these reasons, computer manufacturers rejected interlaced for their monitors, opting instead for progressive scanning.

ITN Independent Television News. An organization created in 1955 for the sole purpose of providing news for British commercial television. Originally non-profit-making and owned by the British regional commercial television franchise holders, now Reuters has a major ownership stake:

ITU International Telecommunications Union. Established in Paris in 1865, when it was known as the International Telegraph Union. As the UN agency charged with regulation and development of international telecommunications, the ITU allocates satellite orbits and operating frequencies.

JCC Japan Communications Satellite Company, licensed by the MPT in 1985.

JSB Japan Satellite Broadcasting, which began pay satellite TV service in 1990, operating as WoWoW. JSB is a shotgun consortium created by the MPT from the thirteen companies which had applied for the one available commercial license.

MII Ministry of Information Industries (China: *Xin Xi Gong Ye Bu*), created in March 1998 out of the merger of the Ministry of Posts and Telecommunications (MPT), the MRFT (see below), the Ministry of Electronic Industries MEI), the Aerospace Industrial Corporation, and the Aviation Industrial Corporation. The MII is a super-agency overseeing telecommunications, multimedia, broadcasting, satellites, and the Internet, reporting directly to the State Council. The traditional rivalry between the MPT and the MRFT has been imported into the new ministry, with little apparent change.

MMDS Multipoint Microwave Distribution System (MMDS), aka MVDS (Microwave Video Distribution system). The use of microwave systems to distribute a television signal over a limited geographical area.

MPHPT Ministry of Public Management, Home Affairs, Posts and Telecommunications (Japan) was set up in January 2001, as part of the Central Government Reform, through the merging of the Management and Coordination Agency, the Ministry of Home Affairs, and the Ministry of Posts and Telecommunications.

MPT Ministry of Posts and Telecommunications. The same title was employed for both China and Japan (*Yuseisho*), though in both cases the ministry has been subsumed into a larger entity (see above).

MRFT Ministry of Radio, Film and Television (China) was a result of the upgrading of the Broadcasting Bureau to the Ministry of Radio and Television in 1982, then to the Ministry of

	Radio, Film and Television (MRFT) in 1985. In 1998 it was swallowed by the new MII (see above), becoming the SARFT State Administration for Film, Radio and Television (*Guang bo dian ying, dian shi guan li ju*).
MSO	Multiple system operators: cable TV system operators offering multiple services, typically including data transfer (Internet) and telephony.
NTSC	Refers to the National Television Standards Committee, the American television standard developed, mostly, by RCA engineers. A 525-line interlaced signal on a 6-megahertz channel, sending 60 frames per second. Used primarily in the United States, Canada and Japan, while the rest of the world favors the PAL system, or its derivatives.
NHK	Nippon Hôsô Kyôkai (Japan Broadcasting Corporation)
PAL	Phase Alternation Line. Television standard used in most of the world outside North America and Japan. See NTSC.
PanAmSat	PanAmerican Satellite Company. Established in 1984 by René Anselmo, who built his fortune in Spanish-language television, as the world's first privately owned international satellite company.
Prasar Bharati	Broadcasting Corporation of India, a statutory autonomous body established in 1997, incorporating AIR (All India Radio) and Doordarshan (Public service television).
Progressive scanning	In "proscan" the entire frame is presented on a screen at one time, making the image stable and easy to read—unlike the interlaced images used in TV—and therefore favored by computer monitor manufacturers. (See Interlaced)
Reuters	British news agency founded in 1851. In 1984 became a private commercial company, with original British, Australian and New Zealand owners retaining an effective veto, designed to maintain editorial independence. Took early lead in IT applications, and became leading financial/business news provider.
SCC	Space Communications Corporation, licensed by the MPT in 1985.
SMATV	Satellite Master Antenna Television. A TVRO shared by a number of final consumers, typically an apartment building or, in China, a work unit.
STAR TV	Launched in 1991 with five television channels, STAR pioneered satellite television in Asia. Now known as 'STAR,' the

company broadcasts 40 services in eight languages. It claims to reach more than 300 million viewers in 53 countries across Asia.

TCP/IP An essential element of the Internet, TCP (transmission-control protocol) refers to messages encapsulated and decapsulated in "datagrams," much as a letter is put into and taken out of an envelope, and sent as end-to end packets, with gateways reading only the envelopes so that only the receiving hosts read the contents. First practical demonstration in 1977.

IP (internet protocol) was a further refinement developed in 1978, responsible for routing individual datagrams. This separation of the protocols made it possible to build fast and relatively inexpensive gateways, which in turn fueled the growth of internetworking.

Transponder Refers to both the channel and to the amplifying hardware on the satellite which are used to receive the uplinking signal from earth and send the downlinking signal back.

TVRO Television Receive Only Earth Station. The original TVROs were massive in size and weight. As satellites have increased in power, so the size and the cost of the receiving "dish" have shrunk.

Visnews TV news service owned by NBC, Reuters, and the BBC. Since 1992 effectively owned by Reuters. Sells to virtually anyone who will pay for news material (including local stations in the States, via INN, and the Sky satellite news channel in Europe).

VOA Voice of America. "VOA broadcasts more than 1,000 hours of news, informational, educational, and cultural programs every week to an audience of some 94 million people worldwide. VOA programs are produced and broadcast in more than 50 languages through radio, satellite television, and the Internet."

WARC '77 The ITU's World Administrative Radio Conference held in 1977, at which for the first time prime orbital positions for satellites were awarded on nation-by-nation basis, regardless of a country's need, ability or desire to use such a position. The assumption was that these slots would be used for DBS satellites.

WTN TV news service owned by ABC, Australia's Channel 9, and ITN. In the U.S. supplies material to ABC, CBS and to the

News Hour (formerly McNeill/Lehrer hour) on PBS. WTN claims to serve some 1,200 television stations worldwide with international news. Their contracts include a multi-million dollar deal with the Japanese national broadcaster, NHK.

WoWoW see JSB.

Notes

NOTES TO INTRODUCTION

1. STAR TV has been renamed simply "Star," but for the purposes of this book I continue to use the original name.
2. For example, see Barnet and Cavanagh (1994) "Global Dreams"; Ohmae (1995) "The end of the nation state"; Friedman (2000) "The Lexus and the Olive Tree"; Hardt and Negri (2000) "Empire." A notable and welcome exception is Vogel (1996) "Freer Markets, More Rules."

NOTES TO CHAPTER ONE

1. For example, in 2002 the Portuguese government threatened to close its second public broadcast TV station, the general interest RTP2, as part of a general cost-cutting move. After protests by staff the compromise was to turn RTP2 into a community access channel dedicated to educational and cultural programming, with a much reduced budget (Radio Netherlands Media Network report for September 8, 2003).
2. Such indicators also invariably fail to account for the off-the-books economy, grey and black, which available information seems to indicate may be equivalent to as least 20% of the "real" economy (see White, 1996). A World Bank report by Friedrich Schneider (2002) concluded that the average size of the "informal economy," as a percent of official GNI in the year 2000, was as high as 41% in developing countries.
3. Interview with David Harvey: "Living in a Global World," 2001, Episode 2.1.
4. There is an apparent contradiction between Giddens' approach and that of Harvey, who proposes the thesis of time-space compression. For Giddens time separates itself away from space and thus allows a 'stretching' of time across space, while Harvey argues that the universalization of time entails space being annihilated by time. I see these as being two sides of the same coin. The 'stretching' of time in fact means connection across space, which is translated into the annihilation of time.
5. References are to the original Japanese language publications. Morita was not credited in the 1991 English-language version published by Simon and Schuster. The title of the Mahathir and Ishihara volume was changed to "The Voice of Asia" when published in English in 1995 by Kodansha.

6. One such company, Iridium, promoted itself as "a global entity, the world's first pan-national corporation" prior to its ignominious collapse. See Bennahum, 1998.
7. As a corollary to this argument, the current decline of CNN might be linked to its becoming more "anchored" after being taken over by Time-Warner, thus losing its status as international gadfly. Another example might be provided by Israel and the Jews. The more deeply "Jewishness" is equated with the state of Israel, rather than with a transnational religion or culture, the greater the loss of international freedom of maneuver, and potentially the diminishment of the concept of an unbounded Jewish culture itself.
8. Interview with Ringo Leung, former Senior Engineer, Hutchison Whampoa (STAR TV), March 4, 1998.
9. Yoshimatsu is at pains to distinguish this example of "external market power (driving) policy change within a state" from *gaiatsu*, the application of direct pressure from foreign governments or firms, often used in Japan to introduce change that might otherwise be unacceptable domestically.
10. An exception may be in geography, in which new approaches are being made to visualize the interconnectedness in the globe, like a multi-dimensional chess board, with vectors and arcs linking points and nodes in economics, health and law (See Langdale 1991 and Luke 1995).
11. The global village does not translate into global uniformity, however. Gladney points out that there was an almost complete disconnect between the two media spheres (of U.S.-British media and media from the Arabic speaking world) in the coverage of the 2003 Iraq war (2004: 18).
12. Anderson (1991: 54) also points out the important role of radio, both as a transition technology between print and television, and as a maker of new nationalisms in the twentieth century: an observation confirmed by the early history of NHK (see Chapter 3), and the use of radio to unify China after 1949 (see Chapter 4).

NOTES TO CHAPTER TWO

1. As defined by Stuart Hall, this debate can be summarized as an emphasis on analyzing the effects of the media on modern society, on the one hand, contrasted with a view that sees the media as directly involved in social construction and legitimation (Hall, 1982).
2. The author had a practical experience of Eco's concept, when he worked in a London movie film developing laboratory. Every night tests were run on the chemical soup in which the film was developed, intended to ascertain whether the colors that emerged would be "accurate." This was of course an entirely subjective judgement, and the Eastman Kodak company had helpfully provided a test strip of a woman's face against which the night managers were supposed to pronounce whether or not the night's work would emerge as a likely representation of reality. A human face was chosen because skin tones are notoriously the most difficult to render satisfactorily. Unfortunately for the British laboratory technicians the face, and its rendition, was plainly American, with noticeably saturated red tones.

Invariably, the face was lightened and made paler. This helps explain the different "feel" of films from different sources: where Americans may favor reds, the British are more interested in greens, while the Russians look at blue and the French seem to prefer a paler, washed-out look, and so on.

3. 'Hegemony' in this context refers to social control by persuasive means, the manipulation of knowledge, norms and values.
4. See, for example, Jerry Mander: "Four Arguments for the Elimination of Television" (1978); Theodor Roszak: "The Cult of Information" (1986) : the works of Sven Birkerts, such as "The Gutenberg Elegies: The Fate of Reading in An Electronic Age" (1994); Clifford Stoll: " Silicon Snake Oil" (1995).
5. Whenever I raised a question about speculative futures in China, Toffler's name was invariably mentioned, as "The Third Wave" has become a "classic" reference text for the social sciences in China.
6. Now known as BBC World.
7. Another seminal work that appeared at the same time was Fritz Machlup's "The Production and Distribution of Knowledge in the United States" (1962), which argued for the key role of information in the economy and indeed human society in general.
8. "Information industries" can be widely interpreted. The former chairman of Monsanto defined biotechnology as "a subset of information technology. It's a way to create value without creating more stuff. I put a gene, which is information, into a cottonseed, and I don't have to spray stuff on the crop in order to control insects. That strategy strikes me as the right one for agriculture, just as it strikes me as the right one for post-industrial society" Specter, 2000: 63.
9. Preston also raises a number of questions concerning information sector studies, including the sometimes loose use of the word "information" in defining (or excluding) specific social sectors, and the tendency to "commodify" information and lump all aspects of it together.
10. I am following Steger's definition of globalism as the "dominant ideological package" of globalization, in effect the neoliberal worldview (Steger, 2002).
11. Information based on their respective web sites and direct correspondence with the organizations. "MTV Networks" includes MTV and Nickelodeon. As of June, 2002, MTV appears in 165 countries and Nickelodeon in 158 countries.
12. However, the early history of broadcasting in the U.S. centered around a vigorous debate between the commercial and the public interest camps. The seminal Radio Act of 1927 was forthright in describing broadcasters as "public trustees," in a privileged position to be station owners, and stating that stations should "be operated as if owned by the public" (Johnson, 2001: 178).
13. In his examination of public hearings convened by the FCC in 1962 to investigate the demise of local television, Curtin places the emergence of a national network television system in the context of capitalism's constant production of new boundaries and new relationships (2001: 351)
14. One reason for the shift in policy was the antipathy of the re-elected Prime Minister Winston Churchill towards the BBC, rooted in memories of leading

a faction in the government of the time which had wished to control coverage of the general strike of 1926, and his overall suspicion of the BBC as being a 'red conspiracy' (Franklin, 1997: 121, 164).

15. According to Peter Chernin, the president of News Corporation: "In almost every TV market in the world, local product has been growing in the past five years, at the expense of American" (Economist, 2002:12).
16. In addition there are three more major agencies. Russia has ITAR-TASS, the successor to the Soviet-era TASS, which was in effect the propaganda arm of the government; China has Xinhua, which continues to operate as a state-controlled government spokesman; and finally there is the Rome-based Inter Press Service, which specializes in Third World News, and is ranked as the sixth-largest agency in the world.
17. NHK was established in the same year, representing an explicit move by the government to control radio, and due in part to lessons learnt from the way the British government had used the media during the General Strike (Kasza, 1986).
18. The legitimation effect also applies to the broadcaster, partly as already explained because television institutions have tended to define themselves by news—and helps explain why they are willing to pay extraordinary sums to obtain rights to cover such events as the Olympics.
19. The language employed by the TV networks is explicit. A CNN press release at the time of the Littleton, Colorado school shootings boasted of its success in delivering viewers: "On April 20, 1999, the network's highest-rated day of the year to date, CNN/U.S. posted total-day increases of 425% in rating and 409% in delivery, averaging a 2.1 rating and delivering 1.6 million homes. The network's delivery among adults 25-34 also increased by 731 percent."
20. Interview with Alan MacDonald, Director, BBC Worldwide, June 20, 1997.
21. Interview with Ping Wei, Director, International Relations, CCTV, April 3, 1997.
22. General surveys of foreign news show that coverage emphasizes the negative. For example, a Media Tenor survey of 5,580 reports on the US TV major networks from May 2000 to August 2001 showed "international coverage . . . dominated by reports on foreign wars, accidents, natural catastrophes, social polices, crimes and other events that were disconnected from American polices and unrelated to American lives" (Media Tenor, 2001).

NOTES TO CHAPTER THREE

1. Figure represents combined morning and evening edition circulations. Newspaper figures are from the Japan Newspaper Publishers and Editors Association (2004) and magazines from the Research Institute for Publications, JETRO (2004), and Shuppan Nyususha (2002, Web Japan Fact Sheet).
2. For example, see Kyogoku (1987), Upham (1987), Ozawa (1994), or Johnson (1995). When the media is featured, it is usually in reference to specific, usually negative incidents, such as Upham's condemnation of the media for self-censorship (1987: 113), or Johnson's account of how the mainstream Japanese media were able to continue reporting on the Cultural

Revolution in China by basically following the official Chinese government view of events (1995: 243). A welcome recent exception is Gatzen (2003).

3. Lebra's "Japanese Social Organization' (1992) also began to describe a vastly more complex society from an anthropological point of view.
4. 'Control of Media of Public Information and Expression in Japan,' 20 Jan. 1945, cited in Tracey, 1998: 130.
5. The exception is TBS, which had started life as a radio station, Radio Tokyo, and had already built up its staff and a network of affiliates before television began. Its parent newspaper, Mainichi, is financially weak: in the 1970s its stockholding dropped to less than one percent (Kitatani, 1988: 181, 2).
6. All recent NHK data is taken from the NHK Annual Report 2004 and from the White Paper on Communications in Japan, 2003, Ministry of Public Management, Home Affairs, Posts and Telecommunications.
7. "Direct Broadcast by Satellite." Please refer to glossary for fuller explanation.
8. In fact the viability of satellite broadcasting had already been demonstrated in 1975 when HBO began satellite transmissions to cable stations around the U.S. and in 1976 when the Palapa A satellites began coverage of Indonesia's 6,000 islands.
9. According to Krauss, "the development and launching of Yuri 2a and 2b cost about Y60 trillion (approximately half a billion US$) of which NHK had borne about 60% of the costs. This represented almost a full ten percent of NHK's yearly budget" (Krauss, 2000: 182).
10. Dupagne and Seel also mention dissatisfaction with the quality of the NTSC signal as a contributing factor. From a technical viewpoint, NTSC, based on 1940s technology, left much to be desired: video engineers used to joke that the initials were an acronym for "Never The Same Color."
11. MUSE stands for multiple sub-nyquist sampling encoding, referring to a compression process.
12. European fears about Japanese intentions did not disappear when they abandoned their analog HDTV system. According to Michel Pelchat, chairman of the 'Association for the Television of the Future,' a lobbying group seeking to merge the US and European plans for a digital transmission system, "They [the Japanese] are going to go gung-ho [into digital HDTV], and this should be feared" Broadcasting & Cable, 1994: 51.
13. Krauss (2000: 187-194) gives a good summary account of the extraordinary lengths to which Japanese industry and government went in attempts to have HDTV accepted as an American system. He even attributes Sony's 1989 purchase of Columbia Pictures and Matsushita's 1990 acquisition of MCA/Universal to the need to have enough film library resources to fuel the anticipated demand for HDTV broadcast material.
14. At the time the MPT first announced that it was thinking of abandoning support for the HDTV system, only 20,000 sets had been sold. Price was the main problem: the cheapest cost $6,000 (Economist, 1994, February).
15. Interview with Spencer Sherman, April 25, 1994.
16. Interview with Yoshihiko Ogaki, Deputy Director, NHK Public Relations Bureau, May 28, 1998.

17. In initial discussions, the BBC was usually mentioned as a partner, a name that would have lent a very high level of credibility to the proposal. However, the BBC never showed any interest, as it was at the time developing its own plans to become an international broadcaster.
18. Interview with Yuanhe Ma, Director General, Foreign Affairs Department, Ministry of Radio, Film and TV. April 1, 1997.
19. One of the Japanese participants in the planning for GNN denied that Tokyo would necessarily have been the Asian center, claiming that Hong Kong could have been an alternative "because we had to try and keep the Chinese happy." Interview with Noriyoshi Fujii, Senior Director, International Relations and Policy Planning, NHK. August 11, 1994.
20. Interview with Steven Herman, Director, Channel Operations & Programming, Discovery Channel-Asia. May 25, 1998.
21. Sherman's charges of pre-censorship at NHK should be balanced by the corporation's willingness to investigate stories that the commercial broadcasters would not touch, such as the gangster-related murder of a Sumitomo banker in September, 1994 (Sender, 1994: 80).
22. Interview with Noriyoshi Fujii, ibid.
23. Interview with Noriyoshi Fujii, ibid.
24. Interview with Noriyoshi Fujii, ibid.
25. NHK was acutely aware of the connection between such sensitivities and international TV. Its DBS broadcasts had spilled over into South Korea and other Asian countries, resulting in an official complaint from Seoul. NHK was forced to shrink its footprint to reduce the extent of reception abroad.
26. Interview with Spencer Sherman, ibid.
27. "Creating Images: American and Japanese Television News Coverage of the Other." The Mansfield Center for Pacific Affairs, 1997.
28. Thatcher and her followers had made something of a crusade out of attacking the BBC, focusing on its Achilles' heel, financing. One of her advisers on communications policy attacked "the chief myth (of public broadcasting) that because an activity fulfills a public service it is not subject to basic laws of economics . . . the principles of supply and demand" (Tracey, 1998: 48).
29. Interview with Yukio Yanagisawa, President, Satellite Magazine Inc., May 28, 1998, and also Shima, 1995 :168-170.
30. After his resignation, Shima set up the "Shima Media Network," primarily a website which acted as a clearing house for "news from exclusive sources without censorship or filtering from government or news agencies."
31. Interview with K. Katoh, Chief Producer, NHK Eisei Hosokyoku. August 9, 1994.
32. Interview with K. Katoh, ibid.
33. One of the many ironies surrounding the failure of GNN was the fact that the BBC had started its own 24-hour news service in Asia just two months before NHK finally gave up its plans.
34. Interview with Katsumi Kuwae, Head of International Department, NHK Joho Network. May 28, 1998.
35. Using only three C-band satellites means the footprints are very wide, often resulting in poor reception. This economical use of satellites was the result

of a conscious decision to cut costs, in anticipation of criticisms from ordinary subscribers or from the Diet about improper use of subscription fee revenues in Japan. In other words NHK still worries about getting its budget passed in parliament (Interview with Yoshihiko Ogaki, Deputy Director, NHK Public Relations Bureau. May 28, 1998).

36. Interview with Yoshihiko Ogaki, ibid.
37. Interview with Katsumi Kuwae, Head of International Department, NHK Joho Network. May 28, 1998.
38. When America's third and fourth largest cable companies, Comcast and MediaOne, announced plans for a merger in March, 1999, the main rationale presented was the potential of broadband cable to deliver high-speed data services, video and telephony on the same menu (Economist, March, 1999). Eventually, MediaOne was bought by AT&T instead: the rationale was the same, however (Economist, May, 1999). In 2002, the tables were turned, and Comcast bought AT&T Broadband. The reasoning was unchanged: "AT&T Comcast could be the first company to make good on the long-awaited promise of broadband" (Lowry, 2002:110).
39. In fact the MPT specifically distinguished between "urban cable TV," meaning systems that offered programming not available on regular TV-the norm for cable TV outside Japan-and cable TV built to alleviate reception problems, usually in rural, mountainous areas.
40. NTT's position at the time was anomalous, because it was forbidden by law from participating in international telecom business. When NTT announced in September 1995 that it would launch its "open computer network" service in 1997, it was thought likely to violate the NTT law because its prime selling point was connecting to the overseas Internet (Yoshimatsu, 1998: 18).
41. Multi-channel "urban-type" systems-comparable to most systems in the United States-had an even lower penetration rate of 4.7% (Kahaner, 1996). The discrepancy is explained by the fact that traditionally most cable systems in Japan were "compensatory," used for re-transmission of terrestrial channels in difficult reception areas.
42. Article 5 of the Cable Television Broadcast Law of 1972 not only explicitly disqualified non-Japanese nationals or organizations from permission to operate a system, but also forbad one fifth or more of voting rights being held by such persons or entities or their proxies.
43. 1994 was also the year in which the British Government White Paper on broadcasting encouraged the BBC to develop its commercial activities, a structural change of like significance.
44. In reality the "reversal of laws" was a relaxation of existing laws. "Since December 1993, the examination standards have become less restrictive." MPT "Manual for Market Entry into Cable TV Business, March, 1998. According to Titus Communications, foreign companies were informed of the change in attitude through an official press release (correspondence, July 2, 1998).
45. Interview with Craig R. Thompson, Chief Operating Officer, Titus Communications Corporation. May 26, 1998.

46. Interview with Thompson, ibid. In fact Thompson made it plain that telephony was the major target for Titus.
47. For example, Itochu and Toshiba had each invested $500 million in Time Warner in 1991.
48. Interview with Yukio Yanagisawa, President, Satellite Magazine Inc. Tokyo. May 28, 1998.
49. Interview with Hiroshi Endoh, Deputy Director, International Affairs Department, Ministry of Posts and Telecommunications, May 26, 1998.
50. The operators had greatly overestimated the potential demand from banks and securities companies, which had been predicted to be the main customers. In the event, the Mitsubishi-controlled SCC had two main customers, the Defense Agency and Tokyo Electric, while JCSAT had NTT, and Nomura and Daiwa Securities (Nikkei Industrial, 1992). The other principal source of business was for news feeds.
51. A major difference between communications and dedicated broadcasting satellites is the power of the signal, with CS much weaker, and thus requiring a larger antenna. What the operators were planning to do was rebroadcast their signals by cable, as the cable head operators were not bothered by the size of the dish. However, later communications satellites greatly increased their output strength, making genuine DBS broadcasts possible.
52. The law revised was the "Wireless Telegraphy Law," which had effectively not only banned the reception of non-cable, uncut international TV broadcasts, but had even banned people from talking about the contents of such programs (Mainichi, 1993: 5).
53. Interview with Paul Smith, Senior Analyst, HSBC Securities Japan. Tokyo, May 15, 1998.
54. Smith (1997:6) attributes this to the fact that majority ownership was held by four trading companies, with no strong ties to major content providers.
55. The fortunes of SCC were in fact heavily dependent on DirecTV, which leased 16 transponders on the SCC Superbird.
56. In February 2000 DirecTV Japan was effectively driven out of business by SkyPerfecTV, which absorbed its subscribers. Its collapse was attributed to failure to build an adequate subscription base, in turn blamed on a lackluster program line-up.
57. Interview with Craig R. Thompson, Chief Operating Officer, Titus Communications Corporation, May 26, 1998.
58. In the case of Fuji TV, one of the shareholders in SkyPerfecTV, the station directly controls only 20% of the dramas they produce, which it claims is typical of the other commercial TV companies in Japan (Interviews with Yoichi Sekine, Senior Director, and Ansei Yokota, Director, International Department, Business Affairs Division, Fuji Television Network, May 26, 1998).
59. Ibid.
60. To an unusual degree advertising companies in Japan are actively involved in Japanese television: as one example, the original concept for "News Station" was developed by an executive of Dentsu, Japan's largest ad agency.
61. Interview with Yukio Yanagisawa, President, Satellite Magazine Inc. Tokyo. May 28, 1998. The same figure was also given by Smith (1997: 14), referring

to an interview given by the President of TBS. Smith points out that TBS has 28 regional affiliates, who would have to share the cost, making the investment theoretically feasible.

62. Interview with Yukio Yanagisawa, ibid.
63. It seems likely that for an initial transition period of at least five years terrestrial digital and analogue services will carry basically the same programs. The new programming needs and opportunities will therefore be on DTH satellite.
64. According to Krauss (2000: 127-130), the status of news inside NHK was completely transformed during the presidency of Maeda Yoshinori (1964-73). Maeda believed that "the soul of public broadcasting is news," and radically upgraded the resources and facilities allocated to news gathering, as well as increasing broadcast hours for news programs.
65. In the mid 1980s NHK's news division had over 1,000 reporters nationwide, of which 800 were based in Tokyo, compared with a key station for one of the big commercial networks, TV Asahi, which had 190 permanent employees, plus 36 freelancers (Krauss, 1998: 664).
66. For the employees of most Japanese companies, in particular the younger ones, custom and peer pressure make it impossible to leave work according to the clock. In addition, rush hour travel in the big cities is so unpleasant that staying in the city until it has cleared is a more attractive option, while commuting time is so long that returning home by 7P.M. is often impossible.
67. By contrast, Reid describes how "News Station" was instrumental in bringing down the 'godfather' of the Liberal-Democratic Party, Shin Kanemaru, by showing how deeply the party boss had been involved in accepting illegal contributions from a yakuza-run trucking company (Reid, 1993:15).
68. In a notorious speech the president of Asahi TV took credit on behalf of his news anchors for the coalition government that emerged after the fall of the LDP from power, resulting in a year-long parliamentary inquiry and threats of Asahi TV losing its license to broadcast.
69. Kenichi Asano, a former investigative reporter and now journalism professor at Doshisha University, identifies lack of professional training as a root cause for the Japanese media's closeness to politicians and bureaucrats. Typically the mass media recruit university seniors direct (after careful vetting by private detectives) on the assumption that they will be trained by the media, rather than go through a journalism school. The other major cause singled out was the press clubs (Wachs, 2001).
70. These values are largely those of "the other Japan," provincial cities and towns and rural areas. As a corollary, the audience for the commercial channels and for the specialist programs offered on cable tends to be found in the major urban conurbations.

NOTES TO CHAPTER FOUR

1. Notable exceptions to this are provided by the work of Dr. Joseph Man Chan and his colleagues in the School of Journalism and Communication of the Chinese University of Hong Kong and Dr. Yuezhi Zhao, whose "Media,

Market and Democracy in China" (1998) provides an invaluable reference work on the paradoxical subject of media in China.

2. Zhao also argues that the media still serves an ideological purpose, which has changed from promotion of reform through class struggle to promotion of national development through the market place. Certainly it remains the intention of the CCP that the media serve as its instruments.
3. The same was true in Japan, where the first regular newspaper, the English-language Nagasaki Shipping List and Advertiser, appeared in 1861, published by an Englishman.
4. One reason for the lack of popularity not mentioned by Lin was the very high rate of illiteracy in pre-revolutionary China. Literacy campaigns were one of the great successes of the communist government. While the Guomindang had only been able to reduce illiteracy from 85 to 75 percent from 1933 to 1948, the PRC cut the 1956 figure of 70 to 34 percent by 1982 (Womack, 1986: 18).
5. This started early. Mao organized a "Plebian's News Agency" in Beijing as part of the May 4th student movement of 1919, acted as editor for several publications in Guangzhou in the 1920s, and frequently wrote articles for Xinhua and for numerous newspapers (Mulligan, 1992: 2).
6. Chang argues that there were some important differences between Soviet and Chinese applications of propaganda, notably the higher degree of central control in the Soviet Union, leading in the 1930s to a move away from persuasion to outright coercion (Chang, 1997: 111).
7. Apparently this situation has not changed. Former Prime Minister Zhu Rongji reportedly identified one of the STAR TV presenters as his favorite, though STAR is theoretically only available in hotels in Beijing [Economist (3), July 3, 1999: 62].
8. This number is not as extraordinary as it might at first appear. In 1954 there were less than 90,000 TV sets in West Germany and 125,000 in France, equivalent to less than three sets per 1,000, in societies with far great economic wealth than China (UNESCO, 1963).
9. Confusingly, a local commercial TV station was founded at the same time, inheriting the name of Beijing TV.
10. The number of sets gives little indication of the number of viewers. Yu suggests that in 1977, when there were only about 3 million TV sets, there was an audience estimated at 47 million, mostly watching at cultural centers or at friend's homes. My wife's family's experience was not unique.
11. Initially advertising was virtually restriction free, at least in terms of product: in 1979 four of the first five advertising accounts on Chinese television were for foreign cigarettes: foreign tobacco and liquor advertising was not banned for another two years (Stross, 1990).
12. By the mid 1980s agricultural reform was already regarded as a success, urban reform had begun, and top leaders including Hu Yaobang and Zhao Ziyang had endorsed the direction of change.
13. A comparison relevant to the United States might be the broadcast of "Roots" in January, 1977, which reached an audience of 130 million, and

"compelled America to face its checkered past" (Entertainment Weekly, 1999: 70).

14. Not only did the Western media favor the protesters to the extent of not reporting widely known but unfavorable facts, for example that many of the student hunger strikers were in fact eating and drinking, but they also downplayed government attempts to be more conciliatory. It is also worth noting that the Chinese authorities did not stop the droves of journalists who arrived prior to June 4, many of them traveling on tourist visas (Barone Center, op.cit: 10).
15. This notion remains popular in Western media coverage of the media in China: see for example Brill (1999: 30) who predicts a time "where the [Chinese] press can challenge authority so fearlessly and so freely that even the top guy has to sit and take it."
16. One of the difficulties faced in trying to track the development of policy in China is that there are effectively two parallel sets of rules: laws promulgated by the National People's Congress and its Standing Committees, and administrative laws, promulgated or approved by the State Council, such as State Council Decree No. 129. It is often unclear which takes priority, and the confusion is deepened by the fact that the laws tend to be general, if not vague, while the regulations are usually specific. To add to the puzzle, an organ like the MRFT and now, apparently, the SARFT, issue 'temporary' administrative regulations to deal with fast-developing situations such as the rapid expansion of cable TV.
17. This strategy of making an intermediary responsible for enforcing the rules was displayed with the regulations governing online publishing, effective from August 1, 2002. The regulations act to consolidate "a system of self-regulation with key positions occupied by editors at different levels just as in other sectors of the news media (and) move towards clearer identification of responsible individuals in the system of production and greater controllability of publication as a result" (China Media Intelligence: 2002).
18. Interview with a manager of Shenzhen ZhongTaiHezi Dianzi Shebei Gonsi situated on Xichang Lu, Kunming. Jan 31, 1997.
19. The benefits offered by different work units are much talked about in China, with higher ranked military being especially well taken care of. In Yunnan the best-reputed work units were attached to the province's richest business: tobacco.
20. In 1996 Yunnan Cable TV was charging a standard fee of eight yuan per month (equivalent to $1). This was broken down as follows: Y 1 to CCTV, Y 2 to Yunnan TV (the regular local broadcast station) and Y 5 to Yunnan Cable.
21. Interview with Ping Wei, Director, International Relations, CCTV, April 3, 1997.
22. Lovelock claims an additional problem, that there was no way to turn off individual connections, in order to penalize recalcitrant subscribers. This seems unlikely, as in reality cable TV is offered as part of the apartment rental package: payment is automatically deducted, regardless of usage.

23. For comparative perspective, on Oahu, with an urban population directly comparable in size to Kunming's, there was one cable operator serving 250,000 households in 1997 (Hawaii Radio & Television Guide, 1998).
24. Interview with Ding Jiacia, Deputy Director, Yunnan Cable TV, and Chairman, Yunnan Cable TV Association. July 3, 1996.
25. Zhou Caifu, Director, Cable TV Department, MRFT, quoted in Liaowang Zhoukan, 12 April 1994, and cited by Lovelock, 1996: 5.
26. Speeches by Li, Kehan, Dep Director, Social Administration Dept, MRFT; Tian, Shenghua, Central Satellite TV Transmission Center; and Zhang, Zhijian, Director of the Science and Technology Committee, MRFT. At China Cable & Satellite Television Summit '96. Beijing. Oct 28-30, 1996. In general the reliability of Chinese official statistical information is low. Smil (2001) reports that the Chinese government "has reported aggregate GDP growth that was 30% too large for the preceding decade (the 1990s) while overlooking half of the country's food-producing land."
27. According to the U.S. Department of State, "the country boasts 5,300 cable operators of which 1,300 are approved by the SARFT," indicating that some 75% of the total operate without such approval (U.S. Department of State 2001).
28. Interview with Yuanhe Ma, Director General, Foreign Affairs Department, Ministry of Radio, Film and TV. April 1, 1997. Liu reports that in March 1993 an MRFT official admitted only 800 out of 2000 cable stations had been officially franchised.
29. This situation not only refers to satellite television or terrestrial overspill, but even to the purchase of imported films and dramas, where cable majors like Beijing and Shanghai compete for 'hot' new programming, regardless of quotas and controls (Liu, 1994: 223).
30. The Ministries of Posts & Telecommunications; Electronic Industries; Radio, Film & Television; Public Security. The commissions of state education; state planning; state economic & trade; state science & technology. The Chinese Academy of Sciences; Xinhua News Agency; Propaganda Department; People's Bank of China; People's Liberation Army; provincial and municipal bodies.
31. As evidence, Lovelock cites the extraordinary growth in subscription levels and the cuts in access fees charged to ISPs (Lovelock, 2000: 7)
32. Interview with Cheong Shin Keong, Assistant General Manager, Television Broadcasts Ltd. March, 2, 1998.
33. Interview with Cheong Shin Keong, Ibid.
34. In the interview with TVB's Assistant General Manager in 1998 (ibid.), two concerns were mentioned: that the situation of piracy should somehow be 'legalized' by the Chinese government, or that the copyright owners of the shows broadcast by TVB but not owned by it should begin to "make a noise." TVB was complaining about it, but "not in a blatant, public sort of way."
35. Interview with Xuan Yu, Beijing TV Reporter, "City Life" program, March 18, 1997.
36. Interview with Wenxiang Gong, Chair, Department of International Communication & Cultural Exchange, School of International Studies, Peking University, March 27, 1997.

37. However, municipal stations like Beijing TV do receive financial aid from the local government, in this case the city of Beijing.
38. Interview with Ping Wei, Director, International Relations, CCTV, April 3, 1997. According to Wei the money went to the Ministry of Finance and to the (then) MRFT.
39. Figures are from a CSM survey (Central Viewers Survey and Consulting Centre and the SOFRES Group), cited in AIM, 1998, pp. 68,9. AIM mentions an additional reason for the remarkable low figures in Guangzhou: the ongoing feud between cable operators in the area and CCTV, as the former have long operated with a remarkable degree of independence-including the blatant pirating of Hong Kong TV signals.
40 There is some speculation that the TV market may be opened further-but only after the 2008 Beijing Olympics, which should be an advertising bonanza for CCTV and regional broadcasters.

NOTES TO CHAPTER FIVE

1. Interviews with David J. Whalen, General Manager, Engineering, Asia Satellite Telecommunications Co. Ltd. March 2, 1998, and with David Manion, President, Hutchison Corporate Access, February 26, 1998. According to Manion, Hutchison was key for another reason: securing Hong Kong government permission to uplink from Hong Kong, which was received in December, 1990.
2. Interview with David J. Whalen, ibid. March 2, 1998.
3. Satellite signals are microwaves. Like the beam of a flashlight, the signal is strongest at the center of the beam, and progressively weaker toward the edges. Satellite designers adjust the size, shape and angle of the beam to optimize signal strength and to maximize signal levels over areas with a high population density. The EIRP (effective isotropic radiated power) contours depicted on maps showing satellite coverage vary according to transponder amplifier power, the size of the coverage area and the beam shape. The strength of the signal from Asiasat-1-and therefore the size of the dish required-varied greatly according to these factors.
4. According to David Manion final decisions on whether STAR TV should be free-to-air or pay-TV had still not been made at the time of its launch (Interview with David Manion, President, Hutchison Corporate Access and Former Distribution Manager, STAR TV. February 26, 1998).
5. Interview with David Manion, ibid.
6. Interview with Alan MacDonald, Director, BBC Worldwide, June 20, 1997.
7. Interview with David Manion, ibid.
8. Interview with Deepak Sahai, General Manager, South Asia and Middle East, Hutchison Corporate Access. Former India representative for STAR TV. February 26, 1998.
9. Interview with Deepak Sahai, ibid.
10. Interview with John ("Ringo") Leung, former Senior Engineer, Hutchison Whampoa (seconded to STAR TV). March 4, 1998 .
11. Interviews with David Manion and Deepak Sahai, ibid. February 26, 1998.

12. By the end of 1994 Murdoch controlled about 70 percent of the newspaper readership in Australia, and 40 percent in Britain. In America he had dozens of media properties, including the 20th Century Fox film studio, Fox Television, TV Guide and the New York Post. He also owned a major publisher, HarperCollins and a pan-Europe satellite station, BSkyB.
13. The third leg of the global strategy was represented by an alliance between News Corp., the Globo Organization of Brazil, Grupo Televisa of Mexica and TCI, an American cable system operator, which resulted in Sky Latin America. This began operations in 1996, broadcasting from Miami. The fourth and most important leg was North America: in 2003 Murdoch succeeded in adding this piece to his global puzzle with the purchase of Hughes Electronics' DirecTV.
14. In 2001 Murdoch had initially lost out in a bidding war for DirecTV to a rival satellite company, EchoStar Communications. Following an intensive lobbying operation, this proposed merger was overruled by the FCC in " a rare instance in which officials appointed by the Bush administration have tried to stop a corporate deal " (Labaton, 2002). Subsequently the FCC approved Murdoch's News Corp's bid in December, 2003.
15. Andrew Neil, the then editor of the Sunday Times, later claimed to be the actual writer of the speech (Vines and Poole, 1997).
16. Interview with Alan MacDonald, Director, BBC Worldwide, June 20, 1997.
17. K. Cooper, "China wants StarTV to drop BBC," Eastern Express, February 17, 1994.
18. According to all the former STAR TV executives interviewed for this book the BBC news was always the least watched of the STAR channels, and consequently the most difficult to sell advertising for. According to Ringo Leung, "Nobody in China was interested in the BBC. It was all in English. Everyone thought it was intended for somewhere else" (Interview March 4, 1998).
19. Early news reports on the partners involved in Phoenix suggested that CCTV was invited to be a shareholder. These stories were later dismissed by CCTV's president as "a completely groundless fabrication" (Keenan, 1996: 56 and South China, 1996).
20. As with StarTV the viewership figures claimed by Phoenix are disputed. In 2000, the ratings agency CVSC-Sofres Media put the viewership at six million. If true, the 42 million figure would make Phoenix the most widely watched foreign channel in China. This would also mean that the bulk of its audience was illegal, receiving its signal via satellite dishes not licensed to receive it.
21. Information on Phoenix is drawn from a variety of sources, including Tech Buddha, 2000, China Online May 16,2001 and May 17, 2001 and the Economist Intelligence Unit, reprinted in China Online October 2000.
22. Such publications seem to be part of a larger policy of gaining favor with senior politicians by publishing their works. HarperCollins had also published Margaret Thatcher's two-volume memoirs, and a book on Chequers, the country retreat of British prime ministers, written by Norma Major, wife of former Prime Minister John Major.

23. The feeling was mutual. In 1994 Governor Patten had given a speech implicitly attacking Murdoch, saying "It would be the most seedy of betrayals for broadcasters or journalists, editors or proprietors, to champion freedom of speech in one country, but to curtail it elsewhere for reasons of inevitably short-term commercial expediency" (Wallen, 1994).
24. According to Granitsas, STAR in 2002 had nine channels, plus a minority stake in India's second largest cable operator.
25. Interview with Deepak Sahai, General Manager, South Asia and Middle East, Hutchison Corporate Access, and former country manager for STAR TV. February 26, 1998.
26. Granting autonomy to Doordarshan apparently did nothing to stop its decline in viewership, or to reduce its top-heavy bureaucracy. In 2001 it had a technical staff of 18,500, compared with a total staff of 5,000 for Star, Sony and Zee TV combined (Vidyasagar, 2001).
27. Star Plus' Hindi content had been restricted by an agreement with the Zee group. As a result, Zee had an average of 10 percent of cable viewers, Sony 8 percent and Star Plus 4.5 percent at the time the partnership between Star and Zee finished (Madhavan, 2000).

NOTES TO CHAPTER SIX

1. Interview recorded on February 16, 2003, for the television series "Living in a Global World," written, directed and produced by the author for the Globalization Research Center, University of Hawai'i.

Bibliography

AIM. 1998. *China: The Media Industry 1998*. Hong Kong: Advisors for International Media (AIM) Asia Ltd.

Alagappa, Muthiah. 1994. "Democratic Transition in Asia: the Role of the International Community." *East-West Center Special Reports*. No.3. October, 1994. p.10.

Alexander, Jeffrey C. and Jacobs, Ronald N. 1998. "Mass communication, ritual and civil society." *In Media, Ritual and Identity*. Eds. Liebes, Tamar and Curran, James. London: Routledge.

Altman, Kristin Kyoko. 1996. "Television and Political Turmoil: Japan's Summer of 1983." *In Media and Politics in Japan*, eds. Susan J. Pharr and Ellis D. Krauss. Honolulu: University of Hawai'i Press.

Anderson, Benedict. 1991. *Imagined Communities*. London: Verso.

Anderson, Philip, Arrow, Kenneth and Pines, David (eds). 1988. *The Economy as an Evolving Complex System*. Reading MA: Addison-Wesley.

Ang, I. 1991. *Desperately Seeking the Audience*. New York: Routledge.

Appadurai, Arjun. 1990. "Disjuncture and Difference in the Global Cultural Economy." In Mike Featherstone ed. *Global Culture: Nationalism, Globalization and Modernity*. Newbury Park, California: Sage.

———. 1996. *Modernity at Large: Cultural Dimensions of Globalization*. Minneapolis: University of Minnesota Press.

Arnason, Johann P. 1990. "Nationalism, Globalization and Modernity." In Featherstone (1990).

Arquilla, John and Ronfeld, David. 1997. *In Athena's Camp: Preparing for Conflict in the Information Age*. Santa Monica, CA: RAND.

Asahi Evening News. 1991. "Japan's TV Networks Fighting News War." *Asahi Evening News*. June 23, 1991: 4.

———. 1991 (2). "NHK Chief Succumbs to Politics." *Asahi Evening News*. July 23, 1991: 4.

Asian Television. 2002. "Japan." www.business.vu.edu.au/bho2250/TV/AsianTV.htm#Japan

Asia Pacific Satellite. 2002. "A new horizon." *Asia Pacific Satellite*: January 2002. wwwiconpub.com/news/story.epml?newsarchive.REF=1840&publication.REF=28.

Auletta, Ken. 1992. *Three Blind Mice*. New York: Vintage Books.

———. 1995. "Awesome." *The New Yorker*. August 14, 1995.

———. 1995 (2). "The Pirate." *The New Yorker*, November 13, 1995.

———. 1996. "The News Rush." *The New Yorker*. March 18, 1996.

Backman, Michael. 2001. "News Corp goes telco networking in China." *theage.com.au*. March 1.

Bagdikian, Ben. 1992. *The Media Monopoly*. Boston: Beacon Press

Bakhshi, Shiv and Bailey, Nathan. 2002. "The Relevance of Framing and Fora to Outcomes: The Case of Debates Over Information Flows."

Barabasi, Albert-Laszlo. 2002. *Linked: The New Science of Networks*. NY: Perseus.

Barnet, Richard J. and Cavanagh, John. 1994. *Global Dreams: Imperial Corporations and the New World Order*. NY: Simon & Schuster.

Barnouw, Erik. 1990. *The Tube of Plenty: The Evolution of American Television*. New York: Oxford University Press.

Barone Center. 1992. "Turmoil at Tiananmen: A Study of U.S. Press Coverage of the Beijing Spring of 1989." The Joan Shorenstein Barone Center on the Press, Politics and Public Policy. Harvard University, June 1992. www.tvsquare.tv/themes/TatT cover.html#anchor263552.

Bateson, Mary C. 1990. "Beyond Sovereignty." *In Contending Sovereignties: Redefining Political Community*. Eds. R.B.J. Walker and Saul H. Mendlovitz. Boulder, CO: Lynne Rienner Publishers.

Baudrillard, Jean. 1990. *Revenge of the Crystal*. London: Pluto Press.

BBC. 1999. *Review of the Future Funding of the BBC*. www.bbc.co.uk/hi/english/static/ bbc_funding_review/report.htm

BBC News. August, 1999. "Beijing says sect stamped out." news.bbc.co.uk/hi/english/world/asia-pacific/newsid_414000/414668.stm. August 8, 1999.

———. May, 2000. "China shuts down website." news.bbc.co.uk/ hi/english/world/asia-pacific/newsid_749000/749027.stm. May 15, 200

———. June 7, 2000. "China arrests internet editor." news.bbc.co.uk/hi/english/world/asia-pacific/newsid_780000/780787.stm. June 7, 2000.

———. June 7, 2000(2). "China to battle internet 'enemies.'"news.bbc.co.uk/hi/english/world/asia-pacific/default.stm. August 9, 2000.

———. August, 2000. "Jiang backs China's net growth." *news.bbc.co.uk/hi/english/world/asia-pacific/*. August 21, 2001.

———. December, 2001. "China's cable TV shake up." *news.bbc.co.uk/hi/english/uk/default.stm*. December 3, 2001.

Bell, Daniel. 1973. *The Coming of Post-industrial Society*. New York: Basic Books.

Bennahum, David S. 1998. "The United Nations of Iridium." Wired 6 (10): 134–201.

Bennett, W. Lance. 1983. *News: The Politics of Illusion*. New York: Longman.

Benzakin, Jocelyne. 1989. *The Gate of Heavenly Peace: Tiananmen Square Incident*. 1989. J.B. Pictures. Produced and directed by Jocelyne Benzakin.

Birkerts, Sven. 1994. *The Gutenberg Elegies: The Fate of Reading in an Electronic Age*. Winchester, MA: Faber and Faber.

Boehlert, Eric. 2001. "Pimping for the People's Republic." www.salon.com/news/feature/20001/03/30/china/ March 30, 2001

Boyd-Barrett, Oliver. 1998. "'Global' News Agencies." In *The Globalization of News*. Eds: Boyd-Barrett, Oliver and Rantanen, Terhi. London: Sage.

Boyd-Barrett, Oliver and Rantanen, Terhi (eds). 1998. *The Globalization of News*. London: Sage.

Boyer, W. 1996. "Across the Americas, 1996 Is the Year When DBS Consumers Benefit From More Choices." *Satellite Communications*, April, 1996.

Branscomb, Anne Wells. 1994. *Who Owns Information?*. New York: Basic Books.

Brill, Steven. 1999. "Cracks in the Great Wall." *Brill's Content*. June 1999:27–30.

Brinkley, Joel. 1997. *Defining Vision: The Battle for the Future of Television*. New York: Harcourt Brace.

Broadcasting & Cable. 1994. "Toward HDTV's 'Immense Alliance.' *Broadcasting & Cable*. v.124. March 7, 1994: 51.

Browne, Donald R. 1989. *Comparing Broadcast Systems: The Experiences of Six Industrialized Nations*. Ames: Iowa State University Press.

Brull, Steven. 1991. "Japan's Global News Dream Fades." *International Herald Tribune*. December 7–8. 1991: 1.

Burawoy, Michael et al. 2000. *Global Ethnography*. Berkeley: University of California Press.

Burns, Tom. 1977. *The BBC: Public Institution Private World*. London: Macmillan.

Burton, Sandra. 1991. "A STAR Is Born over Asia." TIME. October 21, 1991: 50–1.

Buruma, Ian. 1994. *The Wages of Guilt: Memories of War in Germany and Japan*. New York: Farrar Straus Giroux.

Calhoun, Craig. 1989. "Tiananmen, Television and the Public Sphere: Internationalization of Culture and the Beijing Spring of 1989." *Public Culture*. Vol. 2, No. 1: Fall, 1989.

Castells, Manuel. 1997. *The Power of Identity*. Oxford: Blackwell Publishers.

———. 2000. "Information Technology and Global Capitalism." In Chan, Alex. 2002. "From Propaganda to Hegemony: Jiaodian Fangtan and China's Media Policy." *Journal of Contemporary China*. Vol11, No.30, pp. 35–51.

Chan, Joseph Man. 1995. "Calling the Tune without Paying the Piper." *China Review* 1995. Hong Kong: The Chinese University Press.

Chan, Joseph Man, Lee, Paul S.N. and Lee, Chin-Chuan. 1996. *Hong Kong Journalists in Transition*. Hong Kong: Hong Kong Institute of Asia-Pacific Studies, The Chinese University of Hong Kong.

Chan, Samantha. 2000. "Star TV Satellite Joint-Venture Files for GEM Listing." www.myinfoage.com

Chang, Jess T.H. and Dorn, Kevin. 2000. "China's New Cable Network Regulations: Death Knoll for Broadband Operators?" *www.virtualchina.com/news*. February 2, 2000.

Chang, Julian. 1997. "The Mechanics of State Propaganda: the People's Republic of China and the Soviet Union in the 1950s." In Timothy Cheek and Tony Saich, eds., *New Perspectives on State Socialism in China*. NY: M.E. Sharpe.

Chang, Won Ho. 1989. *Mass Media in China: the History and the Future*. Ames: Iowa State University Press.

Chapman, Graham P. 1993. "What do Communication Flows Actually Mean?" *Pacific Telecommunications Review* 15(2): 27–31.

Chase, Michael and Mulvenon, James. 2002. *You've Got Dissent! Chinese Dissident Use of the Internet and Beijing's Counter-Strategies*. Rand Corporation: www.rand.org/publications/MR/MR1543.

Cheek, Timothy. 1997. *Propaganda and Culture in Mao's China: Deng Tuo and the Intelligentsia*. Oxford: Clarendon Press.

China Internet Network Information Center (CNNIC), 2002. "Analysis Report on the Growth of the Internet in China." www.cnnic.net.cn/develst/2002-7e/6.shtml. CNNIC, July, 2002.

China Media Intelligence. 2002. "Internet Publishing : new regulations, new obstacles." Eight and Eight Publication: www. eight-and-eight.com. July 22, 2002.

ChinaOnline. October, 2000. "Phoenix TV: A foreign-owned operation that is illegal in China." Report from the Economist Intelligence Unit. www.chinaonline.com/industry/media_entertainment/News/Archive/Secure/2000/October. October 18, 2000.

———. November, 2000 (1). "Lines are open: Cable, phone companies get go-ahead to lock horns after all." *www.chinaonline.com/industry/infotech/NewsArchive*. November 9, 2000.

———. November, 2000 (2). "Media gatekeeper clarifies new Web site regs." www.chinaonline.com/industry/infotech/NewsArchive. November 9, 2000.

———. December, 2000 (3). "China plots radio, TV empire, but ambitious plan is cast in shadow of doubt." www.chinaonline.com/topstories/001211/1/. December 11, 2000.

———. May, 2001 (1). "Phoenix TV's revenue growth rises, but company loses US$3.19 M in 1Q" www.chinaonline.com/topstories/010516/1/ C01051510. asp, May 16, 2001.

———. May, 2001 (2). "China Cable: The creation of a monopoly." www.chinaonline.com/topstories/010521/1/. May 21, 2001.

———. October, 2001. "Phoenix-CCTV venture to export Chinese programming." www.chinaonline. com/topstories/011031 /c01103102.asp. May 21, 2001.

Chossudovsky, Michel. 1997. *The Globalisation of Poverty, Impacts of IMF and World Bank Reforms*." London: Zed Books.

Clari.Reuters. 1995. "Murdoch back in China's good books with media deal." June 13, 1995.

Clarke, Arthur C. 1984. 1984: *Spring*. New York: Ballantine Books.

Colton, Michael. 1999. "Welcome to my hype-industrial complex, baby." *Brill's Content*. September, 1999. 66–69.

Committee on Foreign Affairs, 1994. "Hearing before the Committee on Foreign Affairs, House of Representatives, April 26, 1994." Washington: U.S. Government Printing Office.

Cooper, Helene. 1998. "Murdoch Blames Unit Executives for Book Debacle." *Asian Wall Street Journal*. March 5, 1998: 2 .

Cooper, K. 1994. "China wants StarTV to drop BBC," *Eastern Express*. February 17, 1994.

Cosper, Amy. 1996. "Asia or Bust." *Satellite Communications*. January 1996: 27.

Credé, Andreas and Mansell, Robin. 1998. *Knowledge societies . . . in a Nutshell: Information Technology for Sustainable Development*. Ottawa: International Development Research Centre.

Croteau, David and Hoynes, William. 2001. *The Business of Media*. Thousand Oaks, California: Sage.

Curtin, Michael. 2001. "Organizing Difference on Global TV: Television History and Cultural Geography." In Edgerton, Gary R. And Rollins, Peter C.

Television Histories: Shaping Collective Memory in the Media Age. Lexington, KY: University Press of Kentucky.

Davis, Jonathan. 1993. "Big Deal." *TV World Guide to Asia*. October 1993.

Davis, L.J. 1995. "Rupert the First." *World Business*. January 1995.

Dayan, Daniel and Katz, Elihu. 1992. *Media Events: The Live Broadcasting of History.* Cambridge, Mass: Harvard University Press.

de Certeau, Michel. 1991. "The Jabbering of Social Life." in *On Signs*. Ed. Marshall Blonsky. Baltimore, MD: The Johns Hopkins University Press.

Decree of the State Council of the People's Republic of China. No. 129. 1993. "Provisions on the Control of Ground Receiving Installations for Satellite Television." October 5, 1993.

Deloitte & Touche, 2001. "Media and Communications." *Express China News*. Issue No.01-1. January/February 2001.

Deutsch, Karl W. 1963. *The Nerves of Government: Models of Political Communication and Control*. London: The Free Press of Glencoe.

Dirlik, Arlif. 1996. "The Global in the Local" in Wilson, Rob and Dissanayake, Wimal eds. *A Borderless World? From Colonialism to Transnationalism and the Decline of the Nation-State*. Durham, N.C.: Duke University Press.

Dittmer, Lowell and Kim, Samuel S. (Eds). 1993. *China's Quest for National Identity*. Ithaca, NY: Cornell University Press.

Duara, Prasenjit. 1995. *Rescuing History from the Nation: Questioning Narratives of Modern China*. Chicago: University of Chicago Press.

Dupagne, Michael and Seel, Peter B. 1998. *High-Definition Television: A Global Perspective*. Ames, Iowa: Iowa State University Press.

Dutton, Michael. 1992. *Policing and Punishment in China*. Cambridge: Cambridge University Press.

Dyke, Greg. 2000. *Greg Dyke's speech in full*. BBC News: *news.bbc.co.uk/hi/english/uk/newsid_896000/896084.stm* August 25, 2000.

———. 2000 (2). *Address to the United Nations Television Forum*. www.bbc.co.uk/info/news/news287.htm. November 16, 2000.

Dyson, Freeman. 1998. *Imagined Worlds*. Cambridge, Massachusetts. Harvard University Press.

Dyson, Kenneth, and Humphreys, Peter, with Negrine, Ralph and Simon, Jean-Paul. 1988. *Broadcasting and New Media Policies in Western Europe*. London: Routledge.

Eco, Umberto. 1991. "How Culture Conditions the Colours We See." In *On Signs*. Ed. Marshall Blonsky. Baltimore, MD: The Johns Hopkins University Press.

Economist, The. 1994. "HDTV, DOA." *The Economist*. February 26, 1994: 65.

———. 1995. "The slow march of progress." *The Economist*. July 15, 1995: 49–50.

———. 1995 (2). "Japan's Internet tangle." *The Economist*. July 15, 1995: 50.

———. 1995 (3). "News of the world." *The Economist*. September 2, 1995: 58.

———. 1996 "Time to adjust your set." *The Economist*. December 24–January 5, 1996: 69.

———. 1996 Extra. "A little local interference." *The Economist*. February 3, 1996: 54.

———. 1996 (2). "Murdoch's Empire: the gambler's last throw." *The Economist*. March 9, 1996: 68.

———. 1996 (3). "Free-Tv-for-all." *The Economist.* June 8, 1996, Turkey survey: 7.

———. 1998. "In praise of paranoia." *The Economist.* November 7th–13th, 1998, Taiwan survey.

———. 1998 (2). "Journey beyond the stars," Dec. 19, 1998:107.

———. 1999. "Sexy cable." *The Economist.* March 27, 1999: 65.

———. 1999 (2). "The carve-up." *The Economist.* May 8, 1999: 65.

———. 1999 (3). "The price of uncertainty." *The Economist.* June 12, 1999: 66.

———. 1999 (4). "The weakling kicks back." *The Economist.* July 3, 1999: 56.

———. 1999 (5). "Rupert's misses." *The Economist.*July 3, 1999: 62.

———. 2002. "Power in your hand: A survey of television." *The Economist.* April 13, 2002.

EIU. 1996. "Illusions of grandeur." *The Economist Intelligence Unit.* Business China. February 19, 1996: 6.

Emmott, Bill. 1997. "Managing the International System Over the Next Ten Years." In *Managing the International System Over the Next Ten Years.* Three Essays by Emmott, B., Watanabe, K. and Wolfowitz, P. New York: The Trilateral Commission.

Entertainment Weekly. 1999. "100 Greatest Moments in Television." *Entertainment Weekly.* February 19–26, 1999: 28–104.

Epstein, Edward. 1974. *News from Nowhere: Television and the News.* New York: Vintage Books.

Fallows, James. 1989. "Containing Japan." *The Atlantic Monthly.* May, 1989.

———. 1994. *Looking at the Sun: The Rise of the New East Asia Economic and Political System.* New York: Pantheon Books.

———. 1996. "Why Americans Hate the Media. " *The Atlantic Monthly.* February, 1996: 62.

Farhi, Paul. 1995. "Rupert Murdoch, Multimedia Mogul." *The Washington Post National Weekly Edition.* February 20–26, 1995: 20.

Farmer, Edward L. 1990. "Sifting Truth from Facts: The Reporter as Interpreter of China." In *Voices of China: The Interplay of Politics and Journalism.* Ed.: Chin-Chuan Lee. New York: The Guilford Press.

FAS. 1998. "Sinosat." Federation of American Scientists Space Policy Project. Updated June 20, 1998. www.fas.org/spp/guide/china /comm/ sinosat.htm

Featherstone, Mike (ed). 1990. *Global Culture: Nationalism, Globalization and Modernity.* London: Sage Publications.

Ferguson, Marjorie. 1990. "Electronic Media and the Redefining of Time and Space." In *Public Communication: The New Imperatives.* Ed.: Marjorie Ferguson. London: Sage Publications.

———. 1994. "Media, Markets and Identities: Reflections on the Global-Local Dialectic: The 1994 Southam Lecture." *Canadian Journal of Communications.* www. cjc-online.ca/BackIssues/Vol. 20.No.4/ erguson.html.

Flournoy, Don and Stewart, Robert. 1997. *CNN: Making News in the Global Market.* Luton: University of Luton Press.

Foreign Press Center. 1986. *Japan's Mass Media.* "About Japan" Series #7. Tokyo: Foreign Press Center.

Forrester, Chris. 2001. "Japan's Pay-TV Picture." *Interspace.* August 15, 2001.

Franklin, Bob. 1997. *Newszak and News Media.* London: Hodder Headline.

Friedland, Jonathan. 1994. "Hard News." *Far Eastern Economic Review*. March 10, 1994: 44–46.
Friedman, Thomas L. 2000. *The Lexus and the Olive Tree*. New York: Anchor Books.
———. (1). 2002. "The Core of Muslim Rage." *The New York Times on the Web*. March 6, 2002.
———. (2). 2002. "Global Village Idiocy." *The New York Times on the Web*. May 12, 2002.
Fukuyama, Eiko. 1997. "Digital wars." *Asahi Evening News*. April 1, 1997: 5.
Gane, Mike. 1991. *Baudrillard: Critical and Fatal Theory*. London: Routledge.
Gans. H. 1979. *Deciding What's News*. New York: Vintage.
Gapper, John. 1998. "News Corp joins Patten book row." *Financial Times*, February 28/March 1, 1998: 7.
Garnham, Nicholas 1986. "Contribution to a political economy of mass-communication." In Collins, Richard et al. *Media, Culture and Society: A Critical Reader*. London: Sage.
Gates, Bill, with Myhrvold, Nathanand Rinearson, Peter.1995. *The Road Ahead*. London: Viking.
Gatzen, Barbara. 2003. "Japan Media: The Stone Unturned." *Japan Media Review*. Posted February 26, 2003. www.ojr.org/japan/media/1043974972.php
Gerbner, George. 1976. "Living with television: the violence profile." *Journal of Communication*. Vol. 26, 1976: 173–99.
Gershon, Richard and Kanayama, Tsutomo. 1995. "Direct broadcast satellites in Japan." *Telecommunications Policy*. Vol. 19, No.3. 217–231.
Giddens, Anthony. 1985. *The Nation State and Violence: Volume 2 of A Contemporary Critique of Historical Materialism*. Cambridge: Polity Press.
Giddens, Anthony. 1990. *The Consequences of Modernity*. Stanford: Stanford University Press.
———. 1991. *Modernity and Self-identity: Self and Society in the Late Modern Age*. Stanford: Stanford University Press.
———. 1994. *Beyond Left and Right: The Future of Radical Politics*. Stanford: Stanford University Press.
———. 1999. "Globalisation." *BBC Reith Lectures 1999: Lecture 1*. //news2.this.bbc.co.uk/hi/english/static/events/reith%5F99/week1
Gill, S.S. 2001. "Directionless Prasar Bharati." *The Hindu*. www.hinduonnet.com/the hindu/2001/07/17/stories/05172523.htm
Gilley, Bruce. 2000. "Star-Crossed." *Far Eastern Economic Review*. www.feer.com/_007_27/p30cover.html. July 27, 2000.
———. 2000 (2). "Letting Off Steam." *Far Eastern Economic Review*. www.feer.com/_0011_09/p020region.html. November 9, 2000.
Ginsberg, B. 1986. *The Captive Public: How mass opinion promotes state power*. New York: Basic.
Gittings, John. 2000. "Shanghai Noon." *The Guardian*. August 24, 2000.
Gladney, Dru C. 1994. "Representing Nationality in China: Refiguring Majority/Minority Identities." *Journal of Asian Studies*. Vol. 53, No.1: 92–123.
Gladney, George Albert. 2004. "Global Village Disconnected?" In Berenger, Ralph, ed. *Global Media Go To War*. Marquette Books: Spokane, Washington.

Gleick, James. 1987. *Chaos: Making a New Science.* New York: Penguin.

Goldberg, Vicki. 1991. *The Power of Photography: How Photographs Changed Our Lives.* New York: Abbeville Press.

Golden, Tim. 2002. "Crisis Deepens Impact of Arab TV News." *The New York Times on the Web.* www.nytimes.com/2002/04/16/international/middleeast/16TELEhtml. April 16, 2002.

Golding, Peter and Elliott, Philip. 1979. *Making the News.* London: Longman.

Goll, Sally. 1994. "Troubled Star Stages a Quiet Comeback." *Asian Wall Street Journal.* August 15, 1994: 1, 5.

Gordon, Kim. 1995. "Raising the red flag." *Broadcast. MIP-TV Supplement.* 7 April 1995: 21–24.

Gould, Stephen Jay. 2002. *The Structure of Evolutionary Theory.* Harvard: Harvard University Press

Grahn, Sven. 2001. "China's first two satellites. Or-Did it ever occur to you how similar to Telstar-1 they look?" www.users.wineasy.se/svengrahn/histind/China12/China12.htm

Gramsci, Antonio. 1995. *Selections from the Prison Notebooks of Antonio Gramsci.* Ed. and translated by Hoare, Quintin and Nowell Smith, Geoffrey. New York: International Publishers.

Granitsas, Alkman. 2000. "Black Hole." *Far Eastern Economic Review.* www.feer.com/_007_27/p36innov.htm.l July 27, 2000.

———. 2002. "How to Make Pay-TV Pay." *Far Eastern Economic Review.* www.feer.com/cgi-bin/prog/printeasy September 5, 2002.

Greenwald, John. 1993. "Rupert's World." *Time.* September 20, 1993.

Greider, William. 1997. *One World, Ready or Not.* New York: Simon & Schuster.

Guillain, Robert. 1957. *600 Million Chinese.* NY: Criterion Books

Habermas, Jürgen. 1989. *The Structural Transformation of the Public Sphere: An Inquiry into a Category of Bourgeois Society.* Trans. Thomas Bürger and Frederick Lawrence. Cambridge: Polity Press.

Hadfield, Peter. 1994. "'Ethnic cleansing' of foreign staff at NHK." No. I Shimbun, *The Journal of the Foreign Correspondents' Club of Japan.* Vol. 26, No.8. August 15, 1994.

Halberstam, David. 1979. *The Powers That Be.* New York: Dell.

Hall, Stuart. 1982. "The rediscovery of 'ideology': return of the repressed in media studies." In Gurevitch, Michael et al, eds. *Culture, Society and the Media.* London: Methuen.

Hamilton, David P. 1993. "Japan Satellite Broadcasting Gets Bailout." *Asian Wall Street Journal.* May 20, 1993: 3.

Hamrin, Carol Lee. 1994. "China's Legitimacy Crisis: The Central Role of Information." In Chin-Chuan Lee, ed. *China's Media, Media's China.* Boulder, Colorado: Westview Press.

Hara, Junjiro. 1995. "Media critic calls for demystification of Japan." *Asahi Evening News.* January 9, 1995: 3.

Hardt, Michael and Negri, Antonio. 2000. *Empire.* Cambridge, Mass: Harvard University Press.

Harvey, David. 1990. *The Condition of Postmodernity.* Cambridge, Mass: Blackwell Publishers.

Hawaii Radio & Television Guide News Over The Air Archive. 1998. "Oceanic Cable To Raise Service Rates." December 6, 1997 news story. www.hawaiiradiotv.com/~archive/HIRATV198.html.

Held, David and McGrew, Anthony, Goldblatt, David and Perraton, Jonathan. 1999. *Global Transformations*. Stanford: Stanford University Press.

Heller, Walter, Starr, Ross and Starrett, David. 1986. *Uncertainty, Information and Communication*. New York: Cambridge University Press.

Herman, Edward S. and Chomsky, N. 1988. *Manufacturing Consent: The Political Economy of the Mass Media* . New York: Pantheon.

Herman, Edward S. and McChesney, Robert W. 1997. *The Global Media: The New Missionaries of Corporate Capitalism*. London: Cassell.

Hertsgaard, Mark. 1989. "China Coverage-Strong on What, Weak on Why." Originally published in *Rolling Stone*, September 21, 1989. www.tsquare.tv/themes/hertsgaard.html.

Hesseldahl, Arik. 2002. "Attack of the Digital Movie." www.forbes.com/2002/03/18/0318digitaldistibution.html.

Hickey, Neil. 2001. "Unshackling Big Media." *Columbia Journalism Review*. www.cjr.org/year/01/4/fcchickey.asp. May/June 2001.

Higgins, Andrew. 1998. "Murdoch in China: The true story." *The Observer Review*. August 3, 1998: 1, 5.

Hobsbawm, Eric and Ranger, Terence (eds). 1983. *The Invention of Tradition*. Cambridge: Cambridge University Press.

Hong, Junhao. 1995. "The evolution of China's satellite policy." *Telecommunications Policy*. Vol. 19, No. 2, pp. 117– 133.

Hood, Marlowe. 1994. "The Use and Abuse of Mass Media by Chinese Leaders During the 1980s." In Chin-Chuan Lee, ed. *China's Media, Media's China*. Boulder, Colorado: Westview Press.

Horkheimer, Max and Adorno, Theodor W. 1972. *Dialectic of Enlightenment*. Trans. John Cumming. New York: Seabury Press.

Horvit, Beverly. 2004. "Global News Agencies and the Pre-War Debate: A Content Analysis." In Ralph D. Berenger, ed. *Global Media Go To War*. Spokane, Washington: Marquette Books.

Howorth Communications & Bloomberg Television. 2001. "Pay TV in Asia Pacific, Mapping the Road Ahead: China."Sandberg Media. www.broadcastpapers.com/broadbiz/HowarthPayTVinAP02htm. November2001.

Hudson, Heather E. 1990 *Communication Satellites: Their Development and Impact*. Macmillan: New York.

Humphreys, Peter J. 1996. *Mass Media and Media Policy in Western Europe*. Manchester: Manchester University Press.

Huntington, Samuel P. 1996. *The Clash of Civilizations and the Remaking of World Order*. New York: Simon & Schuster.

Hutton, Will and Giddens, Anthony. 2000. *Global Capitalism*. New York: New Press.

IDATE. 2000. "Top 50: world ranking of media groups. www.idate.fr/an/cle/media_a.html.

Ikeda, Ken'ichi. 2001. Review of Ellis Krauss, *Broadcasting Politics in Japan: NHK and Television News*. Japanese Journal of Political Science. Vol. 2, Part 2, November 2001.

Innis, H.A. 1951. *The Bias of Communication*. Toronto: University of Toronto Press.
Inoue, Yuko. 1991. "NHK head's resignation may slow network growth." *Japan Economic Journal*. July 27, 1991.
Iritani, Evelyn. 2001. "News Corp. Heir Woos China With Show of Support." *Los Angeles Times*. March 23, 2001.
Ishihara, Shintaro. 1991. *The Japan That Can Say "No.'* New York: Simon & Schuster. Originally published in Japanese as *No to ieru Nihon*, co-authored with Akio Morita, 1989.
Ishihara, Shintaro and Mahathir, Mohamed. 1994. "The Asia That Can Say "No.'" SEE Mahathir, Mohamed and Ishihara, Shintaro. 1995. *The Voice of Asia*. Tokyo: Kodansha.
JIN (Japan Information Network). 2002. "Japan Insight: Japanese population today." www.jinjapan.org/insight/html/in_persctive/urbanization/japane04. html
Japan Media Review. 2003. "Links and Resources." Accessed March 31, 2003. 64.87.25.234/japan/resources/section.php
Japan Times. 1997. "TV Tokyo balks at digital policy." *Japan Times*. March 27, 1997.
Jenner, W.J.F. 1992. *The Tyranny of History: The Roots of China's Crisis*. Penguin: London.
Jiji Press. 1997. "Sony eyes JSkyB for global channel." Interview with Sony President Noboyuki Idei. *Japan Times*. August 7, 1997: 12.
Johnson, Chalmers. 1982. *MITI and the Japanese Miracle: The Growth of Industrial Policy*. 1925–1975. Stanford: Stanford University Press.
Johnson, Chalmers. 1995. *Japan: Who Governs?* New York: W. W. Norton.
Johnson, Haynes. 2001. *The Best of Times*. New York: Harcourt.
Joscelyne, Andrew. 1995. "Revolution in the Revolution." *Wired*. 3.01. January, 1995: 162.
Judis, John. 1990. "A Yen for Approval." *Columbia Journalism Review*. January/February 1990: 42–45.
Jussawalla, Meheroo. 1993. *United States-Japan Trade in Telecommunications*. Westport, Connecticut: Greenwood Press.
Kahaner, D.K. 1996. "Japan's Emerging Cable TV Industry." *Asian Technology Information Program Report 96.103*. www.cs.arizona.edu/japan/www/atip/public/atip.reports.96/atip96.103r.html.
Kallender, Paul. 1999. "DirecTV Hopes Strategy Shift Leads to Profits." *Space News*. January 25, 1999: 10.
———. 1999 (2). "Satellite-Internet Services Advance in Japan." *Space News*. May 3, 1999: 15.
Karp, Jonathan. 1993. "Prime Time Police." *Far Eastern Economic Review*. October 21, 1993.
———.1994. "Do It Our Way." *Far Eastern Economic Review*. April 21, 1994.
Kasza, Gregory. 1986. "Democracy and the Founding of Japanese Public Radio." *Journal of Asian Studies*. Vol. XLV. No. 4: 745–767.
———. 1988. *The State and the Mass Media in Japan*. 1918–1945. Berkeley: University of California Press.
Katz, Jon. 1991. "Collateral Damage to Network News." *Columbia Journalism Review*. March/April 1991. 29

Kaye, Lincoln. 1997. "Fade to Black." *Far Eastern Economic Review*. November 6, 1997: 56–58.

Keenan, Faith. 1996. "Battle of the Titans." *Far Eastern Economic Review*. April 4, 1996: 56.

Kellner, Douglas. 1990. *Television and the Crisis of Democracy*. Boulder, Colorado: Westview Press.

Keng, Lu. 1994. "Press Control in 'New China' and 'Old China.'" In Chin-Chuan Lee, ed. *China's Media, Media's China*. Boulder, Colorado: Westview Press.

Kim, Samuel S. and Dittmer, Lowell. 1993. "Whither China's Quest for National Identity?" in *China's Quest for National Identity*. Dittmer, Lowell and Kim, Samuel S. (Eds) Ithaca, NY: Cornell University Press.

Kishore, Krishna. 1994. "Asiasat 1 and Star TV: Catalysts of the Asian Satellite Communications Market." *Satellite Communications*. April 1994, pp. 16–21.

Kitatani, Kenji. 1988. "Japan." In *International Handbook of Broadcasting Systems*. ed. Philip T. Rosen. New York: Greenwood Press.

Klein, Naomi. 1999. *No Logo*. New York: Picador.

Koelsch, Frank. 1995. *The Infomedia Revolution*. Toronto: McGraw-Hill Ryerson.

Kovach, Bill and Rosenstiel, Tom. 1999. *Warp Speed: America in the Age of the Mixed Media Culture*. New York: Century Foundation Press.

Krauss, Ellis. 1992. *Competition among Japan, the U.S., and Europe over High-Definition Television*. Pew Case Studies in International Affairs: Case 151.

———.1997. "Telling Vision: Explaining American and Japanese Coverage of the Other Nation" in *Creating Images: American and Japanese Television News Coverage of the Other*. The Mansfield Center for Pacific Affairs, University of Montana: 1997.

———.1998. "Changing Television News in Japan." *The Journal of Asian Studies*. 57, no.3. August 1998: 663–692.

———. 2000. *Broadcasting Politics in Japan: NHK and Television News*. Ithaca: Cornell University Press.

Küng-Shankleman, Lucy. 2000. *Inside the BBC and CNN*. London: Routledge.

Kynge, James and Gapper, John. 1998. "Murdoch repairs his links with Chinese leadership." *Financial Times*. December 12, 1998: 20.

Kynge, James. 2001. "Tussle over regulation of telecoms and TV in Beijing." *Financial Times*. July 12, 2001.

Kyodo News, 1997. "Govt allows JSkyB to broadcast on 9 channels." *Daily Yomiuri*. February 26, 1997: 5.

Kyogoku, Jun-ichi. 1987.The Political Dynamics of Japan (Nihon no Seiji). *Tokyo: University of Tokyo Press.*

Labaton, Stephen. 2002. "FCC Blocks EchoStar Deal With DirecTV." *The New York Times*. October 11, 2002: 11.

Lall, Bhuvan. 1997. "ISkyB attacks Indian broadcasting ban." *Screen International*. July 25, 1997: 5.

Lash, Scott and Urry, John. 1987.*The End of Organized Capitalism*. Madison, Wisconsin: University of Wisconsin Press.

Lawson, Stephen. 2001. "Murdoch grabs slice of China broadband operator." www.IDG.net. February 20, 2001.

Lebra, Takie Sugiyama. 1992. *Japanese Social Organization*. Honolulu: University of Hawaii Press.

Ledbetter, James. 1997. *Made Possible By . . . The Death of Public Broadcasting in the United States*. London: Verso.

Lee, Chin-Chuan, ed. 1990. *Voices of China: The Interplay of Politics and Journalism*. NY: Guilford Press. Boulder, Colorado: Westview Press.

Lee, Chin-Chuan, and Chan, Joseph Man. 1990. "The Hong Kong Press in China's Orbit: Thunder of Tiananmen." In Chin-Chuan Lee, ed. *Voices of China*: NY: Guilford Press.

Lee, Chin-Chuan, ed. 1994. *China's Media, Media's China*. Boulder, Colorado: Westview Press.

Lee, Paul and Wang, Georgette. 1995. "Satellite TV in Asia." *Telecommunication Policy*. Vol. 19, No.2, pp. 135–149.

Lee-Young, Joanne. 2000. "Star TV, CyberWorks Spar in India." *The Industry Standard*. www.thestandard.com/article/0,1902,18550.00.html. September 15, 2000.

———. 2001. "The Digital Prince of China." www.idg.net. March 12, 2001.

Leicester, John. 2000. "Student's murder prompts protest at Peking University." www.newstimes.com/archive2000/may24woh.htm. May 24, 2000.

Li, Tsze Sun. 1993. *The World Outside When the War Broke Out*. Hong Kong Institute of Asia-Pacific Studies. Occasional Paper No. 25. July 1993. Hong Kong: The Chinese University of Hong Kong.

Li, Xiaoping. 2002. "Focus (*Jiaodian Fangtan*) and the Changes in the Chinese Television Industry." *Journal of Contemporary China*. Vol.11, No.30, pp. 17–34.

Li Xiguang, and Liu, Kang and others. 1996. *Behind the Demonization of China* (Yao mo hua Zhong guo de bei huo). Beijing: Chinese Social Sience Publisher.

Li, Zhisui. 1994. *The Private Life of Chairman Mao*. NY: Random House.

Lieberthal, Kenneth, 1995. *Governing China: From Revolution Through Reform*. NY: W.W. Norton.

Liebes, Tamar and Curran, James, eds. 1998. *Media, Ritual and Identity*. London: Routledge.

Lin, Yu-Tang, 1936. *A History of the Press and Public Opinion in China*. Chicago: The University of Chicago Press.

Link, Perry. 1992. *Evening Chats in Beijing: Probing China's Predicament*. NY: Norton.

Liu, Sunray. 2001. "China unveils digital broadcast strategy." *EETimes*. www.ee-times.com/story/OEG20010328S0035. March 28, 2001.

Liu, Yu-Li. 1994. "The growth of cable television in China." *Telecommunications Policy*. April 1994. 217– 228.

Living in a Global World. 2001. "The Attacks on the World Trade Center and the Pentagon, and an Interview with David Harvey." *Living in a Global World*, Season 2, Episode 2.1. September 18, 2001. Executive producer: James D. White. Honolulu: the Globalization Research Center.

Long, Mark. 1997. "India's Dream Beam." www.mlesat.com/Articl11.html.July/August, 1997.

Long, Simon. 1992. "The winds that keep blowing: China and its foreign press corps since June 1989." In Robin Porter, ed. *Reporting the news from China*. London: Royal Institute of International Affairs.

Lovelock, Peter. 1995. "Information Highways and the Trade in Telecommunications Services." In John Ure, ed. *Telecommunications in Asia.* Hong Kong: Hong Kong University Press.

———. 1996. *Electronic media.* Unpublished MS.

———. 2000. *China: IP Telephony and the Internet.* Telecommunication Case Study, ITU. www.itu.int/osg/sec/spu/ni/iptel/countries/china/china-iptel.pdf.

Lovelock, Peter and Shoenfeld, Susan. 1995. "The Broadcast Media Markets in Asia." In John Ure, ed. *Telecommunications in Asia.* Hong Kong: Hong Kong University Press.

Lowry, Tom. 2002. "A New Cable Giant." *BusinessWeek.* November 18, 2002. pp.109–118.

Lubbers, Ruud. 1998. *The Dynamic of Globalization.* Paper presented at a Tilburg University seminar on November 26 1998. www.globalize.org/dynamic.html.

Luttwak, Edward. 1998. "Speculative Crimes and Global Punishment." Harper's. December, 1998. 297, No. 1783: 19–23.

Machlup, Fritz . 1962. *The Production and Distribution of Knowledge in the United States.* Princeton, NJ: Princeton University Press.

Madge, Tim. 1989. *Beyond the BBC: Broadcasters and the Public in the 1980s.* Basingstoke: Macmillan.

Madhavan, Narayanan. 2000. "Star TV launches war to win India's Hindi heartland." Yahoo! News/Reuters entertainment news. www.google.com/search?q=Business+Week+Star+TV&binG=Google+Search

Mahathir, Mohamed and Ishihara, Shintaro. 1995. *The Voice of Asia.* Tokyo: Kodansha. Originally published in Japanese as "The Asia That Can Say "No."" ("No" to ieru ajia) 1994.

Mainichi Shimbun. 1993. "Deregulation may allow direct satellite TV into Japan." *Mainichi Daily News.* October 19, 1993: 5.

———. 1994. "Report suggest ways to open broadcast mart." *Mainichi Daily News.* May 26, 1994: 5.

———. 1999. "Diverted cash landed bureaucrat new job." *Mainichi Daily News.* May 29, 1999: 12.

Mander, Jerry. 1978. *Four Arguments for the Elimination of Television.* New York Morrow Quill.

Mansfield Center. 1997. *Creating Images: American and Japanese Television News Coverage of the Other.* The Mansfield Center for Pacific Affairs, University of Montana: 1997.

Marr, Merissa. 2000. "Testing the Tech Limits." abcnews.go.com/sections/sports/DailyNews/olympics-internet_000713.html. July 13, 2000.

Martin, Hans-Peter and Schumann, Harald. 1997. *The Global Trap.* London: Zed Books.

Martinez, Larry. 1985. *Communication Satellites: Power Politics in Space.* Dedham, MA: Artech House, 1985

Marx, Karl and Engels, Friedrich. 1978. "Manifesto of the Communist Party." In *The Marx-Engels Reader*, ed. Robert C. Tucker. New York: W. W. Norton.

MacGregor, Brent. 1995. "Our Wanton Abuse of the Technology: Television News Gathering in the Age of the Satellite." *Convergence.* Spring, 1995. Vol.1, Number 1.

McChesney, Robert W. 1999. "The New Global Media." *The Nation*. November 29, 1999. Pp.11–15.

McDonald, J. Fred. 1990. *One Nation Under Television: The Rise and Decline of Network TV*. New York: Pantheon.

McGregor, Richard. 2000. "China's broadcasters collide on superhighway." *Financial Times Weekend*. August 12/13, 2000: 5.

McLuhan, Marshall. 1965. *Understanding Media: The Extensions of Man*. New York: McGraw-Hill.

McLuhan, Marshall and Fiore, Quentin. 1967. *The Medium is the Massage: an Inventory of Effects*. NY: Bantam Books.

Media Tenor. 2001. "Attacks on America." www.mediatenor.co.za./attacks/attacks_on_america.htm. October 1, 2001.

Merchant, Khozem and Harding, James. 2000. "Star move plugs Indian TV gap." *The Financial Times*. September 13, 2000: 30.

Mermigas, Diane. 1993. "Rupert Murdoch: The Global Strategy." *Electronic Media*. October 11, 1993: 1.

Mignolo, Walter. 2002. "The Zapatistas's Theoretical Revolution: Its Historical, Ethical, and Political Consequences." *Review: Fernand Braudel Center for the Study of Economies, Historical Systems, and Civilizations*. XXV, 3, 2002, 245–75. Binghampton, NY: State University of New York

Miller, David. 2002. "Opinion Polls and the Misrepresentation of Public Opinion on the War with Afghanistan." *Television & New Media*. Vol.3 No.2, May 2002, pp.153–161.

Ming, Ruan. 1990. "Press Freedom and Neoauthoritarianism: A Reflection on China's Democracy Movement". In Chin-Chuan Lee, ed. *Voices of China: The Interplay of Politics and Journalism*. NY: Guilford Press.

Ministry of Posts and Telecommunications. 1998. *Manual for Market Entry into Cable TV Business*. In Japanese and English. Tokyo: Ministry of Posts and Telecommunications. March 1998.

Ministry of Posts and Telecommunications (2). March, 1998. *Broadcast Law As Amended*. Japanese Legislation of Telcommunications, Volume 5. Tokyo: Ministry of Posts and Telecommunications. March 1998.

Mitchell, Pat. 2001. "Real World or 'Reality' Shows?" *The Washington Post*. October 16, 2001: A23.

Mo, Crystl. 2001. "Tuning In To The WTO Means Double Happiness For CCTV." *Asiaweek*. December 7, 2001. www.asiaweek.com/asiawee/magazine/enterprise/o,8782,186253,00.html.

Morikawa, Kathleen. 1992. "NHK Viewers Dodge Monthly Payments." *Asahi Evening News*. August 1, 1992: 5.

Morley, David and Robins, Kevin. 1995. *Spaces of Identity*. London: Routledge.

Mosco, Vincent. 1996. *The Political Economy of Communication*. London: Sage.

Mowlana, H., Gerbner, G. and Schiller, H.I. (eds.) 1992. *Triumph of the Image*. Boulder, Co: Westview Press.

Mowlana, Hamid. 1993. "From Technology to Culture." in Gerbner, G., Mowlana, H. and Nordenstreng, K. *The Global Media Debate: Its Rise, Fall and Renewal*. New Jersey: Ablex

———. 1997. *Global Information and World Communication: New Frontiers in International Relations*. London: Sage.

Mulligan, William A. 1989. *Media Reform in China: After the '89 Turmoil.* Western Conference of the Association for Asian Studies: Selected Papers in Asian Studies. Paper No. 34, 1989. Tucson, Arizona: University of Arizona.

———. . 1992. *The Chinese Press: Journalism under Mao*. Western Conference of the Association for Asian Studies: Selected Papers in Asian Studies. Paper No. 42, 1992. Tucson, Arizona: University of Arizona.

Muranaka, Chizuko. 1996. "Murdoch, Son express no desire to buy more TV Asahi shares." *The Daily Yomiuri*. December 19, 1996: 3.

———. . 1997. "TV deregulation moving slowly but surely." *The Daily Yomiuri*. May 28, 1997: 3.

Murphy, David. 2002. "Very Remote Control." *Far Eastern Economic Review*. August 29, 2002. www.feer.com/cgi-bin/prog/printeasy

Nagel, Joane. 2000. "States of Arousal/Fantasy Islands: Race, Sex, and Romance in the Global Economy of Desire." *American Studies*. Vol. 41: 2/3 (Summer/Fall 2000). Pp. 159–181

Nakamoto, Michiyo. 1995. "Japan and US link in cable TV venture." *Financial Times*. January 10, 1995.

———. . 1996 (1). "Murdoch steps into the Japanese limelight." *Financial Times*, June 14, 1996.

———. . 1996 (2). "Japanese TV loses cosy glow in digital world." *Financial Times*, October 10, 1996.

Nakamura, Yuko. 1988. "Direct Broadcasting by Satellite in Japan: an Overview." In *Satellite Broadcasting*, ed. Negrine, R., 1988.

National Space Development Agency of Japan. 1978. *Outline of Japan's Space Development Policy*. Ministry of Posts and Telecommunications, Tokyo.

Negrine, Ralph, ed. 1988. *Satellite Broadcasting: The Politics and Implications of the New Media*. London: Routledge.

Negrine, R. and Papathanassopoulos, S. 1990. *The Internationalisation of Television*. London: Pinter Publishers.

Negroponte, Nicholas. 1996. *Being Digital*. New York: Vintage.

New Yorker. 1995. "Deng's Daughter: China's Newt?" *The New Yorker*. February 6, 1995: 27.

NHK. April, 1998. *NHK Factsheets*. Series of 18 factshheets. Tokyo: NHK.

———. 2002. "The Red & White Song Contest: New Year's Eve Grand Song Festival." www.nkk.or.jp/bunken/BCRI-rup/h02-d5.html. Accessed February 26, 2002.

NHK Broadcasting Culture Research Institute. 2002. "Evaluation of Public Broadcasting by Country." *BCRI Journal*. No. 19 (New Year, 2002). www.nhk.or.jp/bunken/beri-fr/h19-rl.html

Nikkei Industrial, 1992. "Satellite industry forced to begin restructuring." The Nikkei Industrial Daily, in *Nikkei Weekly*, Oct. 19, 1992.

Nikkei Weekly. 2001. "Government hedges bets on privatization-gambling gets overhaul, but no change at NHK." *Nikkei Weekly*, November 19, 2001.

Nye, Joseph and Owens, William. 1996. "America's Information Edge." *Foreign Affairs*. Vol. 75 No.2. March/April 1996.

O'Brien, Rita Cruise and Helleiner, G.K. 1980. "The Political Economy of Information in a Changing International Economic Order," *International Organization*, 34:4, Autumn 1980.

Ogden, Suzanne. 1989. *China's Unresolved Issues: Politics, Development, and Culture*. New Jersey: Prentice Hall.

Ognianova, Ekaterina and Endersby, James W. 1996. *Objectivity Revisited: A Spatial Model of Political Ideology and Mass Communication*. Columbia, SC: Journalism & Mass Communication Monographs, Association for Education in Journalism and Mass Communication. No. 159, October, 1996

Ohmae, Kenichi. 1995. *The End of the Nation State: the Rise of the Regional Economies*. New York: Free Press.

Ozawa, Ichiro. 1994. *Blueprint for a New Japan: The Rethinking of a Nation*. Tokyo: Kodansha International.

Palmer, Allen. 2002. "Negotiation and Resistance in Global Networks: The 1884 International Meridian Conference." *Mass Communication & Society*. 5 (1), 7–24.

Parker, Richard. 1995. *Mixed Signals: The Prospects for Global Television News*. The Twentieth Century Fund Press: New York.

Parsons, Patrick R. and Frieden, Robert M. 1998. *The Cable and Satellite Television Industries*. Boston: Allyn and Bacon.

Patel, Alpesh. 2001. "Enter the Chinese dragon." *Financial Times*. Weekend September 29/30, 2001: 5.

Pathania, Geetika. 1994. "Ambivalence in a STAR-y Eyed Land: Doordarshan and the Satellite TV Challenge." reenic.utexas.edu/asnic/sagar/spring.1994/geetika.pathan.art.html.

PBS. 1996. *Frontline: Smoke in the Eye*. Correspondent: Daniel Schorr. PBS. April 2, 1996.

Perkins Cole. 2002. "Convergence in China-Divergent Views Persist." www.perkinscole.com/resource/intldocs/convergence.htm

Pew Research Center for the People and the Press. 1998. "Internet News Takes Off". www.people-press.org/reports/ display.php3?ReportID=36

———. 2000. "Internet Sapping Broadcast News Audience." www.people-press.org/reports/ display.php3?ReportID=36

———. 2001. "Missing Intern Stirs Media Frenzy, Lukewarm Public Interest." www.people-press.org/reports/ display.php3?ReportID=7

Pharr, Susan J. 1996. "Media as Trickster in Japan." In *Media and Politics in Japan*. eds. Pharr, Susan J. and Krauss, Ellis D. .Honolulu: University of Hawai'i Press.

Pilger, John. 1998. *Hidden Agendas*. New York: The New Press.

Plate, Tom. 2000. "Why Murdoch knelt to China." *The Honolulu Advertiser*. June 2, 2000: A18.

Pogrebin, Abigail. 1999. "Lack Attack." *Brill's Content*. February, 1999.

Pollack, Andrew. 1997. "Tokyo Speeds Debut Of Digital Broadcasts." *International Herald Tribune*, March 11, 1997: 11.

Poster, Mark. *The Mode of Information: Poststructuralism and Social Context*. (Chicago: University of Chicago Press, 1990).

Postman, Neil. 1986. *Amusing Ourselves to Death*. New York: Viking.

Preston, Paschal. 2001. *Reshaping Communications*. London: Sage.
Prestowitz, Clyde. 1988. *Trading Places*. New York: Basic Books.
Quinn, Steven and Walters, Tim. 2004. "Al-Jazeera: A Broadcaster Creating Ripples in a Stagnant Pool." In Ralph D. Berenger, ed. *Global Media Go To War*. Spokane, Washington: Marquette Books.
Reeves, Jimmie L. and Campbell, Richard. 1994. *Cracked Coverage*. Durham: Duke University Press.
Reich, Robert. 1992. *The Work of Nations: Preparing Ourselves for 21st Century Capitalism*. New York: Vintage.
Reid, T.R. 1993. "Japan's Feisty New Press." *Nieman Reports*. Fall 1993: 15.
Riley, James. 1990. "Launch of a new era." *South China Morning Post*, April 7, 1990:1.
Riodran, Michael and Hoddeson, Lillian. 1997. "Birth of an Era." *Scientific American*.
Ritchie, Ian. 2001. "Ian Ritchie, CEO of Associated Press Television News for Television Journalism". American University in Cairo. www.tbsjounral.com/Archives/Fall01/ritchie.htm.
Robertson, Joanna. 2001. "Berlusconi: Italy's virtual prime minister." *BBC News*. news.bbc.co.uk/ hi/english/world/CHECK/May 23, 2001.
Robertson, Roland. 1992. *Globalization: Social Theory and Global Culture*. London: SAGE Publications.
Robins, Kevin and Webster, Frank. 1999. *Times of the Technoculture: From the Information Society to the Virtual Life*. London: Routledge.
Robinson, William I. 1996. *Promoting Polyarchy: Globalization, US Intervention and Hegemony*. Cambridge: Cambridge University Press.
Rosen, Stanley and Zou, Gary. 1991. "The Chinese Television Documentary "River Elegy" (Part 1)." *Chinese Sociology and Anthropology*. Winter 1991–92. Vol. 24, No.2.
Rosenau, James N. 1990. *Turbulence in World Politics: A Theory of Change and Continuity*. Princeton: Princeton University Press.
Rosenwein, Rifka. 1999. "The News That Dare Not Speak Its Name." *Brill's Content*. October 1999.
Roszak, Theodor. 1986. *The Cult of Information: The Folklore of Computers and the True Art of Thinking*. Cambridge: Lutterworth Press.
Rutenberg, Jim. 2001. "Fox Portrays a War of Good and Evil, and Many Applaud." *The New York Times*. December3, 2001. www.nytimes.com/2001/12/03/business/03FOX.html?todaysheadlines.
Saghieh, Hazem. 2004. "Al-Jazeera: the world through Arab eyes." www.opendemocracy.net/articles. June 17, 2004.
Said, Edward W. 1979. *Orientalism*. New York: Pantheon.
———. 1994. *Culture and Imperialism*. New York: Knopf.
Samuels, Richard J. 1987. *The Business of the Japanese State: Energy Markets in Comparative and Historical Perspective*. Ithaca: Cornell University Press.
Sanger, David E. 1999. "So Much for Grand Theories." *The New York Times*. March 7, 1999. Section 4, p.3.
Sardar, Ziauddin. 1998. *Postmodernism and the Other: The New Imperialism of Western Culture*. London: Pluto Press.

Sasaki, Sei. 1997. "Murdoch sacrifices TV shares to court broadcasting ally." *Nikkei Weekly*. March 10, 1997: 4.

———. . 1997 (2). "JSkyB deal signals media convergence." *Nikkei Weekly*. May 19, 1997: 5.

———. . 1998. "Satellite broadcasting expands its orbit." *Nikkei Weekly*. April 27, 1998: 5.

Sassen, Saskia. 1991. *The Global City*. Princeton, N.J.: Princeton University Press.

———. 2000. "Spatialities and Temporalities of the Global: Elements for a Theorization" *Public Culture*. Durham, NC: Duke University Press. Vol. 12, No. 1, Winter 2000.

Satnews Asia. 2001. "China to Form Satellite Telecoms Group as First Step to Revamp Telecoms Sector . . . Plans to Control and Foreign TV Channel Distribution." November 6, 2001. www.satnewsasia.com/Stories/ 636.html

Satnews Asia. 2002. "Phoenix says China Unified Satellite Plan Delayed." January 17, 2002. www.satnewsasia.com/Stories/718.html

———. . 2002. "China Starts Clampdown After Pirate Satellite Broadcasts." September 5, 2002. www.satnewsasia.com/Stories/ 998.html

Sato, Kyoko. 1992. "National network's new chief gets back to basics." *Nikkei Weekly*. August 1, 1992.

Sato, Michio. 1997. "Mogul Murdoch hits a speed bump." *The Daily Yomiuri*. April 2, 1997: 7.

Scannell, Paddy. 1988. "Radio Times: The Temporal Arrangements of Broadcasting in the Modern World." In *Television and its Audience*. Eds: Drummond, Phillip andPaterson, Richard . London: British Film Institute.

———. . 1992. "Public service broadcasting and modern life." In Scannell, Paddy, Schlesinger, Philip and Sparks, Colin (eds) *Culture and Power*. London: Sage.

Schecter, Danny. 2004. "Counter Programming." Interview with Jehane Noujaim in *Filmmaker*. Winter 2004. www.filmmakermagazine.com/winter2004/ features/counter_programming.html.

Schiller, Herbert I. 1989. *Culture, Inc.: The Corporate Takeover of Public Expression*. New York: Oxford University Press.

———. . 1992. *Mass Communications and American Empire*. (2nd edition). Boulder, Colorado: Westview Press.

Schilling, Mark. 1994. "Japan rushes into an interactive TV future." *Japan Times*. May 30, 1994: 14.

Schlesinger, Jacob M. 1991. "NHK Chief Pushes Global News Network." *Asian Wall Street Journal*. March 26, 1991: 1

———. . 1991 (2). "NHK Abandons Its Plans to Create A Collaborative All-News Network." *Asian Wall Street Journal*. December 9, 1991: 1.

Schneider, Friedrich. 2002. "Size and Measurement of the Informal Economy in 110 countries Around the World." *Rapid Response Unit, World Bank*. July, 2002.

Schreiber, Mark. 2000. "NHK propping up overseas affiliates to preach the word." Translation summary of a report by Tomofumi Yamamoto in the Shukan Asahi. Mainichi Daily News, August 13, 2000.

Schreiber, W.F. 1991. *Fundamentals of Electronic Imaging Systems*. New York: Springer-Verlag.

Schwanhausser, Mark. 2001. "Media feeling the pain." *SiliconValley.Com*. www.siliconvalley.com/docs/news/depth/media092301.htm. September 22, 2001.
Scott, Arran and Fukui, Makiko. 1998. "PerfecTV, JSkyB to Merge On a 50-50 Basis in April." *Asian Wall Street Journal*. February 4, 1998.
Seib, Philip. 1997. *Headline Diplomacy: How News Coverage Affects Foreign Policy*. Westport, Conn: Praeger.
Sen, Amartya. 2002. "How to Judge Globalism." *The American Prospect*. Special Supplement: "Globalism and the World's Poor." Winter, 2002.
Sender, Henny. "Image Problems." *Far Eastern Economic Review*. October 6, 1994: 80.
Shapiro, Michael J. 1991. "Sovereignty and Exchange in the Orders of Modernity." Alternatives. Vol. 16 (1). 447–477.
———. 1992. "Sovereignty, Exchange, and the Politics of Reading." Paper prepared for the 1992 Annual AERA meeting, San Francisco, April 20–24, 1992.
———. 1993. *Reading "Adam Smith": Desire, History, and Value*. Newbury Park, California: Sage Publications.
Shawcross, William. "Planet Murdoch," *South China Morning Post*, July 16, 1994.
Shenon, Philip. 1993. "Star TV Extends Murdoch's Reach." *The New York Times*. August 23, 1993. D1.
Sherman, Spencer. 1994. "East meets West." *Columbia Journalism Review*. April, 1994. 32–36.
———. 1994 (2). "Broadcast Blues." *Tokyo Journal*. September, 1994. 32–37.
Shima, Keiji. 1995. Shima Geji fuunroku/hoso to kenryoku 40nen (The Stormy Record of Shima Keiji: 40 years of broadcasting and politics). Tokyo: Bungei Shunjyu.
Shimizu, Shinichi. 1993. "The Implications of Transborder Television for National Cultures and National Broadcasting: A Japanese Perspective." *Media Asia*. Vol.20 No.4, 1993.
Slack, Edward. 2001. "A Brief History of Satellite Communications." *Pacific Telecommunications Review*. Vol. 22 No. 3, 2001.
Smil, Vaclav. 2001. "It Doesn't Add Up." Asiaweek. November 30, 2001. www.asiaweek.com/asiaweek/magazine/threesixty/0,8782,185600,00. html.
Smith, Adam. 1976. *The Wealth of Nations*., eds. Campbell, R.H., Skinner, A.S. and Todd, W. B. Oxford: Clarendon Press.
Smith, Anthony. 1973. *The Shadow in the Cave*. Urbana, Illinois: University of Illinois Press.
———. 1990. *Towards a Global Culture?* In Featherstone, Mike (ed). 1990. *Global Culture: Nationalism, globalization and modernity*. London: Sage Publications.
Smith, Paul. 1996. "Media Companies." Sector Report for HSBC James Capel. July 5, 1996.
———. 1997. "Broadcasting Boom." Sector Report for HSBC James Capel. May 5, 1997.
Smith, Richard. 1994. *China's Cultural Heritage: The Qing Dynasty, 1644–1912*. Boulder: Westview Press.

Soja, Edward. 1989. *Postmodern Geographies: The Reassertion of Space in Critical Social Theory*. New York: Verso Press.

Song, Qiang, Zhang, Zangzang and Qiao, Bian and others. 1996. *The China that Can Say No*. (Zhong guo Keyi Shuo Bu). Beijing Chinese Commerical Industrial Union.

Soros, George. 1998. *The Crisis of Global Capitalism: Open Society Endangered*. New York: Public Affairs.

South China Morning Post. 1991. "Sunday Money" *South China Morning Post*. April 21, 1991: 10.

———. 1993. "STAR TV buys 49.9pc of key Indian company." *South China Morning Post*. BusinessPost December 24, 1993:1.

———. 1996. "Phoenix fails to take off for Star." *South China Morning Post*. August 18, 1996.

———. 1997. "Phoenix to fly in Guangdong." *South China Morning Post*. May 9, 1997.

Space Daily. 2002. "SINOSAT and Falun Gong: A Propaganda Battle In Space." Unedited article released by the Falun Dafa Information Center. July 11, 2002.

Specter, Michael. 2000. "The Pharmageddon Riddle." *New Yorker*. April 10, 2000. 58–71.

Spiegler, Marc. 1995. "News by Numbers." Wired. 3.06. June, 1995. p.46.

Stockhouse Media Corporation. 2001. "TVB: mainland door ajar." www.financeasia.com/articlesA6C3C842-45CC-11D5-81C8009277E1748.cfm

Stoll, Clifford. 1995. *Silicon Snake Oil: Second Thoughts on the Information Highway*. New York: Doubleday.

Strobel, W. 1997. *Late Breaking Foreign Policy: The News Media's Influence on Peace Operations*. Washington D.C.: U.S. Institute of Peace Press.

Stross, Randall E. 1990. *Bulls in the China Shop and Other Sino-American Business Encounters*. Honolulu: University of Hawaii Press.

Sugaya, Minoru. 1995. "Cable television and government policy in Japan." *Telecommunications Policy*. Vol. 19, No.3.

Sun, Lin. 1999. "Satellite TV Broadcast Market in China." http://www.ptc.org/planetptc/Sun_Lin/paper.htm <CHECK>

Sutcliffe, Bob and Glyn, Andrew. 1999. "Still Underwhelmed: Indicators of Globalization and Their Misinterpretation." *Review of Radical Political Economics*. March 1999. 31 (1): 111–132.

Takashi, Masuko. 1993. "Satellite broadcaster seeks assistance from shareholders." *Nikkei Weekly*. January 18, 1993.

Takashima, Hatsushisa. 1995. "Japanese Television on the World Beat: A Reporter's Perspective." *Japan Review of International Affairs*. Winter, 1995: 17–35.

Tan, Zixiang, Mueller, Milton and Foster, Will. 1997. "China's New Internet Regulations: Two Steps Forward, One Step Back." *Communications of the ACM*. Vol. 40, No. 12. December, 1997.

Tarjanne, Pekka. 1994. *The Globalisation of Telecommunications: Issues and Opportunities in the Evolution of International Telecommunications*. Speech prepared for the October 1994 Asia Pacific Telecommunications Forum, Beijing.

Tasini, Jonathan. 1996 "The Dawn of the Tele-Barons." *The Washington Post National Weekly Edition*. February 12–18, 1996: 22.

Taylor, Philip M. 2001. "Television: The First Flawed Rough Drafts of History." In *Television Histories: Shaping Collective Memory in the Media Age*. Eds: Gary Edgerton and Peter Rollins. Lexington, Kentucky: University Press of Kentucky.

Tech Buddha. 2000. "Upcoming IPO: Phoenix Satellite Television Holdings Ltd." www.techbuddha.com/upcoming/phoenix.html. September 17, 2000.

Tehranian, Majid. 1990. *Technologies of Power: Information Machines and Democratic Prospects*. Norwood, NJ: Ablex Publishing Company.

Thayer, Nathaniel B. 1975. "Competition and Conformity: An Inquiry into the Structure of Japanese Newspapers." In *Modern Japanese Organization and Decision-Making*, ed. Ezra Vogel. Berkeley: University of California Press.

Thomas, J., Grainger, G., Koomen, K., van Vliet, R. 2000. "Governing information and communication technologies." In *World Information and Communication Report 1999/2000*. Paris: UNESCO, 2000.

Thompson, John B. 1990. *Ideology and Modern Culture*. Stanford: Stanford University Press.

Times of India. 2001. "Murdoch's Star TV: Hindi key to Indian success." www.timesofindia.com/070701/07boil11.htm. July 7, 2001.

Togo, Shigehiko. 1998. "The Japan-US Perception Gap and the Media." *Japan Review of International Affairs*. Summer 1998.

Tomlinson, John. *Cultural Imperialism*. Baltimore: The John Hopkins University Press. 1991.

To, Yiu-ming and Lau, Tuen-yu. 1995. "Global Export of Hong Kong Television: Television Broadcasts Limited." *Asian Journal of Communication*. Vol.5, No.2, 1995: 108

Townsend, James and Womack, Brantly. 1986. *Politics in China*. Boston: Little, Brown.

Tracey, Michael. 1998. *The Decline and Fall of Public Service Broadcasting*. Oxford: Oxford University Press.

Tu, Wei-ming. 1991. "Cultural China: The Periphery as the Center." *Daedalus*. Spring 1991, 120 (2), p.5.

TVJapan. 2002. "Program Summary." www.tvjapan.net/eng/index_e.html

Twiston Davies, Simon. 1993. "TVB is primed to fire at China." *South China Morning Post: Business Post*. November 23, 1993: 7.

———. 1994. "When you wish upon a Star." *Eastern Express*. July 11, 1994.

UNESCO. 1963. *Statistics on Radio and Television*, 1950–1960. Paris: UNESCO.

Upham, Frank R. 1987. *Law and Social Change in Postwar Japan*. Cambridge, Mass: Harvard University Press.

Urakami, Keiji. 1994. "Bumpy road ahead for Japan's info highway," *Mainichi Daily News*. April 16, 1994.

U.S. Department of State. *FY2001 Country Commercial Guide: China*. Prepared by U.S. Embassy Beijing and released by the Bureau of Economic and Business in July 2000 for Fiscal Year 2001.

U.S. Embassy China. 1998. New PRC Internet Regulation. January 1998. www.usembassy-china.org.cn/english/sand/netreg.htm

———. . 2000. *Regulations on the Administration of Telecommunication Network Interconnection*. Accessed January, 2000. www.usembassy-china.org.cn/english/commercial/ CCB-Archives/CCB-Vol-2-No-12.htm)

van Wolferen, Karel. 1989. *The Enigma of Japanese Power: People and Politics in a Stateless Nation*. London: MacMillan.

Varadarajan, Tunku. 2001. "Citizen of the World." *The Wall Street Journal*. March 26, 2001.

Varchaver, Nicholas. 1999. "CNN takes over the world." *Brill's Content*. June 1999.

Vidyasagar, N. 2001. "It's a long break for Doordarshan." *The Times of India*. www.times of india.com/160601/16bus17.htm. June 16, 2001.

Vines, Stephen and Poole, Teresa. 1997. "Murdoch dreams of a Chinese empire." *The Independent*. January 10, 1997. p.10.

Vogel, Ezra F. 1979. *Japan as Number One: Lessons for America*. New York: Harper & Row.

Vogel, Steven K.. 1996. *Freer Markets, More Rules: Regulatory Reform in Advanced Industrial Countries*. Ithaca, N.Y.: Cornell University Press.

Wachs, Stewart. 2001. "Media Critic: Asano Kenichi." *Kyoto Journal* No. 46. Winter 2001.

Waldrop, M. Mitchell. 1992. *Complexity: The Emerging Science at the Edge of Order and Chaos*. London: Penguin.

Wallen, David. 1994. "Patten tackles media giants." *South China Morning Post*. March 31, 1994.

Wallerstein, Immanuel. 1987. "World-systems Analysis" In *Social Theory Today*, eds. A. Giddens and J. Turner. Stanford: Stanford University Press.

———. 1992. "A Brief Agenda for the Future of Long-Wave Research." In *New Findings in Long-Wave Research*, eds. Alfred Kleinknecht, Ernest Mandel, Immanuel Wallerstein. London: The Macmillan Press.

Walton, Greg. 2001. "China's Golden Shield: Corporations and the Development of Surveillance Technology in the People's Republic of China." International Center for Human Rights and Democratic Development. 2001. http://www.ichrdd.ca/english/commdoc/publications/globalization/goldenShieldEng.html

Wang, Xiangwei. 2002. "Hong Kong TV coverage of Jiang axed over Falun Gong fears." *South China Morning Post*. July 3, 2002.

Wark, McKenzie. 1994. *Virtual Geography: Living with Global Media Events*. Bloomington: Indiana University Press.

Warner, Fara and Witcher, S. Karene. 1996. "News Corp. Spends Heavily To Remake Television Unit." *Asian Wall Street Journal*. December 17, 1996. pp.1, 9.

Weber, Ian. 2002. "Reconfiguring Chinese Propaganda and Control Modalities: a case study of Shanghai's television system." *Journal of Contemporary China*. Vol11, No.30, pp. 53–75.

Wells, Matt . 2001. "World Service will not call US attacks terrorism." London: The Guardian, Thursday November 15, 2001. www.guardian.co.uk/ukresponse/story/0,11017,593697,00.html

Wessberg, Arne. 2000. "Public Service Broadcasting." In World Information and Communication Report1999/2000. Paris: UNESCO, 2000.

Westney, D. Eleanor. 1996. "Mass Media as Business Organizations." In *Media and Politics in Japan*, eds. Susan J. Pharr and Ellis D. Krauss. Honolulu: University of Hawai'i Press.

Wheeler, Brian. 2003. "Al-Jazeera's cash crisis." BBC News. April 7, 2003. news.bbc.co.uk/go/pr/fr/-/1/hi/business/2908953.stm.

Whipple, Charles. 1995. "Men of Vision."Intersect Japan. August, 1995: 6–7.

Whirligig-tv. 2001. "The Coronation of Queen Elizabeth II." www.whirligig-tv.co.uk/tv/adults/coronation/coronation.htm

White, James D. 1988. *Communicating: a Guide to PR in Japan*. Tokyo: Dentsu PR Center.

———. 1996. "The Map of the City: Putting an Asian Face on Crime" in *Technological Forecasting and Social Change*, Vol.52, Numbers 2 & 3, June/July, 1996. p. 199–219.

White, Lynn T. 1990. "All the News: Structure and Politics in Shanghai's Reform Media." In Chin-Chuan Lee, ed. *Voices of China*. Guildford Press: New York.

White, Lynn and Cheng, Li. 1993. "China Coast Identities: Regional, National, and Global." In *China's Quest for National Identity*. Eds. Lowell Dittmer and Samuel S. Kim. Ithaca, NY: Cornell University Press.

Whittemore, Hank. 1990. *CNN: The Inside Story*. Boston: Little, Brown.

Wicklein, John. 1982. *Electronic Nightmare: The Home Communications Set and Your Freedom*. Boston : Beacon Press.

Wiener, Jon. 1996. "The Cigarette Papers." *The Nation*. January, 1996. p.11.

Wiener, Norbert. 1961. *Cybernetics*. New York: Wiley.

Williams, Holly. 2002. "China's media gets wings." BBC News. July 24, 2002. //news.bbc.co.uk/1/hi/world/asia-pacific/2149508.stm

Williams, Raymond. 1977. *Marxism and Literature*. Oxford: Oxford University Press.

———. 1983. *Towards 2000*. London: Chatto & Windus.

———. 1985. *Keywords*. New York: Oxford University Press.

Wingfield-Hayes, Rupert. 2002. "China loses grip on internet." *BBC News*, June 5, 2002. news.bbc.co.uk/1/hi/world/asia-pacific/2027120.stm

Womack, Brantly., ed. 1986. "Media and the Chinese Public: A Survey of the Beijing Media Audience." *Chinese Sociology and Anthropology*. Spring-Summer, 1986. Vol. XVIII, No. 3–4.

———. 1990. "The Dilemma of Centricity and Internationalism in China. " In Chin-Chuan Lee, ed. *Voices of China*. Guildford Press: New York.

Worsley, Peter. 1990. "Models of the Modern World-System." In Global Culture, ed. M. Featherstone. London: Sage Publications.

Wriston, Walter B. 1992. *The Twilight of Sovereignty*. New York: Charles Scribner's Sons.

World Trade Organization (WTO). 1998. *Audiovisual Services: Background Note by the Secretariat*. WTO, Council for Trade in Services. S/C/W/40. June 15 1998

Wuer, Kaixi, 1989. Student leader in Tianenmen square, interviewed in Benzakin, Jocelyne. *The Gate of Heavenly Peace: Tiananmen Square Incident*, 1989. J.B. Pictures. Produced and directed by Jocelyne Benzakin.

Xu, Xiangmin and Yip, Chlorophyll. 2001. "China's New Telecommunications Regulations: Paving the Way for WTO Accession." *International Financial Law Review*. January, 2001.

Yanagisawa, Tomoko. 1998. "Fear of BS services behind merger of CS broadcasters." *The Daily Yomiuri*. March 12, 1998:2.

Yomiuri Shimbun. 1997. "Digital format chosen for BS-4 satellite." *The Daily Yomiuri*. February 23, 1997: 1.

———. 1999. "NHK posts Y16.7 bil. Surplus in FY98." *The Daily Yomiuri*. May 30, 1999: 3.

———.2000. "Government should accelerate its thrust." *The Daily Yomiuri*. August 3, 2000.

Yoshimatsu, Hidetaka. June 1998. *The Politics of Telecommunications Reform in Japan*. Pacific Economic Paper No. 280. Canberra: Australia-Japan Research Center, The Australian National University.

Yoshimi, Junichi and Arai, Nobuo. 1997. "Behind Murdoch's TV Asahi fiasco." *The Daily Yomiuri*. March 19, 1997: 17.

Yu, Jinglu. 1990. "The Structure and Function of Chinese Television, 1979–1989." In *Voices of China: The Interplay of Politics and Journalism*, ed. Chin-Chuan Lee. New York: The Guilford Press.

Zhang, Zhijian. 1996. "The Development of Satellite Broadcasting in China." Speech given by the Director of the Science and Technology Committee, MRFT. At China Cable & Satellite Television Summit '96. Beijing. October 28–30, 1996.

Zhao, Yuezhi. 1998. *Media, Market, and Democracy in China: Between the Party Line and the Bottom Line*. Urbana and Chicago: University of Illinois Press.

Zou, Dezhen, Wang, Fei and Meiyun, Zheng (sic). 1988. "China." In *International Handbook of Broadcasting Systems*. Ed. Philip T. Rosen. NY: Greenwood Press.

Zwingle, Erla. 1999. *A World Together*. National Geographic. August, 1999: 12–33.

Index

Printed in the United States
by Baker & Taylor Publisher Services

Printed in the United States
by Baker & Taylor Publisher Services